Virginia Woolf & Music

Virginia Woolf & Music

Edited by Adriana Varga

INDIANA UNIVERSITY PRESS   Bloomington & Indianapolis

This book is a publication of

INDIANA UNIVERSITY PRESS
Office of Scholarly Publishing
Herman B Wells Library 350
1320 East 10th Street
Bloomington, Indiana 47405 USA

iupress.indiana.edu

Telephone   800-842-6796
Fax   812-855-7931

© 2014 by Indiana University Press

All rights reserved

No part of this book may be reproduced or utilized in any form or by any means, electronic or mechanical, including photocopying and recording, or by any information storage and retrieval system, without permission in writing from the publisher. The Association of American University Presses' Resolution on Permissions constitutes the only exception to this prohibition.

∞ The paper used in this publication meets the minimum requirements of the American National Standard for Information Sciences–Permanence of Paper for Printed Library Materials, ANSI Z39.48–1992.

*Manufactured in the
United States of America*

Library of Congress
Cataloging-in-Publication Data

Virginia Woolf and Music / edited by Adriana Varga.
    pages cm
    ISBN 978-0-253-01246-3 (hardback) – ISBN 978-0-253-01255-5 (pb) – ISBN 978-0-253-01264-7 (eb) 1. Woolf, Virginia, 1882–1941 – Criticism and interpretation. 2. Music and literature. I. Varga, Adriana.
    PR6045.O72Z89226 2014
    823'.912 – dc23
                            2013046357

1 2 3 4 5   19 18 17 16 15 14

... for the words are continued by the music
so that we hardly notice the transition.

VIRGINIA WOOLF,
"Impressions at Bayreuth," *E*1, August 21, 1909

I always think of my books as music before I write them.

VIRGINIA WOOLF,
The Letters of Virginia Woolf, Vol. 6, September 4, 1940

Contents

- PREFACE *Mihály Szegedy-Maszák* ix
- ACKNOWLEDGMENTS xiii
- LIST OF ABBREVIATIONS xv

- Introduction · *Adriana Varga* 1

PART 1 MUSIC AND BLOOMSBURY CULTURE

1 Bloomsbury and Music · *Rosemary Lloyd* 27

2 Virginia Woolf and Musical Culture · *Mihály Szegedy-Maszák* 46

PART 2 *UT MUSICA POESIS:* MUSIC AND THE NOVEL

3 Music, Language, and Moments of Being: From *The Voyage Out* to *Between the Acts* · *Adriana Varga* 74

4 The Birth of Rachel Vinrace from the Spirit of Music · *Jim Stewart* 110

5 "The Worst of Music": Listening and Narrative in *Night and Day* and "The String Quartet" · *Vanessa Manhire* 134

6 Flying Dutchmen, Wandering Jews: Romantic Opera, Anti-Semitism, and Jewish Mourning in *Mrs. Dalloway* · Emma Sutton   160

7 The Efficacy of Performance: Musical Events in *The Years* · Elicia Clements   180

8 Sounding the Past: The Music in *Between the Acts* · Trina Thompson   204

PART 3 MUSIC, ART, FILM, AND VIRGINIA WOOLF'S MODERNIST AESTHETICS

9 Broken Music, Broken History: Sounds and Silence in Virginia Woolf's *Between the Acts* · Sanja Bahun   229

10 "Shivering Fragments": Music, Art, and Dance in Virginia Woolf's Writing · Evelyn Haller   260

11 Chiming the Hours: A Philip Glass Soundtrack · Roger Hillman and Deborah Crisp   288

· CONTRIBUTORS   311

· INDEX   315

Preface

Mihály Szegedy-Maszák

MUSIC PLAYED A VERY IMPORTANT ROLE IN THE LIFE OF VIRGINIA Woolf. In 1966, when I visited her husband, Leonard Woolf, he kindly showed me some of their favorite gramophone records and spoke of their attachment to specific works by Mozart, Beethoven, and Schubert. Their melomania distinguished them from most of the other members of the Bloomsbury Group, who turned for inspiration to the visual arts. One of the distinguished contributors to this volume quotes a letter by Roger Fry in which he argues that Beethoven's Sixth Symphony reveals "the essential barbarity and want of civilization of the German spirit." Lytton Strachey had little affection for *Le Sacre du Printemps*. Fry, who praised or dismissed paintings for strictly aesthetic reasons, was influenced by politics when speaking about music, and Strachey's contempt for one of the musical chefs d'oeuvre of the early twentieth century suggests a lack of understanding of rhythmic and harmonic innovation. Leonard Woolf's reluctance to acknowledge the avant-garde may have affected his wife's attitude about contemporary music. Their taste was more conservative in music than in literature. In the course of our conversation I became convinced that Leonard Woolf's interest focused on works in diatonic (major-minor) scales, and Virginia shared his admiration for the works composed between the very late sixteenth and the nineteenth centuries. The absence from much of her writing of allusions to the innovative composers of her age seems undeniable. There are relatively few traces of her interest in the activity of those who took the initiative in moving beyond tonality. Since the contemporary British composers whose work she was familiar with represented either late Romanticism (Ethel Smyth) or a kind of conservative nationalism (Vaughan Williams), her involvement in contemporary experimentation may have been limited by their influence. Undoubtedly, modernism is a question-begging concept. As is well known, Arnold Schoenberg (and his disciple Theodor Adorno) had a low opinion of Igor Stravinsky. Outside a narrow circle of experts, few of Virginia's contemporaries could separate the most important achievements from the vast number of second-rate products. In the first decades of the twentieth century, it was not easy to recognize the compositions that would prove most original, especially in a country dominated by eclecticism. One of the merits of the present collection of essays is that it offers a comparison between Virginia Woolf's art and the music of some of her contemporaries.

Inter-art studies represent a wide range of fields. As an amateur musician and reader of scholarly studies by musicologists, I may be too cautious to accept parallels between literary texts and musical compositions. Opera is a hybrid genre. It can be based on a legend that also inspired literary works usually regarded as belonging to "high culture." In such cases the common denominator may be literary. Reflections on the effects of listening to music abound in the works of Virginia Woolf, from *The String Quartet* to *The Years*. References to composers are frequent not only in her autobiographical texts but also in her narrative fiction. In *Night and Day* William Rodney hums a tune out of an opera by Mozart and picks out melodies in *Die Zauberflöte* upon the piano. Clarissa Dalloway remembers Peter Walsh and Joseph Breitkopf discussing Wagner. At the beginning of *Moments of Being*: "Slater's Pins Have No Points" (published in 1928), Miss Craye strikes the last chord of a Bach fugue.

Some people speak of "musical emotion" produced by the novels of Virginia Woolf. They also admit that the media of literature and music are so different that it might be difficult to look for the imitation of musical form. Understandably, the contributors to this volume avoid the temptation of using musical terms without qualifications. The word "counterpoint," for instance, is rarely mentioned, since the simultaneity of voices is hardly feasible in a text that is expected to be read linearly. Music frequently serves as a metaphor in her novels, so the analysis of musical imagery and the aural nature of her prose deserve much attention. Although pause, semantically emancipated or "qualitative" silence, ellipses, spaces of indeterminacy, displaced accents, syncopation, or fragmentation are hardly specific to music, some believe that if repetitions of the signifier (e.g., onomatopoeia, rhyme, assonance, alliteration, parallelism, etc.) are conspicuous, we can speak of the musicality of prose.

Rhythm has not received its deserved attention in the studies devoted to the works of Virginia Woolf, although punctuation choice (e.g., the use of semicolons or dashes) and syntactic structure may be important characteristics of her art. Roger Fry identified rhythm as the distinguishing feature of her art as early as 1918, when despite his dissatisfaction with the ending of her short story "The Mark on the Wall" he praised her first step toward the creation of a language with conspicuous aural characteristics: "Of course there are lots of good writers in one way or another but you're the only one now Henry James is gone who uses language as a medium of art, who makes the very texture of words have a meaning and quality really almost apart from what you are talking about" (198).[1]

Thanks to the contributors to this volume, the reader may learn much about this neglected topic. The following essays reveal the motivation on which Virginia Woolf acts and show that her experience of compositions by J. S. Bach, Mozart, Beethoven, or Wagner helped shape her aesthetic demands and allowed her to realize a spontaneity in writing that is the very antithesis of a cold calculation. The reader realizes that her interest in music gave her a sensitivity to rhythm that makes it possible to quote the words she used when she assessed the style of Congreve: "The more slowly we read [her] and the more carefully, the more meaning we find, the more beauty we discover" (*E6*: 120).

NOTES

1. Spalding, Frances. *Roger Fry: Art and Life* (Norwich: Black Dog Books, 1999).

Acknowledgments

I WOULD LIKE TO THANK OUR EDITORS AT INDIANA UNIVERSITY Press, especially Raina Polivka, Darja Malcolm-Clarke, and Jill R. Hughes, for the wonderful, energetic support they have given this project, and for seeing it come to fruition. In addition, I would like to thank Paula Durbin-Westby for her superior skill and expertise in compiling the volume's index. I am also most grateful to Cornelia and Aurel Varga for their unfailing and generous support throughout the entire editing process of this work. My thankful remembrance also goes to Matei Calinescu, without whom I would not have turned my eye to Virginia Woolf in the first place.

Furthermore, I am indebted to two of the volume's contributors in particular: I am grateful to Mihály Szegedy-Maszák for reading this volume, advising on its compilation, and, most of all, for his inspiring scholarship and lectures at Indiana University–Bloomington, in which he often spoke of modernism and the arts, of Virginia Woolf, Bloomsbury, and music. One result of these lectures, in the late 1990s, was the realization that a collection of essays on this topic was both possible and necessary. His own dissertation, "Virginia Woolf, The Novelist: An Attempt at Appreciation," can be found today in the Special Collections of the University of Sussex Library, the Monks House Papers, where Leonard Woolf, who must have thought highly of it, placed it alongside his own and Mrs. Woolf's personal letters, photographs, and manuscripts. I would also like to offer my special thanks to Trina Thompson, who offered her steadfast encouragement by reading and advising on parts of the manuscript at various stages of the editing process, and by discussing with me music theory and word-music issues as the volume took shape. Many thanks as well to Melody Eotvos, Trina Thompson, and Deborah Crisp for assembling the music examples used in the volume.

I must also acknowledge the support I received from several scholars with whom I discussed aspects of the volume at different times. I am thankful to Susan Gubar for her strong encouragement of the project from the very beginning and throughout the editing process; to Mark Hussey for his most helpful editorial suggestions; to Robert Hatten for his enlightening lectures on Beethoven and music theory at the Jacobs School of Music; to Katherine Linehan and Michael Davis for their extremely helpful comments on the volume's introduction; and to Susan Sellers and Laura Marcus for their illuminating questions and comments on Woolf and music at the Woolf contemporaine / A Contemporary Woolf Colloque de la Société d'Etudes Woolfiennes, Université d'Aix-Marseille I, Aix-en-Provence, September 2010. Finally, I am most thankful to Nazareth Pantaloni, Assistant Director for Copyright and Administration at the William and Gayle Cook Music Library at the Jacobs School of Music; to the Lilly Library librarians at Indiana University, particularly to Rebecca C. Cape, who made available the publications of the Hogarth Press and other Bloomsbury manuscripts; as well as to the Special Collections librarians at the University of Sussex, who kindly helped me research the Monks House Papers, especially Leonard Woolf's "Card Index of Gramophone Recordings" (June 2005).

Abbreviations

Chapters follow the Harcourt Annotated Editions of Virginia Woolf's works unless otherwise noted in each chapter's Works Cited.

AROO	Virginia Woolf, *A Room of One's Own*
BA	Leonard Woolf, *Beginning Again: An Autobiography of the Years 1911–1918*
BP	Virginia Woolf, *Books and Portraits*
BTA	Virginia Woolf, *Between the Acts*
CR1	Virginia Woolf, *The Common Reader*
CR2	Virginia Woolf, *The Common Reader, Second Series*
CSF	Virginia Woolf, *The Complete Shorter Fiction of Virginia Woolf*
D1–5	Virginia Woolf, *The Diary of Virginia Woolf*
DAW	Leonard Woolf, *Downhill All the Way: An Autobiography of the Years 1919–1939*
E1–6	Virginia Woolf, *The Essays of Virginia Woolf*
HL	Hermione Lee, *Virginia Woolf*
JNAM	Leonard Woolf, *The Journey Not the Arrival Matters: An Autobiography of the Years 1939–1969*
JR	Virginia Woolf, *Jacob's Room*
L1–6	Virginia Woolf, *The Letters of Virginia Woolf*
LLW	Leonard Woolf, *The Letters of Leonard Woolf*
LWA1,2	Leonard Woolf, *An Autobiography*
MB	Virginia Woolf, *Moments of Being*
MD	Virginia Woolf, *Mrs. Dalloway*

MELYM	Virginia Woolf, *Melymbrosia: An Early Version of the Voyage Out*
ND	Virginia Woolf, *Night and Day*
O	Virginia Woolf, *Orlando*
PA	Virginia Woolf, *A Passionate Apprentice: The Early Journals 1897–1909*
PH	Virginia Woolf, *Pointz Hall: The Earlier and Later Typescripts of* Between the Acts
QB1, 2	Quentin Bell, *Virginia Woolf: A Biography*
RF	Virginia Woolf, *Roger Fry: A Biography*
S	Leonard Woolf, *Sowing: An Autobiography of the Years, 1880–1904*
TG	Virginia Woolf, *Three Guineas*
TL	Virginia Woolf, *To the Lighthouse*
VO	Virginia Woolf, *The Voyage Out*
W	Virginia Woolf, *The Waves*
Y	Virginia Woolf, *The Years*

Introduction

Adriana Varga

AS EARLY AS 1901, VIRGINIA WOOLF WAS WRITING TO HER COUSIN Emma Vaughan, "The only thing in this world is music – music and books and one or two pictures" (L1: 35). And as late as 1940, she was writing to her friend, the gifted violinist Elizabeth Trevelyan, about the structure of *Roger Fry: A Biography:*

> Its odd, for I'm not regularly musical, but I always think of my books as music before I write them. And especially with the life of Roger, – there was such a mass of detail that the only way I could hold it together was by abstracting it into themes. I did try to state them in the first chapter, and then to bring in developments and variations, and then to make them all heard together and end by bringing back the first theme in the last chapter. Just as you say, I am extraordinarily pleased that you felt this. No one else has I think. (L6: 425–26)

Such confessions may be surprising, coming from an author whose works are more often associated with the visual arts than with music. They point to the significant role music played in Woolf's writing and aesthetics throughout her life. In her 1939 memoir "A Sketch of the Past," Woolf also described one of her first childhood memories at Talland House, St. Ives, as a "colour-and-sound" moment in which sound, rhythm, image, and scent were fully interconnected. Life itself seemed to have unfolded out of these synesthetic moments the child experienced, which the writer, later, at the height of her creative power, refrained from calling "pictures" because "sight was then so much mixed with sound that picture is not the right word" ("Sketch" 67). These autobiographical details reveal early, consciousness-shaping synesthetic experiences that formed some of the author's most treasured memories.[1] Despite numerous musical references and connections that enrich her fiction, essays, letters, and diaries, readers have most often focused on comparisons with the visual arts, often failing to "hear" Woolf's novels – to use Jane Marcus's insightful words – and ignoring Woolf's "longing to imitate music with words, to build a structure to house the human longing for sublimity as Wagner had done," to "compose her novel," and "above all to bring forward the chorus" (*Languages of Patriarchy* 51).

In the Stephen-Jackson family, music was a practiced art. Woolf remembered, in "A Sketch of the Past," that her mother "could play the piano and was musical" (86), and that her older half sister, Stella Duckworth, "was taught the violin by Arnold Dolmetsch and played in Mrs Marshall's orchestra" (97). Stella would record in her diary (August 18, 1893), as Hermione Lee points out, that "Ginia did her music" while she herself practiced Beethoven sonatas (33). Mihály Szegedy-Maszák reminds us that the seventeen-year-old Virginia and Vanessa used to play fugues on the harmonium (L1: 27). The two sisters did receive a fairly standard female childhood instruction in piano, singing, and dancing, but, while Vanessa whimsically complained about it,[2] in Woolf's case this early training seems to have nourished and enhanced her unusual sensitivity to rhythm and the pleasure of sound she recalled from her childhood, which were so closely interrelated to her linguistic ingenuity. Despite Quentin Bell's assertion that Virginia could not read music "with any deep comprehension" (149), and despite Leonard Woolf's conviction that his wife "had no deep knowledge of [music's] construction" (for a discussion of this point, see Jacobs 232), it is safe to assume that Virginia Woolf could read music and not only understood musical form and structure but also, most importantly, used them creatively in her own writing – as her own description of the structure of *Roger Fry: A Biography* suggests.

Within the last decade, we have been witnessing concerted efforts among Woolf scholars to reconsider the writer's musical background, the direct influence music had on Woolf's aesthetics and politics, and connections between music and her fictional and critical writings. Joyce E. Kelly discusses Woolf's "continual enjoyment of and interest in musical performance" (417); Emilie Crapoulet argues that Woolf "undoubtedly had a fair share of technical musical knowledge" (201); and, more importantly, Emma Sutton points to a "paradigm shift" in Woolf criticism, which "has returned us in one respect to the position of many of Woolf's original readers, to whom the parallels between her work and some contemporary music were self-evident" (278). Woolf's interest in music was all the more enriched by her almost systematic attendance of classical music concerts from an early age (Szegedy-Maszák, chapter 2, this volume), and later by listening to music practically every day in her own home as well as reading, discussing, writing, and publishing music criticism. She planned to host her own private concerts during the autumn of 1925, and borrowed a piano from Edward Sackville West for this purpose (L3: 195). Although critical of the BBC as breeding "a new monster, the middlebrow" (Caughie 339), Woolf, as Pamela Caughie explains, listened in "with great pleasure" for being able to "sit at home & conduct The Meistersinger myself" (D4: 107), thus partaking of what became an active form of listening: "highly attentive to technique; sensitive to nuances of voice; selective in tuning in certain kinds of programmes and tuning out distractions, including the sound of the technology itself. Listening became a skill, producing a heightened critical awareness and independence of thought" (Caughie 338). Most of all, Woolf found the cultural milieu of Bloomsbury receptive to music as part of a modernist aesthetic that fed into her ongoing fascination with color-sound art (see Bahun; Haller in the present volume).

In her September 14, 1925, diary entry, Woolf also described an important purchase: "I shall aim at haphazard, bohemian meetings, music (we have the algraphone, & thats a heavenly prospect – music after dinner while I stitch at my woolwork)" (D3: 42).[3] The Algraphone was a cherished possession because it allowed her to listen to her music in private, without the usual distractions that disturbed her listening experience at public performances.[4] This was also an important purchase for Leonard Woolf, who reviewed classical gramophone recordings for the *Nation and Athenaeum* between 1926 and 1929. In his "New Gramophone Records" column, he reviewed a variety of works by composers ranging from Giovanni Pierluigi da Palestrina and Johann Sebastian Bach to Joseph Haydn, Wolfgang Amadeus Mozart, Ludwig van Beethoven, Franz Schubert, Robert Schumann, Richard Wagner, Anton Bruckner, Claude Debussy, Richard Strauss, Frederick Delius, and many others.

As a result, the Woolfs built up an impressive record collection, a small portion of which is today part of the Charleston Trust.[5]

At about the same time, between 1927 and 1930, the Hogarth Press published several books about music history and musicology – Robert Hull's *Contemporary Music* (1927) and *Delius* (1928); Basil de Selincourt's *The Enjoyment of Music* (1928); Ralph Hill and Thomas J. Hewitt's two-volume *An Outline of Musical History* (1929); Erik Walter White's *Stravinsky's Sacrifice to Apollo* (1930); and a sixth, inter-art study, White's *Parnassus to Let: An Essay about Rhythm in the Films I* (1928). These works address the "common reader," but they also offer comprehensive musical analyses. They were part of the *Hogarth Essays*, a series the Woolfs began to publish in 1924 that included works such as *Mr. Bennett and Mrs. Brown* (Virginia Woolf), *The Artist and Psycho-Analysis* (Roger Fry), *Henry James at Work* (Theodora Bosanquet), and *Homage to John Dryden* (T. S. Eliot) (Willis 108). By 1941 the Hogarth Press had published thirteen such series. That music was a subject that featured prominently alongside literature, art, politics, law, and history shows the serious interest the Woolfs took, as publishers, in music history and musicology.[6]

Equally important is Virginia Woolf's interest in music criticism and performance history, as her essays, diaries, and letters attest. She expressed this interest in one of the earliest essays she wrote about musical performance, "Impressions at Bayreuth" (August 1909), in which she stated her concern for music criticism, decrying "the lack of tradition and of current standards" in writing about what she called "new music" (E1: 288). Having made the Covent Garden Opera House "her college" (Marcus, *Languages of Patriarchy* 51), Woolf was able to compare what she saw in London with what she saw in 1909 Bayreuth and Dresden,[7] discerning what few music critics would have been able to realize at the time about performance practice: "In the final impression of Bayreuth this year, beauty is still triumphant, although the actual performances (if we except *Götterdämmerung*, which remains to be heard) have been below the level of many that have been given in London" (E1: 292).

Her slightly earlier article "The Opera" (April 1909) reflects a complex understanding of musical performance, reception, and criticism. She divides the operagoing public into three groups: those who prefer *Traviata* to *Walküre*, that is to say, the bel canto tradition to Wagnerian opera; those "who disapprove of opera altogether, but, go, cynically enough, for the sake of what they term its bastard merits" (E1: 270) – a reference to the dispute between the supporters of absolute music (instrumental, non-programmatic music without words) and the supporters of opera; and a third party, "which opposes Gluck to Wagner" (270). In her opinion, this latter difference is the one "most worthy of discussion" (270), because it has to do exactly with the relationship between text and music: in Christoph Willibald Gluck's case, Woolf argues, emotions arise directly from the music itself, while in Wagnerian opera, emotions "flash out in men and women, as the story winds and knots itself, under the stress of sharp conflict" (270). Woolf then continues to examine different ways of relating to and understanding Wagner's works, but what interests her most is the relationship between word and music as played out to the fullest in Wagnerian opera. She returns to this topic again in "Impressions at Bayreuth," where she describes the opera *Parsifal*'s music as "intimate in a sense that none other is; one is fired with emotion and yet possessed with tranquility at the same time, for the words are continued by the music so that we hardly notice the transition" (289).

LITERATURE AND MUSIC

In December 1940, Woolf wrote to her friend Ethel Smyth about her intention "to investigate the influence of music on literature." She asked the composer to write her own "loves and hates for Bach Wagner etc out in plain English," because none of the books on music that Woolf was reading could give her a hint of how she might investigate that influence (L6: 450).[8] It is significant that she was planning to investigate the relationship between music and literature herself, unwilling to rely on existing criticism, finding "[Hubert] Parry all padding" and Donald Francis Tovey "too metaphysical" (450).

Questions concerning musical form and meaning as well as the problematic literature-music relationship are extremely complex, and they have been debated ever since music itself became a subject of discourse, with disagreements over attempts to establish even basic analogies between musical score and literary text. Are music and language completely different and separate media, or do they share certain characteristics? Are there areas where they overlap? Ian Cross and Elizabeth Tolbert point to diachronic, historical transformations in the ways music, language, and meaning have been understood and defined in the Western intellectual tradition. They trace these transformations from the classical Greek philosophical tradition, to the medieval world, to the early modern, Romantic, modernist, and postmodern periods.[9] Along similar lines, several articles included in the present volume (Szegedy-Maszák; Stewart; Varga; Thompson; Manhire) analyze Woolf's awareness of these historical developments as well as the various ways she employed them in her fiction and discussed them in her essays and diaries. *Between the Acts*, for instance, could be seen as an interweaving of melodic, fundamentally human musical activities with theories based, in the classical Greek philosophical tradition, on the natural laws of number "viewed as reflecting abstract and immanent aspects of the universe," "the principles of natural order, or the workings of the divine" (Cross and Tolbert 26) – the celestial music (harmonies and dissonances) that Mrs. Swithin muses on during her circular tours of the imagination. While in novels such as *The Voyage Out* and *The Waves*, as well as in several short stories,[10] Woolf explores the tension between music viewed in terms of human passion and affects and music viewed as an autonomous art, important for its own sake, not only different from language but also resisting linguistic description.[11]

Music theorists may ground their arguments in aesthetic considerations, in semantic theories, or in attempts to understand music and musical meaning within the social and cultural contexts in which they have developed. These differing perspectives have resulted in a wide variety of approaches to the process of exploring musical and linguistic meaning and their possible interconnections. In an article included in this volume, Trina Thompson summarizes these views and draws a particularly useful classification through three types of inquiry: (1) Is music like a language? (2) How do text and music relate within a work such as an art song or opera? (3) How can a work of art in one media be "translated" into another media? It is against this background that Woolf's own approach to exploring relationships between music and literature can be situated. In her fictional and critical works, Woolf follows similar directions of inquiry into the dilemmas of musical meaning and the connections between music, language, literature, and community.

MUSIC AND MODERNISM

The paradigm shift in "Woolf and music" scholarship, signaled by the most recent studies on the topic,[12] is paralleled by another shift: a reconsideration of the reception of modernist music in Great Britain in the early twentieth century. Even though the repertoire of British music before the 1960s is usually seen as having considerably lagged behind continental modernist developments in classical music, and even though British composers themselves were decrying the backward state of music in England during the first half of the twentieth century, critics have recently begun to point out that modernist continental music was known in London in the first decades of the twentieth century. Works by Arnold Schoenberg, Manuel de Falla, Igor Stravinsky, Béla Bartók, and Maurice Ravel premiered in London, sometimes conducted by the composers themselves; works by the composers of the Second Viennese School were frequently broadcast by the BBC during the interwar period;[13] and "modern music" was reviewed, debated, and seriously considered in the British press and music journals (Riley 2).

This latter point deserves attention in the context of this study because, as Deborah Heckert has shown, at the beginning of the twentieth century, debates about the performance and reception of modernist music in England were expressed through and connected to the theoretical language of visual modernism as developed and coined by Roger Fry and Clive Bell: "We can see resonances of Fry's art criticism of 1910–13 in the positive critical reactions to Schoenberg and other performances of Continental avant-garde music in 1913–14, around the time of the second performance of the *Five Orchestral Pieces* [January 1914]" (Heckert 62). Although the first performance of this work was harshly criticized in London, after its second performance, conducted by the composer himself, British critics began to consider the possibility that the work was "a 'next step' in an evolving musical language" (62) and, in doing so, they made recourse to Fry's aesthetic language. They were considering, among other things, "the importance of form and the structural characteristics of the artwork in creating an emotional and expressive impact," and "they echoed Fry's themes and adapted them to explain the new music, attempting to justify these works to the London public in terms that were increasingly familiar across the spectrum of emerging modernist styles in the visual arts, literature and music" (62). If the question Woolf began "Impressions at Bayreuth" with in 1909, concerning what she called the ambiguous state of musical criticism for both "new" and "old" music (E1: 288), could have received an answer at all, it would have received it by way of the aesthetics of Fry and Bell. While genetic criticism points to the conclusion that Woolf was much more familiar with and, therefore, influenced by the classical style (by the First rather than the Second Viennese School), her very early appreciation of Wagner's music and exposure to Richard Strauss[14] as well as her familiarity with the latest developments in visual-art criticism of the Bloomsbury Group bring her aesthetics in line with those of her contemporary modernist musicians and artists. This opens up new critical perspectives and comparative approaches, allowing scholars such as Sanja Bahun, Evelyn Haller, Roger Hillman, and Deborah Crisp to consider Woolf's works in their interrelations with modernist and later twentieth-century music and art.

Such reconsiderations also raise the question of how we may interpret Woolf's interest in the classical style in light of neoclassical developments in early twentieth-century classical music. Reflecting back in 1941 on Stravinsky's *Octet* (1923), Aaron Copland observed that this work "was destined to influence composers all over the world in bringing the latent objectivity of modern music to full consciousness by frankly adopting the ideals, forms, and textures of the preromantic era" (Taruskin 447). Woolf's interest in the classical style may be seen not as anachronistic but, rather, as resonating with modernist musical developments (see Lloyd 35, and Szegedy-Maszak 63, this volume). Richard Taruskin goes as far as to affirm that it is neoclassicism that marks the beginning of "the history of twentieth-century music as something esthetically distinct from that of the nineteenth century" (448). If twentieth-century musical and literary aesthetics may be interpreted as a recycling of both classicism and romanticism, the point remains that *Octet* ushered in neoclassicism as "a new creative period, not only for Stravinsky but for European and Euro-American 'art music' generally," these "musical manifestations" being "symptoms in turn of a pronounced general swerve in the arts that reflected a yet greater one in the wider world of expressive culture" (448).

SIGNIFICANT FORM: MUSICAL STRUCTURE IN WOOLF'S SHORT FICTION

Returning to the question of how Woolf approached text-music comparisons, one of the short stories that has received intense critical attention, "The String Quartet," shows Woolf's reluctance to draw imitative analogies between music and literature. It also illustrates how she used the short-story genre as a space in which she could explore various topics – in this case the text-music relationship – in a smaller, restrained space, which she would then develop on a larger scale in her novels. Included in the collection *Monday or Tuesday* (1921), this story marks the beginning of a period of searching, experimentation, and fervent creativity, in which Woolf even compared herself to "an improviser with his hands rambling over the piano" (*D*3: 37–38), and which produced *Jacob's Room* (1922), *Freshwater* (1923), *Mrs. Dalloway* (1925), and *To the Lighthouse* (1927). "The String Quartet" is a distillation of these experiments, a perfect example of what Woolf would describe in "Poetry, Fiction and the Future" (1927, reprinted by Leonard Woolf as "The Narrow Bridge of Art") as the need to "dramatize some of those influences which play so large a part in life, yet have so far escaped the novelist – the power of music, the stimulus of sight, the effect on use of the shape of trees or the play of colour [...]. Every moment is the centre and meeting-place of an extraordinary number of perceptions which have not yet been expressed" (*E*4: 439).

The story's early reception is one of success, with praise from Lytton Strachey, Roger Fry, and T. S. Eliot (*D*2: 109, 125). Yet the story's musical references have also provoked a variety of divergent interpretations. The narrative is so deceptively simple that Avrom Fleishman argued that it has a circular A-B-C-B-A structure patterned on a Mozart quartet, concluding that it is simply "an exercise in imitative form" that could not be considered one of the most important tales (67). Peter Jacobs astutely pointed out that the clue that Mozart's music is heard in the story is ironic (243), yet he also interprets the story as having a "straightforward bithematic A-B-A-B-A-B-A scheme" (244–455). Emilie Crapoulet, in turn, has argued that Schubert's "Trout" Piano Quintet in A major, D. 667, is the musical composition that inspired the story, and not a Mozart quartet ("Beyond Boundaries" 208), basing her interpretation on Woolf's diary entry of March 9, 1920 (D2: 24n13).[15] However, the story's title itself refers to a quartet, and in a short paragraph Woolf omitted from the published text, which is extant in the typescript (see CSF 140n2), the author mentioned Mozart for what would have been a second time in the story. Even allowing for the assumption that, if the story's characters envision fish swimming in the Rhône while they hear a musical performance, it must mean they are listening to Schubert's "Trout" Quintet, by mentioning Mozart's name, Woolf pointed to her characters' failure to recognize the composer they have just heard – a criticism of musical performance as a purely social event in which attention focuses on everything but the music itself. More importantly, this also means the author intentionally provided ambiguous or inconclusive clues about exactly which composition should be associated with this short story. Had she wanted, Woolf could have easily singled out a particular composition – as she did with Beethoven's Sonata, op. 111, in *The Voyage Out*. Beyond any imitation of musical structure or desire to capture and convey musical meaning, this discrepancy between the use and mention of music in "The String Quartet" points to a metafictional engagement with classical music, postmodern in its playfulness (see Manhire 147, this volume). In fact, the story's narrator (or one of the story's narrators) asks herself: "But the tune, like all his tunes, makes one despair – I mean hope. What do I mean? That's the worst of music!" (CSF 139). Musical meaning is ineffable. If the first reaction to music invokes a "conglomeration of fish all in a pool," later passages suggest a transcendence of the indoor concert experience – "'these are the embraces of our souls.' The lemons nod assent. The swan pushes from the bank and floats dreaming into midstream" (CSF 30) – while the very end of the story describes an entirely different, synesthetic and visionary experience reminiscent of Lucy Swithin and Isa Oliver's musings in *Between the Acts*: "the green garden, moonlit pools, lemons, lovers, and fish" dissolved "in the opal sky across which, as the horns are joined by trumpets and supported by clarions there rise white arches," like the architecture that arises from Rachel's playing, "firmly planted on marble pillars ... Tramp and trumpeting. Glang and clangour. Firm establishment. Fast foundations. March of myriads. Confusion and chaos trod to earth" (CSF 141).

Woolf's approach to exploring the relationship between music, language, and literature may therefore be situated against the background of a dispute that reflects two distinct perspectives on this relationship: an aesthetic one, valuing music as autonomous with a meaning detached from linguistic semantics or social value (an expression-based approach [Cross 27]); and an approach that assumes comparisons between music and language can be naturally drawn, linguistic and musical meaning often intersect, and "the relationship between a page of print and the poem it represents is analogous to that between a score and the music it represents" (Brown 7). Critiquing the latter approach,[16] Suzanne Langer argued that reading a score is not equivalent to reading a text, because, while in music the passage of time is made audible by "purely sonorous elements," which exist for the ear alone,[17] the elements of literature are not sounds as such: "Instead of being pure sense objects that may become 'natural' symbolic forms, like shapes and tones, they are symbols already, namely 'assigned' symbols, and the artistic illusion created by means of them is not a fabric of *tönend bewegte Formen*, but a different illusion altogether" (*Feeling* 135).[18]

The argument is based on analyses Langer had made earlier in *Philosophy in a New Key* (1942), where she explained that the actual function of meaning calls for permanent contents. Music, as opposed to language, is an "unconsummated symbol" – it articulates without asserting (240). It is a point Virginia Woolf had made in her 1909 essay "Impressions at Bayreuth," when she briefly tried to discuss the difference between musical and linguistic expression: "Apart from the difficulty of changing a musical impression into a literary one, and the tendency to appeal to the literary sense because of the associations of words, there is the further difficulty in the case of music that its scope is much less clearly defined than the scope of the other arts. [...] Perhaps music owes something of its astonishing power over us to this lack of definite articulation; its statements have all the majesty of a generalization, and yet contain our private emotions" (E1: 291).[19]

The similarities with Langer's discussion of the difference between music and language are striking, yet they should not surprise: Langer's aesthetic approach to musical meaning relies heavily on Clive Bell and Roger Fry's "Significant Form,"[20] a concept Woolf was well acquainted with. While she did not seek to imitate musical structure, Woolf not only found inspiration in musical form when structuring her own writing, as she explained in her letter to Elizabeth Trevelyan, but she also understood and emphasized literary form in a way that brought it close to musical form as described by Langer: "Articulation is its life, but not assertion; expressiveness, not expression. The actual function of meaning, which calls for permanent contents, is not fulfilled; for the *assignment* of one rather than another possible meaning to each form is never explicitly made" (*Philosophy* 240). The "Impressions at Bayreuth" passage quoted above continues with a comment about Shakespeare that shows Woolf was thinking of authors who attempted to bring the quality of the English language close to that of music: "Something of the same effect is given by Shakespeare, when he makes an old nurse the type of all the old nurses in the world, while she keeps her identity as a particular old woman" (E1: 291). The debates with Arnold Bennett centered precisely on an emphasis, on Woolf's part, on form and formal expressiveness rather than meaning and plot. While she was not interested in imitating musical form, the constant attention Woolf devoted to form in writing; her awareness that form can drive articulation/utterance in ways that are significantly different from assertion and explanation; and the importance she placed on rhythm, sound, and silence in her writing bring her textual praxis close to musical form in the sense Langer meant it, as exhibiting "pure form not as an embellishment but as its very essence" (*Philosophy* 209).

Woolf was certainly well aware of the pitfalls of indiscriminately comparing music and text. She stated quite early her belief that descriptions of music were "worthless" and "rather unpleasant" (D1: 33). She also affirmed, metafictionally, through the heroine of her first novel, that it would be better to write music instead of novels (VO 212). At the same time, as several contributors to this volume (Szegedy-Maszák; Manhire; Varga) point out, Woolf was fascinated by the ideal of *ut musica poe-*

sis and was influenced by Walter Pater's "School of Giorgione" maxim, "All art constantly aspires towards the condition of music." As early as 1905, she recorded in her diary that she was passionately studying Pater's works "not to copy [. . .] but to see how the trick's done" (PA 251). In Woolf's fiction and in her writings on music and literature there are tensions similar to those arising from debates about where the boundaries that separate the arts can be drawn. When discussing the "Laocoön problem" – the problem of "discovering how strongly the boundaries separating the various artistic media manage to repel transgression" (Albright 6–7) – Daniel Albright points out that alleging that all media are one paradoxically calls attention to their recalcitrance and, vice versa, that "artists who deliberately seek divergence among the constituent arts sometimes discover that the impression of realness, *thereness*, is heightened, not diminished" (7).[21]

Several scholars have written about the influence of music on Woolf's works – most notably, Mark Hussey in *The Singing of the Real World: The Philosophy of Virginia Woolf's Fiction* (1986); Jane Marcus in *Virginia Woolf and the Languages of Patriarchy* (1987); and Patricia Laurence in *The Reading of Silence* (1991) – and over the past fifteen years a few well-regarded essays treating aspects of the topic have appeared, some authored by scholars who are also contributors to this volume.[22] Prior to 1980 one finds only very few essays that touch on the subject of Woolf and music, usually more oriented toward narrative method and isolated textual readings than researched considerations of the role music played in the intellectual and cultural milieu of the Bloomsbury Group in general and in Woolf's development in particular. Surprisingly, until now no collection of essays has focused primarily on the relationship between music, language, and the other arts in Virginia Woolf's writings. *Virginia Woolf and Music* fills this gap by focusing on how Woolf's use of music led to her breaking with traditional forms of representation in her novels at various stages of her aesthetic development and by exploring the inter-arts and interdisciplinary aspects of her modernist fictional experimentation. The essays gathered here examine various aspects of Virginia Woolf's musical culture as well as the rich and deeply musical nature of her works from several different perspectives:

1. Contextual – the importance of music in the Bloomsbury milieu and its role within the larger framework of modernism and early twentieth-century culture (Lloyd; Szegedy-Maszák; Haller; Bahun);
2. Biographical – Woolf's involvement with music as a listener and concertgoer, her musical knowledge and aesthetics (Szegedy-Maszák; Varga; Manhire; Clements);
3. Comparative – Woolf's own use of music as metaphor, motif, or trope in her writing as well as connections between classical, modernist, and contemporary music and Woolf's fictional and critical writings (Stewart; Manhire; Sutton; Clements; Thompson; Bahun; Hillman and Crisp).

The introductory section of the volume examines the importance of music for Cambridge and Bloomsbury intellectuals from G. E. Moore to Roger Fry, thus offering a setting in which Virginia Woolf's own musical culture can be discussed. In the opening essay Rosemary Lloyd explains that even though for many of Woolf's contemporaries music may have taken a secondary place to the fine arts, especially under Fry's influence, for some of them, most notably Woolf herself, music was a source of sensual delight and intellectual stimulation that informed their writing and aesthetic convictions.

Woolf's interest in music was all the more enriched by her attendance of classical music concerts from an early age, by reading about music, and, later, by listening to music practically every day in her own home. Mihály Szegedy-Maszák's essay focuses our attention on the important role music played in Woolf's life and writings. Contrary to what critics have previously argued, Szegedy-Maszák sees continuity between Woolf's early concert- and operagoing experiences, the interest she took in Wagner, and her later interest in the works of Beethoven, arguing that a major artist never forgets the inspiration of early, formative years.

The middle section of the volume includes essays that discuss aspects of the music-literature relationship in Virginia Woolf's fiction, with a focus on the novel, showing that this can be done from a variety of angles and from sometimes diverging perspectives. In my own contribution, I trace transformations in the text-music relationship from

The Voyage Out (1915) to *The Waves* (1931) and *Between the Acts* (1941) and discuss Woolf's interest in exploring the interconnections of rhythm, sound, and language in these particular works. Woolf's musical "voyage out" led to the highly experimental forms of her later fiction, in which she reconfigured the relationship between reader, text, and context; actor, audience, and performance.

Jim Stewart draws attention to Woolf's early interest in drama, particularly to her keen awareness of singing Greek choruses, which she discussed in her essays, and which clearly influenced her first novel, *The Voyage Out*. Using Friedrich Nietzsche's *Birth of Tragedy* as a cross-reference to Virginia Stephen's intellectual practice, Stewart argues that between 1899 and 1905, Woolf's musical sensibility and her insight of writing as a form of rhythm was influenced partly by the form of the Greek music-drama and partly by Wagnerian opera.

It is to the "worst of music" that Vanessa Manhire responds in her essay, in which she shows that Woolf does not attempt to reproduce musical form but, rather, to transpose indeterminacy of meaning into linguistic play. Looking at the novelist's treatment of music in *Night and Day* (1919) and in the "The String Quartet," Manhire explores Virginia Woolf's use of music in order to problematize the relationship between the external world and the world of the mind. She explains that Woolf used music as a model for representing interiority, and suggests that Woolf's development of stream-of-consciousness narrative techniques owes much to her thinking about the effects of playing and listening to music – a shared social experience, but one that simultaneously allows for the individual movement of imagination.

Emma Sutton also discusses Richard Wagner's influence on Woolf, and explores the ways in which *Mrs. Dalloway* (1925) is informed by Wagner's *Der fliegende Holländer* (1843). Sutton's approach to the topic relies on the double perspective of discussing *Mrs. Dalloway*'s intertextuality with Wagner's Romantic opera and of considering the role and representation of Jewish religious practice – particularly the Jewish mourning practice of shivah – amplifying, in this way, Woolf's critique of the Wagnerian intertext. Sutton considers Woolf as expressing in her fiction both indebtedness and resistance to the Wagnerian operatic model of tragedy.

The Years (1937), Elicia Clements argues, is Woolf's most overtly political novel, and at the same time, it "turns up the volume" by foregrounding aurality in new and ubiquitous ways. In her essay Clements explains that the two foci – political and musical – converge in both the novel's subject matter and methods. One of the reasons Woolf values music as an art form is that it is performative by its very nature. As with theater, it traverses a continuum between efficacy (or effective acts that produce change, as in ritual) and entertainment (symbolic gestures for an aesthetic purpose).

Opera is again a subject of discourse in Trina Thompson's essay, this time in reference to Woolf's last novel, *Between the Acts*. Thompson argues that the structural poetics of Woolf's novel and the emergence of opera share a parallel genetic evolution: in cinquecento Italy, musical entertainments were performed during the intermissions of the primary theatrical piece. Composers of these interludes believed that the social and moral power of the ancients was a function of *musical* drama – verbal utterance soldered to music's dynamic force. Opera was created as a genre between the acts, and, likewise, the conflicted societal collective of Pointz Hall finds its voice between historical moments. Through this prism, *Between the Acts* can be interpreted as an "experiment with historically infused genres," recapitulating Woolf's engagement with the past and her explorations of alternatives to traditional historiography.

The last section of the volume is concerned with exploring inter-art connections between Virginia Woolf's fiction and twentieth-century music, the visual arts, and film. Sanja Bahun begins this section with an appraisal of Woolf's knowledge of and involvement with modernist music and explains how Woolf's writing changed substantially in terms of expression and mood after reaching its most resonant pitches with *The Waves* and *The Years* – a shift in representation that parallels contemporary developments in modern classical music. By focusing on Woolf's *Between the Acts* as a unique formal articulation of its moment of production, Bahun highlights the cross-sections between sociohistorical content, philosophic and artistic practice in compositions by Schoenberg and Stravinsky, and Woolf's fiction. Woolf's last novel becomes a study in the emancipation of sound similar to that carried out in "ultramodern" music.

Evelyn Haller begins her contribution to this volume by citing connections among aspects of art – specifically sound in music as well as language, sculpture and painting, and movement as further epitomized by dance. What have the rambunctious Italian Futurists or the shorter-lived English Vorticists to do with Virginia Woolf or Bloomsbury? Reviewing criticism that both affirms and denies Woolf's associations with Vorticism, Haller explains that in her eagerness to collapse artistic conventions of time and space, Woolf was also interested in aspects of modern life and mechanization. Haller focuses on the aurality of Woolf's novels: the sound of the skywriting airplane in her war-haunted *Mrs. Dalloway*; the sound of "the sea" she intended to be heard "all through" *The Waves*; street noises in *The Years*.

In the final essay, film studies scholar Roger Hillman and musicologist Deborah Crisp join forces for an analysis of the interplay between music, image, and text at work in all three stages of the adaptive process leading to Stephen Daldry's 2002 film *The Hours* – the two previous stages being Michael Cunningham's 1998 novel, *The Hours*, and Woolf's *Mrs. Dalloway*, from which Cunningham took his inspiration. Through musical examples, the authors show how Philip Glass's music creates the underlying connection between the narrative strands of the film (with a screenplay by David Hare). But they also interweave comparative examples from Woolf's fiction (*Mrs. Dalloway*), her biography, Cunningham's novel, and Daldry's film, showing how these works stem out of and influence each other in a mise-en-abîme-like effect that is connected and amplified through textual and aural musical references.

The essays gathered in the present volume have the advantage of reconsidering and opening up the question of how Virginia Woolf made music bear on her writing, by addressing it from several, differing perspectives rather than from a single, homogenous point of view. In biographical, historical, and conceptual terms, they advance the discussion about music in the Bloomsbury environment and the evolution of Woolf's own musical knowledge and textual praxis, interweaving modernist poetics with classical and contemporary music. As well, they address esthetic, theoretical, and political issues about how comparisons between music, literature, the visual arts, and film prove (im)possible and what the musical intertexts add to the ethical dimensions of Woolf's writing.

NOTES

1. In the same memoir, Woolf also describes the thrill of her first childhood writing success: "How excited I used to be when the 'Hide Park Gate News' was laid on her [Julia Stephen's] plate on Monday morning, and she liked something I had written! Never shall I forget my extremity of pleasure – it was like being a violin and being played upon – when I found that she had sent a story of mine to Madge Symonds" ("Sketch" 95). Jane Marcus comments on this moment in her excellent analysis in "Virginia Woolf and Her Violin: Mothering, Madness, and Music" (*Languages of Patriarchy* 96).

2. In her notes for the *Memoir Club* after Virginia's death, Vanessa Bell wrote that music "naturally, since we were girls, had to be drummed into us, and the piano mistress succeeded in reducing us to complete boredom."

3. Woolf "was embroidering a cross-stitch chair cover from a design by Vanessa Bell" (*D*3: 42n8).

4. On February 13, 1915, for example, she described hearing a "divine" concert at Queen's Hall (also attended by Oliver Strachey, Bernard Shaw, and Walter Lamb), where "they played Haydn, Mozart no 8, Brandenburg Concerto, & the Unfinished" (*D*1: 33), but expressed her annoyance at the neighbors' behavior: "a young man & woman next me who took advantage of the music to press each other's hands; & read 'A Shropshire Lad' & look at some vile illustrations. And other people eat chocolates, & crumbled the silver paper into balls" (34). She often remarked sarcastically on the show of toilettes and furs during such occasions, and years later she wrote to Ethel Smyth: "I couldnt go to Londonderry House to hear Nadia [Boulanger], as invited; but I heard her on the wireless. Cant bear music mixed with peerage" (*L*6: 301, Nov. 9, 1938).

5. The Leonard Woolf Records Collection at Charleston contains forty-five HMV, Columbia Gramophone, and Decca "Polydor Series" records: Béla Bartók Quartet in A minor, op. 7; Ludwig van Beethoven Trio no. 3 in C minor, Quartet in F minor, op. 95, Quartet in F major, op. 135; Johannes Brahms Quintet in G major, op. 111, Quartet in A major, op. 26, Quartet in C minor, op. 51, Trio no. 2 in C major, op. 87; W. A. Mozart Quartet in E flat major, Quartet in C major, Quartet in D minor, Quartet in D major, Oboe Quartet in F major part 2 and 4, Quartet in G major no. 19; Franz Schubert Trio no. 1 in B flat, op. 99; Pyotr Ilyich Tchaikovsky Quartet in D, op. 11.

6. In his introduction to *A Checklist of the Hogarth Press, 1917–1946*, J. Howard Woolmer explains that between 1927 and 1930, the Woolfs' only assistant at the press was young Richard Kennedy. Judging by the record of his impressions, *A Boy at the Hogarth Press* (1972), Kennedy was not the kind of assistant who was able to help with making decisions about accepting or rejecting manuscripts, so during this time it is safe to assume that Virginia and Leonard were entirely responsible for reading, selecting, and editing the manuscripts submitted to them. Virginia herself was involved directly with the printing of the books: George (Dadie) Rylands, who was their assistant during the summer of 1924, recalls working in the basement of the Woolfs' Tavistock Square residence, where he "had many happy hours setting up type with Virginia and helping Leonard with the hand press" (Woolmer xxvii–xxviii; Letter to author June 29, 1965).

7. In 1908, for example, János (Hans) Richter conducted an English-language production of Wagner's *The Ring* at London's Covent Garden.

8. At the time, she was reading Hubert Parry's *Art of Music* (1894) and Donald Francis Tovey's *Essays in Musical Analysis* (1935–1939).

9. Cross and Tolbert suggest diachronic, historical transformations in the concept of musical meaning in the Western intellectual tradition. They trace them from the classical Greek philosophical tradition – in which one aspect of music was a melodic, fundamentally human activity, while another aspect involved theories based on the natural laws of number "viewed as reflecting abstract and immanent aspects of the universe," "the principles of natural order, or the workings of the divine" (26) – to the medieval world, in which this dichotomous view of music gained complexity "as it was refracted through the multiple prisms of early Christian thought" (27). In the late seventeenth and early eighteenth centuries, the meanings of music "had come to be largely theorized in terms of human passion or affects," music aligning itself with rhetoric and its forms mirroring "those of the linguistic prosody, though the structures that music could articulate also became more important for their own sake" (27). By the eighteenth century, "music's forms became more and more intelligible in terms of theories of harmony, related to either, and sometimes to both the findings of physical acoustics, and abstract principles or architectonic structure" (27). As a consequence, musical meaning no longer required reference to words it would have accompanied, or to "prosody" – "the ways in which it conveyed those words" – and thus "instrumental music came to be conceived of as equally capable of bearing meaning in its own right" (27). Downing A. Thomas further explains, in the same *Oxford Handbook of Music Psychology,* that most mid- to late eighteenth-century philosophers who wrote about music assumed it was a kind of language (5), an assumption that would be overturned at the end of the eighteenth century by the notion of music as autonomous, as having value in its own right (Cross and Tolbert 27).

10. Stories such as "The Journal of Mistress Joan Martyn," "The String Quartet," "A Simple Melody," and "Moments of Being: 'Slater's Pins Have No Points.'"

11. In such expression-based theories, "music's capacity to engender aesthetic experience does not rely on, and is not expressible in the same terms as the capacity that language possesses of bearing meaning by expressing complex propositions that have determinable sense and reference" (Cross and Tolbert 28).

12. See Emilie Crapoulet, *Virginia Woolf: A Musical Life,* and Emma Sutton, "Music."

13. See Jennifer Doctor's *The BBC and Ultra-Modern Music, 1922–1936.*

14. Woolf heard Richard Strauss's *Symphonia Domestica* in 1905 with Henry Wood conducting the Queen's Hall Orchestra and, more importantly, after attending concernts in Bayreuth, in August 1909, Woolf traveled – with her friend Saxon Sydney-Turner and with her brother Adrian Stephen – to Dresden, where she heard Strauss's *Salome* (1905) (E1: 292n2).

15. Woolf noted: "On Sunday I went up to Campden Hill to hear the S[c]hubert quintet – to see George Booth's house – to take notes for my story – to rub shoulders with respectability – all these reasons took me there, & were cheaply gratified at 7/6" (D2: 24). It may be somewhat problematic to make the assumption that the Schubert quintet was the "Trout," as neither Woolf nor George Booth refer in their diaries to this particular composition.

16. Brown responded to Langer's criticism in several articles published in the *Yearbook of Comparative and General Literature* in the 1980s.

17. "All the musical helps to our actual perception of time are eliminated and replaced by tonal experiences in the musical image of duration" (Langer, *Feeling and Form* 135).

18. In addition, the step between inward and actual hearing in music is occupied by another phase of artistic production, performance itself, which, for Langer, "is as creative an act as composition" (*Feeling and Form* 139). While silent reading may occur both when reading a score and reading a text, it has "different values in the two respective contexts" (135).

19. Mark Hussey is one of the earliest scholars to discuss the role of the arts, particularly that of music, in Woolf's works in his 1986 monograph, *The Singing of the Real World: The Philosophy of Virginia Woolf's Fiction*. He discusses Susanne Langer's concept of "significant form" in the same context (see particularly *The Singing* 67–68).

20. Music is significant form, Langer argued, "in the peculiar sense of 'significant' in which Mr. Bell and Mr. Fry maintain they can grasp or feel, but not define; such significance is implicit, but not conventionally fixed" (*Philosophy* 240–41).

21. Gotthold Ephrain Lessing, for instance, challenged Horace's "*Ut pictura poesis*" (*Ars poetica* 333–65) and was himself challenged by some of his contemporaries. Herder in particular disapproved of the narrowness of Lessing's taste and his "rigid segregation of temporal from spatial," while Diderot, and later Wagner and others, devised "serious arguments concerning the unity of the arts" (Albright 10, 8).

22. Elicia Clements's "Virginia Woolf, Ethel Smyth, and Music" and "Transforming Musical Sounds in Words: Narrative Method in Virginia Woolf's *The Waves*" appeared in separate journals: *College Literature* and, respectively, *Narrative*. Emma Sutton's "'Within a Space of Tears': Music, Writing, and the Modern in Virginia Woolf's *The Voyage Out*" appeared in *Music and Literary Modernism;* her chapter, "Music," in *Virginia Woolf in Context;* as well as "Shell Shock and Hysterical Fugue, or why Mrs Dalloway Likes Bach," appeared in *Literature and Music of the First World War*. Joyce Kelley's "Virginia Woolf and Music" is included in *The Edinburgh Companion to Virginia Woolf and the Arts*. Emilie Crapoulet's "Beyond the Boundaries of Language: Music in Virginia Woolf's 'The String Quartet'" appeared in *Journal of the Short Story in English*, while her wonderful analysis *Virginia Woolf: A Musical Life* was published in the Bloomsbury Heritage Series by Cecil Woolf. Tracey Sherard published "'Parcival in the forest of gender': Wagner, Homosexuality, and *The Waves*," and Joycelyn Slovak published "Mrs. Dalloway and Fugue: 'Songs without Words, Always the Best...'" at Unsaid (http://www.unsaidmag.com/display_lit.php?issue=2&file_url=slovak.html/). Three groundbreaking studies that began the shift in Woolf and music scholarship are Jane Marcus's "Enchanted Organs, Magic Bells: *Night and Day* as Comic Opera," in *Virginia Woolf Revaluation and Continuity;* Melba Cuddy-Keane's "Virginia Woolf, Sound Technologies, and the New Aurality," in *Virginia Woolf in the Age of Mechanical Reproduction*, which discusses, among other things, the challenge of "listening" to a book and differences between the linguistic representation and conceptualization of sound; and Pamela Caughie's "Virginia Woolf: Radio, Gramophone, Broadcasting," in *The Edinburgh Companion to Virginia Woolf and the Arts*. Peter Jacobs's "The Second Violin Tuning in the Ante-room: Virginia Woolf and Music" is an exceptionally brilliant piece dealing with music in an otherwise visual

arts-oriented set of essays, *The Multiple Muses of Virginia Woolf*, edited by Diane F. Gillespie. Two of the most fruitful earliest articles on the topic – Gerald Levin's "The Musical Style of *The Waves*" (1983), and Harold Fromm's "*To the Lighthouse:* Music and Sympathy" (1968) – are also well worth mentioning in this context.

WORKS CITED

Albright, Daniel. *Untwisting the Serpent: Modernism in Music, Literature, and Other Arts*. Chicago: University of Chicago Press, 2000. Print.

Bell, Clive. *Art*. Ed. J. B. Bullen. Oxford: Oxford University Press, 1987. Print.

Bell, Quentin. *Virginia Woolf. A Biography*. Vol. 1. London: Hogarth, 1972. Print.

Brown, Calvin. "The Writing and Reading of Music: Thoughts in Some Parallels between Two Artistic Media." *Yearbook of Comparative and General Literature* 33 (1984): 7–18. Print.

Bullough, Edward. "'Psychical Distance' as a Factor in Art and as an Aesthetic Principle." *British Journal of Psychology* 5 (1912): 87–117. Print.

Caughie, Pamela L. "Virginia Woolf: Radio, Gramophone, Broadcasting." *The Edinburgh Companion to Virginia Woolf and the Arts*. Ed. Maggie Humm. Edinburgh: Edinburgh University Press, 2010.

Clements, Elicia. "Transforming Musical Sounds into Words: Narrative Method in Virginia Woolf's *The Waves*." *Narrative: The Journal of the Society for the Study of Narrative Literature* 13.2 (May 2005): 160–81. Print.

———. "Virginia Woolf, Ethel Smyth, and Music: Listening as a Productive Mode of Social Interaction." *College Literature* 32.3 (July 2005): 51–71. Print.

Crapoulet, Emilie. "Beyond the Boundaries of Language: Music in Virginia Woolf's 'The String Quartet.'" *Journal of the Short Story in English. Les Cahiers de la nouvelle* 50 (Spring 2008): 201–15. Print.

———. *Virginia Woolf: A Musical Life*. Bloomsbury Heritage Series, no. 50. London: Cecil Woolf, 2009. Print.

Cross, Ian, and Elizabeth Tolbert. "Music and Meaning." *The Oxford Handbook of Music Psychology*. Ed. Susan Hallam, Ian Cross, and Michael Thaut. Oxford: Oxford University Press, 2009. Print.

Cuddy-Keane, Melba. "Virginia Woolf, Sound Technologies, and the New Aurality." *Virginia Woolf in the Age of Mechanical Reproduction*. Ed. Pamela L. Caughie. New York: Garland, 2000. Print.

Fleishman, Avrom. "Forms of the Woolfian Short Story." *Virginia Woolf: Revaluation and Continuity*. Ed. Ralph Freedman. Berkeley: University of California Press, 1980. Print.

Fromm, Harold. "*To the Lighthouse:* Music and Sympathy." *English Miscellany: A Symposium of History, Literature, and the Arts*. Ed. Mario Praz. Rome: Edizioni di Storia e Letteratura, 1968. Print.

Gendron, Bernard. "Music." *A Companion to Modernist Literature and Culture*. Ed. David Bradshaw and Kevin J. H. Dettmar. Malden: Blackwell, 2006. Print.

Hussey, Mark. *The Singing of the Real World: The Philosophy of Virginia Woolf's Fiction*. Columbus: Ohio State University Press, 1986. Print.

Iser, Wolfgang. *Walter Pater: The Aesthetic Moment*. Trans. David Henry Wilson. Cambridge: Cambridge University Press, 1987. Print.

Jacobs, Peter. "'The Second Violin Tuning in the Ante-room': Virginia Woolf and

Music." *Multiple Muses of Virginia Woolf*. Ed. Diane F. Gillespie. Columbia: University of Missouri Press, 1993. Print.

Kelley, Joyce E. "Virginia Woolf and Music." *The Edinburgh Companion to Virginia Woolf and the Arts*. Ed. Maggie Humm. Edinburgh: Edinburgh University Press, 2010. Print.

Langer, Susanne K. *Feeling and Form*. New York: Scribner's, 1953. Print.

———. *Philosophy in a New Key: A Study in the Symbolism of Reason, Rite, and Art*. 1942. New York: Mentor, 1951. Print.

Lee, Hermione. *Virginia Woolf*. New York: Knopf, 1997. Print.

Levin, Gerald. "The Musical Styles of *The Waves*." *Journal of Narrative Technique* 13.3 (1983): 164–72. Print.

Marcus, Jane. "Enchanted Organs, Magic Bells: *Night and Day* as Comic Opera." *Virginia Woolf Revaluation and Continuity*. Ed. Ralph Freedman. Berkeley: University of California Press, 1980. Print.

———. *Virginia Woolf and the Languages of Patriarchy*. Bloomington: Indiana University Press, 1987. Print.

Nattiez, Jean-Jacques. *Fondements d'une sémiologie de la musique*. Paris: Union générale d'éditions, 1975. Print.

———. *Music and Discourse: Toward a Semiology of Music*. Trans. Carolyn Abbate. Princeton: Princeton University Press, 1990. Print.

Sherard, Tracey. "'Parcival in the forest of gender': Wagner, Homosexuality, and *The Waves*." *Virginia Woolf: Turning the Centuries. Selected Papers from the Ninth Annual conference on Virginia Woolf*. Ed. Ann Ardis and Bonnie Kime Scott. New York: Pace University Press, 2000. Print.

Slovak, Joycelyn. "Mrs. Dalloway and Fugue: 'Songs without Words, Always the Best . . .'" *Unsaid* 2. Web. Sept. 23, 2013. http://www.unsaidmag.com/display_lit.php?issue=2&file_url=slovak.html/.

Sutton, Emma. "Music." *Virginia Woolf in Context*. Ed. Bryony Randall and Jane Goldman. Cambridge: Cambridge University Press, 2012. Print.

———. "'Within a Space of Tears': Music, Writing, and the Modern in Virginia Woolf's *The Voyage Out*." *Music and Literary Modernism: Critical Essays and Comparative Studies*. 2nd ed. Ed. Robert P. McParland. Newcastle upon Tyne: Cambridge Scholars, 2009. Print.

Taruskin, Richard. *The Oxford History of Western Music*. Oxford: Oxford University Press, 2005. Print.

Thomas, Downing A. *Music and the Origins of Language: Theories from the French Enlightenment*. Cambridge: Cambridge University Press, 1995. Print.

Willis, J. H., Jr. *Leonard and Virginia Woolf as Publishers: The Hogarth Press, 1917–41*. Charlottesville: University Press of Virginia, 1992. Print.

Woolf, Leonard. *Beginning Again: An Autobiography of the Years 1911–1918*. London: Hogarth, 1964. Print.

———. *Letters of Leonard Woolf*. Ed. Frederick Spotts. San Diego: Harcourt, 1989. Print.

Woolf, Virginia. *The Diary of Virginia Woolf*. Vol. 1: *1915–1919*. Ed. Anne Olivier Bell. New York: Harcourt, 1977. Print.

———. *The Diary of Virginia Woolf*. Vol. 2: *1920–1924*. Ed. Anne Olivier Bell. Assist. Andrew McNeillie. London: Hogarth, 1978. Print.

———. *The Diary of Virginia Woolf*. Vol. 3: *1925–1930*. Ed. Anne Olivier Bell. New York: Harcourt, 1980. Print.

———. *The Essays of Virginia Woolf*. Vol. 1: *1904–1912*. Ed. Andrew McNeillie. London: Hogarth, 1986. Print.

———. *The Flight of the Mind: The Letters of Virginia Woolf*. Vol. 1: *1888–1912*. Ed. Nigel Nicolson. London: Hogarth, 1975. Print.

———. *Leave the Letters Till We're Dead: The Letters of Virginia Woolf*. Vol. 6:

1936–1941. Ed. Nigel Nicolson. London: Hogarth, 1980. Print.

———. "The Narrow Bridge of Art." *Collected Essays*. Vol. 2. Ed. Leonard Woolf. London: Chatto & Windus, 1967. Print.

———. "A Sketch of the Past." *Moments of Being*. Ed. Jeanne Schulkind. 2nd ed. San Diego: Harcourt, 1985. Print.

———. *The Voyage Out*. San Diego: Harcourt, 1968. Print.

———. *The Waves*. San Diego: Harcourt, 1978. Print.

Woolmer, J. Howard. *A Checklist of the Hogarth Press, 1917–1946*. With a short history of the press by Mary E. Gaither. Revere: Woolmer/Brotherson, 1986. Print.

PART ONE

Music and Bloomsbury Culture

ONE

Bloomsbury and Music

Rosemary Lloyd

LOOKING BACK ON THE HEADY DAYS IN CAMBRIDGE WHEN MANY of those who would come to be known as the Bloomsbury Group first met, Leonard Woolf recognized how important music had been for himself and his friends. He affirms in his biography that they were "intellectuals, intellectuals with three genuine and, I think, profound passions: a passion for friendship, a passion for literature and music (it is significant that the plastic arts came a good deal later), a passion for what we called the truth" (S 173). If the heyday of Bloomsbury can be seen as starting in March 1905, when the four young Stephens – Vanessa, Thoby, Virginia, and Adrian – opened their home in Gordon Square for Thursday evening gatherings, and continuing until the end of World War I, a calamity that, according to Vanessa Bell at least, also killed Bloomsbury (*Selected Letters* 364), its origins date back to 1899, when Lytton Strachey, Thoby Stephen, and Leonard Woolf first met at Cambridge University, and it continued in an altered form until 1939, when the dark days of World War II loomed.[1] Clever, witty, and sexually unconventional, the Bloomsberries, as they called themselves, were associated above all with new movements in art and literature. As a group, they reveled in free and open discussions, attempting to reach a less stuffy, less hypocritical form of ethics than the previous generation and to shape their lives and their thinking around love and beauty, giving value to what Leonard Woolf termed the "passion for friendship" (S 173). Rebelling against the stuffiness of their parents' generation, they turned to forms of art that exalted the sensual. For many of them, the family home had had little of aesthetic interest and the family ethos had been driven by a scornful rejection of aesthetic values. Although Virginia Woolf would later assert that her father had "no feeling for pictures; no ear for music; no sense of the sound of words" (MB 68), the other members of the Stephen family were to some extent an exception to this position, with Virginia's mother and her half sister, Stella, revealing a lively interest in music. The passion for photography revealed by her great-aunt, Julia Margaret Cameron, no doubt influenced her own practice of that art,[2] and both Virginia and Vanessa, like most young women of their class, were given music and ballet lessons from an early age. For most of the Bloomsbury Group, however, the discovery of visual and aural beauty during their Cambridge years, passed on to the women through brothers at the university, became a formative experience that would shape their later aesthetics. The early passion for music that Leonard Woolf reveals may have faded for many of them in comparison with the discovery of the plastic arts, especially under the guidance of Roger Fry, but music nevertheless remained an important part of their lives, both intellectually and emotionally.

Turning to the period 1911–1918 in the volume of his autobiography titled *Beginning Again*, Leonard Woolf captures the excitement the Bloomsbury Group felt in the vital artistic year 1913, the year that saw New York's Armory Show inaugurate a new era in modern art; when Roger Fry established the Omega Workshop in Fitzroy Square, London, to produce textiles and furniture designed by artists; and when the London Group of artists held its first exhibition. It was the year when Sigmund Freud, a central figure for so many of the group, would publish his interpretation of dreams as well as *Totem and Taboo* and when Marcel Proust would transform the image of the novel form by publishing the first volume of *In Search of Lost Time*. Leonard Woolf evokes the excitement of the year in the following revealing terms:

> On the stage the shattering impact of Ibsen was still belatedly powerful and we felt that Ibsen had a worthy successor in Shaw as a revolutionary. [. . .] In painting we were in the middle of the revolution of Cézanne, Matisse, and Picasso. [. . .] And to crown all, night after night we flocked to Covent Garden, entranced by a new art, a revelation to us benighted English, the Russian ballet in the greatest days of Diaghilev and Nijinsky.[3]

What appears to be missing from this enthusiastic list is music, yet these were also heady days for music lovers, and several of those who frequented Bloomsbury were indeed passionate about certain aspects at least of that art. Nineteen thirteen, after all, saw the tumultuous first presentation in Paris on May 29 and in London on July 11 of Igor Stravinsky's *Rite of Spring,* while the years between 1905 and 1912 were dominated by the first performances of several Gustav Mahler symphonies (no. 6 in 1906, no. 7 in 1908, no. 8 in 1910, and no. 9 in 1912). The year 1905 witnessed the first Bloomsbury gatherings and also saw the premieres of Mahler's *Kindertotenlieder* and Debussy's *La Mer.* In 1905, too, Thomas Beecham came to London.[4] He had already conducted the Hallé Orchestra in Manchester, and now, in addition to conducting the New Symphony Orchestra, he played an essential role in introducing Richard Strauss to an English audience and in inviting to the capital many leading performers, composers, and companies, most significantly, perhaps, the Ballets Russes. In 1907 Frederick Delius's opera *A Village Romeo and Juliet* had its premiere, although significantly, perhaps, in Berlin rather than London, and in 1908 Edward Elgar's first symphony and his violin concerto were both given their opening performance, the second with Fritz Kreisler playing the solo part. In 1911 Mahler's *Das Lied von der Erde* was performed for the first time, as was Elgar's second symphony, and the following year saw the first performance of Arnold Schoenberg's expressionist *Pierrot Lunaire* with its groundbreaking use of the twelve-tone chromatic scale.

Despite these momentous musical events, it was ballet that struck most of the Bloomsberries as the most radical artistic form, largely through Thomas Beecham's powerful promotion of that art. This is not entirely surprising, given the highly innovative works that Diaghilev and the Ballets Russes were bringing to London. We need to bear in mind, moreover, not only that the Ballets Russes themselves brought pioneering music with them, but also that it was much more difficult to hear groundbreaking music in those days before radio and recording studios made it so much more widely available. Music was known primarily through concerts, sheet music, the pianola (or player piano), and only later the gramophone, a device that Virginia Woolf so wonderfully described as opening "one little window" in their lives (D3: 151). Besides, as she revealingly wrote in an essay for the *London Times* of August 21, 1909: "The commonplace remark that music is in its infancy is best borne out by the ambiguous state of musical criticism. It has few traditions behind it, and the art itself is so much alive that it fairly suffocates those who try to deal with it" ("Impressions at Bayreuth," BP 18). The conflation of music with its criticism is both characteristic of her primary focus on language and intrinsically interesting in that it draws attention to the degree to which the general public, even those as intelligent as the Bloomsbury Group, relied on the critics to guide them and shape their appreciation of music, whereas in other artistic domains they would feel more confident of relying on their own judgment.

What Woolf points to as particularly problematic for those writing or even talking about contemporary music was the lack of precedents: "A critic of writing is hardly to be taken by surprise, for he can compare almost every literary form with some earlier form and can measure the achievement by some familiar standard. But who in music has tried to do what Strauss is doing, or Debussy?" (BP 18). As a result, she argues, "We are miserably aware how little words can do to render music. When the moment of suspense is over, and the bows actually move across the strings, our definitions are relinquished, and words disappear in our minds" (21). Even for the highly articulate members of the Bloomsbury Group, finding a way of talking about music, especially of modern music, posed problems they did not seem to encounter, or at least not so severely, when they discussed art, literature, or the ballet.

Yet long before that seminal period and the gramophone's opening of the little window, music had begun to play a shaping role in Bloomsbury's aesthetic world and left its trace in the letters, diaries, and memoirs of many of its members. Of course, music formed an essential part of the education and social lives of the middle classes at this period, a time when, as Virginia Woolf crisply puts it in *Three Guineas,* women were taught to tinkle on the piano but not allowed to join an orchestra (TG 45), and yet the intensity of Leonard Woolf's passion for music, a passion shared by several leading figures in the English modernist movement, goes well beyond those standard paradigms. The pleasure Leonard Woolf derived from music was, as is often the case, closely related to the enjoyment he gained from mathematics: "This satisfaction which I got from mathematics is, I think, closely related to the aesthetic pleasure which came from poetry, pictures, and, most of all, in later years from music" (S 95). For Leonard Woolf, moreover, music is clearly part of a nexus of memories and responses associated with friendship, intelligence, intensity, and intellectual passion. There can be little doubt, as well, that its close association with those formative and magical years in Cambridge conferred on it an added prestige for him in later life.

Moreover, a major force in creating such enthusiasm for music among these undergraduates was, less cerebrally, the pivotal figure of the philosopher George Moore. Moore's influence over their thinking, especially through his book *Principia Ethica,* has often been noted,[5] and the charm he exerted clearly played a vital role in conveying his own love of music to his friends and disciples. According to Leonard Woolf, for instance,

> [Moore] played the piano and sang, often to Lytton Strachey and me in his rooms and on reading parties in Cornwall. He was not a highly skilful pianist or singer, but I have never been given greater pleasure from playing or singing. This was due partly to the quality of his voice, but principally to the intelligence of his understanding and to the subtlety and intensity of his feeling. He played [Beethoven's] Waldstein sonata or sang [Schumann's] "Ich grolle nicht" with the same passion with which he pursued truth; when the last note died away, he would sit absolutely still, his hands resting on the keys, and the sweat streaming down his face. (S 150)

Lytton Strachey, too, in a letter to Virginia Stephen, stressed the interrelationship of Moore's magnetic personality and his musicality: "Moore is a colossal being and he also sings and plays in a wonderful way" (Levy, *Letters* Apr. 23, 1908, 141). It is not just that Moore seemed to have acquired for many of the Apostles, the Cambridge University secret society dedicated to intelligent conversation, an aura that attached itself to anything he did, including music, but that he embarked on all of his activities with such passion that his enthusiasm became highly contagious.

While Moore may have exerted the greatest musical influence over those in the Apostles society, Leonard Woolf had another group of Cambridge friends who were also music lovers, friends so different in outlook and even behavior that he kept a sharp divide between them and his Apostles companions. The brief pen-portrait of his friend Harry Gray, for example, brings out both the characteristic enthusiasm and the different way in which it found expression in him as compared to Moore: "He was absorbed in two things, but with an almost impersonal absorption, medicine and music. [...] He was already, as an executant[e], a first-class pianist. His playing was brilliant, but singularly impersonal and emotionless, and, when he was not working, he would usually be found playing the piano. It was characteristic of him that he was usually playing Chopin" (s 190).

Perhaps even more important than Moore in forming the early musical taste of this element of Bloomsbury was the enigmatic Saxon Sydney-Turner, whose genius they long took on trust and whose literary style Virginia Woolf once described as "the envy of my heart" (L3: 411), but who was never able to produce the great works of which he and they dreamed. Sydney-Turner was an ardent Wagnerite, who no doubt played an essential role in introducing to his Bloomsbury friends the German composer and his image of the *Gesamtkunstwerk*, the all-embracing art work that combined music, libretto, scenery and costumes into a coherent whole. We catch glimpses of Sydney-Turner in Adrian Stephen's journal, where he is wittily described as "talking about good and evil and playing the pianola" (HL 237) or traveling to Bayreuth with Adrian (see, for instance, V. Bell, *Letters* 68). Adrian and Sydney-Turner were joined in 1909 by Virginia, who initially confided in her sister, Vanessa, that *Parsifal* "seems to me weak vague stuff, with the usual enormities" (L1: 404), but later said that it moved her almost to tears and that she judged it "the most remarkable of the operas; it slides from music to words almost imperceptibly" (406). If Sydney-Turner's influence is perceptible here, his irritation when they praised composers other than Wagner is also evident: "We went to Salome (Strauss, as you may know) last night." Virginia reported to her sister: "I was much excited, and believe that it is a new discovery. He gets great emotion into his music, without any beauty. However, Saxon thought we were encroaching upon Wagner, and we had a long and rather acid discussion" (L1: 410). Writing to Clive Bell in 1907, Lytton Strachey reported with his characteristic malice as well as typical stylistic bravura: "Poor Turner's volcanic energy has deserted him. His lava flows no more. It is all dust and ashes now, and decrepitude and sciatica. [...] He showed me the MS of his opera this evening. Will its final resting-place be the British Museum, beside the notebooks of Beethoven? Well! At any rate *we* shall never know" (Levy, *Letters* 122). In 1908 Vanessa Bell chose to portray Saxon Sydney-Turner, according to Michael Holroyd, "seated slightly bent before a pianola, and peering through his spectacles at some sheet of music with an expression of rapt, self-obvious concentration" (144–45).[6] The link between music and mathematics that Leonard Woolf charts with such energetic enthusiasm becomes almost caricatural in Sydney-Turner, who combined it with a love of puzzles, especially crossword puzzles, and whose extraordinary memory together with his passion for Wagner made him capable of comparing countless performances and recalling the exact dates on which he had seen them, but did not lead to any creative production.

Other members of the Bloomsbury Group had a less passionate but nevertheless decisive response to music. For Lytton Strachey, for instance, music had been a familiar part of family life since his childhood. Virginia Woolf's unflattering likeness of him in her character St. John Hirst in *The Voyage Out* rather unkindly says that he had "no taste for music, and a few dancing lessons at Cambridge had only put him in possession of the anatomy of a waltz, without imparting any of its spirit" (VO 157). But Strachey's ungainly walk and elongated body probably had more to do with this little caricature than with any truth about his musical sensibilities. According to Holroyd, Strachey's mother, Jane Maria Strachey, "enjoyed classical music, sitting Lytton on her knee while she played songs on the piano" (6), while his brother Oliver, hoping to become a professional concert player, had studied piano with the famous teacher Theodor Leschetizky in Vienna, thus becoming one of only two Englishmen to attend Brahms's funeral in that city's central cemetery (Levy, *Letters* 47). Their younger brother James, who has become best known as the general editor of Freud's works in English, was also an authority on Haydn, Mozart, and Wagner, and in the 1950s contributed notes and commentaries for the Glyndebourne opera programs (Holroyd xv).

In a letter to the *Times* in 1924, protesting at attempts to prevent the proposed visit of the Vienna State Opera Company to Covent Garden, Lytton Strachey clearly included himself among the "lovers of music in England" (Levy, *Letters* 533), although his main purpose in writing may well have been political rather than aesthetic. Certainly some of his accounts of the operas that he attended focus more on the audience than the opera itself. Take, for instance, a letter of 1918 about a performance of *The Magic Flute*, in what he refers to as a performance that was "even more preposterous than usual," and during which Strachey's attention seems to have been directed far more toward "an attractive young man, in evening dress" who turned out to be Duncan Grant (*Letters* 198–99).[7]

In letters to Leonard Woolf during Woolf's long absence in Ceylon, Strachey frequently refers rather more seriously to music. "Alas!" he writes soon after Woolf's departure, "Beethoven thunders in vain for you, and the ocean has swallowed up Mozart!" (Levy, *Letters* 36), while later he expatiates on the beauties of Christoph Gluck, only to fall silent when he faces the challenge that Virginia Woolf's *Times* essay addresses, that of the inadequacy of words to evoke music. "They're now with me more almost than Racine. Pure beauty and grandeur – elysian airs, exquisite crescendos, inimitable heights. There is a ballet in the third act of Orfeo – but what's the good of talking?" (*Letters* 85).[8] Unpredictably, perhaps, he also delighted in Gilbert and Sullivan, reporting on *Iolanthe* that the "astounding thing about Iolanthe is the acting of Mr. Workman, who really does reach the most magnificent tragic heights. It's impossible to believe that a Lord Chancellor in love with a fairy can be anything but ridiculous, but one goes, and when the moment comes, it's simply great. The audience was completely mastered, and I believe many of them were in tears" (*Letters* 131). A letter to Ottoline Morrell on April 23, 1916, indicates a more predictable familiarity with Mozart: "The Magic Flute was considerably slewed [note: others read "slimed"] over by Beecham's vulgarity but the loveliness came through" (*Letters* 290). His biographer, Michael Holroyd, also argues that music played a central, if metaphorical, role in the sexual relationship between Strachey and Roger Senhouse: "When they listened to Mozart together, chamber music mostly, it almost seemed as if Roger and he were the instruments themselves" (582). Yet however important music may have been for Strachey, it is notable that his tastes in that art were far more conservative and classical than in other areas, rarely moving far beyond the middle of the nineteenth century.

As for the painter Duncan Grant, his love of music, together with his general aesthetic sensibility, had come to him from his father (Holroyd 130–31). David Garnett notes in his chatty and rather superficial autobiography that Grant "was always buying and playing gramophone records – especially Mozart" (*Flowers of the Forest* 29). Although he had no formal training in music, Grant enjoyed playing the piano and had a particular gift for dancing. Far more significantly and adventurously, Grant was familiar with the experiments of the French Postimpressionists and the Italian Futurists, as well as more specifically the French poet Guillaume Apollinaire, known for his *Calligrammes*, poems written such that the words – evoking a dove or rain, for example – form the shapes they evoke, and the Russian composer and pianist Alexander Scriabin, whose compositions draw inspiration from a color system ascribing different colors to the keys of a keyboard. Under their influence, Grant created his 1914 "Kinetic Scroll," which Frances Spalding describes as "a fourteen foot long scroll decorated with rectangular abstract coloured shapes, which he intended should be viewed through an aperture, as it was slowly wound past to the accompaniment of music by J. S. Bach" (*Roger Fry* 168).[9] The music selected was the Brandenburg Concerto no. 1. With this kind of experimentation, drawing on both art and music, Grant was creatively responding to such synesthetic creations as that produced in 1912 by the joint efforts of designer Leon Bakst, impresario Sergei Diaghilev, and dancer Vaslav Nijinsky when they staged their famous ballet based on Claude Debussy's sensuous response to Stéphane Mallarmé's beautiful poem "L'Après-midi d'un faune." Whereas Mallarmé had wanted the scenery to consist of trees made of zinc, Bakst chose to recreate the barbaric splendor of the Tartar, Russian, and Persian despots of the Middle Ages, while Nijinsky's choreography blended the archaic style of dancing found in Greek bas-reliefs with frank eroticism, ending with a final masturbatory gesture that shocked the critics. While Grant's choice of Bach might seem outdated in such an experiment, it should be remembered that this was the beginning of a period of renewed interest in Bach's music, reflected in the neoclassical compositions of, among others, Erik Satie, Sergei Prokofiev, and Igor Stravinsky.

No doubt the most progressive of all the Bloomsbury intellectuals, where an awareness of modern art and modernist movements in Europe and the United States was concerned, was the artist and art critic Roger Fry, of whom Kenneth Clark so memorably remarked: "Insofar as taste can be changed by one man, it was changed by Roger Fry" (Fry, *Last Lectures* ix). Indeed, Virginia Woolf saw his importance as a guide and influence over Bloomsbury's awareness of art, particularly of color, as so great that she later lamented that she had not dedicated to him *To the Lighthouse* with its affirmation of beauty and its rejection of Mr. Ramsay's blindness to the external sensory world (L3: 385). Through him, she insists, "The old skeletal arguments of Bloomsbury about art and beauty took on flesh and blood" (MB 175). Although his Quaker upbringing rejected music as an acceptable pastime, Fry was certainly familiar with the works of the classical composers. In 1891, for example, he wrote to his friend, the historian Goldie [Goldsworthy Lowes] Dickinson, from Florence that the Lorenzo Library and the Chapel of the Medici "make me quite certain that Michelangelo was much the greatest architect that has lived since Greek times; it is a perfectly new effect produced by the most subtle arrangement in proportion, and expresses an idea at least as complete and intelligible as a sonata of Beethoven's, which indeed it much resembles" (Fry, *Letters* 141). Thirty years later, again in a letter to Dickinson, Fry waxes lyrical about the operas and concerts he can attend in Vichy, although his response to them is, not surprisingly, sharply influenced by his own personality. Of Wagner's *Valkyrie* he comments:

> At first I thought I should never stick it out because they began at once to get to the last pitch of emotion over nothing in particular and of course his want of proportion is simply scandalous – also the puerile psychology, the sentimental education of a board school or *Daily Mail* journalist, but I did manage by disregarding all he was trying to express to get great pleasure out of the music. I think the *Valkyrie* is a lucky one because the amorous interest is slight and he's to me unendurable over that. (615)

In the same letter he makes the following curious comment on Beethoven's *Pastoral Symphony,* an observation clearly influenced by national prejudices associated with the First World War: "[The symphony] shocked me profoundly and shows the essential barbarity and want of civilization of the German spirit and the worst of it is he's such a musician" (615).

Most importantly, Fry drew on musical analogies in his art criticism, asserting, for example, of the artist Wassily Kandinsky's innovative abstract paintings at the Allied Artists' Salon of 1913 that "the improvisations become more definite, more logical and more closely knit in structure, more surprisingly beautiful in their colour oppositions, more exact in their equilibrium. They are pure visual music." And he added, revealingly, "I cannot any longer doubt the possibility of emotional expression by such abstract visual signs" (Reed 152). Fry's coinage of the term "visual music" was to have a lengthy and distinguished history, inspiring artists and critics alike in attempts both to forge synesthetic connections among the arts and to create a form of painting that aspired to the condition of music.[10] No doubt Fry's thinking about music was also strongly influenced by his interest in the French poet Stéphane Mallarmé, whose demanding and difficult poems he translated into English and whose highly intelligent, articulate, and imaginative responses to music in general and Wagner in particular he would have found both challenging and stimulating.

An anecdote recounted by George Bernard Shaw suggests a further dimension to Fry's appreciation of music. According to Shaw, Fry and the English composer Edward Elgar were both present at a luncheon in 1917:

> Elgar talked music so voluminously that Roger had nothing to do but eat his lunch in silence. At last [Roger] began in his beautiful voice: "After all, there is only one art; all the arts are the same." I heard no more, for my attention was taken by a growl from the other side of the table. It was Elgar, with his fangs bared and all his hackles bristling, in an appalling rage. "Music," he spluttered, "is written on the skies for you to note down. And you compare that to a DAMNED imitation." There was nothing for Roger to do but either seize the decanter and split Elgar's head with it, or else take it like an angel with perfect dignity. Which latter he did. (qtd. in RF 208)

As Christopher Reed asserts, this anecdote reveals Fry's belief in the unity of the arts, his conviction that "we cannot hold our theory for music and architecture and drop it for poetry and drama" (278). Reading Fry's theoretical writings, it becomes clear that what most appeals to him in music, as for such other members of the Bloomsbury Group as Leonard Woolf and Saxon Sydney-Turner, is its formal quality and above all its representation of order. "Why," he asks in "The Artist and Psycho-Analysis," "are we moved deeply by certain sequences of notes which arouse no suggestion of any experience in actual life?" His response is that "there is a pleasure in the recognition of order, of inevitability in relations, and that the more complex the relations of which we are able to recognize the inevitable interdependence and correspondence, the greater is the pleasure" (Reed 364–65). This attitude clarifies the absence from much of his writing, and indeed from that of much of the Bloomsbury Group, of contemporary composers, many of whom were driven by an imperative to seize and reproduce the disordered and chaotic nature of a postwar world, one in which the inevitability of rational order was no longer a central conviction. Wagner, whom so many of those associated with Bloomsbury admired, is far closer than these contemporaries to Fry's image of order and relation as central to the pleasure of music.

One final aspect of Fry's response to music appears most clearly in a 1911 lecture he gave on the topic of Postimpressionism. His aim in the lecture, he explains, is to discover

> what arrangements of form and colour are calculated to stir the imagination most deeply through the stimulus given to the sense of sight. This is exactly analogous to the problem of music, which is to find what arrangements of sound will have the greatest evocative power. But whereas in music the world of natural sound is so vague, so limited, and takes, on the whole, so small a part of our imaginative life, that it needs no special attention or study on the part of the musician; in painting and sculpture, on the contrary, the actual world of nature is so full of sights which appeal vividly to our imagination – so large a part of our inner and contemplative life is carried on by means of visual images, that this natural world of sight calls for a constant and vivid apprehension on the part of the artist. (Reed 100–101)

For Roger Fry, at least, the world of sight was simply much more vivid than the world of hearing, and music, as a result, appeared to him as vague and limited in comparison with the intense stimulus he obviously received from vision and therefore from painting and sculpture. Given Fry's extensive influence over the Bloomsbury Group, judgments like these must have carried considerable weight in forming members' tastes and developing their impressions of the arts.

Other figures associated with the Bloomsbury Group have less clearly articulated responses to music. For example, although in later life E. M. Forster was delighted and honored to be invited by Benjamin Brittan to write the libretto for *Billy Bud,* he leaves few echoes of his enjoyment of music in either his public or his private writing. In 1908, for instance, he attended at least the *Götterdämmerung* part of the Ring Cycle being performed at Covent Garden but mentions it only in passing. In addition, Quentin Bell, in his *Bloomsbury Recalled,* offers the following amusing but not particularly informative shred of evidence:

Q: It seems to me, Morgan, that you were near but not exactly *in* Bloomsbury.

M: What makes you think that?

Q: Well, you preferred Beethoven to Mozart.

M: (smiling) Ah, but I was young then. (144–45)

Vanessa Bell and Dora Carrington seem to have had little time for music, focusing far more on the visual. When she does mention concerts, Vanessa is far more likely to comment on the audience than the performance. In a letter to her son Quentin, for example, she describes a performance of Ethel Smyth's Mass at the Albert Hall: "The Queen was there attended by Timmy [Gerald Chichester], and the Dame went and had a long conversation with her in the Royal Box and made her laugh a good deal. I don't wonder. The Dame was in her best wig and tricorn hat and an 'Ascot frock' bought at Stagg and Mantles for 16/6. The Queen was dressed in much the same sort of way and they really made an imposing couple. As for the music, I have no views, but it seemed brilliantly amorphous" (*selected Letters* 377). "Brilliantly amorphous" suggests a musical appreciation that was significantly different from Roger Fry's search for pattern and order, something rather closer to her sense of artistic values. Maynard Keynes, for his part, had little affection for music. According to his biographer, Robert Skidelsky, "There was nothing in the Keynes family home to stimulate the aesthetic sensibilities. [. . .] Nor was music then part of their lives, except for an occasional visit to a Gilbert and Sullivan, though [Keynes's father] later collected records of operatic arias" (31). His closest friend during his years at King's College, Cambridge, Robert Furness, who went on to become a distinguished translator, was an ardent Wagnerite but did not succeed in passing that enthusiasm on to the economist, although like many of the Bloomsberries, Keynes did attend the 1906 performance of *Tristan und Isolde* in London. Even his love affair with the *mélomane* Duncan Grant failed to instill in him any great pleasure in music (see, for instance, Skidelsky 119), and if he came to appreciate the ballet it was above all because it gave him an opportunity to "view Mr. Nijinsky's legs" (154), as he put it in a letter to Lytton Strachey in July 1911, and later as a medium associated with his wife, Lydia Lopokova, rather than for ballet's interpretation of music. After the First World War he entered the same social circle as Sir Thomas

Beecham, but the relationship seems to have been purely social rather than being based on aesthetic concerns.

The fervent views of music we find in certain members of the Bloomsbury circle must therefore be counterbalanced by the responses of other elements within the group who not only regarded music with considerably less enthusiasm but also considered concerts more as an opportunity for observing human behavior than as an aesthetic experience. In discussing Bloomsbury, after all, it is always advisable to bear in mind the journalist and critic Desmond MacCarthy's caveat that "in taste and judgment 'Bloomsbury' from the start has been at variance with itself. Indeed, here lay its charm as a social circle" (Rosenbaum 67). It is worth underlining MacCarthy's description of it as a social rather than an intellectual or a cultural circle, although there are many critics who would argue that it also deserved those epithets. And MacCarthy's argument notwithstanding, where music is concerned there are certain shared assumptions, interests, and experiences that run through the letters, diaries, and memoirs of those who made up the Bloomsberries, even if those assumptions are somewhat less progressive than some of their other views about the arts. Indeed, for many of them, the music that played an important part in their social life was mainly, although far from exclusively, well-established classical music. Raymond Mortimer, who joined the group after the First World War, may be taking matters too far when he provocatively claims in his "London Letter" written for the American journal *Dial* in 1928, that Bloomsbury tended to exalt the classical in all the arts: "Racine, Milton, Poussin, Cézanne, Mozart and Jane Austin have been their more cherished artists" (Rosenbaum 311). Nevertheless, he has a point. The operas of Richard Wagner were for many of them the most innovative addition to the standard repertoire. The sensitivity to the radical changes in the plastic arts that the group embraced, promoted, and delighted in, together with that sharp awareness of the changes in social mores that Virginia Woolf playfully dates to around December 1910, seems to have found an equivalent in music only in the case of a few of the Bloomsberries, most notably Virginia Woolf herself.

Indeed, contemporary music tends to be treated with distaste or scorn, as when Strachey, encountering the English composer Roger Quilter at a party, focuses on the outward appearances without seeming to listen to the music at all: "I went to the 'Friday Club'[...]. The proceedings were curious and unpleasant. Nearly everyone – male and female – sat on the floor back to back, while Walter Creighton sang Brahms or posed with a cigarette, and his friend Mr. Roger Quilter – a pale young man with a bottle nose – played his own compositions on the piano" (Levy, *Letters*, Dec. 7, 1905, 86). And although there are allusions to Diaghilev's ballets, Stravinsky's epoch-making *Rite of Spring*, first performed in Paris in 1913, apparently passed many of them by largely unnoticed. Lytton Strachey did attend a performance in July 1913 but described it as "one of the most painful experiences of my life," explaining that he "couldn't have imagined that boredom and sheer anguish could have been combined together at such a pitch" (Holroyd 291). By 1919, however, Diaghilev's company was being lionized by Bloomsbury (and others), and in 1926 Vita Sackville-West writes of attending a Stravinsky ballet with Virginia Woolf, although her main attention seems to have been focused on Virginia's extraordinary outfit (HL 495).

Music as social exercise and fairly lighthearted entertainment is what most strikes a reader of the correspondence of many of the Bloomsbury Group, including Virginia Woolf's letters, even those she exchanged with the feminist and composer Ethel Smyth. But then, as she puts it to Gerald Brennan in 1923, letter writing for her was often a "tossing of omelettes" (L3: 80). At one point, perhaps to avoid the embarrassment of having to offer evaluations of her correspondent's music, Virginia insisted that she could not judge music (L5: 135). Of course there is in any writer's correspondence a sense of delight in seizing opportunities to test techniques or to indulge in displays of virtuoso description that often distorts the real seriousness with which the subject matter might normally be taken. Thus, in a letter of 1903, she paints an amusing picture of Adrian playing the pianola for their own pleasure but as a result affecting the moods and behavior of the servants:

> A fresh lot of tunes came today chosen by Adrian and a very mixed set – Bach and Schumann and the Washington Post, and the Dead March in Saul, and Pinafore and the Messiah. We find the difference in quality a very good thing because all our servants sit beneath the open drawing room window all evening while we play – and by experiment we have discovered that if we play dance

music all their crossnesses vanish and the whole room rings with shrieks and then we tame them down so sentimentally with Saul or bore them with Schumann. (L1: 88)

The pianola also features in Duncan Grant's memoir of Virginia Woolf, in which it is described in the following comic manner:

> In the back part of the [drawing] room there was an instrument called a Pianola, into which one put rolls of paper punctured by small holes. You bellowed with your feet and Beethoven or Wagner would appear. Anyone coming into the room might have thought Adrian was a Paderewski – the effort on the bellows gave him a swaying movement very like that of the great performer, and his hands were hidden. (Rosenbaum 99)

Although Grant notes that he could not remember having seen Virginia play on this instrument, he adds that "it must have played a part in her life, for Adrian on coming home from work would play in the empty room by the hour" (99).

Playing a pianola in an empty room might indeed seem a curiously apt metaphor for the musical tastes of many of those associated with Bloomsbury, a group whose verbal skills and visual imaginations seem to have relegated music to an activity at best appreciated at second hand and in private. But that very verbal skillfulness can be misleading: when we read their letters or essays, it can frequently seem that the desire to amuse can outweigh any intention of seriousness in conveying a response to a musical experience, yet the ways in which the Bloomsberries depicted music in their works of art can suggest a different and more serious appreciation. Diverse in their tastes, forthright in the expression of their aesthetic judgments, witty and iconoclastic, the Bloomsbury Group reveals a response to music that was as varied and idiosyncratic as were its individual members. While many of them were not as innovative in their musical taste as in their appreciation of literature and the visual arts, some of them, notably Virginia Woolf, found in music a source of sensual delight and intellectual stimulation that informed their aesthetic convictions and in turn fed into their writings. It is this more profound appreciation of music that this collection of essays on Virginia Woolf sets out to explore. Setting her responses against, or at least in the context of, those of the wider Bloomsbury circle illuminates her own independence of spirit and her originality.

NOTES

1. On the nature and chronology of the Bloomsbury Group, see among many others, Clive Bell, *Civilization and Old Friends*, 2: 126–37; Leon Edel; Frances Spalding, *Bloomsbury Group*; and Hermione Lee, *Virginia Woolf*, 258–59.

2. See, for instance, Humm.

3. Leonard Woolf, *Beginning Again*, 35–37, qtd. in Skidelsky, *John Maynard Keynes*, 148.

4. Curiously, his now-famed wit seems not to have appealed to Strachey, who seems to have found Beecham as stuffy as the eminent Victorians whose lives and reputations he would later so critically reexamine. "What a pompous bounder!" he wrote of Beecham to Ottoline Morrell in 1917 (Levy, *Letters* 170). Beecham's name does not even figure in the index of Holroyd's biography of Strachey.

5. See, for instance, Holroyd; Regan; and Watt.

6. In 1917 Vanessa Bell gave this portrait to Barbara Bagenal, who bequeathed it to the Charleston Trust. It may be seen online at http://www.charlestoncollection.org.uk/index.asp?page=item&mwsquery=%7BIdentity%20number%7D=%7BCHA/P/6%7D. On Sydney-Turner, see also Hall and Lee.

7. Of course the flippant nature of this letter may have far more to do with a desire to entertain its recipient than with any real response to the opera.

8. The famous dance of the blessed spirits is in fact in the second act. Virginia Woolf shared Strachey's love of Gluck's *Orfeo*, which she described at one point as "the loveliest opera ever written" (*L*5: 259). By a strange irony, the funeral directors at Virginia Woolf's cremation chose to play excerpts from this opera without consulting Leonard, who was furious because the opera promised a reunion he knew to be impossible.

9. The film can be viewed at www.tate.org.uk/archivejourneys/bloomsburyhtml/art_grant_modernism.htm.

10. See, for instance, Brougher and Mattis.

WORKS CITED

Banfield, Ann, *The Phantom Table: Woolf, Fry, Russell, and the Epistemology of Modernism*. Cambridge: Cambridge University Press, 2000. Print.

Banks, Joanna Trautmann, ed. *Congenial Spirits: The Selected Letters of Virginia Woolf*. New York: Harcourt, 1989. Print.

Bell, Clive. *Civilization and Old Friends*. 2 vols. in one. Chicago: University of Chicago Press, 1973. Print.

Bell, Quentin. *Bloomsbury Recalled*. New York: Columbia University Press, 1995. Print.

Bell, Vanessa. *Selected Letters of Vanessa Bell*. Ed. Regina Marler. London: Bloomsbury, 1993. Print.

Brooke, Rupert, and James Strachey. *Friends and Apostles: The Correspondence of Rupert Brooke and James Strachey, 1905–1914*. Ed. Keith Hale. New Haven: Yale University Press, 1998. Print.

Brougher, Kerry, and Olivia Mattis. *Visual Music: Synaesthesia in Art and Music since 1900*. London: Thames & Hudson, 2005. Print.

De Salvo, Louise, and Mitchell A. Leaska, eds. *The Letters of Vita Sackville-West* to Virginia Woolf. New York: Morrow, 1985. Print.

Dunn, Jane. *A Very Close Conspiracy: Vanessa Bell and Virginia Woolf*. London: Jonathan Cape, 1990. Print.

Edel, Leon. *Bloomsbury: A House of Lions*. Philadelphia: Lippincott, 1979. Print.

Fry, Roger. *Last Lectures*. Cambridge: Cambridge University Press, 1939. Print.

———. *Letters of Roger Fry*. Ed. Denys Smith. 2 vols. London: Chatto & Windus, 1972. Print.

Garnett, David. *Carrington: Letters and Extracts from her Diaries*. New York: Holt, 1970. Print.

———. *The Flowers of the Forest*. London: Chatto & Windus, 1955. Print.

Gerzina, Gretchen. *Carrington: A Life*. New York: Norton, 1989. Print.

Hall, Sarah M. *Before Leonard: The Early Suitors of Virginia Woolf*. Chester Springs: Peter, 2006. Print.

Holroyd, Michael. *Lytton Strachey: The New Biography*. New York: Farrar, 1994. Print.

Humm, Maggie. *Modernist Women and Visual Cultures: Virginia Woolf, Vanessa Bell, Photography, and Cinema*. New Brunswick: Rutgers University Press, 2003. Print.

Largo, Mary, and P. N. Furbank, eds. *Selected Letters of E. M. Forster*. 2 vols. London: Collins, 1983. Print.

Lee, Hermione. *Virginia Woolf*. New York: Knopf, 1997. Print.

Levy, Paul, ed. *The Letters of Lytton Strachey*. London: Viking, 2005. Print.

Marler, Regina. *Selected Letters of Vanessa Bell*. London: Bloomsbury, 1993. Print.

Morrell, Ottoline. *Ottoline at Garsington: Memoirs of Lady Ottoline Morrell, 1915–1918*. Ed. Robert Gathorne-Hardy. New York: Knopf, 1975. Print.

Reed, Christopher. *A Roger Fry Reader*. Chicago: University of Chicago Press, 1996. Print.

Regan, Tom. "Moore and Bloomsbury: The Myth and the Man." *The British Tradition in 20th Century Philosophy*. Ed. Jaakko Hintikka and Klaus Puhl. Vienna: Hölder-Pichler-Tempsky, 1995. 43–59. Print.

Rosenbaum, S. P., ed. *The Bloomsbury Group: A Collection of Memoirs and Commentary*. Toronto: University of Toronto Press, 1995. Print.

Scott, Bonnie Kime, ed. *The Gender of Modernism*. Bloomington: Indiana University Press, 1990. Print.

Seymour, Miranda. *Ottoline Morrell: Life on the Grand Scale*. London: Hodder & Stoughton, 1992. Print.

Skidelsky, Robert. *John Maynard Keynes, 1883–1946: Economist, Philosopher, Statesman*. Harmondsworth: Penguin, 2003. Print.

Spalding, Frances. *The Bloomsbury Group*. London: National Portrait Gallery, 2005. Print.

———. *Roger Fry: Art and Life*. Berkeley: University of California Press, 1980. Print.

———. *Vanessa Bell*. London: Weidenfeld and Nicolson, 1983. Print.

Spotts, Frederic, ed. *Letters of Leonard Woolf*. New York: Harcourt, 1989. Print.

Watt, Donald J. "G. E. Moore and the Bloomsbury Group." *English Literature in Transition (1880–1920)* 12: 119–34. Print.

Woolf, Leonard. *Beginning Again*. London: Hogarth, 1964. Print.

———. *Sowing: An Autobiography of the Years 1880–1904*. London: Hogarth, 1960. Print.

Woolf, Virginia. *Books and Portraits*. Ed. Mary Lyon. London: Hogarth, 1977. Print.

———. *The Diary of Virginia Woolf*. Ed. Anne Olivier Bell. 5 vols. 1915–1941. San Diego: Harcourt, 1980. Print.

——— *The Letters of Virginia Woolf*. Ed. Nigel Nicolson and Joanna Trautmann. 6 vols. 1975–1980. New York: Harcourt. Print.

——— *Moments of Being*. Ed. Jeanne Schulkind. New York: Harcourt, 1976. Print.

——— *Roger Fry: A Biography*. New York: Harcourt, 1940. Print.

——— *Three Guineas*. London: Penguin, 1977. Print.

TWO

Virginia Woolf and Musical Culture

Mihály Szegedy-Maszák

ALTHOUGH VIRGINIA WOOLF WAS SKEPTICAL OF THE MERITS of any verbal approach to music, she was fascinated by the ideal of *ut musica poesis*. As she listened to a concert in 1915, she decided that "all descriptions of music are quite worthless" (D1: 33), yet she constantly drew inspiration from music. There is good reason to believe that as early as 1905 (PA 251) she became familiar with Walter Pater's celebrated statement "All art constantly aspires towards the condition of music" (86), echoed by Oscar Wilde's declaration in the preface to *The Picture of Dorian Gray:* "From the point of view of form, the type of all the arts is the art of the musician" (17). "Its odd, for I'm not regularly musical, but I always think of my books as music before I write them," she remarked toward the end of her life. "I want to investigate the influence of music on literature," she added a few months before her death (L6: 426, 450).

Any insight we might have into Woolf's musical canon will help us to approach her style and the structure of her novels, although this relation must not be confused with a unidirectional causal one. Just because the two questions cannot be fully separated, I have to acknowledge that by entering into the less ambitious while staying away from the more, my discussion will be fragmentary. On the one hand, the evidence I have found in her autobiographical writings may be incomplete; on the other hand, the analysis of prose rhythm would ask for the ear of a native speaker.

Can a comparison of music and literature lead to a better understanding of Virginia Woolf's works? The issues involved are complex;

one must move carefully and tentatively in this area. A comparison of the two arts might mean a number of different things.

How can the sister arts "appear" in a work of literature? One could begin by drawing a distinction between the ideal types of "use" and "mention." Gérard Genette gives the following examples: "In the sentence 'Paris is a great city,' the word Paris is used transitively [. . .]; in 'Paris consists of two syllables,' the name of the city is mentioned (cited)" (235–36). The actual presence of the sister arts in a literary work can never be a clear-cut case of use or mention. Having made this general statement, I would risk the hypothesis that the verbal description of a painting is more feasible than the literary imitation of a musical structure. Whether this is true or not, it cannot be denied that Virginia Woolf was surrounded by visual artists (such as her sister, Vanessa, and the painter Duncan Grant), and the two theoreticians whose aesthetic views exerted a profound influence on her, Roger Fry and Clive Bell, focused on the visual arts. That may be a partial explanation for the fact that an imaginary landscape plays a more important role than the tune played by an old fiddler in Woolf's story titled "A Simple Melody" (written around 1925).

How can one characterize the impact of music on her writing? "We do not have much of a factual base to start from," as one of the critics who has attempted to address this question has noted (Jacobs 228). The information one can collect from the diaries, the essays, the correspondence, and other publications is so fragmentary that only tentative conclusions can be drawn. Let it suffice to mention one example: On January 16, 1929, Virginia and her husband went for a week to Berlin, where they were joined by her sister, Duncan Grant, and her younger nephew, Quentin Bell. "We spent most of our time at the opera," she wrote to a cousin (L 4: 126), but her diary and correspondence contain no reference to any performance, and Quentin Bell's biography describes the Berlin holiday as a dismal failure and makes no mention of any operatic experience. Given such gaps in our knowledge, it is difficult to assess Virginia Woolf's musical culture.

In the late nineteenth century children in an upper-middle-class English family were expected to acquire some knowledge of the visual arts and music. The author's mother "could play the piano and was musical" (MB 100). "Last night we went to the first of our four operas," Virginia Stephen informed her elder brother, Thoby, in June 1898. A letter to a friend dated August 12, 1899, indicates that the children "perform Fugues on the Harmonium." "I draw for hours every evening after dinner," she wrote to another friend in December 1904 (L1: 17, 27, 170). "My old piano" is mentioned as early as 1901. A year later there is a reference to a pianola recently purchased. Her younger brother, Adrian, seemed to be the most musical in the family; he brought sheet music into the household by J. S. Bach, George Frideric Händel, and Robert Schumann (L1: 41, 55, 88). After she had started reviewing books, Virginia devoted some attention to works on music: in 1905 she reviewed the fifth volume of *The Oxford History of Music* in the *Guardian,* and in 1909 her article "The Opera" appeared in the *London Times* (E1: 373–74, 269–72). She continued to be very critical of the shortcomings of musical life in Britain: in 1918 she dismissed the "incredible, pathetic stupidity of the music hall" (D1: 144) and attacked those who regarded the oratorio as the "only permissible form of art" (E2: 262). As late as 1932 her friend Dame Ethel Mary Smyth, speaking of someone with musical talent, complained about the inferiority of the status of music in British culture in comparison with Germany, saying, "He's a phenomenon. How I pity him! Forced to live in England with that gift – you don't know the loneliness" (D4: 69).

Among the members of the larger family there were some who could play instruments. "[When] we asked if she could play, [...] she strummed through a Beethoven sonata, with the tramp of a regiment of dragons," the young Virginia wrote about her cousin Helen Stephen (1862–1908) (L1: 343). Determined to make up for the lack of musical culture in London, Emma Vaughan (1874–1960), one of Virginia's early friends, spent several months studying in Dresden.

Although there are many publications about those who knew the young Virginia Stephen, they contain surprisingly little information on music, and indeed they are sometimes unreliable. One scholar, for instance, mentions that Oliver Strachey (1874–1960), Lytton's elder brother, "studied the piano with Lechititsky in Vienna" (Jacobs 229), and the reader may assume that the reference is to the influential Polish instrumentalist Teodor Leszetycki, known in the German-speaking countries as Theodor Leschetizky (1830–1915), one of the few who established a highly original school of interpretation, an alternative to the tradition of Ferenc Liszt.

Among the Cambridge friends of Virginia's brothers there were amateur musicians. "It was characteristic of him that he was usually playing Chopin," Leonard Woolf wrote about Harry Gray, who in later life became a well-known surgeon (LWA 112), and the philosopher G. E. Moore "sang *Adelaide,* Schubert songs, or the *Dichterliebe,* or [...] played the *Waldstein* or the *Hammerklavier* sonata" (BA 42), works that demand considerable virtuosity.

While all these people may have helped the young Virginia acquire good taste in music, the most important influence must have been that of Saxon Sydney-Turner (1880–1962), a regular visitor to chamber music concerts, who "kept a record, both on paper and in his head, of all the operas he had ever been to" (LWA 66). In fact, it is possible to argue that this Wagnerite played a major role in the musical education of the young writer until her future husband appeared on the scene and took a firm stand against the legacy of Richard Wagner. Back from Ceylon, in 1911 Leonard Woolf discovered that the musical life of the British capital was dominated by foreigners. "Among the frequenters of the Russian Ballet there was, strangely enough, a vogue for Wagner – strangely, because one can hardly imagine two products of the human mind and soul more essentially hostile" (BA 49). These words, written two decades after the death of Virginia Woolf, express a deep-seated resentment of the cult of Wagner that had been built up by intellectuals and musicians such as George Bernard Shaw, Sir Thomas Beecham, Albert Coates, or the Hungarian-German János (Hans) Richter (1843–1916), the conductor of the first performances in Bayreuth and one of the musical directors of the Covent Garden in the first decade of the twentieth century.

The earliest references to Wagner in Virginia Stephen's written legacy are in "A Sketch of the Past," which contains a passage about a performance of *Der Ring des Nibelungen* in June 1900 (MB 155), and in a 1904 letter written in Paris to her closest friend, Violet Dickinson. During a dinner with Clive Bell and the painter Gerald Kelly, Beatrice Thynner "expounded theories on Wagner," creating a hot debate (L1: 140). At the beginning of the next year she reviewed a two-volume work on Wilhelmine of Prussia, markgravine of Brandenburg-Bayreuth, in which she remarked that the markgravine not only founded a university but even "anticipated the present opera house" – that is, the Festspielhaus (E1: 90). Two years later Virginia saw a performance of *Die Meistersinger* and listened to her younger brother, Adrian, spell out Wagner on the piano. Her affirmation that "nothing will induce me to sacrifice my Richter" indicates that she valued the Wagner performances of the Covent Garden (L1: 294, 308, 312). In a sketch written in 1909 she drew a portrait of Miriam Jane Timothy (1879–1950), a member of the London Symphony Orchestra, who was, according to Richter, "as excellent on the harp as on the lute" (V. Woolf, *Carlyle's House* 23). In 1908 she praised a "very fairly satisfactory performance of *Götterdämmerung*" and declined an invitation from Lady Robert Cecil, because "our opera began at 4:30." In that year she went "almost nightly to the opera" and "in the afternoon" studied German (L1: 329, 330, 331, 333). Her obvious goal was to understand the texts of Wagner's works. Sydney-Turner sent her an authentic portrait of Hans Sachs, and she asked him to get tickets for her (352, 362).

In 1909 she visited Bayreuth, accompanied by Sydney-Turner and Adrian. "Now we are going to read *Parsifal*, and then lunch, and then we shall hear the immortal work," she wrote to her sister, Vanessa, on August 7. The next day she summarized her impressions in the following terms: "Saxon and Adrian say that it was not a good performance, and that I shan't know anything about it until I have heard it 4 times. [. . .] We have been discussing obscure points in *Parsifal* all the morning" (L1: 404). On August 11 she saw another performance of Wagner's last work. On this occasion she felt "within a space of tears" and reached the conclusion that "it is the most remarkable of the operas; it slides from music to words almost imperceptibly" (406). In that year Siegfried Wagner and Karl Muck were the conductors. The few available recordings with them suggest a fundamental difference between their interpretations: the composer's son, Siegfried (himself a composer), tended toward more transparency in orchestral playing (*Siegfried Wagner Conducts Wagner*, Archipel 0288), whereas Muck was instrumental in creating a long tradition of slow performances that stressed heaviness (Richard Wagner: *Parsifal*, Naxos Historical 8.110049–50). It would be interesting to know which of the two versions appealed more to Virginia Stephen.

While she wrote to her sister that *Lohengrin* was "a very dull opera" (L1: 409) before actually seeing that performance in Bayreuth on the evening of August 19, 1909, her comment may need some explanation. The impressions of a young and relatively inexperienced person should perhaps not be taken too seriously, but it is worth noting that *Parsifal* is not an easily accessible work, so she may have sensed some of the distinct qualities of Wagner's art if she enjoyed it. It must be borne in mind that she could give only the "impressions as an amateur" in her article published in the *Times* on August 21. The remarkable thing is that she ascribed the superiority of *Parsifal* over *Lohengrin* to the fact that in the later work "the words are continued by the music so that we hardly notice the transition" (E1: 289), a feature that echoes Wagner's own intentions. Needless to say, *Lohengrin* can be called an outstanding achievement from at least two perspectives: (1) as the culmination of the German Romantic opera represented by E. T. A. Hoffmann, Carl Maria von Weber, Heinrich August Marschner, and Albert Lortzing, or (2) as a model for the Expressionism of Bartók's *Duke Bluebeard's Castle*, composed in 1911, a one-act opera with an opposition between darkness and light (an F sharp and C polarity) comparable to the contrast underlying the structure of *Lohengrin,* and a blood motif inspired by the music associated with Ortrud in Wagner's work. For different reasons, both of these contexts were unknown to Virginia Stephen.

From Bayreuth, Sydney-Turner, Adrian, and Virginia Stephen went to Dresden, where they saw a performance of *Salome* by Richard Strauss. "I was much excited, and believe that it is a new discovery. He gets great emotion into his music, without any beauty" (L1: 410). Once more, an insight might be detected beneath the surface of Virginia's statement: the realization that expressivity can be attained without an appeal to conventional beauty.

Back in London Virginia may have heard a performance of *Tristan und Isolde* in 1910 (L1: 425) and *Elektra* (HL 239), a work that deploys dissonance in a more radical way than *Salome,* and may also have attended *Der Ring* in 1911. It seems almost certain that she saw few Wagner performances after her marriage to Leonard in 1912. A letter to Katherine Cox written in May 1913 testifies to the influence of Virginia's husband: "We came up here 10 days ago to attend the *Ring* – and I hereby state that I will never go again[...]. My eyes are bruised, my ears dulled, my brain a mere pudding of pulp – O the noise and the heat, and the bawling sentimentality, which used once to carry me away, and now leaves me sitting perfectly still. Everyone seems to have come to this opinion, though some pretend to believe still" (L2: 26). In 1923 she wrote about her loss of enthusiasm to a younger woman in terms that suggest a focus on the action rather than on the music: "I went to *Tristan* the other night; but the love making bored me. When I was your age I thought it the most beautiful thing in the world – or was it only in deference to Saxon?" (L3: 56). Two years later, in a letter addressed to Sydney-Turner, Virginia seemed to express a more qualified view: "I have been to the *Walküre*, and to Lords: at both places I looked for you in vain. [...] *Walküre* completely triumphed, I thought; except for some boredom – I can't even enjoy those long arguments in music – when it is obviously mere conversation upon business matters between Wotan and Brunhilde: however, the rest was superb. The fire is terrible: I saw at once that it was made of red silk, and that used to be done quite satisfactorily. Also I missed the ride of the horses" (L3: 186). Aside from the reservations that refer to the visual components of the production, the characterization of act 2, scene 2 suggests an inability to recognize the turning point of *Der Ring*: the dramatic function of Wotan's outburst of despair caused by the realization that he is unable to create a human being who could have the freedom of will that is denied to the gods. Virginia failed to understand why the composer once described this as "the most important scene in the whole tetralogy" (Donington 155). Wotan's monologue, moving gradually from almost unaccompanied speech to a complex musical texture in which singing is combined with orchestral development, functions as a self-examination that sheds light on the contradictions of his past. As Pierre Boulez remarked, "La totale confession de Wotan devant Brünnhilde (La Walkyrie, acte II) s'impose comme indispensable à la compréhension de son caractère, qui s'y révèle beaucoup plus profondément qu'au moyen de quelque autre procédé plus *actif*" (176) [Wotan's full confession before Brünnhilde (*The Walkyrie*, Act II) imposes itself as indispensible to the understanding of his character, which reveals itself here much more profoundly than by means of some other more *active* method].

Although shortly after this performance of *Die Walküre* she conversed with the Jewish stockbroker Sydney J. Loeb (1876–1964), who was the son-in-law of Hans Richter and an ardent Wagnerian (D3: 26), in one of the stories composed around the same time Virginia made a guest of Clarissa Dalloway refer to the *Meistersinger* (CSF 194), and in 1931 she listened to Ethel Smyth's lengthy argument about *Parsifal* (D4: 49). She missed the 1935 performance of *Tristan und Isolde* as well as *Der Ring* of 1937 and 1938 conducted by Wilhelm Furtwängler, with superb singers in the leading roles such as Frida Leider, Kirsten Flagstad, Maria Müller, Tiana Lemnitz, Margarete Klose, Franz Völker, Max Lorenz, Lauritz Melchior, Herbert Janssen, and Rudolf Bockelmann. The British press was enthusiastic, and the surviving recorded parts of the two cycles (*Wilhelm Furtwängler Conducts Excerpts from Götterdämmerung*, Music & Arts CD-1035 and Eklipse EKR 62) suggest that these performances may have been the most powerful in history. It would perhaps not be far-fetched to conclude that Virginia stopped learning German and lost her interest in Wagner under her husband's influence. She may have felt some loss; "There was a time when I went out to operas, evening concerts &c, at least 3 times a week," she noted with regret in 1915 (D1: 19). In her later years she rarely attended performances of operas composed after 1800. In 1928 she saw Christoph Gluck's *Armide*, a work she found not too interesting (L3: 497); in 1931 she went to Cambridge for a performance of *The Fairy Queen*, Purcell's longest semi-opera, a work she enjoyed (L4: 290, 292); in 1932 she went to *Dido and Aeneas* at the Sadler's Wells Theater and thought it "absolutely and entirely satisfying"; and in December she attended Gluck's *Orfeo ed Euridice* at Sadler's Wells (possibly sung in English), which she described as "the loveliest opera ever written" (L5: 135, 259). Her diary refers mainly to Mozart performances: in 1918 she saw *Don Giovanni* and *Die Zauberflöte*, in 1926 *Le Nozze di Figaro*, in 1930 *La Finta Giardiniera*, in 1931 *Die Zauberflöte*, and in 1933 she took her niece, Angelica Bell, to *Don Giovanni* at Sadler's Wells. In 1934 she heard *Le Nozze di Figaro* in Glyndebourne, conducted by Fritz Busch, with Willi Domgraf-Fassbänder in the title role and Aulikki Rautawaara and Luise Helletsgruber as the Contessa and Cherubino, respectively. The next year she also went there to a concert and to *Die Zauberflöte*, conducted by the same music director.

It is possible that after her early experience of *Salome* Virginia never heard any of the major operas of the post-Wagnerian era. In 1926 she may have seen a concert performance of Nikolai Rimsky-Korsakov's *The Legend of the Invisible City of Kitezh* (D3: 72), and in 1931 she was taken to see Ethel Smyth's *The Wreckers* by Vita Sackville-West and the composer (D4: 48), an opera she had seen for the first time conducted by Thomas Beecham in 1909, three years after the first performance in Leipzig. Neither of these works made a deep impression on her, not even the British composer's three-act opera, appreciated by such eminent conductors as Arthur Nikisch and Bruno Walter, and based on the legends of Cornwall, the region where the Stephen family spent several summers. Her relative lack of familiarity with the music of her age may explain why she dismissed *Ariane et Barbe-bleue* as "a faded arty opera" when she heard it performed at Covent Garden by a French company conducted by Philippe Gaubert (D5: 81). Paul Dukas's only opera, first performed in 1907, was highly regarded by Schoenberg and Berg, who must have realized that although it contains quotes from *Pelléas et Mélisande* and *La mer*, it has elements that are closer to Expressionism than to Debussy's orchestral idiom. In 1936 Olivier Messiaen characterized it as "le chef-d'oeuvre incompris" and praised especially the central act, "ce génial crescendo de l'ombre à la lumière qui fait du 2e acte le chef-d'oeuvre de Paul Dukas et un des chefs-d'oeuvre de la musique" (79, 84).

Although Virginia's relations with Sydney-Turner had cooled considerably over the years, her dependence on his expertise continued. In a letter written in January 1920 she asked him about an episode in *The Voyage Out:* "I wonder if you would once more tell me the number of the Beethoven sonata that Rachel plays in the *Voyage Out* – I sent the copy I marked to America, and now they're bringing out a new edition here – I can't remember what you told me – I say op. 112 – It can't be that" (L2: 418). The fact that she did not seem to remember that op. 112 was the cantata "Meeresstille und glückliche Fahrt" clearly indicates that Sydney-Turner was her main source of information. He occasionally took her to concerts, and in 1923 they heard "a divine Bach," the secular cantata "Geschwinde, geschwinde ihr wirbelnden Winde" (BWV 201) (L2:39).

It would be a mistake to deny the impact of Wagner on Virginia's formative years. "I doubt whether she really enjoyed the tense atmosphere of her Bayreuth holiday," remarked one of her critics (Jacobs 234). Such assumptions are in contradiction with the characterization of the activity of the public "between the acts" and the description of the site in the article "Impressions at Bayreuth." One might think of passages such as the following: "when the opera is over, it is quite late; and half way down the hill one looks back upon a dark torrent of carriages descending, their lamps wavering one above another, like irregular torches." In fact, the article also refers to the impact of the atmosphere of the city: "we wander with *Parsifal* in our heads through empty streets at night, where the gardens of the Hermitage glow with flowers like those other magic blossoms, and sound melts into colour, and colour calls out for words, where, in short, we are lifted out of the ordinary world and allowed merely to breathe and see" (E1: 289–92). One should avoid making the false assumption that early influences are obliterated by what comes later in an artist's career, for this may lead us to misinterpret the early works.

Let me illustrate with one example how commentaries may do the works a disservice. Rachel Vinrace, the heroine of *The Voyage Out*, is an amateur musician. In *Melymbrosia*, the first version of the novel, she has a late Beethoven sonata "spread upon the little piano," and she is reading an "engaging passage":

> Der zagend vor dem Streiche
> sich flüchtet, wo er kann,
> weil eine Braut er als Leiche
> für seinen Herrn gewann!
> Dünkt es dich dunkel,
> mein Gedicht?
> (MELYM 36)

Isolde's ironic and self-reflexive words in act 1, scene 2 suggest that Tristan is reluctant to face her, because he is taking her as a bride for another man. In the next chapter Clarissa Dalloway opens the score of *Tristan und Isolde* that lies on the table of the salon and remembers Bayreuth: "I shall never forget my first *Parsifal* – a grilling August day, and all those fat old German women, come in their stuffy high frocks, and then the dark theatre, and the music beginning [...]. It's like nothing else in the world!" (MELYM 54).

In the later version only the scene in which Rachel Vinrace is playing a Bach fugue is preserved. Mrs. Dalloway knocks at the door and enters. "The shape of the Bach fugue crashed to the ground" (VO 61). "Rachel's maturity reflects Woolf's own as she began to leave behind the popular Wagner for the older works of Beethoven, Bach and Mozart," argues a critic in a recent essay (Kelley 422). The relevance of this explanation can be questioned on at least three grounds. First, in the early version Wagner is presented as continuing the tradition of Beethoven, very much in the spirit of the later composer's influential essays on his predecessor. Second, before World War I Wagner's music was hardly more popular than that of Mozart or Beethoven. Third, in *Melymbrosia* the focus is on the text and not the music. The passage quoted might have appealed to Virginia Woolf as poetry because of its somewhat enigmatic character.

Woolf's interest in the legend of Sir Tristram and the Lady Iseult can be traced back to her short fiction known as "The Journal of Mistress Joan Martyn," composed in August 1906. In what I would regard as her most interesting short narrative before "The Mark on the Wall" (1917), Master Richard tells the story, "in a high melodious voice":

> He dropped his gay manner, and looked past us all, with straight fixed eyes, as though he drew his words from some sight not far from him. And as the story grew passionate his voice rose, and his fists clenched, and he raised his foot and stretched forth his arms; and then, when the lovers part, he seemed to see the Lady sink away from him, and his eye sought farther and farther till the vision was faded away; and his arms were empty. And then he is wounded in Brittany; and he hears the Princess coming across the seas to him. (CSF 55–56)

Melymbrosia may indicate Virginia Stephen's interest in the way Wagner added to the complexity of the love story. Be that as it may, the focus is on the text rather than on the music.

To return to the passage cited above from Leonard Woolf's autobiography, according to which Diaghilev's company represented a modernity different from that of Wagner, I have to admit that I have found no reference in the diaries or correspondence of Virginia Woolf to the most significant ballets of the early twentieth century. *L'Oiseau de feu* was "not given until Diaghilev's third British season," on June 18, 1912, at the Royal Opera House, Covent Garden; *Petrushka* was given its British premiere on February 4, 1913; and *Le Sacre du Printemps* premiered at the Theatre Royal, Drury Lane, on July 11, 1913 (Thomas 69, 70, 72). Quentin Bell remarks that the Woolfs went to the Russian Ballet at the beginning of July 1913 but does not mention the performance they attended (QB2: 12). Although *Le Rossignol* was conducted by Emile Cooper in 1914 (Stravinsky 52), I have not found any reference suggesting that the Woolfs attended the performance of Stravinsky's first opera, a work begun in 1908, before his compositional style had been considerably modified.

Most of the ballets Diaghilev presented had music that represented a far more traditional and even sentimental romanticism than that of the Bayreuth master. "The London public were much excited at the prospect of seeing Pavlova in *Giselle*. [...] The other 'sensation' of our autumn season in London was the début of Kchessinska in *Le Lac des Cygnes*" (Grigoriev 69). The musical idiom of Tchaikovsky is certainly very different from that of Wagner, but it can hardly be called more "advanced" in terms of harmony or structure, and it would be superfluous to compare Wagner and Adolphe Adam. Diaghilev may have believed that the British public was unprepared for his most experimental productions. In 1918 Virginia Woolf could see only the ballet-pantomime *Le Carnaval* and the one-act choreographic drama *Shéhérézade* (D1: 222, 288), two of the earliest productions of the company, first performed in 1910, with music by Robert Schumann (orchestrated by Nikolay Rimsky-Korsakov, Anagtol Liadov, Alexander Glazounov, and Alexandre Tchérépnine) and Rimsky-Korsakov, respectively. On the evidence of Virginia's correspondence (L2: 367), it can be assumed that in 1919, when Diaghilev's company returned to London, what she saw was an eclectic production, *La Boutique Fantastique,* based on "a collection of odd pieces by Rossini," orchestrated by Respighi and danced by Lydia Lopokova and Léonide Massine (Grigoriev 154–55). Five years later she attended a performance of *Les Tentations de la Bergère ou l'Amour Vainqueur,* choreographed by Bronislava Nijinska (1891–1972), with décor and curtain designed by the Cubist painter Juan Gris (1887–1927). Virginia Woolf called it "a less popular but a more interesting ballet than 'Cimarosiana' and 'Le Train Bleu,'" respectively a one-act ballet based on a suite of dances by Cimarosa and an "opérette dansée" with scenario by Jean Cocteau and music by Darius Milhaud. In the two paragraphs she wrote about *Les Tentations* for the "From Alpha to Omega" column in *Nation and Athenaeum* (E6: 399–400), the focus is on the visual experience and no mention is made of the music of the Baroque composer Michel Pignolet de Montéclair (1667–1737), restored and orchestrated by Henri Casadesus (1879–1947), instrumentalist, conductor, and composer, one of the founders of the Société des Instruments Anciens. According to Hermione Lee, in 1926 Virginia Woolf and Vita Sackville-West "went to Stravinsky's new ballets at the Haymarket" (HL 501), but Diaghilev's *régisseur* mentions only the performance of *Les Noces* at His Majesty's, in his chronicle of the Russian Ballet (Grigoriev 229).

Unlike G. E. Moore, Sydney-Turner, or Virginia's younger brother, Adrian, Leonard Woolf was not an amateur musician. He never tried to compose and played no instrument. He went to concerts, but his taste was limited by strong ideological considerations. As he admitted in his late autobiography, "In 1911 I knew nothing about Wagner, but I saw that it was time for me to set about him seriously. I therefore took a box in Covent Garden for the *Ring* in October, and Virginia came to *Das Rheingold, Siegfried,* and *Götterdämmerung*, with Adrian and Rupert Brooke to *Die Walküre*" (BA 50). Although his memory was overshadowed by later historical events, it can be safely assumed that he regarded the works of Wagner as detrimental from the outset. In his writings he almost seemed to avoid addressing the music itself and paid little attention to technical considerations: "I see that in its way the *Ring* is a masterpiece, but I dislike it and dislike Wagner and his art. [...] The Germans in the 19th century developed a tradition, a philosophy of life and art, barbarous, grandiose, phoney. Wagner was both cause and effect of this repulsive process which ended in the apogee and apotheosis of human bestiality and degradation, Hitler and the Nazis" (BA 50).

In the later 1920s he reviewed gramophone records for the *Nation and Athenaeum*. Some of the records selected were of considerable interest. He paid some attention to the activity of the Dolmetsch family, probably because he knew that Stella Duckworth, Virginia's half sister, who died in 1897, "was taught the violin by Arnold Dolmetsch" (MB 113), and in 1917 Dolmetsch made a virginal for Roger Fry (today in the Courtauld Gallery), but he failed to see the importance of period instrument interpretation. It is hardly understandable why he limited his choice to five labels (Parlophone, Beltona, His Master's Voice, Columbia, and Decca) and ignored the products of important companies like Telefunken, Homocord, Odeon, Polydor, or Gramophone. In any case, some 50 percent of the items he discussed were insignificant. The finale of act 1 of *Lohengrin* and the king's prayer sung in English and conducted by Sir Hamilton Harty certainly do not represent a memorable contribution to the history of interpretation. Although the reviewer's short evaluations cannot be dismissed as entirely worthless, his remarks on the technical strengths and weaknesses of the recording (e.g., the emphasis on the balance between orchestra, chorus, and singers) dominate. The relatively long notice on Felix von Weingarten's Columbia version of the *Symphonie fantastique*, for instance, contains no characterization of the specific features of the art of the great conductor.

In addition to extramusical considerations, Leonard Woolf's approach to music was hampered by misinformation and the impact of fashionable views. He attributed the song titled "Die beiden Grenadiere" to Schubert (*DAW* 201) and constantly praised the late string quartets of Beethoven. Since he reviewed the recordings of these works made by the Léner and Capet Quartets (L. Woolf, "New Gramophone Records," May 18; July 20), it seems likely that these were the versions known to Virginia Woolf. In his autobiography Leonard insisted that she was especially fond of one of these quartets:

> I had once said to her that, if there was to be music at one's cremation, it ought to be the cavatina from the B flat quartet, op. 130, of Beethoven. There is a moment at cremations when the doors of the crematorium open and the coffin slides slowly in, and there is a moment in the middle of the cavatina when for a few bars the music, of incredible beauty, seems to hesitate with a gentle forward pulsing motion – if played at the moment it might seem to be gently propelling the dead into eternity of oblivion. Virginia agreed with me.

Incidentally, "the music of the 'Blessed Spirits' from Gluck's Orfeo was played" at the cremation (*JNAM* 95–96), but it is undeniable that the late Beethoven quartets seemed to be the most important musical experience for the Woolf couple in the 1920s and 1930s.

Several documents demonstrate that Leonard Woolf's gestures of praise for these works were far from original in the interwar period. One of them is the reminiscences of Stravinsky. Here is Stravinsky's somewhat malicious description of his meeting with a writer for whom Virginia Woolf had great admiration: "After the premières of Mavra and Renard in June 1922, I went to a party [...]. Marcel Proust was there also. Most of the people came to that party from my première at the Grand Opera, but Proust came directly from his bed [...]. I talked to him about music and he expressed much enthusiasm for the late Beethoven quartets – enthusiasm I would have shared were it not a commonplace among the intellectuals of that time and not a musical judgment but a literary pose" (102).

At any rate, if the prewar years for Virginia Woolf were marked by operatic experiences, the next decades were dominated by concerts and recordings. "There was a concert where they played Mozart," says the narrator of "Sympathy" (written in 1919), and the name of the same composer occurs in "The String Quartet" (1920) (CSF 140). In the second of these stories a character refers to Mozart as the composer of the work performed. Since the character may be wrong, there is no contradiction with the diary entry that suggests the notes for this text were taken during a performance of a quintet by Schubert (D2: 24).

Painted Roofs, the first part of a novel cycle by Dorothy Miller Richardson was published by Duckworth some six months after *The Voyage Out*. The heroine of this novel, a governess sent to Germany, is an amateur pianist who is impressed by "the music that was everywhere all the week" (Richardson 1: 66) in Hanover. The description of the performance of compositions by Beethoven, Weber, and Chopin may have inspired Virginia Woolf when she was writing "The String Quartet."

Although an afternoon concert she attended at the Queen's Hall in 1915, conducted by Sir Henry Wood (1869–1944), included some Wagner, and on another occasion César Franck's Symphony in D minor and three movements of Lalo's *Symphonie Espagnole* were performed (D1: 5, 20), Wood's programs focused on the Viennese classics. The most remarkable feature of his Promenade Concerts was an emphasis on works by J. S. Bach, an approach that could be considered outdated from the perspective of the twenty-first century. Woolf also regularly attended the chamber concerts held at Shelley House (the Chelsea house belonging to St. John Hornby). In 1919 she heard the Allied String Quartet in Wigmore Hall (D1: 307). During a Beethoven Festival Week, April

25–30, 1921, at the Aeolian Hall she heard all the Beethoven string quartets played by the London String Quartet (D2: 113). Two of Schubert's chamber works, the Octet and the String Quintet, also made a deep impression on her (D1: 63; D2: 24).

With some exaggeration it could be argued that the conservative eclecticism of the British music of the period might be blamed for the limitations of Virginia's taste. Although she found the music of Ethel Smyth "too literary – too stressed – too didactic" (D4: 12), she felt an obligation to listen on the wireless to a Promenade Concert conducted by Smyth in 1930 that included the *Anacreontic Ode* composed in 1908 and some of her songs. Woolf described them as "very satisfying" in a letter addressed to Smyth (L4: 209). Furthermore, at the beginning of 1931 the Woolfs were present at the first performance of Smyth's oratorio, *The Prison*. Two years later Virginia listened to a "Serenade Concert" that included some of Smyth's music broadcast from the Canterbury Festival of Music and Drama, and she assured her friend that she liked her music "very much." At the beginning of 1934 she sent her congratulations to the composer after a concert devoted entirely to her music conducted by Sir Thomas Beecham. "And then I hope the Smyth festival is over," she wrote, expressing her relief in a letter to her nephew Quentin Bell on January 10. On March 3, 1934, she attended a performance of Smyth's late *Romantic Mass in D*, premiered in 1893 and later revised (L5: 193, 267, 269, 280). Virginia Woolf's reluctance to attend a concert that included the Prelude to Ethel Smyth's *The Wreckers* at the Queen's Hall in 1935 can be felt in the opening words of a letter addressed to the composer: "Yes, I'll come if I can, on the 3rd, but I cant be dead sure; and oh Lord how I hate afternoon concerts. But as I say, if I can, from love of you, I'll come" (L5: 370).

Since Virginia Woolf was related to Vaughan Williams by marriage, she went to concerts with his works on the program. Lord Berners was an acquaintance, so she tried to appreciate his music, and similarly personal reasons made her attend the first performances of *Façade*, a collaborative effort of the British literary figures Edith, Osbert, and Sacheverell Sitwell and William Walton (D2: 245–46), or *Pomona*, a twenty-minute ballet by Leonard Constant Lambert (1905–1951), with set and costumes designed by Vanessa Bell (D4: 144). In 1934 the Woolfs were taken to the premiere of an opera by Lawrence Collingwood (1887–1982), the principal conductor of Sadler's Wells Opera, by Mary Hutchinson, a cousin of Lytton Strachey and a lover of Clive Bell (D4: 207).

All in all, the most innovative examples of twentieth-century music may have been virtually unknown to Virginia Woolf. Two performances of Ravel's String Quartet in F major, composed in 1903 and revised in 1910 (D1: 226; D2: 39); an early performance of Debussy's Sonata for Flute, Viola, and Harp, inspired by Rameau's *Pièces de clavecin en concerts* and composed in 1915–1916 (L2: 140); a theatrical production of Stravinsky's *L'Histoire du Soldat* held in 1928 (E4: 564); and the performance of some excerpts from *Petrushka* during Sir Thomas Beecham's "Season of the Russian Opera and Ballet" (D4: 31) were among the exceptions. A letter addressed to Clive Bell suggests that Virginia planned to see *Petrushka* in 1919 (L2: 375), but as far as I know there is no evidence proving that she actually went to the performance at the Alhambra Theatre. In view of the fact that the "season at the Alhambra ended on 30 July" (Grigoriev 157), and that on October 27 Virginia Woolf was still hesitating to see "the Russian dancers" because they "were so expensive" (L2: 393), it seems likely that she had no chance to see Stravinsky's second folk-influenced ballet. In 1921 *Le Sacre du Printemps* had two further performances in London: it was given first at a concert conducted by Leon Aynsley Goossens (1893–1962) with the composer present and later at a theater by the Diaghilev company. On June 10 the world premiere of the *Symphonies d'instruments à vent à la mémoire de Debussy* in the vast arena of Queen's Hall turned out to be a disastrous failure. "Both my work and Koussevitzky," the conductor, were "victimized," Stravinsky wrote some fifteen years later (94, 96). In June 1927 the composer himself conducted his opera-oratorio *Oedipus Rex* and a gala performance of his ballets was given by Diaghilev (133). Had Virginia Woolf attended these performances, there would be some trace of them in her diary. Sources unknown to me might invalidate that hypothesis.

"Do you like folk music?" she asked Ethel Smyth, and her own answer to that question suggested that she was reluctant to see the benefits of the folk culture revival both in music and in literature: "To my thinking they're the ruin of all modern music – just as Synge and Yeats ruined themselves with keening Celtic dirges" (L4: 406). In a letter written in

1934 she called a work by Ethel Smyth "cacophonous" (L5: 360). One may even suppose that the neoclassicism of Walton and Lambert might have made some impact on the work of Virginia Woolf in the 1930s, when she turned back to what she herself called "the representational form," "fact recording," "objective, realistic, in the manner of Jane Austen: carrying the story on all the time" (D4: 142, 147, 168). Lambert took a firm stand against both Schoenberg and Stravinsky, and Virginia Woolf repeatedly asked Ethel Smyth to let her publish an essay in which she discussed his music (L4: 214, 215, 226). The ballet *Pomona,* consisting of pastiches titled Prelude, Corante, Pastorale, Menuetto, Passacaglia, Rigadoon, Siciliana, and Marcia, was the work of an artist for whom "the true guardian of the music of the future" was Jean Sibelius, the Finnish composer "whose shadow strides across Walton's First Symphony (1935)" (Wood 156). Lambert's ballet was composed in 1927, but the performance Virginia Woolf attended was given in January 1933, when she was trying to finish *Flush* and was struggling with *The Pargiters,* the first version of *The Years,* works that she herself called "cuckoos in my nest" (D4: 143). One could add that the "new" compositions Stravinsky presented to the British public in the 1920s and 1930s, the ballets *Apollon Musagète* and *Le Baiser de la Fée* or the *mélodrame Perséphone,* works he conducted in London in 1927, 1929, and 1934, respectively, imitate earlier styles and confirm a neoclassical outlook the contemporary British public could accept without serious reservations. None had the originality of the works he composed in the 1910s. As he himself admitted, he tried a style and orchestration "by means of which the music could be appreciated at the first hearing" (Stravinsky 149).

Although Virginia Woolf missed the most outstanding operatic performances of the interwar period, she heard some celebrated instrumentalists: in 1919 she heard Alfred Cortot (1877–1962) perform, both as pianist and as chamber musician; in 1924 she became acquainted with Brahms's *Lieder* in the interpretation of the great German mezzo-soprano Elena Gerhardt (1883–1961) and heard the famous Portuguese cellist Guilhermina Suggia (1888–1950). In 1932 she went to the Wigmore Hall concert of the Busch Quartet, who played Brahms, Dvořák, and Beethoven, and the following year she heard four concerts by the same ensemble (D1: 311; D2: 298, 320; D4: 78, 147) and listened to Jelly Arányi

(1893–1966) (the artist to whom Ravel dedicated *Tzigane*, Bartók his two sonatas for violin and piano, Holst his Double Concerto, and Vaughan-Williams his "Concerto Accademico"), playing J. S. Bach in Westminster Abbey. In 1934, the first year of the Glyndebourne Festival, she also heard an afternoon concert conducted by Fritz Busch, and in 1939 she heard another recital by the Busch Quartet at the Wigmore Hall that included Schubert's early Quartet in B flat major (D. 112), Mozart's G minor Quintet (K. 516), and Beethoven's Op. 131 in C sharp minor, the quartet that Wagner regarded as one of his main sources of inspiration, in which "das innerste Traumbild wird in einer lieblichsten Erinnerung wach" (Wagner, *Gesammelte Schriften* 97).

Virginia Woolf was often far from enthusiastic about, and indeed at times was quite critical of, the quality of the music she heard. In 1918 she disliked Mozart's great Symphony in G minor (K. 550) as conducted by Julian Clifford (1877–1921), finding it slow and sentimental, "with a lugubrious stickiness," and she disapproved of the "vulgarity" of Henry Wood's rendering of works by J. S. Bach, Beethoven, Mozart, Gluck, and Dvořák (D1: 142, 206). She found the theatrics of conductors – for example, the "grimaces, attenuations, dancings, swingings" of Sir Thomas Beecham – superfluous and disturbing (D4: 284). She expressed reservations about some of the performances heard on the radio; "they play too slowly," she remarked about the all-female Macnaghten Quartet playing Haydn (L6: 54).

With the rise of the recording industry, the Woolfs more often listened to music at home instead of going to concerts. A reference to Artur Schnabel's Beethoven recitals in a letter written on November 8, 1932, may suggest that the risk of fainting in the heat, heart troubles, and an intermittent pulse may have prevented Virginia from attending concerts (L5: 122). Her diary and correspondence such as the following may give one some idea of their daily routine: "Home to music"; "And soon the bell will ring, and we shall dine & then we shall have some music [...]"; "delightful as this letter is, I must go and put my pie in the oven [...]. Then we turn on the loud speaker – Bach tonight"; "Black clouds while we played Brahms"; "Bach at night"; "we'll play bowls; then I shall read Sévigné; then have grilled ham and mushrooms for dinner; then Mozart" (D3: 108, 247; L5: 88; D4: 107, 241, 336; L6: 286).

Although the world premiere of Schoenberg's *Five Orchestral Pieces* (op. 16) in London on September 3, 1912, met with an "extremely hostile reception" (Heckert 49), the works of this composer had numerous performances in the British capital, and from November 1923 they were often broadcast (Doctor 337–51), his name does not appear in the published diaries, letters, or biographies of Virginia Woolf. Between 1929 and 1936 Anton von Webern conducted nine concerts for the BBC. According to a booklet designed and edited by Lewis Foreman for Continuum Records (*Webern Conducts Berg: Violin Concerto*, Continuum Testament, SBT 1004), the programs included works by J. S. Bach, Beethoven, Schubert, Brahms, Johann Strauss Jr., Bruckner, Wolf, Mahler, Krenek, Milhaud, as well as by the three major composers of the Second Viennese School (Schoenberg, Webern, and Berg). There is reason to believe that the London audience appreciated Berg's works more than the music of Schoenberg and Webern. Before the memorial concert for Berg conducted by Webern on May 1, 1936, a concert performance of *Wozzeck* was held on March 14, 1934. Among the large number of Virginia Woolf's diary entries about music heard on the radio, there is not a single one referring to any of these concerts.

In the acutely troubled period of the late 1930s, under the influence of preparations for war and her husband's growing involvement in the activity of the Labour Party, Virginia came to view music as "our one resource against politics" (L6: 19). Even during the air raids they used their gramophone in the evenings, as the last words of the diary entry of October 22, 1940, suggest: "reading, music, bed" (D5: 333).

Since the catalog of the records the Woolfs owned is now archived with the papers of Leonard Woolf at the University of Sussex, and in some cases he noted the dates on which they listened to certain recordings, it seems possible to have some hypothesis concerning the core of their repertoire. In the 1930s they listened mainly to HMV recordings of works by J. S. Bach as performed by Edwin Fischer and Alfred Cortot; Beethoven string quartets played by the Busch, Capet, and Léner quartets; Artur Schnabel's, Adolf Busch's, and Fritz Kreisler's interpretations of Beethoven sonatas; the Pro Arte Quartet's Haydn series; and Mozart's violin sonatas played by Szymon Goldberg and Lily Kraus. The catalog also includes Debussy's *Violin Sonata* and some compositions by Richard

Strauss, Ravel, and de Falla, but it is not possible to determine whether these recordings were acquired before 1941. The only major twentieth-century work that Leonard Woolf mentions and includes a date on which they listened to it (April 10, 1935) is Bartók's *First String Quartet* (op. 7), composed in 1908–1909.

Under the influence of such recordings, Virginia's working method changed gradually. "I do a little work on it in the evening when the gramophone is playing late Beethoven sonatas." "It occurred to me last night while listening to a Beethoven quartet that I would merge all the interjected passages into Bernard's final speech." Such statements may suggest that listening to music may have helped her in the writing of *The Waves* (D3: 139, 339). Whatever the case, it is certainly true that in the final decades of her life she regarded the string quartets of Beethoven as masterpieces comparable to the greatest works by Shakespeare. "Hamlet or a Beethoven quartet is the truth about this vast mass that we call the world," she wrote at the end of her life (MB 84).

Though I would by no means deny the inspiration drawn from music in her works composed from the mid-1920s, I nonetheless would be somewhat reluctant to accept E. M. Forster's claim that *To the Lighthouse* is "a novel in sonata form" (381), the assumption that Virginia Woolf's biography of Roger Fry has a "sonata structure" (Jacobs 199, 253), or even the suggestion that "the conception of the long-lived Orlando" was inspired by *The Rite of Spring* (Haller 226). One of the numerous articles attempting to link her work to music suggests that more caution might be needed. At the outset of his essay, Gerald Levin asserted that in *The Waves* Virginia Woolf achieved "contrapunctal style," but later he himself pointed out the fundamental weakness in this argument by stating that "voices in the novel cannot be heard simultaneously" (165, 166). The monologues of the six characters can be read only consecutively, so the comparison with a fugue would be a little presumptuous. Some of those who insist that her later works can be explained with the help of the thesis that Wagner's influence had been replaced by that of Beethoven have tried to find British sources for Virginia Woolf's interest in the late string quartets of the earlier master. They may not realize that such works as, for instance, *Beethoven: His Spiritual Development* (1927), by the mathematician J. W. Sullivan (1886–1937), may have been inspired by

Wagner's longest essay on Beethoven (1870), a much more professional discussion of these works that contains a profound analysis of the C sharp minor Quartet (op. 131).

"I am writing *The Waves* to a rhythm not to a plot," Virginia Woolf wrote in her diary (*D*3: 316). In a letter to Ethel Smyth she even revealed her awareness that such an approach to writing represented a radical departure from the generic conventions of the novel: "my difficulty is that I am writing to a rhythm and not to a plot. Does this convey anything? And thus though the rhythmical is more natural to me than the narrative, it is completely opposed to the tradition of fiction" (*L*4: 204). While working on *Between the Acts* (provisionally titled *Pointz Hall*), she observed "that it is the rhythm of a book that, by running in the head, winds one into a ball: and so jades one. The rhythm of PH. (the last chapter) became so obsessive that I heard it, perhaps used it, in every sentence I spoke" (*D*5: 339). In 1930, in a letter to Ethel Smyth, Virginia Woolf remarked with regret that there were no "accents to convey tone of voice" (*L*4: 225–26), and in an essay published in 1936, she insisted that "the prose writer, although he pretends to walk soberly in obedience to the voice of reason, nevertheless excites us by perpetual changes of rhythm" (*L*6: 418). Louie Everest, the "cook-general" at Monks House noted that when Virginia was having her bath, one could hear her talking to herself. "On and on she went, talk, talk, talk [...]. When Mr Woolf saw that I looked startled he told me that Mrs Woolf always said the sentences out loud that she had written during the night. She needed to know if they sounded right and the bath was a good, resonant place for trying them out" (Noble 189).

Undoubtedly, tone, voice, and the disposition of forms play a major role in *To the Lighthouse, The Waves,* and *Between the Acts,* but it would be an exaggeration to link them to specific musical genres or structures. Tentative explanations might be attempted in more general terms. Since the stylization of *The Waves* has characteristics usually associated with verse rhythm, it is possible to argue that we can "*hear* the difference between the characters rather than visualise them" (Caughie 345). Lily Briscoe is driven by "some rhythm which was dictated to her," but this rhythm is at least as spatial as musical, echoing Roger Fry's thesis that "rhythm is the fundamental and vital quality of painting, as of all the arts" (Reed 102). In her painting Virginia "attained a dancing rhythmical movement, as if the pauses were one part of the rhythm and the strokes another, and all were related" (TL 184, 182).

Contrary to what some may believe, a major artist never forgets the inspirations of her early years. In the case of Virginia Woolf, it is an exaggeration to believe that there was a rift between her early experiences of Wagner's stage works and her later interest in the works of Beethoven. In *Jacob's Room* a character thinks that Brangäne is "a trifle hoarse" in a performance of *Tristan und Isolde* (JR 68). In 1926 the sight of the burning of the gorse on the moor reminded Virginia of the death of the hero in *Götterdämmerung* (L3: 309). In a letter written to Ethel Smyth five years later, she refers to rhythm as the most distinctive element of the "Waldweben" ("forest murmurs") section of act 2 of *Siegfried:* "The loudspeaker is pouring forth Wagner from Paris. His rhythm destroys my rhythm [. . .]. All writing is nothing but putting words on the backs of rhythm" (L4: 303). In *The Years, Siegfried* is called Kitty's "favorite opera" (Y 196). The suggestion that in this case act 1of the "Zweiter Tag" of Wagner's tetralogy is used "to illustrate dictatorship and aggression" (HL 242) suggests that sometimes textual (and intermedial) evidence is being distorted to fit an ideological preconception. Although the reader of the Covent Garden scene of Virginia's longest novel may not refute the argument that in presenting a performance the focus is on the audience rather than on the music, since observations "on the latter outnumber appreciations of music and performers" (Jacobs 241), in a more general sense music may have helped her realize that a "sense of rhythm," a quality the significance of which she pointed out in her early essay "Street Music," published in 1905 (E1: 30), was a sine qua non of prose writing. Insofar as Leslie Stephen, "one of the great pioneers of Victorian unbelief," professed the "ideal of disengaged, instrumental reason," music in general and Wagner's Romantic "expressivism" (Taylor 402, 413) in particular may have helped Virginia Woolf in her protest against the scientific rationality of her father's generation. The only possible conclusion is that it was at least partly thanks to the inspiration drawn from music that she was able to become a major artist.

WORKS CITED

Bell, Quentin. *Virginia Woolf: A Biography*. New York: Harcourt, 1972. Print.

Boulez, Pierre. *Regards sur autrui (Points de repère, tome II)*. Textes réunis et présentés par Jean-Jacques Nattiez et Sophie Galaise. Paris: Bourgois, 2005. Print.

Caughie, Pamela L. "Virginia Woolf: Radio, Gramophone, Broadcasting." *The Edinburgh Companion to Virginia Woolf and the Arts*. Ed. Maggie Humm. Edinburgh: Edinburgh University Press, 2010. 332–47. Print.

Doctor, Jennifer. *The BBC and Ultra-Modern Music, 1922–1936: Shaping a Nation's Tastes*. Cambridge: Cambridge University Press, 1999. Print.

Donington, Robert. *Wagner's "Ring" and Its Symbols*. 3rd ed. London: Faber, 1974. Print.

Forster, E. M. "Virginia Woolf." *Modern British Fiction*. Ed. Mark Schorer. New York: Oxford University Press, 1961. 376–90. Print.

Genette, Gérard. *Figures IV*. Paris: Seuil, 1999. Print.

Grigoriev, S. L. *The Diaghilev Ballet, 1909–1929*. Trans. and ed. Vera Bowen. Harmondsworth: Penguin, 1960. Print.

Haller, Evelyn. "Her Quill Drawn from the Firebird: Virginia Woolf and the Russian Dancers." *The Multiple Muses of Virginia Woolf*. Ed. Diane F. Gillespie. Columbia: University of Missouri Press, 1993. 180–226. Print.

Heckert, Deborah. "Schoenberg, Roger Fry, and the Emergence of a Critical Language for the Reception of Musical Modernism in Britain, 1912–1914." *British Music and Modernism, 1885–1960*. Ed. Matthew Riley. Farnham: Ashgate, 2010. 49–66. Print.

Jacobs, Peter. "'The Second Violin Tuning in the Ante-Room': Virginia Woolf and Music." *The Multiple Muses of Virginia Woolf*. Ed. Diane F. Gillespie. Columbia: University of Missouri Press, 1993. 227–60. Print.

Kelley, Joyce E. "Virginia Woolf and Music." *The Edinburgh Companion to Virginia Woolf and the Arts*. Ed. Maggie Humm. Edinburgh: Edinburgh University Press, 2010. 417–36. Print.

Lee, Hermione. *Virginia Woolf*. London: Vintage, 1997. Print.

Levin, Gerald. "The Musical Style of *The Waves*." *Journal of Narrative Technique* 13 (1983): 164–71. Print.

Messiaen, Olivier. "Ariane et Barbe-Bleue." *La Revue Musicale* 132–36 (1936): 79–86. Print.

Miller, J. Hillis. "Mr. Carmichael and Lily Briscoe: The Rhythm of Creativity in *To the Lighthouse*." *Modernism Reconsidered*. Ed. Robert Kiely. Cambridge: Harvard University Press, 1983. 167–89. Print.

Noble, Joan Russell, ed. *Recollections of Virginia Woolf*. London: Sphere, 1975. Print.

Pater, Walter. *The Renaissance: Studies in Art and Poetry*. Ed. and intro. Adam Phillips. Oxford: Oxford University Press, 1986. Print.

Reed, Christopher, ed. *A Roger Fry Reader*. Chicago: University of Chicago Press, 1996. Print.

Richardson, Dorothy M. *Pilgrimage*. Intro. Walter Allen. New York: Popular Library, 1976. Print.

Stravinsky (I. F.). *In Conversation with Robert Craft*. Harmondsworth: Penguin, 1962. Print.

Taylor, Charles. *Sources of the Self: The Making of the Modern Identity*. Cambridge: Harvard University Press, 1989. Print.

Thomas, Gareth. "Modernism, Diaghilev, and the Ballets Russes in London,

1911–1929." *British Music and Modernism, 1895–1960*. Ed. Matthew Riley. Farnham: Ashgate, 2010. 67–91. Print.

Wagner, Richard. *Gesammelte Schriften und Dichtungen: Neunter Band*. Herausgegeben von Wolfgang Golther. Berlin: Bong & Co., n.d. Print.

Wilde, Oscar. *The Complete Works*. Intro. Vyvyan Holland. London: Collins, 1984. Print.

Wood, Hugh. "English Contemporary Music." *European Music in the Twentieth Century*. Ed. Howard Hartog. Rev. ed. Harmondsworth: Penguin, 1961. 145–70. Print.

Woolf, Leonard. *An Autobiography: With an introduction by Quentin Bell*. Vol. 1: *1880–1911*. Oxford: Oxford University Press, 1980. Print.

———. *Beginning Again: An Autobiography of the Years 1911–1918*. London: Hogarth, 1964. Print.

———. *Downhill All the Way: An Autobiography of the Years 1919–1939*. London: Hogarth, 1967. Print.

———. *The Journey Not the Arrival Matters: An Autobiography of the Years 1939 to 1969*. New York: Harcourt, 1975. Print.

———. "New Gramophone Records." *Nation and Athenaeum*, May 18, 1929, 252. Print.

———. "New Gramophone Records." *Nation and Athenaeum*, July 20, 1929, 543. Print.

Woolf, Virginia. *Carlyle's House and Other Sketches*. Ed. David Bradshaw. London: Hesperus, 2003.

———. *A Chance of Perspective: The Letters of Virginia Woolf*. Vol. 3: *1923–1928*. Ed. Nigel Nicolson. London: Hogarth, 1977. Print.

———. *The Complete Shorter Fiction*. Ed. Susan Dick. 2nd ed. San Diego: Harcourt, 1989. Print.

———. *The Diary*. Vol. 1: *1915–1919*. Ed. Anne Olivier Bell. Intro. Quentin Bell. Harmondsworth: Penguin, 1979. Print.

———. *The Diary*. Vol. 2: *1920–24*. Ed. Anne Olivier Bell. Harmondsworth: Penguin, 1981. Print.

———. *The Diary*. Vol. 3: *1925–30*. Ed. Anne Olivier Bell. Harmondsworth: Penguin, 1982. Print.

———. *The Diary*. Vol. 4: *1931–35*. Ed. Anne Olivier Bell. Harmondsworth: Penguin, 1983. Print.

———. *The Diary*. Vol. 5: *1936–1941*. Ed. Anne Olivier Bell. Harmondsworth: Penguin, 1985. Print.

———. *The Essays*. Vol. 1: *1904–1912*. Ed. Andrew McNeillie. San Diego: Harcourt, 1986. Print.

———. *The Essays*. Vol. 2: *1912–1918*. Ed. Andrew McNeillie. San Diego: Harcourt, 1987. Print.

———. *The Essays*. Vol. 3: *1919–1924*. Ed. Andrew McNeillie. San Diego: Harcourt, 1988. Print.

———. *The Essays*. Vol. 4: *1925–1928*. Ed. Andrew McNeillie. Orlando: Harcourt, 1994. Print.

———. *The Essays*. Vol. 6: *1933–1941*. Ed. Stuart N. Clarke. London: Hogarth, 2001. Print.

———. *The Flight of the Mind: The Letters of Virginia Woolf*. Vol. 1: *1888–1912*. London: Hogarth, 1975. Print.

———. *Jacob's Room: The Waves*. New York: Harcourt, 1959. Print.

———. *Leave the Letters Till We're Dead: The Letters of Virginia Woolf*. Vol. 6: *1936–1941*. Ed. Nigel Nicolson. London: Hogarth, 1980. Print.

———. *Melymbrosia*. Ed. and intro. Louise DeSalvo. San Francisco: Cleis, 2002. Print.

———. *Moments of Being: Unpublished Autobiographical Writings*. Ed., intro., and notes by Jeanne Schulkind. Frogmore: Triad Panther, 1978. Print.

———. *A Passionate Apprentice: The Early Journals of Virginia Woolf*. Ed.

Mitchell A. Leaska. London: Hogarth, 1992. Print.

———. *The Question of Things Happening: The Letters of Virginia Woolf.* Vol. 2: *1912–1922.* Ed. Nigel Nicolson. London: Hogarth, 1976. Print.

———. *A Reflection of the Other Person: The Letters of Virginia Woolf.* Vol. 4: *1929–1931.* Ed. Nigel Nicolson. London: Hogarth, 1978. Print.

———. *The Sickle Side of the Moon: The Letters of Virginia Woolf.* Vol. 5: *1932–1935.* Ed. Nigel Nicolson. London: Hogarth, 1979. Print.

———. *To the Lighthouse.* Intro. D. M. Hoare. London: Dent, 1963. Print.

———. *The Voyage Out.* London: Hogarth, 1965. Print.

———. *The Years.* London: Hogarth, 1937. Print.

PART TWO

Ut Musica Poesis:
Music and the Novel

Understanding a sentence is much more akin to
understanding a theme in music than one may think.

LUDWIG WITTGENSTEIN,
Philosophical Investigations

THREE

Music, Language, and Moments of Being

FROM *THE VOYAGE OUT* TO *BETWEEN THE ACTS*

Adriana Varga

IN HER MEMOIR, "A SKETCH OF THE PAST" (1939), VIRGINIA WOOLF described one of her "first impressions in pale yellow, silver, and green" (66), in which the perception of sound and image was undivided: "Everything would be large and dim; and what was seen would at the same time be heard; sounds would come through this petal or leaf – sounds indistinguishable from sights" (66). These "colour-and-sound memories" (66) she called "these moments of being of mine" (73) reflect not only the interest Woolf took at the height of her artistic maturity in exploring the interconnections between rhythm, sound, sight, and language but also an awareness that her experience of these interconnections had occurred simply and naturally in childhood, at Talland House, St. Ives:

> Sound and sight seem to make equal parts of these first impressions. [...] The quality of the air above Talland House seemed to suspend sound, to let it sink down slowly, as if it were caught in a blue gummy veil. The rooks cawing is part of the waves breaking – one, two, one, two – and the splash as the wave drew back and then it gathered again, and I lay there half awake, half asleep, drawing in such ecstasy as I cannot describe. (66)

It is this synesthetic quality that Woolf remained interested in exploring in her fiction and essays throughout her life, yet, while the importance of the visual arts in her works has been widely recognized and researched, music and rhythm have not received their deserved attention despite the influence they had on a writer who confessed that she always thought of her books as music before writing them (L4: 425). It should come as no surprise, then, that the heroine of her first novel, *The Voyage Out*, is a pianist. Because she recognizes that language, while necessary for expression, restricts and narrows it, Rachel resorts to music. Woolf experiments with and expands the boundaries of language in this novel by looking at it through the prism of her heroine's musical experience in the effort to impart the sense of that "reality dwelling in what one saw and felt, but did not talk about" (vo 35). In this essay I trace changes in the role music plays in three novels spanning Woolf's writing career – *The Voyage Out* (1915), *The Waves* (1931), and *Between the Acts* (1941) – showing that these changes reflect an evolution in Woolf's modernist experiment and textual praxis.

The most aesthetically innovative sections of Woolf's first novel are those that express Rachel Vinrace's thoughts and perception of reality. These moments are unusual not only because Rachel's mind is "as the landscape outside when dark beneath clouds and straitly lashed by wind and hail" (vo 223) but also because she is a pianist. What she cannot find in books and in her social interactions, she is able to find in music. Woolf does posit, through her heroine, a gulf between music and language as forms of expression: the novel, being made of words and not of notes, fails to express in the same way as music does. Yet, paradoxically, Woolf creates and describes moments in which time and space expand and contract in ways that parallel Rachel's own piano playing, presenting reality, like music, as transitory as "a light passing over the surface and vanishing" (125).

While exploring the relationship between music and language in her first novel, Woolf also revisited Walter Pater's famous "School of Giorgione" dictum, "All art aspires toward the condition of music."[1] Both Pater and Woolf discuss the "moment" of being as the kernel of aesthetic perception as well as expression, and they both describe such "moments" in terms of music. However, as Wolfgang Iser has pointed out, there are also important differences between the ways in which Pater and Woolf conceptualize the "moment":

> In her novels, [the moment] gives a kaleidoscopic form to the way in which experience is mirrored in human consciousness, whereas for Pater the moment does not have a potential power to give form to anything. It is impossible to describe Pater's concept of the moment in any positive terms – he himself could only delineate it negatively. His moment remains embedded in the flow of time, whereas Virginia Woolf lifts it out of time, or rather she sees it as cutting across the

sequence of past, present and future to which Pater adheres so rigidly. For her it is a mode through which time-transcending forms of human consciousness may be captured, while for Pater it remains an atom that can only be perceived in the abstract. (*Walter Pater* 138)

Furthermore, while Pater saw the individual as experiencing such moments in isolation, for Woolf the "moment" is always embedded within a particular community and cultural context, taking place as an interaction between reader and text, performer and audience.

Woolf returns to exploring the connection between music, language, and the moment of being again in *The Waves*, yet the way music is experienced as well as the function it plays within the fictional work is significantly transformed. Through her performance, Rachel Vinrace had inspired her audience to feel ennobled and see "themselves and their lives, and the whole of human life advancing very nobly under the direction of music." Rhoda's experience of a chamber performance in *The Waves* (163) is very different from that of Rachel. It is no longer shared by an entire audience, but has become abstract and isolated. If in 1915 Rachel Vinrace's music could inspire her audience to envision a vast structural design, by 1931 the beetle-shaped men with their violins inspire Rhoda to imagine a very different kind of architecture, one whose purpose no longer allows the performer and listeners to see "themselves advancing very nobly under the direction of music." Rhoda's square placed upon the oblong has become an abstract modernist experience of much more restrained gestures and proportions.

By 1941 this modernist experience changes again significantly. In *Between the Acts* the source of music is a gramophone, whose strains can make the audience either disperse or "sink down peacefully" (84). Yet, as planned by Miss La Trobe, the musical experience transcends a mechanical device, producing unusual reveries, and can unite, even if only momentarily, nature and man:

> The view repeated in its own way what the tune was saying. The sun was sinking; the colours were merging; and the view was saying how after toil men rest from their labours: how coolness comes; reason prevails; and having unharnessed the team from the plough, neighbours dig in cottage gardens and lean over cottage gates.
>
> The cows, making a step forward, then standing still, were saying the same thing to perfection.

> Folded in this triple melody, the audience sat gazing; and beheld gently and approvingly without interrogation, for it seemed inevitable, a box tree in a green tub take the place of the ladies' dressing-room. (92)

Music has become public again, but it no longer evokes Rachel Vinrace's building with spaces and columns succeeding each other. In Woolf's last novel, reality is modeled on a musical experience that can both create and break the bonds between performance, audience, and the world. The triple melody is synesthetic and enfolds the world itself: the sinking sun, the merging colors, the unharnessed plough team, toil and rest.

The experience of music, and the relationship between text, reader, music, performer, and audience, change dramatically from Woolf's first novel to her last one. In order to understand these transformations, I consider both how Woolf discusses music and how she explores relationships between music and language in her fiction. Following Albert Gier's music/literature triangle (itself patterned on the semiotic triangle), Siglind Bruhn distinguishes three ways in which literature relates to music: (1) on the level of the denoted (thematizing music) – verbal utterance *about music;* (2) on the level of the signified (emulating a compositional technique or a type of structural organization typical for music) – verbal utterance *following musical designs;* and (3) on the level of the signifier (imitating the sound, the typical surface patterns, or the aesthetic self-sufficiency of music) – verbal utterance *as music* (82). In some cases, language in Woolf's fiction may be seen as an example of what Bruhn calls musical ekphrasis: "a transformation of a message – in content and form, imagery and suggested symbolic signification – from one medium into another" (drama – music) (xvi). Virginia Woolf's interest in music, as well as the ways in which she investigated the relationship between text, music, performance, and reception on these three levels, changed dramatically from her first novel to the last one. In this process, Woolf also reconfigured the relationship between reader and text; actor, performance, and audience.

RACHEL VINRACE AND *THE VOYAGE OUT*: WORD AND MUSIC

In her first novel Woolf set up a dispute between music and language at the core of which lies the question of whether language is an adequate means of communication, especially when compared to music, and of whether language can capture and express the ineffable aspects of human experience – the sense of that reality one saw and felt (*VO* 35). Woolf created in the heroine of her very first novel a passionate although youthful pianist who questions her fiancé's interest in writing novels and urges him to write music instead: "Music, you see [. . .] music goes straight for things. It says all there is to say at once. With writing it seems to me there's so much [. . .] scratching on the matchbox" (212). In love for the first time, Rachel discovers that books and language cannot adequately describe her experience, that "her sensations had no name" (223). The most aesthetically innovative sections of *The Voyage Out* express moments when Rachel takes refuge in music and in a kind of musical experience of reality. Woolf does posit a gulf between music and language as very different forms of expression,[2] yet she also creates moments in which time and space are dilated or contracted, through language, in ways that parallel Rachel's thought processes as well as her music making.

Long before she meets her future fiancé, while still traveling the seas aboard the ship that bears the name of one of the three Graces, Euphrosyne, the goddess of mirth, grace, and beauty, Rachel thinks of her life with her aunts back in Richmond and of her life now, only to realize that "nobody ever said a thing they meant, or ever talked of a feeling they felt, but that was what music was for" (*VO* 37). It is only through music that Rachel can accept "her lot" and subside – and it is precisely at this moment that she thinks of Beethoven's last piano sonata:

> Absorbed by her music she accepted her lot very complacently, blazing into indignation perhaps once a fortnight, and subsiding as she subsided now. Inextricably mixed in dreamy confusion, her mind seemed to enter into communion, to be delightfully expanded and combined, with the spirit of the whitish boards on deck, with the spirit of the sea, with the spirit of Beethoven Op. 111, even with the spirit of poor William Cowper there at Olney. Like a ball of thistledown it kissed the sea, rose, kissed it again, and thus rising and kissing passed finally out of sight. The rising and falling of the ball of thistledown was represented by the sudden droop forward of her own head, and when it passed out of sight she was asleep. (37)

This passage suggests a trajectory of ascent and transformed descent – a pattern to which I will return when discussing *The Waves* – that characterizes not only Rachel's consciousness but also the direction of the novel itself. Yet, if the mention of Beethoven's Piano Sonata no. 32 in C minor, op. 111, at this particular moment allows for any interpretation of the text through prism of this composition, this can be done only implicitly, because Woolf, who believed that "all descriptions of music are quite worthless" (D1: 33), never explained exactly the meaning or significance of this sonata in the context of her novel. The preference for use rather than explanation of this musical example was a bold and original choice on the author's part, because the famous sonata was often discussed, its "meaning" elucidated in the twentieth-century novel.

One of two such famous examples is Thomas Mann's *Doctor Faustus* (1947), in which the author devotes several pages to an analysis of Opus 111 delivered by the stuttering, Pennsylvania-born genius Wendell Kretzschmar. The latter interprets the entire sonata "as a dreadful journey" full of "fury, tenacity, obsessiveness, and extravagance," which ends in "the most touching, comforting, poignantly forgiving act in the world" (Mann 59). Stuttering significantly on the word "death," Kretzschmar tries to explain why Beethoven never wrote a third movement to his last sonata: the farewell of the second movement could not possibly be followed by a new beginning. When Kretzschmar plays the sonata, the music, punctuated by the shouts and explanations of the overexcited lecturer, both terrifies and amuses his small audience.

Quite different is the interpretation assigned to the same work almost forty years earlier by E. M. Forster. In *A Room with a View* (1908), Lucy Honeychurch performs Opus 111 unexpectedly at a social event at Tunbridge Wells, "where the upper classes entertain the lower" (Forster 53). Here, the relationship between performer and audience is strained both because, as a musician, Lucy is indifferent to the audience and tends to retreat to the pleasure of her own performance (53), and because the audience is insensitive to the music itself. In Forster's interpretation, Beethoven's last sonata signifies a victory that parallels Lucy's triumphant marriage to George Emerson at the end of the novel. Through their characters, Mann and Forster assign meaning to Opus 111: fury followed by poignant forgiveness in the former case, and victory not easily understood by an ordinary audience in the latter. It is to Woolf's merit that although she purposefully mentions Opus 111 in her novel, she does not offer any explicit commentary on this sonata, even though her correspondence with R. C. Trevelyan and Saxon Sydney-Turner shows that the work was probably often discussed in the Bloomsbury circle (L2: 418).[3] At the same time, while Woolf mentions the sonata by opus number without any commentary, the context in which she places it is highly significant: Opus 111 is connected precisely with those moments of temporal and spatial dilation Woolf wanted to create in the novel by describing Rachel Vinrace's states of mind.

Beethoven's last sonata, completed on January 13, 1822, combines three compositional styles that had became increasingly important in the composer's late period, characteristics that are also found in his late string quartets: fugal writing, the theme and variation form, and the use of extended trills. This sonata is also a perfect example of Beethoven's late experimentation with the number of movements in his musical compositions: it has only two movements, the first in sonata-allegro form with a strongly fugal texture; the second, the Arietta, in theme and variation form, a theme with four variations and a coda. Critics have commented on the transcendental quality attained at the end of the second movement, after the turbulent first movement, an effect achieved through the transition from the inherently unstable, foreboding C minor key of the first movement, to the C major of the second movement.[4] However, the C minor to C major progression no longer signifies the tragic-to-triumphant trajectory that had characterized Beethoven's middle period best exemplified in the Fifth Symphony. Rather, in the works Beethoven composed in his final years, during his so-called late period,

> the tragic-to-triumphant genre appears to be interpretable in terms comparable to the theatrical category of religious drama – namely, tragedy that is transcended through sacrifice at a spiritual level. The pathos of the tragic may be understood as stemming from a kind of Passion music, depicting a personal, spiritual struggle; and the "triumph" is no longer a publicly heroic "victory" but a transcendence or acceptance that goes beyond the conflicts of the work (after having fully faced them). (Hatten 79)

The tragic-to-transcendent trajectory of Opus 111 and the fact that Beethoven chose not to add a third movement are significant.[5] The ending of the Arietta is characterized by the arrival at a sense of stasis. This sense of motionlessness is created through the accumulation of more and more notes in each variation, combined with a heightened rhythmic activity and minimal harmonic action leading to the dissolution of rhythm into the trills of the coda, where polarities disappear.[6] A temporal and spatial dilation is achieved, paradoxically, by intensifying movement and sound. It is through expressing her heroine's peculiar way of perceiving reality that Woolf also produces, linguistically, effects of temporal and spatial dilations that can be compared to those of the Arietta. By referring to Beethoven's Opus 111 precisely at the moment when her heroine, "absorbed by her music," can "enter into communion," her mind "delightfully expanded and combined" (VO 37), Woolf creates a parallel between music and language in her novel experiment.

Another example (among many) of the kind of linguistic experimentation Woolf was undertaking in the novel by creating and exploring "moments of being" is Rachel's stroll by the riverbed after the dance party with Gibbon in one hand and Balzac in the other. Even though no particular musical composition is mentioned, the effect is similar to the example described above. This purely poetic moment of emotion recollected not in tranquility, as Wordsworth would have had it, but in exultation, allows Rachel to behold a tree in such a way that it "appeared so strange that it might have been the only tree in the world" (VO 174):

> Dark was the trunk in the middle, and the branches sprang here and there leaving jagged intervals of light between them as distinctly as if it had but that second risen from the ground. Having seen a sight that would last her for a lifetime, and for a lifetime would preserve that second, the tree once more sank into the ordinary ranks of trees, and she was able to seat herself in its shade and to pick the red flowers with the thin green leaves which were growing beneath it. She laid them side by side, flower to flower and stalk to stalk, caressing them for, walking alone, flowers and even pebbles in the earth had their own life and disposition, and brought back the feelings of a child to whom they were companions. (174)

One of Rachel's defining characteristics is exactly her ability to "miraculously" dilate and prolong the moment of perception from instance to permanence. She attains this by looking at nature and people with a kind of childlike wonder – a perception that brings her close to young Louis in *The Waves* and to little George in *Between the Acts* – as if seeing them for the first time.

Woolf would later describe, in her 1926 essay "Impassioned Prose," an effect of temporal and spatial dilation in the writings of Thomas De Quincey in exactly such terms: "His confession is not that he has sinned but that he has dreamed. Hence it comes about that his most perfect passages are not lyrical but descriptive. They are not cries of anguish, which admit us to closeness and sympathy; they are descriptions *of states of mind in which, often, time is miraculously prolonged and space miraculously expanded*" (E 4: 367; my emphasis). As Woolf knew well, Sir Leslie Stephen considered De Quincey "the inventor and sole performer on a new musical instrument – for such an instrument is the English language in his hands" (Stephen 326). The musical comparison continues: "The most exquisite passages in De Quincey's writing are all more or less attempts to carry out the idea expressed in the title of the dream fugue. They are intended to be musical compositions, in which words have to play the part of notes" (329).

Similarly, Rachel prolongs the moment as she contemplates flowers and pebbles on the ground, and as her gaze moves upward and hovers there before descending. The gaze moves rhythmically upward and downward, like a musical gesture, beholding the tree from where it rises from the ground, up its dark trunk, to its branches that leave "jagged intervals of light between them" (VO 174).

> Looking up, her eye was caught by the line of the mountains flying out energetically across the sky like the lash of a curling whip. She looked at the pale distant sky, and the high bare places on the mountaintops lying exposed to the sun. When she sat down she had dropped her books on the earth at her feet, and now she looked down on them lying there, so square in the grass, a tall stem bending over and tickling the smooth brown cover of Gibbon, while the molted blue Balzac lay naked in the sun. (174)

Rachel's eyes do not simply follow the contours of the landscape. Her gaze has direction – a movement of ascent and descent – and it has rhythm: it flies energetically through jagged intervals from leaves to mountaintops. The rhythm of the prose itself produces this pattern. The seemingly unending pause between the end of the second sentence and the beginning of the third functions as the apex of this passage. The gaze that remains suspended there and the moment of suspension itself, before Rachel sits and looks down again, are not qualified in any way. As in a musical composition, a pause is crucial and silence implies everything. It is for the reader's imagination to experience and fill in – an example of how silence may be used in the novel, perhaps an allusion to Terence Hewet's desire to create a novel made of silence.

Harold Fromm discusses "the achievement of communication through silence – or, at any rate, through something other than words" (189) in *To the Lighthouse*, as musical. Since language is different from music, Fromm argues, literature cannot literally imitate musical forms, or it can only try to do so with unfortunate results. However, certain literary passages in Woolf's novels can produce "musical emotion" (188): "The effects are musical to the extent that the emotions they produce are like, or the same as, the emotional effects of music: that is, they are sub-rational, more frequently found in poetry than in the novel" (183). I would like to advance this argument and suggest that during such moments of perception as described above, the musical "effect" is an expression of language, which, full of rhythms and directions, sounds and silences, creates "gesture" as in a musical composition. The elongated moment of soaring and silence between two sentences transforms everything and makes the descent particularly poignant. Rachel's perception of the world tends to follow musical patterns and rhythms, and dilates or contracts both in time and space. It is exactly this kind of perception that becomes more and more emphatic in Woolf's later novels and becomes central in *The Waves* and *Between the Acts*. In *The Waves* it is Rhoda, always lagging behind her companions, seemingly passive, who knows best how to look at reality the way Rachel does. And Rachel shares with Lucy of *Between the Acts* a propensity to imagine the world undivided.[7] What Rachel and Lucy have in common is precisely the ability to experience the world musically.

Through her performance and experience of music Rachel also exemplifies G. E. Moore's arguments in the last part of his *Principia Ethica*,[8] a book Helen Ambrose reads during the sea voyage and Richard Dalloway comments on ironically as "Metaphysics and fishing" (VO 74): while good is indefinable, the greatest goods are personal affection and aesthetic enjoyment. For Rachel, who longs to ask questions (59), the two become indistinguishable. The musical performance enables her to communicate with her listeners in ways that are impossible in everyday language. At the end of the dance party on the island of Santa Marina, Rachel reinvigorates the dancers with her music. Passing from John Peel to Bach, she brings the dispersed audience back around her piano:

> As they sat and listened, their nerves were quieted; the heat and soreness of their lips, the result of incessant talking and laughing, was smoothed away. They sat very still as if they saw a building with spaces and columns succeeding each other rising in the empty space. Then they began to see themselves and their lives, and the whole of human life advancing very nobly under the direction of the music. They felt themselves ennobled, and when Rachel stopped playing they desired nothing but sleep. (167)

A musical performance not only involves score and player, but it also requires an audience – in this case one inspired to discern the architecture of sound. By describing the way Rachel and, in her later novels, Rhoda, Bernard, Isa, and Lucy Swithin experience music, Woolf explores the connections between word and music as well as between reader and text, audience and performance. The building "with spaces and columns succeeding each other rising in the empty space," which may also be seen as a symbol of the novel itself, is not a static, finished construction but one in a state of constant transformation, an artistic form that is also capable of transcending its own boundaries toward the other arts. The novel, as Woolf envisions it, requires a reader who is both interpreter and performer: "The reading process always involves viewing the text through a perspective that is continually on the move, linking up the different phases, and so constructing what we have called the virtual dimension" (Iser, *Implied Reader* 280).

Beyond the realm of music, Rachel's relationship with the outside world is never clarified, and, after her engagement to Terence Hewet, her musical practice changes. Her attempts to play are constantly interrupted by Terence, in whose presence music is no longer communicative but has become a laborious, Sisyphus-like exercise: "Rachel said nothing. Up and up the steep spiral of a very late Beethoven sonata she climbed, like a person ascending a ruined staircase, energetically at first, then more laboriously advancing her feet with effort until she could go no higher and returned with a run to begin at the very bottom again" (*VO* 291). The state of spiritual transcendence is reached only temporarily in the world of Virginia Woolf's first novel. Beethoven's Sonata, op. 111, functions rather as a foil to Rachel's vision, as a reflection of her aspirations. The inability to communicate, musically and verbally, at the end of the novel is not simply the failure of a particular individual but is generally symbolic of the failure of language itself to bridge the gap between human consciousness and its exterior. When Rachel performed her music successfully, such rifts were momentarily transcended. What role does music play, then, when reality, at least as Rachel sees it, is "only a light passing over the surface and vanishing, as in time she would vanish" (125), and when "words are made of wood" (124)? In *The Voyage Out* language takes on musical rhythms and gestures during "moments of being" explored through Rachel Vinrace's perception of reality. Even if Rachel affirms, metafictionally, the failure of language, the linguistic exploration of such moments of perception creates spaces in which communication is enabled by rules and principles different from those of ordinary verbal exchanges. By exploring the relationship between the subject, music, language, and the world, Virginia Woolf works out in her first novel a very different model of perceiving reality from that of her Edwardian predecessors.

FROM *THE VOYAGE OUT* TO *THE WAVES*: THE NOVEL AS MUSICAL CONVERSATION

In *The Waves* Rhoda's experience and reflections on music bring her, of all six characters in Woolf's 1931 novel, closest to Rachel Vinrace's musical perception of the world. As she falls behind her companions, on a walk at Hampton Court, Rhoda muses and her thoughts move rhythmically, through repetitions and pauses, from the present moment to a wider space, remembered or imagined:

> Let me visit furtively the treasures I have laid apart. Pools lie on the other side of the world reflecting marble columns. The swallow dips her wing in dark pools. But here the door opens and people come; they come towards me. Throwing faint smiles to mask their cruelty, their indifference, they seize me. The swallow dips her wings; the moon rides through blue seas alone. I must take this hand; I must answer. But what answer shall I give? I am thrust back to stand burning in this clumsy, this ill-fitting body, to receive the shafts of his indifference, and his scorn, I who long for marble columns and pools on the other side of the world where the swallow dips her wings. (W 75–76)

Rhoda's repeatedly expressed longing appears as a recollection of the vision Rachel Vinrace had inspired in her audience. Such a vision is possible in *The Waves* only as a dream to soothe one's terror. Rachel's performances in *The Voyage Out* recalled a nineteenth-century aesthetic that conceived of music, above all arts, as able to communicate directly and build a human communion that would otherwise be impossible.[9] By the time Rhoda attends a chamber performance in *The Waves*,[10] her experience of music has become a very different one:

> There is a square; there is an oblong. The players take the square and place it upon the oblong. They place it very accurately; they make a perfect dwelling-place. Very little is left outside. The structure is now visible; what is inchoate is here stated; we are not so various or so mean; we have made oblongs and stood them upon squares. This is our triumph; this is our consolation. (118)

The musical experience has become individual, isolated, and abstract, suggesting a very different musical architecture and narrative architectonic. Two important changes took place as Woolf continued to explore the tendency of language toward the condition of music through "moments of being." If Rachel Vinrace's music could raise, for her audience, a vast but all-unifying structural design, by 1931 the beetle-shaped men with their violins inspire in Rhoda an abstract modernist experience of much more restrained gestures and proportions, reminiscent of Lily Briscoe's painting in *To the Lighthouse*. Furthermore, in *The Waves* music plays a significant role in building up the structure of the novel.

The Waves *and Quartet Op. 131*

Letters and diaries dating from this period show that Woolf seriously pursued the question of how to organize her novel and bring together the characters, voices, episodes, and interludes of this highly experimental work. Two diary entries in particular, from 1927 and 1930, show that Woolf was listening to Beethoven's late sonatas and quartets while working on *The Waves*, and that these compositions strongly influenced both the conception and the structure of her novel.[11] In the first entry, what would become *The Waves* is described as a "play-poem idea" envisioned as "some continuous stream" while listening to late Beethoven sonatas on the gramophone (*D*3: 139). The second entry reveals that Beethoven's

Example 3.1. Ludwig van Beethoven, String Quartet no. 14 in C sharp minor, op. 131 (1826). 1. Adagio ma non troppo e molto espressivo, mm. 1–2.

quartets played a role in shaping this play-poem: "It occurred to me last night while listening to a Beethoven quartet that I could merge all the interjected passages into Bernard's final speech, and end with the words O solitude: thus making him absorb all those scenes and having no further break" (339). Bernard, the character who illustrates the author's method of creation, identifies with Beethoven and even buys his portrait in a silver frame. A Beethoven quartet serves as inspiration for structuring and ending the author's "play-poem."

While Woolf does not identify a particular quartet in this diary entry, a comparison with the composer's favorite, Quartet no. 14 in C minor, op. 131, yields rich results. Completed in 1826, this composition was meant to be performed with no interruptions between its seven movements (Ratner 235). Beethoven achieved unity within this work by using various compositional strategies, perhaps most significantly a distinctive melodic motto that is generally associated with his late works.

The four-note motto is stated in the first bars of the quartet's first movement and then restated and reworked throughout the entire composition, only to be restated in its original tonal order in the finale, giving "a final assertion of melodic unity to the quartet" (Ratner 236). This short motivic element is extremely important because it is also a representation of the musical up/down gesture, in which the stress falls on the down step, characterizing the entire quartet that "progresses in accentuation from weak to strong, from light to heavy. It forms a broad iambic unit, end-oriented to build periodicity" (235).

The up/down gesture of what has been characterized as a traditional *pathetique* figure is reminiscent of the musical gesture I described above in connection with Beethoven's last sonata, Opus 111, and with Rachel Vinrace's musical experience of ascent and transformed descent.[12] Yet, if in Woolf's first novel the up/down gesture described Rachel Vinrace's flights of imaginations as well as an ascent from struggle to transcendence paralleling Rachel's aesthetic endeavors, in Woolf's 1931 novel this gesture plays an essential role in structuring the novel itself. It can be recognized in the small, breathlike movements of the waves (small motivic elements that provide structural unity and move both characters and reader through the space of the novel, forward as well as backward) as well as in the overarching rising and setting of the sun, symbolizing the passing of a day, of the seasons, and of a life cycle. The novel, like Opus 131, is structured upon a unifying motif that runs through all of its interludes and episodes. As the themes Woolf states, varies, and develops throughout this work come together defiantly in Bernard's final speech, the overall accentuation of the novel is, as with Beethoven's motto, iambic, from light to heavy, from weak to strong, despite the fact that both a day and human lifetime come to an end.

The Waves *as Musical Conversation*

Another important transformation from *The Voyage Out* to *The Waves* is the interweaving, in the latter novel, of multiple voices and perspectives brought together as Bernard explains in his last summing-up soliloquy: "The illusion is upon me that something adheres for a moment, has roundness, weight, depth, is completed. This, for the moment, seems to be my life" (w 238). In his seminal work, *Problems of Dostoevsky's Poetics* (1929), Mikhail Bakhtin applied the concept of polyphony to fiction (6), describing it as the representation of a variety of ideological positions that engage freely in dialogue. Looking at musical polyphony as a source of inspiration for Woolf's "play-poem" provides a very different reading model. In *The Waves* polyphony does not describe an interaction of characters representing clearly definable ideological positions. Rather, in Woolf's novel, polyphony entails a texture of themes and motifs that are developed and intertwined as they are stated by various characters whose voices combine in a "continuous stream" to form an organically unified work that shares characteristics with drama and poetry as well as with music. Musical polyphony, in this sense, may be used to explain a move from monophony, from one character's experience expressed melodically, to a way in which voices may interact with one another to form a multilayered expression. In *The Waves* every character is a voice that develops as a result of interacting with other voices and is part of a whole.

Moreover, in this novel, themes and motifs, "images and phrases" do not characterize any one particular character exclusively. They are, rather, exchanged between characters much like a musical theme passes from instrument to instrument. The polyphonic texture of this work is created as an interweaving of themes and motifs exchanged by the six voices of *The Waves* as in a musical conversation. Mara Parker's interpretation of the quartet as a particular kind of musical conversation helps explain how the quartet as a musical genre, rather than an ensemble, may have influenced Woolf in structuring her novel:

> A musical conversation is not just strict imitation as in a fugue or canon, but describes a condition where an idea, which turns and changes, can be passed from voice to voice. In a true musical conversation, each voice is differentiated by contrasting melodic shapes, phrase lengths, and rhythms. The ability to distinguish individual lines in itself does not guarantee an ensemble with four equal parts. A truly democratic quartet is only possible once the voices have achieved an *interchangeability of function*. At this point, specific roles and stratified pitch layers are pushed aside, thus allowing the composer to assign to any of the four instruments any of the roles discussed by Koch: the leading voice, the bass, or one of the inner voices. (23; my emphasis)

It is this kind of discourse that also occurs between characters in *The Waves*. In such a "conversation" there are no assigned roles: "Any voice may play any line and/or function [accompanimental, melodic, or participatory] at any given moment. The ability to predict what line will be heard in which instrument is gone" (Parker 281). What matters is the "condition where an idea, which turns and changes, can be passed from voice to voice" (123).

Virginia Woolf herself was envisioning "a gigantic conversation" as a way to conclude and "pull together" all the interludes and voices in her play-poem (*D*3: 285). In the spirit of such a "conversation," I look, in the following two sections, at the complex texture of *The Waves* in two different ways: following themes as they interact creating the polyphonic texture of the novel, and following the transformations of a single motif as it moves through different contexts and acquires different affects. My intention is not to show that *The Waves* imitates a particular musical structure or composition, but simply to understand how voices interact in this novel in ways that suggest musical polyphony – as opposed to monophony or homophony. Such an interaction could acquire a vertical, contrapuntal quality, keeping in mind that the separation of linear activity from counterpoint is impossible and that a listener and a reader may experience both at the same time.

Polyphonic Texture in The Waves

The second-to-last section of the novel, in which six friends reunite for dinner at Hampton Court late in the autumn of their lives, offers a particularly good example of the novel's polyphonic texture. Bernard frames this section with his monologues, giving the tone for the characters' coming together and departing one last time. The main themes of the novel – meeting, identity, self-definition, and friendship; childhood, youth, and middle age; memory, the flow of time, death – are stated separately by each character, then restated and varied by other characters before Bernard is ready to "merge them into his final speech" of the last episode, as Woolf had described in her December 22, 1930, diary entry.

Considering the prologue as a separate, prelude-like part, it is possible to see this section as divided into five monologues and two dialogues. A structural pattern emerges, which I have traced separately (see the appendix to this chapter). Here, I would simply like to show how the first theme is stated, exchanged between the six friends, and varied, as in a musical conversation, while the other three themes are also introduced one by one and acquire shape and dimension within a context. Bernard, who notices patterns as they form and change as he tries to capture them in language, feels an identity change about to take place as he joins the others and states "the shock of meeting":

> They have come together already. In a moment, when I have joined them, another arrangement will form, another pattern. What now runs to waste, forming scenes profusely, will be checked stated. I am reluctant to suffer that compulsion. Already at fifty yards' distance I feel the order of my being changed. The tug of the magnet of their society tells upon me. I come nearer. They do not see me. Now Rhoda sees me, but she pretends, with her horror of the shock of meeting, that I am a stranger. (W 154)

Next, Neville picks up this theme and colors it with his longing for Percival, who will no longer come: "'Now sitting side by side,' said Neville, 'at this narrow table, now before the first emotion is worn smooth, what do we feel? Honestly, now, openly and directly as befits old friends meeting with difficulty, what do we feel on meeting? Sorrow. The door will not open; he will not come. And we are laden'" (155). A character is defined through his or her interaction with the others. Neville introduces the next theme, the question of self-definition: "Being now all of us middle-aged, loads are on us. Let us put down our loads. What have you made of life, we ask, and I? You, Bernard; you, Susan; you, Jinny; and Rhoda and Louis? [. . .] I feel in my private pocket and find my credentials – what I carry to prove my superiority. I have passed" (155).

As the episode progresses, each character compares and contrasts himself or herself with the others, and self-definition ensues out of this conversation like a "clash of antlers" (158). When Susan takes on the themes of the shock of meeting and self-definition, she combines them with a third one: "remembering childhood." The present moment is intertwined with the past, a return to the beginning of *The Waves*: "'There was the beech wood,' said Susan, 'Elvedon, and the gilt hands of the clock sparkling among the trees'" (157). The statement immediately following Susan's soliloquy comes as a summing up of this first section, as a break between the prelude, the meeting and salute of old friends, and what is to follow. Rhoda then picks up the same theme and brings her own contribution to the present moment: "The gold has faded between the trees [. . .] and a slice of green lies behind them" (158). Her short paragraph is a transition to the second part of this section, in which the first three themes are restated. Woolf has created a texture in which themes are stated, varied, given different hues by each voice that carries them, and interwoven with other themes.

The Looking Glass: Motivic Transformations

It is also possible to look at the structure of this work by tracing a particular motif that runs horizontally throughout various parts of the novel, cutting across the polyphonic texture described above. A motif that is particularly important in this context is that of the looking glass holding the scene immobile "as if everlasting in its eye" (*w* 153). It appears for the first time in the third prelude as if it were an eye opening in the morning:

"the looking-glass whitened its pool upon the wall" (53). It disappears again when everything is covered "with vast curtains of darkness" and the precise brush stroke becomes "swollen and lopsided" (174). The mirror can "reflect" only when consciousness awakens. It stands for the age of artistic maturity, offering the only antidote, even if temporary, against the passage of time.

In the eighth episode this motif appears first as Jinny's possession: "I have sat before a looking-glass as you sit writing, adding up figures at desks. So, before the looking-glass in the temple of my bedroom, I have judged my nose and my chin […] Now I turn grey; now I turn gaunt; […] But I am not afraid" (162). In a moment of reflection Jinny can visualize her entire life. The mirror is a foil for the character who might be seen as the most superficial of the six, were it not for her almost mystical "burnings" (163). Jinny's concern with surfaces becomes symbolic of the ritual preparations she keeps up even in the face of aging and death:

> "Who comes?" says Jinny; and Neville sighs, remembering that Percival comes no more. Jinny has taken out her looking-glass. Surveying her face like an artist, she draws a powder-puff down her nose, and after one moment of deliberation, has given precisely that red to the lips that the lips need. Susan, who feels scorn and fear at the sight of these preparations, fastens the top button of her coat, and unfastens it. What is she making ready for? For something, but something different. (166)

If the looking glass is a symbol of vanity, it also reflects the inevitable passage of time, a hope for rebirth, for a continuation of life through art. Furthermore, the mirror is a reference to Woolf's own childhood: in "A Sketch of the Past," the author describes the "small looking-glass in the hall at Talland House" (67) as one of her most significant early childhood memories. It symbolizes both her strong affinity to beauty – the aesthetic – and an element of guilt and shame she felt and associated with the spartan, ascetic, puritanical streak in her family and in her upbringing (68). Perhaps not coincidentally, Leslie Stephen's affectionate nickname for Virginia was "Jinny."[13]

In the interlude that begins the eighth episode, the looking glass captures the garden elongated with shadows "made portentous" by the setting sun. It captures time itself and temporarily stops its flow: "Rimmed in a gold circle the looking-glass held the scene immobile as if everlasting in its eye" (W 153). The looking glass is a symbol of artistic creation, the only thing that has permanence, like Keats's Grecian urn. Yet it is also inscribed in a scene that will soon be engulfed in darkness, mirroring characters in the autumn of their life, in a novel soon to come to an end. The human act of creation is limited. What began as a white pool upon the wall (53) will end "pale as the mouth of a cave shadowed by hanging creepers" (174). In lectures published only two years before the publication of *The Waves,* Virginia Woolf associated the mirror with the novel as well as with the act of writing:

> If one shuts one's eyes and thinks of the novel as a whole, it would seem to be a creation owning a certain looking-glass likeness to life, though of course with simplifications and distortions innumerable. At any rate, it is a structure leaving a shape on the mind's eye, built now in squares, now pagoda shaped, now throwing out wings and arcades, now solidly compact and domed like the Cathedral of Saint Sofia at Constantinople. (AROO 71)

The looking glass, as one of the motifs that run across the polyphonic structure of *The Waves,* stands for the novel itself – yet this is not a mirror carried along a high road, as it had been in Stendhal's *The Red and the Black.* The impulse to create and record usually associated with Bernard, the writer, is also associated, through the looking glass, with Jinny, as it is in other parts of the novel with Neville, the poet. Characters in this novel do not play well-delineated roles, but are voices, ready to share or exchange registers and rhythms at different times in a performance that lasts both a day and a lifetime. Themes and motifs interweave and run through the novel as in a conversational musical composition and bring the separate sections of this play-poem together, creating a tightly unified whole.

BETWEEN THE ACTS: MUSIC, LANGUAGE, AND COMMUNITY

Rachel Vinrace and Rhoda seem naturally inclined to perceive the world musically and to synthesize movement and stasis, time and space. Such moments of experience, however, occur in isolation. By contrast, in *Between the Acts* the moment of aesthetic perception – defined by both Pater and Woolf as inextricably connected to music – has been transformed from an individual experience to a moment in which an entire linguistic, cultural, and historical community participates. This work offers a response to the conflict between language and music that Woolf set up in her first novel: language and music have now become interconnected, and every word attracts attention to the fact that it can do something, that it has performative powers. To give just one example, the trees Rachel had contemplated on her walks in *The Voyage Out* are no longer simply visual but have become aural representations.[14] They can "syllable," and the rhythmical and alliterative qualities of the language that describes them convey this:

> For I hear music, they were saying. Music wakes us. Music makes us see the hidden, join the broken. Look and listen. See the flowers, how they ray their redness, whiteness, silverness and blue. And the trees with their many-tongued much syllabling, their green and yellow leaves hustle us and shuffle us, and bid us, like the starlings, and the rocks, come together, crowd together, to chatter and make merry while the red cow moves forward and the black cow stands still. (vo 83)

No longer linear, descriptive, monophonic, narrative has become an explosion of voices and rhythms. Trees speak "in tongues" and their music connects flower, rook, and cow with Cobbet of Cobbs Corner, the simple villager.

Woolf had explored very early the idea that music and language are interrelated. After hearing Wagner's *Parsifal* in Bayreuth in August 1909, she wrote to her sister, Vanessa, that the opera could slide from music to words almost imperceptibly (L1: 406; E1: 293). But musical experience in *Between the Acts* has moved from the concert hall – as it had been in *The Voyage Out* and *The Waves* – outdoors. Woolf's last novel opens with birdsong and several characters take on birdlike qualities. When Isa, who possesses a most powerful poetic imagination, makes her appearance for the first time, she enters "like a swan swimming its way" and wears "a dressing-gown with faded peacocks on it" (BTA 4). A bit later, under the spell of her father-in-law's reciting Byron, Isa's powerful emotions for Mr. Haines move them "like two swans down stream" (4–5). Goose-eyed Mrs. Haines, aware of the emotion circling them, will destroy it "as a thrush pecks the wings off a butterfly" (5). Poetic sensibility and the ability to inhabit and be possessed by language, rhythm, and music belong only to such bird-people and not, for example, to Giles Oliver, who has "no command of metaphor" and does not tread the same ground as Isa, Lucy, Bart, and Miss La Trobe. In contrast to the urban, mechanized, war-waging world of the city that Giles travels to and returns from every day, the realm of Pointz Hall is populated by bird-people, listeners who are also singers, spectators who are also actors.

At the beginning of October 1940, as she was finishing *Between the Acts*, Woolf began to jot down ideas for two essays: "Anon" and "The Reader."[15] Although unfinished, these essays show her interest in writing a different kind of literary history and in rethinking the relationship between reader, author, and text. Since Woolf explored these topics in her last novel, the two essays may also be considered companion pieces to and commentaries on *Between the Acts*. In "Anon" Woolf asks whether the desire to sing did not come "to one of those huntsmen because he heard the birds sing, and so he rested his axe against the tree for a moment" (E6: 581), suggesting that the creative moment comes into existence inspired by birdsong and only while the axe is at rest – between the acts – in times of peace. While in "The Reader," she explains that when the reader's "attention is distracted, in times of public crisis, the writer exclaims: I can write no more" (E6: 601). Reader and writer, performer and audience are inextricably bound together. Furthermore, in "Anon" Woolf describes the moment of creation as the moment of performance: "The audience was itself the singer; 'Terly, terlow' they sang; and 'By, by lullay' filing in the pauses, helping out with a chorus. Every body shared in the emotion of Anon's song, and supplied the story" (581).

In "The Politics of Comic Modes in Virginia Woolf's *Between the Acts*," Melba Cuddy-Keane argues that characters in this novel fulfill a function similar to that of the chorus in Greek drama. The collective choric voice places this work in the tradition of the comic genre. Instead of interpreting the work as "a portrait of social collapse" that is defective because it lacks an effective leader, the narrative advocates, precisely through its collective choric voice, a decentering of authority (274): "What defines this ritual group is the fluid bond of giving utterance to collective emotion, not the stricter unity of adhering to a common belief" (275). Language and music provide this fluid bond and momentarily bring together the members of a community soon to be ravaged by war. In this way the very nature of the novel is restructured, patterned as it is on rhythm and music rather than following a linear, teleological narrative development.

The Music of the Spheres

In one of her earliest essays, "Street Music" (1905), Woolf described a kind of "music in the air for which we are always straining our ears and which is only partially made audible to us by the transcripts which the great musicians are able to preserve. In forests and solitary places an attentive ear can detect something very like a vast pulsation, and if our ears were educated, we might hear the music also which accompanies this" (E1: 31). That the revolution of the planets produced an unheard music was a notion writers throughout the Middle Ages and the Renaissance, including Milton and Shakespeare, contemplated and wrote about (Grout 6). Virginia Woolf may have also been familiar with these ideas via Walter Pater's *Plato and Platonism;* the 1898 edition of this work was in the Woolf library at their 24 Victoria Square, London, residence (Holleyman Index 45). Woolf's own description of the all-encompassing harmony meant for a gigantic ear resonates with the way Pater speaks of Pythagora's doctrine of number (*Plato* 45). In *Between the Acts*, Woolf returns to this idea and develops it through Lucy Swithin, the only character whose ear seems attuned to a "vast pulsation," to universal harmonies meant for a gigantic ear attached to a gigantic head.

Lucy, whom the servants also call "Old Batty," is "given to increasing the bounds of the moment by flights into past or future" (BTA 7), which makes her imagination of a mettle with that of Rachel Vinrace. Like Rachel, Lucy can dilate time and space and thinks of the world in musical terms:

> Mrs. Swithin caressed her cross. She gazed vaguely at the view. She was off, they guessed, on a circular tour of the imagination – one-making. Sheep, cows, grass, trees, ourselves – all are one. If discordant, producing harmony – if not to us, to a gigantic ear attached to a gigantic head. And thus – she was smiling benignly – the agony of the particular sheep, cow, or human being is necessary; and so – she was beaming seraphically at the gilt vane in the distance – we reach the conclusion that all is harmony, could we hear it. And we shall. Her eyes now rested on the white summit of a cloud. Well, if the thought gave her comfort, William and Isa smiled across her, let her think it. (119)

Lucy's gaze follows the same up/down trajectory that had suspended the passage of time for Rachel Vinrace. However, if Lucy shares many similarities with Rachel, both age and narrative technique have transformed the former character. While Rachel was "narrated" in the third person by a narrator who was highly sympathetic to her way of perceiving reality, Lucy Swithin's innermost thoughts are no longer expressed by a narrator who shares her point of view. Her thoughts, "seraphic" like the song of the burning ones who praise God in the Hebrew Bible, remain unheard by the untrained ear. They can be only guessed at by her favorites, Isa and William, who watch her, smiling with benevolent irony. They can only imagine that she, caressing her cross in her "one-making" circular tour of the imagination, has access to places where they can no longer go, that she can hear the kind of music about which they can only "reach the conclusion." The scene is set up to reflect the rift existing even between those who feel most kindred: between Lucy and her generation and that of William and Isa. Yet it also posits, by way of imagining what Lucy might be thinking, that everything discordant produces an all-encompassing harmony meant for a gigantic ear attached to a gigantic head. Music – harmony/disharmony – bridges the separation set up by both individual isolation and narrative perspective.

This is a concept that also finds echoes in Romanticism, as Mitchell Leaska shows (PH 225), sending to a comparison with Book I of Wordsworth's *The Prelude*:

> Dust as we are, the immortal spirit grows
> Like harmony in music; there is a dark
> Inscrutable workmanship that reconciles
> Discordant elements, makes them cling together
> In one society.

Woolf expresses it, through Lucy's longing, as an attempt of an older generation to capture the harmonious moment when birdsong, lyric, and community were one.[16] Yet this private longing is also expressed publicly in the pageant. Miss La Trobe places it at the center of her play: in the second act, Queen Anne – under whose reign England and Scotland united into a sovereign state, and with whom the spectators identify England itself ("Was she England or Queen Anne? Both perhaps" [PH

129]) – proclaims: "'At my behest the armed warrior lays his shield away. [. . .] Beneath the shelter of my flowing robe' (here she extended her arm) 'the arts arise. Music for me unfolds its heavenly harmony'" (129). Demonstrating the reality of such harmonies is less important than recognizing that a longing for their existence is placed at the very center of the village pageant and of the novel itself.

Language, Music, Moments of Being

Multiple meanings and voices are created and heard in Woolf's last novel: the celestial harmony Lucy's ear is attuned to; the syllabling trees; a chattering of inner voices; the ping-ping of the telephone; the sounds wafting from the hidden gramophone; the "brave music" that awakens, gives sight, joins the broken (BTA 83); and the "mad music" Isa hears when she feels herself carrying "the burden that the past laid on me, last little donkey in the long caravanserai crossing the dessert" (106). Through her pageant, Miss La Trobe creates a diachronic representation of history, but it is Isa who recognizes the multiplicity of voices and understands that no voice stands alone:

> Voices interrupted. People passed the stable yard, talking.
> "It's a good day, some say, the day we are stripped naked. Others, it's the end of the day. They see the Inn and the Inn's keeper. But none speaks with a single voice. None with a voice free from the old vibrations. Always I hear corrupt murmurs; the chink of gold and metal. Mad music." (106)

Music and language create a history and provide intrinsic connections for a community that, even under the threat of war, still faithfully reenacts its existence as it has done for centuries. An individual's song is laden with the burden of many generations. No individual can sing alone, "free from the old vibrations," and any song sung presently belongs to the past and to the future.

Superimposed onto these multiple meanings and suggestions is the musicality of the prose itself, created through repetition, parentheses, onomatopoeia, rhythm, and rhyme. During an intermission the spectators' dialogue itself becomes a song – a lament in trochee – as they stream across lawns and down paths as in a dance. Prose may also be read as poetry:

Mrs. Manresa took up the strain. *Dispersed are we.* "Freely, boldly, fearing no one" (she pushed a deck chair out of her way). "Youths and maidens" (she glanced behind her; but Giles had his back turned). "Follow, follow, follow me.... Oh Mr. Parker, what a pleasure to see *you* here! I'm for tea!" "Dispersed are we," Isabella followed her, humming. "All is over. The wave has broken. Left us stranded, high and dry. Single, separate on the single. Broken is the three-fold ply... Now I follow" (she pushed back her hair) "that old strumpet" (she invoked Mrs. Manresa's tight, flowered figure in front of her) "to have tea." Dodge remained behind. "Shall I," he murmured "go or stay? Slip out some other way? Or follow, follow, follow the dispersing company?" *Dispersed are we,* the music wailed; *dispersed are we.* Giles remained like a stake in the tide of the flowing company. "Follow?" He kicked his chair back. "Whom? Where?" He stubbed his light tennis shoes on the wood. "Nowhere. Anywhere." Stark still he stood. (BTA 66–67)	*Dispersed are we.* (Mrs. Manresa) Freely boldly, fearing no one Youths and maidens follow, follow follow me.... Oh Mr. Parker, what a pleasure to see *you* here! I'm for tea! Dispersed are we. (Isabella) All is over. The wave has broken. Left us stranded, high and dry. Single, separate on the shingle. Broken is the three-fold ply... Now I follow that old strumpet to have tea. (William) Shall I go or stay? Slip out some other way? Or follow, follow, follow the dispersing company? Dispersed are we, dispersed are we. (Giles) Follow? Whom? Where? Nowhere. Anywhere. (BTA 66–67)

The tendency toward the "more and more" poetic writing Jane Goldman has identified in Woolf's novel writing from *Mrs. Dalloway* to *The Waves* (Goldman 49) can also be extended to *Between the Acts*.[17] The poetic and dialogic characteristics of the prose show the strong interconnections Woolf drew between the language of the novel, of the lyric, and of drama.

Returning to the chorus, the concept that introduced this section, it should be mentioned that in volume 1 of his *Outline of Musical History*, published by Hogarth Press (1929), Thomas J. Hewitt traced a direct connection between music, drama, and the modern opera, which could not have escaped Woolf's notice: "The tragedies of Aeschylus (525–456 BC), Sophocles (497–406 BC), and Euripides (480–407 BC) contained choruses, which were sung or recited to a kind of chant based on the modes.

For this reason they may be accounted the forerunners of modern opera" (14). The music's rhythm, Hewitt argued, was dependent on that of the verse, and each syllable was "clothed with a sound" (14). Yet Woolf had been thinking even earlier about the intrinsic links between music and language. When visiting Bayreuth in 1909, it was during the intermissions that she felt most strongly the interconnections between music, drama, the visual arts, and the community that creates them. What happens "during the intervals between the acts" (E1: 289) is as much a part of the performance as the music itself. Experience becomes synesthetic:

> It has been possible, during these last performances [of *Parsifal*], to step out of the opera house and find oneself in the midst of a warm summer evening. [...] One may sit among rows of turnips and watch a gigantic old woman, with a blue cotton bonnet on her head and a figure like one of Dürer's, swinging her hoe. The sun draws out strong scents from the hay and the pine trees, and if one thinks at all, *it is to combine the simple landscape with the landscape of the stage. When the music is silent the mind insensibly slackens and expands,* among happy surroundings: heat and the yellow light, and the intermittent but not unmusical noises of insects and leaves smooth out the folds. (E1: 290; my emphasis)

In Woolf's description, sounds, scents, colors, rhythms, and images – be they the natural settings she sees or the Dürer paintings she is inspired to remember – are an essential part of the operatic performance, the *Gesamtkunstwerk*. Furthermore, the work of art stems from and is dependent on the context – language, community, culture, history, landscape – in which it is created. The process of reading/interpreting is bound to the process of creation. Music allows Woolf to envision not only a different kind of novel but also a different kind of reading experience. The author expressed her reader-oriented approach in several essays, perhaps most memorably in *A Room of One's Own*:

> This shape, I thought, thinking back over certain famous novels, starts in one the kind of emotion that is appropriate to it. But that emotion at once blends itself with others, for the "shape" is not made by the relation of stone to stone, but by the relation of human being to human being. [...] The whole structure, it is obvious, thinking back on any famous novel, is one of infinite complexity, because it is thus made up of so many different judgments, of so many different kinds of emotion. (70)

Theorists such as Wolfgang Iser have recognized in Woolf's approach to the novel an affinity with reader-response and reception aesthetics

(*Walter Pater* 276). In her essay on Jane Austen, for instance, Woolf argued that it is the indeterminate space of the "trifle," the "trivial," and the "unfinished" – the gaps or blanks of meaning (*Leerstellen*) – that the reader's imagination feels most free to explore and inhabit. It is within such spaces that the reading experience becomes three-dimensional. In Woolf's last novel these spaces of indeterminacy become very important, occurring during moments when the boundaries between performance and reality disintegrate. The intervals between the acts have become of central importance: they emphasize the linguistic, cultural, and literary history of a community, as well as the individual's relationship with that shared past. By exploring the relationship between the subject, music, language, and community, Virginia Woolf works out – from her first to her last novel – a very different model of perceiving reality. From *The Voyage Out* to *Between the Acts,* Woolf explores ways in which the language of the novel itself aspires toward the condition of music.

APPENDIX: THEME AND VARIATION IN *THE WAVES* – AN EXAMPLE

Part 1: "The shock of meeting."

BERNARD: Theme 1 (The shock of meeting) (154–55).

NEVILLE: Theme 1 and Theme 2 (self-definition) (156–57); the "I" against "you"; "Change is no longer possible" (157).

SUSAN: Themes 1, 2 and Theme 3 (childhood remembered) (157–58).

Transition: Rhoda: comments on the end of the day (158).

Part 2: Is the self "fixed irrevocably"? (158) Themes 1, 2, 3 restated.

BERNARD: Theme 2 and 3 (159); Bernard's variation: from the perspective of one who is "wrapped round with phrases" (159).

LOUIS: Theme 3 and Theme 1 (160–61); Louis's variation: the perspective of one who wants "to reduce these dazzling, these dancing apparitions to one line capable of linking all in one" (160). Louis compares himself with Jinny.

JINNY: Theme 2 (161–63); Jinny's variation: her "imagination is the body's" (161). She compares herself with Louis.

RHODA: Synthesis of Themes 1, 2, 3; Rhoda's bubble: "Yet there are moments when the walls of the mind grow thin; when nothing is unabsorbed, and I could fancy that we might blow so vast a bubble that the sun might set and rise in it and we might take the blue of midday and the black of midnight and be cast off and escape from here and now" (164).

Part 3: The moment captured, time has stopped in the looking glass, death.

BERNARD: Theme 4 (time) "drop upon drop [...] silence falls," "anxiety is at rest" (164–65).

Quick accompanying exchange: S, J, R, L: silence, time has stopped, death has occurred (165). Bernard's nose brings them back to life: time returns (tick, tick, hoot, hoot) the moment of defiance and resistance (166).

(A)(Rhoda and Louis): parenthetical dialogue (166).

Part 4: A walk through the gardens at Hampton Court; recovering the sense of time.

BERNARD: Theme 4 varied: from personal to historical time (166–67).
From private to public experience
Our English past – one inch of time

NEVILLE: Theme 4 reversed: time comes back; the present moment acquires huge dimensions: "Three hundred years now seem more than a moment vanished against that dog" (167).

LOUIS: Synthesis of Themes 4 and 3: the present moment and childhood become one: "It is difficult not to weep, calling ourselves little children, praying that God may keep us safe while we sleep. It is sweet to sing together, clasping hands, afraid of the dark, while Miss Curry plays the harmonium" (167).

Quick accompanying exchange: L, J, S, R, B, L, J, B: momentarily escaping time (167–68).

(B)(Rhoda and Louis): parenthetical dialogue: "The still mood, the disembodied mood is on us [...] and we enjoy this momentary alleviation (it is not often that one has no anxiety) when the walls of the mind become transparent" (168). "All seems alive [...] I cannot hear death anywhere tonight" (169). The bubble destroyed when the others return (171). Quick accompanying exchange: B, N, J, S: gaping, unsatisfied, like young birds, for something that has escaped (171).

Part 5: Conclusions

BERNARD: returning to London, resuming daily life (171–73).

NOTES

1. Various scholars, from Lord David Cecil, to Perry Meisel, to Wolfgang Iser, and to Emma Sutton, have argued that Pater's aesthetics had a significant influence on Woolf's works, on her criticism in particular. Brenda Silver points out that *The Renaissance* was among Woolf's list of books from 1905 and that in *Moments of Being* Woolf recollects reading *Marius the Epicurean: His Sensations and Ideas* with relish at least as early as 1903 (Meisel 17). Meisel makes the convincing argument that even though she wrote no essays exclusively on Pater, and even though in her diaries and essays references to him are scant, the Oxford critic was an important, if unacknowledged, influence on Woolf. Despite Sir Leslie Stephen's aversion to Pater, Woolf studied Latin and Greek with the critic's sister, Clara Pater, very likely on her father's recommendation, in 1898 and 1899–1900, before becoming Janet Case's student. Woolf's personal library contained the 1900–1901 nine-volume Edition de Luxe of Pater's *Works* (London: Macmillan) signed "A.V.S.," Adeline Virginia Stephen, probably purchased in 1905 (Meisel 17).

2. In *The Singing of the Real World* Mark Hussey discusses the role of the arts and of music – in particular, in Woolf's novels. He concludes that the logical discrimination of symbols prevents language from sharing the quality of "significant form" with music (67–68).

3. Because of a printer's error, Opus 111 was printed as Opus III – although, this way of printing also appears in early editions of Forster's *A Room with a View*, where the same sonata is mentioned. Therefore, there has been some controversy about the opus number Woolf intended to use. That Louise DeSalvo has suggested that Opus 112 is preferable to Opus 111 is intriguing because Beethoven's Opus 112 happens to be the cantata *Meerestille und glückliche Fahrt* (*Calm Sea and Prosperous Voyage*), based on two poems by Goethe. DeSalvo associates the poem with Isolde, "the corpse-like Bride," and Rachel's "brooding preoccupation with death associated with water" (10). However, this

question seems to have been answered by Woolf's own January 25, 1920, letter to Saxon Sydney-Turner:

My dear Saxon,
I wonder if you would once more tell me the number of the Beethoven sonata that Rachel plays in *The Voyage Out* – I sent the copy I marked to America and now they're bringing out a new edition here – I can't remember what you told me – I say op. 112 – It can't be that. (L2: 418)

To R. C. Trevelyan she writes: "I am altering op. 112 to op. 111. The goats certainly are mysterious" (L2: 419). James Hafley reconsiders DeSalvo's arguments concerning the change from Opus 112 to Opus 111: "Opus numbers are almost invariably written in Arabic rather than Roman numerals . . . : also, Rachel is of course a pianist. Is it not reasonable, then, that as she falls asleep she is thinking neither of Op. 3, the routine little string trio in E-flat, nor of Op. 112, the exceptionally obscure cantata, but rather of Op. 111, the celebrated last of the piano sonatas, and that 'Op. III' was a printer's misreading of a correction for the understandably erroneous 'Op. 112' or the Ms and the first edition?" (Hafley 4). Besides Woolf's own clarification, there may be an additional reason why the celebrated last Beethoven sonata fits the context of this novel better than Opus 112. Since Rachel Vinrace's identification with music is powerful and unmediated while her relationship with language is tentative and strained, it is appropriate that she play a sonata, a purely instrumental work and a piece "played," rather than a cantata, a piece "sung," even if the latter is set on two Goethe poems about a sea voyage.

4. See, for example, Martin Cooper (200); Lawrence Kramer (55–56); Robert Hatten (79); and Maynard Solomon (209).

5. The two-movement sonata puzzled Beethoven's publishers, and when Schindler questioned the master, the latter replied that he did not have the time to write a third movement. Beethoven appears to have planned a third movement but may have found it unnecessary. In any case, whether the composer's reply was facetious became less important as musicians began to wonder less about the number of movements of this last sonata and more about the significance and interconnections between the two existing movements (see Newman 536).

6. Variation I begins with three notes per measure; Variation II has twelve; Variation III, twenty-four; and Variation IV, twenty-seven. In the fourth variation, "unbroken sequences of thirty-second-note triplets, without accents or phrase markings, metamorphose from shakes at the interval of the fifth into oscillating octaves (mm. 80–81), at which point they condense into a shimmering sonic barrier that blurs any distinction between rapid movement and the depths of stasis" (Solomon 209).

7. For instance, after a conversation with Richard Dalloway, Rachel realizes that "the attempt at communication had been a failure" (VO 66), and her next step is to override time and leap, like Lucy, into a primordial world that has not yet been dispersed: "She was haunted by absurd jumbled ideas – how, if one went back far enough, everything perhaps was intelligible; everything was in common; for the mammoths who pastured in the fields of Richmond High Street had turned into paving stones and boxes full of ribbon, and her aunts" (67).

8. Woolf's August 3, 1908, letter to Clive Bell shows that she was working on the first variant of *The Voyage Out, Melymbrosia,* while also reading G. E. Moore (L1: 340).

9. This experience is encountered in other places in Woolf's fiction, perhaps

most memorably in the short story "The String Quartet" (1921): "For me it sings, unseals my sorrow, thaws compassion, floods with love the sunless world, nor, ceasing, abates its tenderness, but deftly, subtly, weaves in and out until in this pattern, this consummation, the cleft ones unify; soar, sob, sink to rest, sorrow and joy" (CSF 140).

10. Rhoda's experience seems almost a replay of the entrance of the musicians in "The String Quartet" (W 139), but with some significant differences: "Then the beetle-shaped men come with their violins; wait; count; nod; down come their bows. And there is ripple and laughter like the dance of olive trees and their myriad-tongued grey leaves when a seafarer, biting at wig between his lips where the many-backed steep hills come down, leaps on shore" (163).

11. Critics like Gerald Levin and Robin Gail Schulze have argued for either a pantonal style or, respectively, an atonal, serial structure for *The Waves*. However, there is no evidence that Woolf was familiar with and intentionally followed such structures.

12. Leonard Ratner explains that "this motto has an affinity with a traditional figure described in Kirkendale's *Fugue and Fugato* as a *pathetic type (1)*" (235).

13. Woolf remembers, after her mother death, how in the past she had often waited anxiously for her mother's return, only to be told "reprovingly" by her father, "You shouldn't be so nervous, Jinny" ("Sketch" 84).

14. See, for example:

On the bank grew those trees which Helen had said it was worth the voyage out merely to see. April had burst their buds, and they bore large blossoms among their glossy green leaves with petals of a thick wax-like substance coloured and exquisite cream or pink or deep crimson. [...] She did not see distinctly where she was going, the trees and the landscape appearing only as masses of green and blue, with an occasional space of differently coloured sky. (VO 174)

15. Woolf established a concrete connection between "Anon" and *Between the Acts:* she begins the essay by quoting an early medieval lyric, Poem No. XXXIII (E. K. Chambers and F. Sidgwick's *Early English Lyrics*), fragments of which can also be recognized in Lucy Swithin's musings throughout the novel.

16. Later in "Anon" Woolf contrasts the communal aspects of early artistic creation with the isolation of the individual writer who emerged in the Renaissance (E6: 601).

17. The Monks House Papers collection at the University of Sussex (see also PH 567) contains several pages of verse that are related to and resonate with the language of Woolf's last novel. These poems – which, arguably, form a cycle – may also be read as short dramatic compositions, exemplifying, like *Between the Acts*, the strong interconnections Woolf wanted to draw between prose, poetry, and drama.

WORKS CITED

Aronson, Alex. *Music and the Novel: A Study in Twentieth-Century Fiction.* Totowa: Rowman and Littlefield, 1980. Print.

Bakhtin, Mikhail. *Problems of Dostoevsky's Poetics.* Ed. and trans. Caryl Emerson. Minneapolis: University of Minnesota Press, 1984. Print.

Barford, Philip T. "Beethoven's Last Sonata." *Music and Letters* 35.4 (1954): 320–31. Print.

Briggs, Julia. "The Novels of the 1930s and the Impact of History." *The Cambridge Companion to Virginia Woolf*. Ed. Sue Roe and Susan Sellers. Cambridge: Cambridge University Press, 2000. Print.

Bruhn, Siglind. *Musical Ekphrasis: Composers Responding to Poetry and Painting*. Hillsdale: Pendragon, 2000. Print.

Chambers, E. K., and F. Sidgwick, eds. *Early English Lyrics: Amorous, Divine, Moral and Trivial*. London: Sidgwick and Jackson, 1921. Print.

Cooper, Martin. *Beethoven: The Last Decade, 1817–1827*. London: Oxford University Press, 1970. Print.

Cuddy-Keane, Melba. "The Politics of Comic Modes in Virginia Woolf's *Between the Acts*." *PMLA* 105.2 (1990): 273–85. Print.

DeSalvo, Louise. "A Textual Variant in *The Voyage Out*." *Virginia Woolf Miscellany* 3 (1973): 9. Print.

Forster, Edward Morgan. *A Room with a View*. Norfolk: Knopf, 1922. Print.

Fromm, Harold. "*To the Lighthouse*: Music and Sympathy." *English Miscellany: A Symposium of History, Literature, and the Arts*. Ed. Mario Praz. Rome: Edizioni di Storia e Letteratura, 1968. Print.

Goldman, Jane, "From *Mrs. Dalloway* to *The Waves*: New Elegy and Lyric Experimentalism." *Cambridge Companion to Virginia Woolf*. Ed. Susan Sellers. Cambridge: Cambridge University Press, 2010. Print.

Grout, Donald U., and Claude V. Palisca. *A History of Western Music*. 6th ed. New York: Norton, 2001. Print.

Hafley, James. "Another Note on Rachel and Beethoven in *The Voyage Out*." *Virginia Woolf Miscellany* 4 (1975): 4. Print.

Hatten, Robert. *Musical Meaning in Beethoven: Markedness, Correlation, and Interpretation*. Bloomington: Indiana University Press, 1994. Print.

Hewitt, Thomas J. *An Outline of Musical History*. Vol. 1. London: Hogarth Press, 1929. Print.

Holleyman, G. A. *Catalogue of Books from the Library of Leonard and Virginia Woolf Taken from Monks House, Rodmell, Sussex and 24 Victoria Square, London and now in possession of Washington State University Pullman, U.S.A.* Brighton: Holleyman & Treacher, 1975. Print.

Hussey, Mark. *The Singing of the Real World: The Philosophy of Virginia Woolf's Fiction*. Columbus: Ohio State University Press, 1986. Print.

Iser, Wolfgang. *The Implied Reader: Patterns of Communication in Prose Fiction from Bunyan to Beckett*. Baltimore: Johns Hopkins University Press, 1974. Print.

———. *Walter Pater: The Aesthetic Moment*. Trans. David Henry Wilson. Cambridge: Cambridge University Press, 1987. Print.

Jacobs, Peter. "'The Second Violin Tuning in the Ante-room': Virginia Woolf and Music." *Multiple Muses of Virginia Woolf*. Ed. Diane F. Gillespie. Columbia: University of Missouri Press, 1993. Print.

Kramer, Lawrence. *Music as Cultural Practice, 1800–1900*. Berkeley: University of California Press, 1990. Print.

Levin, Gerald. "The Musical Styles of *The Waves*." *Journal of Narrative Technique* 13.3 (1983): 164–72. Print.

Mann, Thomas. *Doctor Faustus: The Life of the German Composer Adrian Leverkuhn as by a Friend*. New York: Knopf, 1997. Print.

Meisel, Perry. *The Absent Father: Virginia Woolf and Walter Pater*. New Haven: Yale University Press, 1980. Print.

Newman, William S. *The Sonata in the Classic Era*. New York: Norton, 1983. Print.

Parker, Mara. *The String Quartet, 1750–1797: Four Types of Musical Conversation*. Aldershot: Ashgate, 2002. Print.

Pater, Walter. *Plato and Platonism: A Series of Lectures*. New York: Macmillan, 1893. Print.

———. *The Renaissance*. Oxford: Oxford University Press, 1986. Print.

———. *The Renaissance: Studies in Art and Poetry, the 1893 Text*. Berkeley: University of California Press, 1980. Print.

Ratner, Leonard G. *The Beethoven String Quartets: Compositional Strategies and Rhetoric*. Stanford: Stanford Bookstore, 1995. Print.

Rosen, Charles. *Beethoven's Piano Sonatas: A Short Companion*. New Haven: Yale University Press, 2002. Print.

Solomon, Maynard. *Late Beethoven: Music, Thought, Imagination*. Berkeley: University of California Press, 2003. Print.

Sutton, Emma. "'Within a Space of Tears': Music, Writing, and the Modern in Virginia Woolf's *The Voyage Out*." *Music and Literary Modernism: Critical Essays and Comparative Studies*. 2nd ed. Ed. Robert P. McParland. Newcastle-upon-Tyne: Cambridge Scholars, 2009.

Winter, Robert, and Robert Martin, eds. *The Beethoven Quartet Companion*. Berkeley: University of California Press, 1994. Print.

Wittgenstein, Ludwig. *Philosophical Investigations: The German Text, with a Revised English Translation*. Trans. G.E.M. Anscombe. Oxford: Oxford University Press, 2001. Print.

Woolf, Virginia. "'Anon' and 'The Reader:' Virginia Woolf's Last Essays." Ed. Brenda R. Silver. *Twentieth-Century Literature* 25.3–4 (1979): 356–441. Print.

———. *Between the Acts*. Annot. and intro. Melba Cuddy-Keane. Gen. ed. Mark Hussey. Orlando: Harcourt, 2008. Print.

———. *The Complete Shorter Fiction of Virginia Woolf*. Ed. Susan Dick. 2nd ed. San Diego: Harcourt, 1989. Print.

———. *The Diary of Virginia Woolf*. Vol. 1: *1915–1919*. Ed. Anne Olivier Bell. New York: Harcourt, 1977. Print.

———. *The Diary of Virginia Woolf*. Vol. 2: *1920–1924*. Ed. Anne Olivier Bell. London: Hogarth, 1978. Print.

———. *The Diary of Virginia Woolf*. Vol. 3: *1925–1930*. Ed. Anne Olivier Bell. New York: Harcourt, 1980. Print.

———. *The Essays of Virginia Woolf*. Vol. 1: *1904–1912*. Ed. Andrew McNeillie. London: Hogarth, 1986. Print.

———. *The Essays of Virginia Woolf*. Vol. 3: *1919–1924*. Ed. Andrew McNeillie. London: Hogarth, 1988. Print.

———. *The Essays of Virginia Woolf*. Vol. 4: *1925–1928*. Ed. Andrew McNeillie. London: Hogarth, 1986. Print.

———. *The Essays of Virginia Woolf*. Vol. 6: *1933–1941 and Additional Essays, 1906–1926*. Ed. Stuart N. Clarke. London: Hogarth, 2011. Print.

———. *The Flight of the Mind. The Letters of Virginia Woolf*. Vol. 1: *1888–1912*. Ed. Nigel Nicolson. London: Hogarth, 1975. Print.

———. *Leave the Letters Till We're Dead: The Letters of Virginia Woolf*. Vol. 6: *1936–1941*. Ed. Nigel Nicolson. London: Hogarth, 1980. Print.

———. *Monks House Papers (Virginia Woolf)*. University of Sussex Library Special Collections. B.4 Fragments. Mss and tss in a folder containing verse related to *Between the Acts*. 4 pp ts. Web. March 4, 2011. http://www.sussex.ac.uk/library/speccoll/collection_catalogues/monks.html/.

———. *Pointz Hall: The Earlier and Later Typescripts of* Between the Acts. Ed., intro., annot., and afterword by Mitchell

A. Leaska. New York: University Publications, 1983. Print.

———. *The Question of Things Happening: The Letters of Virginia Woolf.* Vol. 2: *1912–1922.* Ed. Nigel Nicolson. London: Hogarth, 1976. Print.

———. *A Room of One's Own.* Annot. and intro. Susan Gubar. Gen. ed. Mark Hussey. Orlando: Harcourt, 2005. Print.

———. "Sketch of the Past." *Moments of Being.* Ed. Jeanne Schulkind. 2nd ed. San Diego: Harcourt, 1985. Print.

———. *The Voyage Out.* San Diego: Harcourt, 1968. Print.

———. *The Waves.* Annot. and intro. Molly Hite. Gen. ed. Mark Hussey. New York: Harcourt, 2006. Print.

Will truth be quicker found because
we stop our ears to music [...] ?

VIRGINIA WOOLF,
"On Not Knowing Greek"

FOUR

The Birth of Rachel Vinrace from the Spirit of Music

Jim Stewart

THIS STUDY DISCUSSES THE IMPLIED MUSIC OF SONGS FROM Sophocles's *Antigone* and Milton's *Comus*, which Virginia Woolf quoted verbatim near the opening and close of her first novel, *The Voyage Out* (1915).[1] Circumstantial evidence framing the novel's composition suggests Woolf was well aware of what this music meant for Sophocles's and Milton's texts and for her own. Her sense of the Greek song is clearer when considered in the light of her Aristotle readings, and her awareness of the Milton song was enhanced by her participation in an amateur performance of *Comus*. Nietzsche's ideas about Dionysian music drama were influential during Woolf's formative period; in his seminal work, *The Birth of Tragedy from the Spirit of Music*; and later, in *The Case of Wagner*; and it is likely that the diffusion of his ideas helped shape her own thinking about, on one hand, Dionysian music such as accompanies Sophocles's choruses and, on the other, Wagner's wish for a neoclassical music drama, not to say (by contrast) Milton's musical anti-Dionysianism. The study keys these implied Sophoclean and Miltonic musical praxes to Woolf's tragic characterization of Rachel Vinrace and to Rachel's fate.

THE CHORIC SONG AND ITS MUSIC

In chapter 3 of *The Voyage Out*, the innocent reader is surprised by the following passage:

πολλὰ τὰ δεινά, κοὐδὲν ἀν-
θρώπου δεινότερον πέλει.

τοῦτο καὶ πολιοῦ πέραν
πόντου χειμερίῳ νότῳ
χωρεῖ, περιβρυχίοισι
περῶν ὑπ' οἴδμασι

The excerpt transcribes Sophocles's *Antigone*, lines 332–37. It is neither transliterated nor translated. In her essay "On Not Knowing Greek," first published in *The Common Reader* (1925), Woolf for the most part translated her quoted Greek passages (CR1: 27, 33, 36). But William Pepper, the uncommon reader whose lines of dialogue these are, and who shares a classical education with Ridley Ambrose, knows his Sophocles by heart and has no problem reciting impromptu. It is understandable if today's readers skip the lines and move to the next English words, which are, appropriately, "Mrs. Dalloway looked at him with compressed lips." Some, who may not know Aeschylus from *Antigone*, may feel, with her, "'I'd give ten years of my life to know Greek,'" and may vicariously welcome Ambrose's assurance – "'I could teach you the alphabet in half an hour [...] and you'd read Homer in a month'" – for the passage is unmediated, and uncompromising. Mrs. Dalloway's thoughts reveal misgivings that are not untypical, these days, of the common reader of Woolf's novel.

Had she so wished, Woolf could have either translated this passage in the ensuing dialogue or bypassed its Greek altogether at the moment of utterance. She did neither. It remained to witness to the differing aims and results of male and female education, as well as to the inevitable – and gendered – clash of high culture with ignorance. Ambrose's offer could have allayed Mrs. Dalloway's diffidence. But it also called her bluff. In addition to lack of knowledge, she has no passion for the task and has been infantilized anyway by marriage to a Christ-figure husband. Virginia Stephen, by contrast, did have such passion. She wrote to Emma Vaughan in 1900: "Greek [...] is my daily bread, and a keen delight to me" (L1: 35). She had been feeding her hunger. From 1897 she studied Greek with some formidable scholars, in classes run by the Aeschylus translator George Warr, and from 1899 with Clara Pater. She received "vigorous" tuition from 1900 with the classicist Janet Case.[2] In 1901 she singled out one play for special praise: "I have read the Antigone [...] I should rather like to read the Antigone again [...] I find to my immense pride that I really *enjoy* not only admire Sophocles" (L1: 42). So although the passage originally given to Pepper was the *Odyssey* I. 63–66, it would be the *Antigone*'s first choric ode that would supplant Homer in *The Voyage Out* (MELYM 52).[3] Virginia Stephen also read Latin at this time, but in 1905 she thought Virgil's *Georgics* was "without the vitality of my dear old Greeks" (Leaska 238).

Included in her 1905 reading was Aristotle's *Poetics* – which, she enthused, "will fit me for a reviewer!" *Poetics* excited her. It was a "really excellent bit of literary criticism! – laying down so simply & surely the rudiments both of literature & of criticism [...] Aristotle said the first & the last words on this subject." Reading him was a pleasure. He "remains singularly interesting & not at all abstruse, & yet going to the root of the matter as one feels" (PA 240–41, 242). She later hoped, in her 1909 Wagner essay "Impressions at Bayreuth," that somebody might yet do for music "what Aristotle did 2000 years ago for poetry." But it would not be her. She was not Aristotle and was "not disposed to go to the root of the matter" in judging Wagner's opera (E1: 288). Even so, early in 1905 she was gratefully reading the philosopher's ideas on the tragic mythos or plot and, incidentally, on the chorus and its music. She then turned to Aristotle's paradigm, Sophocles's *Oedipus Tyrannos,* and "unearthed some gems" from that "fine play" (PA 245, 248, 250). She would have seen that, for Aristotle, music was as natural to humans as imitation (mimesis). In formal tragedy, therefore, he thought language should be "enriched" by "music or song." If "spectacle is [...] essential" to drama, so were "song and diction, these being the medium of representation." He believed "music [to be] the most important of the pleasurable additions to the play" and acknowledged "choral song" as "common to all tragedies" (*Poetics* 35, 39, 41, 47). The *Antigone* chorus quoted in *The Voyage Out* is such a song. It is a standing song, not a walking entry or exit song. Bernard Knox qualifies, "Of course the chorus is not actually stationary; its members dance in formation as they sing" (397). The music for this singing and dancing mattered. P. E. Easterling writes of "the immediate sensuous appeal of the choral performance, the *thelxis,* or enchantment [as] a major reason why the musical element did not vanish from Greek tragic plays as the spoken part became more complex and elaborate" ("Form and Performance" 156).

Aristotle was very decided about the chorus. It "should be regarded as one of the actors […] and should assume a share in the action, as happens in Sophocles, but not in Euripides." He was thinking of the music as much as the sentiment.

> With other playwrights [than Sophocles] the choral songs may have no more to do with the plot in hand than with any other tragedy; they are mere choral interludes […] But what difference is there between the singing of interpolated songs like these and the transference of a speech or a whole episode from one play to another? (*Poetics* 57)

It was praiseworthy in Sophocles that his choric songs integrated themselves with the mythos or plot. They were as important as any speech or episode. Aristotle's "pleasurable additions" were not ornamental, then. These insights were undoubtedly part of what Virginia Stephen found "really excellent" and "singularly interesting" in the *Poetics* (CR1: 29). Aristotle's influence continued to make itself felt a full two decades later, in her essay "On Not Knowing Greek."

> To grasp the meaning of the play the chorus is of the utmost importance. One must be able to pass easily into those ecstasies, those wild […] utterances […] [Sophocles's] choruses grow naturally out of his situations, and change, not the point of view, but the mood. (MB 186)

Hence it was that Aristotle, and Virginia Woolf, too, singled out the fully integrated Sophoclean chorus for praise.

But not long before reading *Poetics*, in 1904 (according to her later memoir), she "had lain [ill] in bed […] thinking that the birds were singing Greek choruses." Hermione Lee is skeptical about this and thinks that Woolf, struggling to find language for what happened to her in 1904, retrojected later metaphors onto her 1904 illness. Around when Woolf made this claim, Lee reminds us, she was preparing "On Not Knowing Greek," in which (Lee quotes) Greek choruses "sing like birds." The motif also entered the thoughts of Septimus Smith in *Mrs. Dalloway*, which Woolf was then beginning. So for Lee, Woolf's account is dramatized, not literal. This is an interesting caveat. Yet it has a kind of deafness. Referring to this choric Greek birdsong, Lee twice alludes to "these Greek-*talking* birds" and, once, to "those Greek-*speaking* birds" (195–97; emphases added). The paraphrases show she does not register the singing or the music. Woolf, by contrast, had known since the later 1890s what Greek choruses did. Well before 1904, neither George Warr, nor Clara Pater, nor Janet Case, nor her own original and passionate interest left her unaware that Greek choruses *sang*. She would have taken this as given.

As William Scott observes, "Music and sound were indispensable features of fifth-century [BCE] Athenian theatre" and were "continuous during the choral songs" (21). Virginia Stephen, as she kept her Greek notebook between 1906 and 1908, annotating Aristophanes's *Frogs* and other texts, cannot have failed to note that "Aristophanes in his critique of Aeschylus and Euripides in his *Frogs* devotes special attention to their music" (*HL* 144; West 17). Indeed, in having Ridley Ambrose translate Pindar, she introduced an ancient Greek "composer" from a musical family, himself "a professional musician" (West 344, 13; Michaelides 258). But Pindar's presence was in striking contrast to the Sophoclean chorus whose Greek she quoted; Pindar was a musical "conservative" who "showed no interest in the innovations of his time" (Michaelides 258), whereas Sophocles was famed for the opposite, credited (as M. L. West says) with "introducing the Phrygian mode to tragedy and using it in a rather dithyrambic [that is, frenzied] manner." West cites Aristotle's *Politics* on the Phrygian mode as "exciting (*orgiastika*) and emotional" (352, 180, 181). Aristotle asserts in the *Politics*": The Phrygian mode is held to give inspiration and fire [...] the effect of [it] is religious excitement and general emotion [including] Dionysiac frenzy [...] melodies which are in the Phrygian mode are the vehicle suitable for such states of mind" (344, 351). Solon Michaelides confirms this, saying the Phrygian mode was "pre-eminently Dionysiac" (255). In turn, the link to Dionysus had been stated with particular clarity by the ancient musicologist Proclus: "The dithyramb is tumultuous and appears in a highly ecstatic manner with the choral dance; it is suited to the passions most proper to the god; it is hurried along by its rhythms" (Mathiesen 74). Those choric songs, in this frenzied mode, were part of Sophocles's outstanding contribution to tragic form. Obtruding a Sophoclean choric outburst upon, as it were, a conservatively Pindaric background, Woolf commanded attention for that excited, emotional, and agitated song. Important enough to give in the original, it became doubly salient.

According to Thomas Mathiesen, "In the drama, Greek music found its fullest and most powerful expression [... in] the dynamic combination of text, music, instrumental accompaniment [and] dance" (125). And within that drama, as Virginia Stephen knew, choric songs were events in their own right, Sophoclean songs in particular being musically innovative. They were a formal departure. The Dionysian was foregrounded and realized materially in the fraught dithyrambic rhythms Sophocles brought into tragedy. West says notation did not figure in rehearsal: "poet-composers taught choruses by singing to them," and for Sophocles this would be apt, given his break with tradition (270). Peter Arnott comments on the advantages of this: "We know enough about Greek music [...] to be aware of the subtle range of moods and feelings that such choral music could induce [...] Greek drama['s] unique combination of music, dance, and the spoken word [...] was an intimate one, with the poet serving as his own composer, and his own choreographer too" (26–27). Choric instruction was viva voce: Sophoclean choruses enacting excitement were shown how to sing in the mode appropriate to their agitation. On the tempo for agitation, the "dramatic chorus [...] expressing [...] excitement [...] would have gone quicker than a solemn hymn" (West 153). Whatever the nature of any given "excitement," then, the melody existed (more so in Sophocles) to assist the tragedy's larger pulse. More immediately, the meters aided the techniques governing bodily movement (Michaelides 201, 291, 207). Woolf's *Antigone* quotation therefore has a resonance in *The Voyage Out* that partly subsists in what the author knew of the Sophoclean chorus. As we will see, that opening strophe from the *Antigone*'s first standing song is wondering, astonished, apparently laudatory. But the song is troubled and succumbs to a stunned dismay. We should pause to look at it and briefly consider how its overall structure and metrics reveal mood. We may take note of its instrumental accompaniment and draw conclusions about its implied music. In the last part of this essay, we can ponder how the song's implicit music, along with the music from one of the songs from Milton's *Comus,* informs the larger, agonistic rhythm of *The Voyage Out.*

To start with the shape of the *Antigone*'s first standing song, Robert Murray comments on a standing song's structure: "The [...] structure of the choral ode [...] is singularly appropriate for drama, since the [...] strophe and antistrophe can serve to set forth a miniature aesthetic parallel of the larger dramatic antagonisms" (328). On those "larger dramatic antagonisms," compared with the *Antigone,* Elizabeth Wyckoff claims, "no other Greek play is so fast off the mark" in its development (179).

To turn from the song's shape to its metrics and how these reveal mood, H. D. F. Kitto renders and annotates the song like this:

> (*glyconics*) Wonders are many, yet of all
> Things is Man the most wonderful.
> He can sail on the stormy sea
> Though the tempest rage, and the loud
> Waves roar around, as he makes his
> Path amid the towering surge.
> (13, ll. 330–35)[4]

How the meter at this point feeds into song and choreography depends on those "*glyconics.*" Kitto describes the gaiety of glyconic meter, but adds, "The glyconic is often used where gaiety is out of the question, as for example in the [first standing song] of the *Antigone*" (152). If the lively meter is not associated here with a "gaiety [that] is out of the question," this is because it expresses frenzied agitation. The horrified chorus goes on to sing:

> What evil spirit is abroad? I know
> Her well: Antigone. But how can I
> Believe it? Why, O you unlucky daughter
> Of an unlucky father, what is this?
> Can it be you, so mad and so defiant,
> So disobedient to a King's decree?
> (14–15, ll. 370–75)

These lines introduce an even higher level of disturbance as the chorus sings its judgment of this intransigent and misbegotten madwoman.

The chorus had cause to be disturbed. As Knox explains, they are "thinking of the daring and ingenuity of the person who gave Polynices' body symbolic burial. This does not mean that they are expressing approval of the action; the wonders of the world, of which man is the foremost, are 'terrible wonders'" (397). Hence the chorus "drives along," "fast off the mark" to the crisis involving Antigone. The accompaniment would be the aulos, a double pipe giving drone and melody. Aristotle linked this pipe with Dionysian music, because the aulos was orgiastic: "the effect of [the aulos] is religious excitement and general emotion" (*Politics* 351). The *Antigone*'s chorus fear the coming political storm. The nature of the melody furthering this choric agon would not have been lost on Virginia Stephen, who had her novel's larger rhythm to consider.

We can draw these observations together. Pepper's Sophocles quotation reflects what Stephen called the "vitality" of the Greeks. That vitality was instanced, she would write in 1925, in "the choruses[which are] the undifferentiated voices who sing." In "On Not Knowing Greek," and with a revealing relation of object to verb, Woolf said of the ancient tragedian: "Music and dancing he would need" (CR1: 29, 25). Sophocles's "dancing" chorus in the *Antigone*'s first standing song did indeed "need" its "music." Its song (to apply one criterion from antiquity) was "hurried along by its rhythms," making it go "quicker," as West commented, all the more so here, in the *Antigone*, "fast[er] off the mark" than any comparable play. As for the choric "ecstasies, those wild [...] utterances," to use Woolf's 1925 phrasing, these were what Aristotle called "agitations of the mind" (*Politics* 351) associated with Dionysus, and that was what made the musical mode and the frenzied meter suitable for the song's melody. Sophocles, praised for his artistic integrity, had brought these songs, this music, and this mode into tragedy as a "miniature aesthetic parallel of the larger dramatic antagonisms" (Murray 328). Pepper's Sophocles quotation, then, was originally sung to aulos music and induced unease,[5] and Virginia Stephen, with her keen awareness of "singing Greek choruses," would have known this.

THE DIONYSIAN IN MUSIC

"Heartily sick" (in August 1899) of her own "feeble word painting" of natural scenes, the seventeen-year-old Virginia Stephen wondered which of "all the Arts" was best suited to "imitate" the real. For an aspiring writer, she drew a difficult conclusion: "Somehow ink [...] seems to me the least effectual method of all – & music the nearest to truth." But she would pursue that contrast, with a view to transcending it. Obviously, she could not incorporate music in her fictions. But music had features other than melody, such as rhythm. By 1905 she had "got a book about the relations of poetry & music" (PA 143, 221). And in that same year, she made the following important connection in her published essay "Street Music": "We should invent – or rather remember – the innumerable [classical Greek] metres which we have so long outraged, and which would restore both prose and poetry to the harmonies that the ancients heard and observed" (E1: 31). In this assessment, the rhythm of contemporary writing could be replenished by classical Greek meters, in a process combining memory with invention.

On March 26, 1905, she also wrote of attending her "weekly concert" at the Queen's Hall on Sunday afternoons, happily going to still another concert the day after (PA 257). During those years, 1899–1905, her musical sensibility was growing, influenced in part by the Greek music drama to which she was increasingly sensitive as a form. It is instructive, for example, to note her 1903 journal on the troubling power of "dance music": "It stirs some barbaric instinct – lulled asleep in our sober lives – you forget centuries of civilisation in a second, & yield to that strange passion which sends you madly whirling round the room – oblivious of everything save that you must keep swaying with the music" (257). She wrote of "the ecstasies of the waltz." But given long enough, she said, the dance would take "possession of" the dancers. When it did, "all joy & life has left it, & it is diabolical, a twisting livid serpent, writhing in cold sweat & agony, & crushing the frail dancers in its contortions" toward the end of a "dark & tragic" night (165–67). Formally, this was not the kind of "dancing" the *Antigone* chorus, frantic with apprehension, would have done. But it was equally maenadic, just as "exciting (*orgiastika*) and emotional," and with the same deadly animation. Despite her disclaimer in March 1905 that Greek mythology was "a subject of which I know nothing," in 1903 Stephen held it against perfunctory musicians that they were "not inspired Gods, calling men to a more joyous & passionate existence" (166). To reflect on her terms is to gather a strong impression of this "dance music" so liable to bring "possession" by the "diabolical." The terms are callow and overdone but are those of a natural ecstatic. Whatever "inspired" deity presided here, he was not Apollo.

It was these 1903 journal impressions that Virginia Stephen later decanted into her published 1905 essay "Street Music." In that piece "a trance of musical ecstasy" is owing to "a god [...] within [...]; for music [like this] takes possession of the soul" and is distinct from other kinds of music that have only a "facile eloquence." The entranced singer or musician "is possessed by a spirit which [...] is clearly very potent." This spirit goes "in the disguise of animals," is "the wildest of all the gods," and, followed by his "fanatic worshippers," can "breathe madness into our brains." Such "music is dangerous," and what makes it so is not its "safest and easiest attribute – its tune," but rather its "rhythm, which is its soul." In "the power of rhythm" was heard "the voice of the god," and rhythm ensured that "the art of writing" is "nearly allied to the art of music" (E1: 28, 29, 30, 31, 32). These private and then public meditations on the role of rhythm are from a 1903 journal and a 1905 essay. They have accidental sympathy with the breakthrough represented in Stravinsky's *Rite of Spring*, which he was composing in the years up to 1912 (Salzman 29).

This insight – that writing is a form of rhythm and that rhythm enables risks – was seminal for Virginia Stephen. As the ancient resources of meter and rhythm must along with the music contribute to a larger, overall rhythm, so too "both prose and poetry" could find such procedures restorative. This was no simple appeal for sonority, but for a rigorous reimagining of writing from its rhythms outward. Stephen was not just looking for lyricism, either. She wanted to reproduce writing by a process to which ancient meter and melody had strongly contributed. It was not a question merely of finding new ways of organizing one's writing. If that were so, Apollo would be the presiding deity. It was as much, if not more, the following of an original creative passion, hence her gestures of homage to the Dionysian. This project, which she abstracted from the ancient praxes, is implicit in William Pepper's untranslated Sophoclean choric outburst. In the larger rhythm of *The Voyage Out*, his early declamation's implied melodic and literal metric unease forebode a tragic catastrophe, involving just the kind of sacrifice that had been on Sophocles's mind.

Of course, a major, and unignorable, theory of the Dionysian in music had been circulating in Europe throughout Virginia Stephen's formative years, which she cannot but have encountered. It had appeared in Nietzsche's *The Birth of Tragedy from the Spirit of Music*, which was translated into English in 1909 (M. Bell, "Nietzscheanism" 58). In that very year, she heard for herself a major attempt (initially much praised by Nietzsche) to produce a neoclassical music drama. For she was then in Bayreuth, listening to Wagner, albeit complaining, "I can only read the German with great difficulty." Her brother Adrian and their friend the "fervent Wagnerian" Saxon Sydney-Turner tried to "make [her] read the libretto in German, which trouble[d her] a great deal" (L1: 404, 407).[6] She would not have attempted Nietzsche untranslated before 1909. But as Michael Bell notes, Nietzsche had "immense vogue" in Europe at the time, and "the major modernist writers had absorbed the Nietzschean spirit or recognitions independently before having their own thoughts focused by him." It was a "relation of anticipation rather than influence" between Nietzsche and early modernism ("Nietzscheanism" 56, 64, 66). In the absence of demonstrable impact, Nietzsche's *Birth of Tragedy* is still a suitable cross reference to Virginia Stephen's thinking, which will have comprised, as Bell remarks elsewhere, "a coming to terms with the lines of thought associated with [. . .] Nietzsche" ("Metaphysics" 9). In the company of fluent German readers, men of ideas like her friend and family, she was not ignorant of Nietzsche's "immense vogue" and indeed could well have read him in English after 1909.

Quentin Bell says Virginia Stephen attended the 1909 Bayreuth Wagner festival (her one and only) mainly at Sydney-Turner's prompting. But he also conceded that about this time she was "very frequently at the opera" (149). The habit went back further still. Mitchell Leaska shows that in June 1897 alone she attended two operas and that she knew Wagner from at least January 1905 (94, 99, 222). In April 1909, in her piece "The Opera," she thought Wagner's music was more "essentially dramatic" than that of Gluck, but it did not always reach its goal, and there were failures of "cleavage between the drama and the music" (E1: 270). Her singling out of Gluck and Wagner is interesting. Peter Burian notes how both composers were self-consciously building on the template of Greek music drama – in Wagner's case with ambitions of renewing it (244–47). Yet by May 1913 Stephen had turned against Wagner while admitting she had been formerly transported: she complained to Katherine Cox of his "bawling sentimentality, which used once to carry me away, and now leaves me sitting perfectly still" (L2: 26). Peter Jacobs pithily says, "Virginia's feeble admiration for Wagner [...] did not last long" (235). Her 1909 letters to her sister from Bayreuth reveal disdain for Wagner's "gross symbolism," which she found ridiculous. What was happening "between the acts" seemed as absorbing as the stage action of some "heroine in a nightgown, with a pig tail on each shoulder, and watery eyes ogling heaven." "Between the acts" were intervals, and the substantial breaks could mean Wagner's operas did not survive as unities (with the exception of *Parsifal*, a judgment repeated in her "Bayreuth" piece) (L1: 404, 406, 407, 409; E1: 289, 290).

Her response to Wagner is a minor version of Nietzsche's own trajectory. The conclusion to *The Birth of Tragedy* is "the worst part of the book [...] with its effusive appreciation of Wagner," according to one translator (Nietzsche, *Wagner* 603). Nietzsche advocated Wagner's opera as a "rebirth of tragedy" (*Tragedy* 96, 98). He then believed Wagnerian music drama "absorbs the highest musical ecstasies, and thus brings music to a state of true perfection" (100). But this had given way to disillusion, and in 1888 Nietzsche published his repudiation, *The Case of Wagner*. "Is Wagner a human being at all?" he wondered. "Isn't he rather a sickness?" The symptoms were "hysterics" and "overexcited sensibility." While "Wagner is above all an actor," this did not mean he was dramatic: "drama requires *rigorous* logic: but what did Wagner ever care about logic?" (620, 622, 630–31, 636). Music drama had been displaced by mere theater in Wagner's opera, and musicality had been commandeered by histrionics. That was what happened if the Dionysian declined contact with "*rigorous* [dramatic] logic." If Nietzsche's turnaround was exemplary, Virginia Stephen may have had her "own thoughts focused by him," for one might entertain hopes of Wagnerian form, only to have to abandon them.

Jane Marcus once asserted that Virginia Stephen's "1909 visit [to Bayreuth] had filled her with the desire to make fiction aspire to the condition of Wagner's opera," because that opera was "epic theatre for ordinary people" (82–83). But Wagner's opera did not on balance go down well with Stephen. Her continually satirizing the audience in letters to Vanessa suggests she thought them anything but "ordinary." They were not ordinary; they were Wagnerians. That spring, before going to Bayreuth, she called them "strange men and women" with "something primitive in the look of them" (E1: 271). At Bayreuth, even *Parsifal*, though "a very mysterious emotional work, unlike any of the others I thought," had "emotions [that] are all abstract" and a libretto consisting of "weak vague stuff, with the usual enormities" (L1: 404). The sentiment was repeated by Rachel Vinrace; on reaching the question in the romance of *Tristan* (source of "the most extreme opera ever written" [Boyden 246]), "'Seems it so senseless what I say?' [Rachel] cried that it did, and threw down the book" (VO 29). Despite those "enormities," Stephen heard *Parsifal* twice. The second time, "it was much better done." But she was short of deeply moved: "I felt within a space of tears. I expect it is the most remarkable of the operas" (L1: 406). The praise is conditional. Wagner had failed to deliver something in which Stephen was greatly interested, namely, a genuinely neoclassical music drama, though her disappointment lacked Nietzsche's violence.

Stephen's absorption in the *thelxis* or enchantment of music, and "very frequently" (Q. Bell 149) of opera, was in character. Sensuous by nature, capable of intense anguish and keen delight, she had strong capacities for all the emotions music evokes. Music seems to grant immediate and truthful access to feeling, and she could hardly be indifferent to music that brought her "within a space of tears." But music also requires formal properties if it is to be recognizable, and these need some shaping intelligence that is intimately at one with its materials. Schopenhauer, quoted at length in *The Birth of Tragedy*, showed how strong musical illusion may be, in his claim that "music [...] provides the innermost kernel preceding all form" (78). But if we only recognize as "music" sound that has already assumed form, music can make us forget this: its form seems to vanish into content. As Stephen said privately of her second hearing of *Parsifal*, "it slides from music to words almost imperceptibly," or, in her rephrasing for the "Bayreuth" essay, "the words are continued by the music so that we hardly notice the transition" (E1: 289). For the renovative literary project that was on her mind, music was a powerful exemplar. Its aesthetic truth could be presented with consummate invisibility of form. To this formal need, *Parsifal* "almost" answered, with its verbal and musical transitions, which we "hardly" notice. Nietzsche's exploration of the Dionysian therefore articulated what Virginia Stephen was independently feeling. He suggested "Attic tragedy" as "the work of art that is as Dionysiac as it is Apolline." Elaborating on this, he styled Apollo as the shaping, formal god presiding over the organization of life and art and said that music, insofar as it embodied "rhythms," was felt by the ancients to be "an Apolline art." But of course there were other rhythms. There was Dionysus, presiding over "ecstatic reality," whose "music [...] induced feelings of awe and terror" worked off "in the complete gesture of the dance." Attic tragedy fused these influences. Plays required form, and they evinced arrangement and choreography. But the choral songs could be, as Virginia Stephen had noted, "ecstasies" or "wild utterances," and in the hands of Sophocles, who integrated his songs with his overall tragic form, the Dionysian assumed a crucial role. In Nietzsche's summary, "The sublime and esteemed work of art [...] is *Attic tragedy*[,] and the dramatic dithyramb [is] the common goal of the two impulses" (*Tragedy* 14–21, 27, 32).

On the kind of musicality to which language itself might aspire, Nietzsche was discouraging. "[Language] can never uncover the innermost core of music but, once it attempts to imitate music, always remains in [merely] superficial contact with it, and no amount of lyrical eloquence can bring its deepest meaning a step closer" (*Tragedy* 35). But as we have noted, Virginia Stephen was not in pursuit of "lyrical eloquence" pure and simple. In "Street Music" she claimed that "rhythm [...] is [the] soul" of music, not melody or lyricism. "The art of writing" was "nearly allied to the art of music" in its rhythm (*E*1: 30, 31). For Nietzsche, regularity of rhythm was an Apolline feature, because it was a principle of government. Yet it was also indispensable to Dionysian music. Stephen's term "soul" here may approximate Nietzsche's "Geist." She referred to the spirit of music in her "Bayreuth" article; some "music is too rigidly serene and too final in its spirit," she said (*E*1: 289). As she understood matters, rhythm was the "spirit" of any music, Dionysian or Apolline, and it was also for Nietzsche music's "innermost core," its "deepest meaning." Nietzsche became convinced that Wagner's was a false Dionysianism, but he scorned too "the arithmetical abacus of the fugue and contrapuntal dialectics" for their unmodulated Apollinism (*Tragedy* 95). He therefore would have dismissed some aspects of Rachel Vinrace's musicianship, which are addressed later in this essay.

Thinking of Rachel and her fate, it is well to recall Nietzsche's ambition for a true music drama: "Only from the spirit of music can we understand delight in the destruction of the individual" as distinct from the more communal values of the chorus (*Tragedy* 79). This general point is complicated by the fact that the *Antigone* male chorus whose song Woolf quoted was appalled not just by the individuation they faced in Antigone but by her sex. The Dionysianism Sophocles brought into tragedy through his frenzied choric songs was in this instance masculine. Helene Foley cautions that Creon and Antigone "are not precisely representative of their respective genders," but she allows that Greek culture "does not normally permit adult moral autonomy to the female agent." More than that, "Antigone's wildness and rawness is conventionally characteristic [...] of young and unmarried girls." And worse still, "mythical virgins who reject marriage," as Antigone does, may "become wandering maenads for Dionysus" (172, 181, 199). Better then (one might say) to be a Clarissa in thrall to Richard Dalloway, or a Helen dancing affectionate attendance on Ridley Ambrose, than to be unwed. Hence the meter, rhythm, and implied melody of the choric standing song, Dionysian in themselves, expressed a dread that female self-determination might lead to a feminized Dionysianism outside male control. This worry reflected Attic democracy's denial of voting citizenship to women, as well as its institutionalizing and maintenance of the Dionysus cult, which women favored. Virginia Stephen structured this choric masculine unease into an overall, agonistic rhythm that produced Rachel Vinrace as tragic, as remains to be shown. It is worth noting in passing, that while Nietzsche incriminated Wagner as "a master of hypnotic tricks [who] manages to throw down the strongest like bulls," Stephen herself was neither mesmerized nor overthrown. Her critical distance meant she was no easy Wagner conquest, no accessory to what Nietzsche styled "Wagner's *success* – his success with nerves and consequently women" (*Wagner* 622).

THE BIRTH OF RACHEL VINRACE FROM THE SPIRIT OF MUSIC

Nietzsche's subtitle for *The Birth of Tragedy* had been *aus dem Geiste der Musik*. Virginia Stephen's 1905 essay had likewise conceived music as having a "soul," which for her was its "rhythm." Choric music's melodic and rhythmic content had assisted the larger rhythms of ancient tragedy. Rachel Vinrace is a tragic figure, so this essay substitutes her name for the "tragedy" of Nietzsche's title in order to imply that she is made possible within a greater novelistic rhythm owing something to an implied music. This has meant looking at the Dionysian melody of the gendered choric song Woolf quoted and also at her formal interest in music drama, ancient and Wagnerian. The question is whether the Dionysian and Apolline are fused in Rachel on her own terms. To what extent is a presumptive melodic content needful to that larger novelistic rhythm within which Rachel is constituted as tragic?

We might ask first whether the configuring of implied melody and musical rhythm that helps form Rachel's fictional character combines those Nietzschean values of the Apolline and Dionysian and, if so, whether in combination they produce a character who is *perforce* tragic. To address this, we should consider Rachel's own musicality. She is "a fanatic about music," we are told (*VO* 27). We are introduced to the music she usually plays and alerted to its attractions:

> It was [...] Bach and Beethoven, Mozart and Purcell [...] In three minutes she was deep in a very difficult, very classical fugue in A, and over her face came a queer remote impersonal expression of complete absorption and anxious satisfaction [...] an invisible line seemed to string the notes together, from which rose a shape, a building. She was [...] far absorbed in this work, for it was really difficult to find how all these sounds should stand together, and drew upon the whole of her faculties. (53)

When Mrs. Dalloway entered the room, "the shape of the Bach fugue crashed to the ground" (53). For this was "very difficult" art music, the architectonics of which were hard to master. It demanded focus, allowing Rachel to abstract, to become de-individuated and "impersonal" despite the skill involved. Her "satisfaction" was largely private and "anxious," not easy to reprise after interruption. "The arithmetical abacus of the fugue" of Nietzsche's contempt in fact pleased Rachel. But to entertain Nietzsche's point, Rachel's music does seem more Apolline than Dionysian here, its performance requiring great self-government. If this were the sum of Rachel's resources, her music would be simply Apolline. She would then seem to lack capacity for the Dionysian. That might be regrettable, but it would not be tragic.

BIRTH OF RACHEL VINRACE FROM THE SPIRIT OF MUSIC 127

Yet Rachel does not lack capacity for the Dionysian. To see this, we need only contrast her art music with the hotel dance scene, some aspects of which were anticipated by the 1903 journal and the 1905 "Street Music" essay: "After the lancers there was a waltz; after the waltz a polka; and then a terrible thing happened; the music [...] stopped suddenly [... and] the musicians [...] looked bored and prosaic." Rachel was asked to rescue the situation. When someone protested that what she was playing was "not a dance," she insisted they "'invent the steps.' Sure of her melody she marked the rhythm boldly so as to simplify the way." Helen Ambrose and Miss Allan were then among the first who "whirled round the room." This was a dance "'for people who don't know how to dance.'" Rachel here rehearsed a free-form choreography: "The tune changed to a minuet [...] the tune flowed melodiously [...] The tune marched [...] Once their feet fell in with the rhythm they showed a complete lack of self-consciousness." In prose itself dependent upon marked rhythms, two of the company "galloped round and round the room with [...] impetuosity." This was finally followed by "the great round dance," in which "they swung faster and faster and faster," ending up "breathless and unkempt" (VO 170–72). As in the 1903 journal, dawn ended the dancing. Here we see a spontaneous Rachel, improvising, and her music is not "very difficult," but accessible and social. Unlike the highly structured art music she mastered in private, this was visceral music for the body not the mind, its melody subservient to Rachel's "mark[ing] the rhythm boldly." For anyone reading this in its year of publication, 1915, and who happened to have caught the Paris or London premier of Stravinsky's *Rite* two years previous, the passage may have had a certain familiarity. Here was a Dionysian Rachel, producing music both "exciting (*orgiastika*) and emotional." Not to be forgotten either is her social role in this scene. Dionysian music had enabled her to become de-individuated, more communal than solitary, and she had achieved this by insisting on her own musical and social terms.

There is no doubt that Rachel can and does synthesize her Apolline and Dionysian musical capacities. If her doing so speaks of empowerment, we are shown as much in the dance scene: "'No wonder [the musicians] get sick of playing stuff like this,' she remarked, reading a bar or two; 'they're really hymn tunes, played very fast, with bits out of Wagner and Beethoven' [... , but] As very soon she had played the only pieces of dance music she could remember, she went on to play an air from a sonata by Mozart" (170–71). From Mozart, she proceeded without a break to the physicality of the improvisations just noted. For dance purposes she altered the tempo and rhythm of traditional art music. She, too, offered a range of melodies "played very fast." It was not just Sophocles, then, who "marked the rhythm boldly" and whose frenzied melodies and meters had been "hurried along by [their] rhythms." As "fast off the mark" as any Sophoclean mythos, Rachel's benign music was born of a comic and festive spirit. It was effectively a reclamation of the female Dionysian, through just the sort of combination of memory and invention advocated in "Street Music."

We will not locate the tragic, either, in Rachel's engagement to an aspiring novelist, as if his plots must inevitably eclipse her music. It is she who teased Terence over this: "'Why do you write novels? You ought to write music. Music, you see [...] music goes straight for things. It says all there is to say at once. With writing it seems to me there's so much [...] scratching on the match-box'" (VO 220). But later in that friendly conversation, "they tried to invent theories [of music and writing] and to make their theories agree. As Hewet had no knowledge of music, Rachel took his stick and drew figures in the thin white dust to explain how Bach wrote his fugues" (232). This was companionable, indeed harmonic. There is no sense here that either party's art would have to be sacrificed for the other's.

If we are looking to understand how Woolf's overall novelistic rhythm produces Rachel as *tragic*, then, we will have to combine the effect of the Sophoclean song's implied melody and meter with that of still another song recited within earshot of Rachel's catastrophe. Rachel's fictional empowering through Dionysian dance music is not to be confused with the aims of Virginia Stephen's own larger fictive rhythm. Stephen was not ignorant of the Dionysian as palliative, a rehearsal of nonexistence. She would know (at least after her March 1905 studies in the origins of Greek mythology [PA 249]) what was the wisdom of old Silenus, father of the Dionysian satyrs, and the revelation he gave Midas: that it is best not to have been born (Easterling, "Show for Dionysus" 52–53).

She also would have noted Aristotle's claim that tragedy emerged from the Dionysian satyr dance (*Poetics* 37).

Accordingly, at the other end of the novel from the frenzied notional music of that Sophoclean choric song, Terence is found reading Milton's *Comus* to Rachel when she develops the headache that betokens her untimely death. Specifically, it is a song he is reading when the headache sets in beyond doubt. There had been an earlier *Comus* passage quoted, as spoken by Milton's Attendant Spirit (VO 347, 348, 350). In the original 1634 performance, this Attendant Spirit was played by Henry Lawes, who also "wrote the music that survives for the masque" and who was a singing teacher and court musician. The Spirit then breaks into the song "Sabrina fair," given in full in Terence's reading and symbolically framed by the onset of Rachel's headache. The Lady of the masque, the object of Comus's attention, has her own song, "Sweet Echo." Sabrina the river nymph, summoned to help the Lady against Comus, also sings "By the rushy-fringed bank" (Campbell 58, 72–73, 74). As Cedric Brown notes, "The name Comus [...] means revelry, though in the New Testament the word is used in the negative sense of 'riot, and ill-managed merriment,' which is what the Lady thinks she heard in the wood." Hence, says Brown, "the godly Lady, in addition to being [...] carefully trained in music, resists Comus's arguments as he has never been resisted before" (26, 27, 29–30, 31).

Virginia Stephen was fairly familiar with all of these Miltonic songs. She probably knew that (in Brown's words) at court masques "they had a ball" and that "when things go wrong in princely halls, they evidently go the whole way." So she would see how the Lady's "well schooled, godly principles of temperance" (high in Milton's scale of values) counteracted those Dionysian tendencies (Brown 26, 30). Stephen's brother-in-law, Clive Bell, started a play-reading group in December 1907, and *Comus* was undertaken by their troupe. In that performance, "Virginia played [...] the Lady and Sabrina [and] the song summoning 'Sabrina fair' would haunt her, and she [would] put it into *The Voyage Out*," as Hermione Lee reminds us (252). She did not herself recite, in her group's *Comus*, the song she later got Terence to read to Rachel, but she had lyrics to deliver, doubling as the Lady and Sabrina. As Brown comments, those roles and their songs offered stiffly critical resistance to what Comus stood for, namely, the Dionysian, which was viewed as definitively masculine. A woman's Miltonic role was to resist the Dionysian, in the interest of a patriarchal idea of moderation. This counter-reveling, patriarchal musical ethos enters the novel symbolically, at the moment Rachel begins to die.

We therefore note two poles of melodic and rhythmic meta-reference in Woolf's overall scheme. Near the novel's outset, we have the frenzied, apprehensive, and gendered Dionysian music that is implied in the quotation of a standing song from the *Antigone*. Close to the end, we have the Apolline, anti-Dionysian, equally gendered musicality of Milton's *Comus* song. But the Sophoclean semi-dirge against female autonomy, combined with the Miltonic hymns to female moderation, bode ill for Rachel. Woolf's mythos had been moving Rachel toward a greater and more sufficient individuation, which was at the same time communal. Simultaneously, Rachel's personal life moved toward deeper assimilation to convention, through the institution of patriarchal marriage as exemplified in the Dalloways and Ambroses. This larger rhythm, this oscillation, makes for a palpable tension, which must seek resolution or catastrophe. Rachel faced, through the conventions of bourgeois marriage, the prospect of an Apolline or supervised version of the female Dionysian. The implied frenzied melody of the *Antigone* song was unhappy about the woman who is singular, whereas the tacit melodic content of the *Comus* song sought a harmony only attainable if the female-musical became an instrument of patriarchal moderation. As we have seen, Rachel herself comprehended Apolline and Dionysian impulses and was well able to modulate these, synthesizing as required. That was no tragic rhythm, but empowering and productive. However, it is overlaid by the novel's larger rhythm. In that more fundamental fictive pulse, the choric music agitated by a menacingly solo female agent, and the rational masque song summoning all female agency to the cause of social balance, impose tempi and architectonics that Rachel would find much harder to master than Bach. She would not find that fugue so manageable or its arithmetic calculable.

In the words of one of Nietzsche's biographers, "Anyone who knows how to listen [to music] properly also hears it come to an end. True music is a swan song" (Safranski 132). For the fictional musician Rachel

Vinrace, the music of standing song and masque song is (as it had to be) withheld. But Woolf made a virtue of this necessity, and the music in the novel is implicit. Pindar's songs too, doggedly Englished by Ambrose, were lyrics in the derived sense, not sung to the lyre as anciently. The *Tristan* libretto was foreshadowed, but rejected by Rachel as "senseless." There is an evanescent line from Ariel's Song in *The Tempest* (VO 50). All of these songs or arias were of course unaccompanied, but they implied their musical settings both as music and as absence. Rachel's own music is silenced at the last, every bit as unheard as the melodies accompanying standing song and masque, libretto and stage song. Woolf's first novel thus choreographed radical tensions, producing movement and counter-movement, and the agon between these helped bring Rachel Vinrace to birth as a tragic figure. Woolf's praxis achieved this through what was, in her view, the prose analogue of music's "soul" or spirit, namely, "rhythm," in the form of a reimagined, musically informed narrativity.

NOTES

1. The thematic relevance of the *Antigone* to *The Voyage Out* is summarized by Jane Wheare. Regarding usage, I will refer to "Virginia Woolf" or to "Woolf" when discussing her finished and published first novel or when referring to her life's work. When discussing the first novel as a work in progress or referring to her earlier life, I will call her "Virginia Stephen" or "Stephen."

2. Hermione Lee mentions Homer, Plato, and Xenophon in connection with Clara Pater, and Aeschylus, Euripides, Sophocles, Plato, Homer, and Aristophanes in relation to the lessons with Case (143–44).

3. In the *Odyssey* passage, Zeus denies victimizing Odysseus, blaming instead the sea god Poseidon, and this links the Homer text to Sophocles's song about humans daring stormy seas. Mrs. Dalloway's mention of Clytemnestra prompts Pepper's quotation of a passage in which the gods discuss the assassinations of Agamemnon and Clytemnestra (*MELYM* 52).

4. Kitto 13. His lineation differs slightly from that of the Greek text.

5. Mendelssohn tried, in his 1841 *Antigone,* "to replicate the metres of the Greek, and [. . .] paid close attention to metre when he composed his orchestral settings," but this experiment was not thought wholly satisfactory. Virginia Stephen heard Mendelssohn's music in March 1897 and January 1905, but it is not clear that she knew of this piece (Wiles 145–46; *PA* 59–60, 222).

6. Q. Bell, 1: 149.

WORKS CITED

Aristotle. *On the Art of Poetry* [*Poetics*]. *Classical Literary Criticism: Aristotle,*

Horace, Longinus. Trans. T. S. Dorsch. Harmondsworth: Penguin, 1986. Print.

———. *The Politics of Aristotle*. Trans. Ernest Barker. Oxford: Oxford University Press, 1978. Print.

Arnott, Peter D. *Public and Performance in the Greek Theatre*. London: Routledge, 1991. Print.

Bell, Michael. "The Metaphysics of Modernism." *The Cambridge Companion to Modernism*. Ed. Michael Levenson. Cambridge: Cambridge University Press, 1999. Print.

———. "Nietzscheanism: 'The Superman and the All-Too-Human.'" *A Concise Companion to Modernism*. Ed. David Bradshaw. Oxford: Blackwell, 2003. Print.

Bell, Quentin. *Virginia Woolf: A Biography*. Vol. 1: *Virginia Stephen, 1882–1912*. St. Albans: Triad, 1976. Print.

Boyden, Matthew. *Opera: The Rough Guide*. London: Penguin, 1997. Print.

Brown, Cedric. "Milton's Ludlow Masque." *The Cambridge Companion to Milton*. Ed. Dennis Danielson. Cambridge: Cambridge University Press, 1999. Print.

Burian, Peter. "Tragedy adapted for stages and screens: The Renaissance to the Present." *The Cambridge Companion to Greek Tragedy*. Ed. P. E. Easterling. Cambridge: Cambridge University Press, 1997. Print.

Campbell, Gordon, ed. *John Milton: The Complete Poems*. London: Dent, 1980. Print.

DeSalvo, Louise. *Melymbrosia: A Novel by Virginia Woolf*. San Francisco: Cleis, 2000. Print.

Easterling, P. E. "Form and Performance." *The Cambridge Companion to Greek Tragedy*. Ed. P. E. Easterling. Cambridge: Cambridge University Press, 1997. Print.

———. "A Show for Dionysus." *The Cambridge Companion to Greek Tragedy*. Ed P. E. Easterling. Cambridge: Cambridge University Press, 1997. Print.

Foley, Helene P. *Female Acts in Greek Tragedy*. Princeton: Princeton University Press, 2001. Print.

Grant, Donald J., and Claude Palisca. *A History of Western Music*. 6th ed. New York: Norton, 2001. Print.

Hall, Michael. *Leaving Home: A Conducted Tour of Twentieth-Century Music with Simon Rattle*. London: Faber, 1996. Print.

Jacobs, Peter. "'The Second Violin Tuning in the Ante-Room': Virginia Woolf and Music." *The Multiple Muses of Virginia Woolf*. Ed. Diane F. Gillespie. Columbia: University of Missouri Press, 1993. Print.

Kitto, H. D. F. *Sophocles: Three Tragedies*. Oxford: Oxford University Press, 1973. Print.

Knox, Bernard. Introduction to *Sophocles: The Three Theban Plays*. Trans. Robert Fagles. New York: QPBC, 1994. Print.

Leaska, Mitchell A. *A Passionate Apprentice: The Early Journals, 1897–1909*. London: Hogarth, 1990. Print.

Lee, Hermione. *Virginia Woolf*. London: Chatto, 1996. Print.

Marcus, Jane. *Art and Anger: Reading Like a Woman*. Columbus: Ohio State University Press, 1988. Print.

Mathiesen, Thomas J. *Apollo's Lyre: Greek Music and Music Theory in Antiquity and the Middle Ages*. Lincoln: University of Nebraska Press, 1999. Print.

Michaelides, Solon. *The Music of Ancient Greece: An Encyclopedia*. London: Faber, 1978. Print.

Murray, Robert D. "Greek Poetry." *Princeton Encyclopedia of Poetry and Poetics*. Ed. Alex Preminger. London: Macmillan, 1975. Print.

Nietzsche, Friedrich. *The Birth of Tragedy*. Trans. Shaun Whiteside. London: Penguin, 1993. Print.

———. *The Case of Wagner: Basic Writings of Nietzsche*. Trans. Walter Kaufmann. New York: Modern Library, 2000. Print.

Safranski, Rudiger. *Nietzsche: A Philosophical Biography*. London: Granta, 2003. Print.

Salzman, Eric. *Twentieth-Century Music: An Introduction*. Englewood Cliffs: Prentice Hall, 1988. Print.

Scott, William C. *Musical Design in Aeschylean Theatre*. Hanover: University Press of New England, 1984. Print.

West, M. L. *Ancient Greek Music*. Oxford: Clarendon, 1992. Print.

Wheare, Jane. "Introduction to *The Voyage Out*." *Virginia Woolf: Introductions to the Major Works*. Ed. Julia Briggs. London: Virago, 1994. Print.

Wiles, David. *Greek Theatre Performance. An Introduction*. Cambridge: Cambridge University Press, 2000. Print.

Woolf, Virginia. *The Flight of the Mind: The Letters of Virginia Woolf*. Vol. 1: *1888–1912*. London: Hogarth, 1975. Print.

———. "Impressions at Bayreuth." *The Essays of Virginia Woolf*. Vol. 1: *1904–1912*. Ed. Andrew McNeillie. London: Harcourt, 1986. Print.

———. "Old Bloomsbury." *Moments of Being*. Ed. Jeanne Schulkind. N.p.: Triad, 1976. Print.

———. "On Not Knowing Greek." *The Common Reader: First Series*. London: Hogarth, 1984. Print.

———. "The Opera." *The Essays of Virginia Woolf*. Vol. 1: *1904–1912*. Ed. Andrew McNeillie. London: Harcourt, 1986. Print.

———. *The Question of Things Happening: The Letters of Virginia Woolf*. Vol. 2: *1912–1922*. London: Hogarth, 1976. Print.

———. "Street Music." *The Essays of Virginia Woolf*. Vol. 1: *1904–1912*. Ed. Andrew McNeillie. London: Harcourt, 1986. Print.

———. *The Voyage Out*. London: Hogarth, 1992. Print.

Wyckoff, Elizabeth, trans. *Sophocles: Antigone. Greek Tragedies*. Vol. 1. Ed. David Grene and Richmond Lattimore. Chicago: University of Chicago Press, 1968. Print.

FIVE

"The Worst of Music"

LISTENING AND NARRATIVE IN *NIGHT AND DAY* AND "THE STRING QUARTET"

Vanessa Manhire

VIRGINIA WOOLF'S ACKNOWLEDGED INTEREST IN INTERDISciplinary approaches to literature, her love of music, and her assumed position as "common listener" rather than musical expert offer fruitful angles into her early fiction: her groundbreaking reworking of narrative conventions depends heavily upon her explorations of the ways in which music works, especially for its listeners.[1] Woolf engages directly and critically with the social and literary norms of late nineteenth-century society, placing explicit emphasis on musical scenes as subject matter from which to build this critique, and using music to problematize the relationship between the external world and the world of the mind. This essay discusses Woolf's treatment of music in her second novel, *Night and Day* (1919), and the short story "The String Quartet" (1921), focusing on scenes of musical performance as well as Woolf's questioning of music's representational capacities. Stylistically, these texts are polar opposites: one heavy, conventional, and Victorian, the other light, experimental, and modernist. Yet in very different ways they both explore music as a potential model for the representation of interiority. Following Pater's idea of music as embodying the perfect relationship between form and content, Woolf draws on music as a vehicle for the exploration of language. Woolf's development of stream-of-consciousness narrative techniques, I suggest, owes much to her thinking about the effects of listening to music, a shared social experience but one that simultaneously allows for the individual movement of the imagination.

While less explicitly than in *The Voyage Out*,[2] the idea of music is of central importance in *Night and Day*; in fact, it takes on two seemingly contradictory functions. While the plot highlights the ways music is embedded in social grids of meaning, the language of the novel foregrounds metaphors of music as creating the possibility of seeking new patterns and meanings. On the level of content, musical scenes in the novel work as static visual tableaux illustrating nineteenth-century social rituals: in this respect, classical music is part of the domestic performance that *Night and Day* exposes as restrictive and obsolete. The music hall, by contrast, with its modern, urban mix of registers and styles, is figured as a site of imaginative potential. Yet Woolf also draws heavily on musical imagery to represent thought and communication, using it as a key metaphor for the movement of the mind. Music's dual nature in the novel thus exemplifies the tensions between social settings and the individual construction of meaning at the heart of Woolf's development of new models of narration.

Night and Day initially casts music as a conservative, backward-looking pursuit: the values of its music-loving characters seem stuck in the nineteenth century. For Mrs. Hilbery, music takes center stage in the romanticized narratives of her childhood: she sings an "absurdly and charmingly sentimental" setting of her father's poetry and recalls her mother "singing till the little ragamuffin boys outside stopped to listen" (ND 108, 92). Her daughter, Katharine Hilbery, who has "no particular liking for music" (267), has been called "Rachel Vinrace's opposite" (Dick 179). The piano playing of Katharine's cousin Cassandra Otway, by contrast, fits squarely within the drawing-room marriage market. Cassandra's brother Henry plays both piano and violin, has half-finished an opera, and makes a patchy living teaching provincial young ladies (ND 95, 182, 186). Musicianship is thus figured as a somewhat ludicrous relic of Victorian society – an appropriate part of general education, desirable for a young woman, yet not a proper profession for a gentleman. William Rodney takes classical music as a stable marker of class and culture. A Mozart opera is always open on his piano – first *Don Giovanni*, then *The Magic Flute* (64, 267). He sees music as cultural capital that is capable of regulating emotion, citing it as one of the few civilizing influences preventing him from emigrating (63). William repeatedly turns to rhythm and melody to impose order on his feelings and sets out to educate Cassandra in the "great tradition" of music (267). It thus plays an important part in his courtship of Cassandra, whom he figures as "some inimitably graceful species of musical mole" (267). After their engagement, Cassandra's piano playing also helps temper Katharine's parents' disapproval (462, 483).

Night and Day depicts music, then, largely as an old-fashioned and static social rite. As such, it deploys key contrasts between the novel's two couples: if Cassandra and William's relationship is both propped up and encumbered by the social niceties and heavy furniture of Victorian domesticity, Katharine and Ralph are drawn together by their shared impulse to move. Although their initial meeting is in the "remote and still" Cheyne Walk drawing room (8), their friendship is continually worked out in incongruous, usually public, places. They march down the Strand, meet at Kew, wander the city at night, with a lot of to-ing and fro-ing, both literal and figurative: they undertake difficult negotiations between public and private, ideal and real, questioning what love, work, and marriage mean in a changing world. Cassandra and William, by contrast, are almost always safely inside. Their courtship, a series of tableaux set in domestic interiors, seems to Katharine and Ralph uncomplicatedly conventional: "the melody of Mozart seemed to express the easy and exquisite love of the two upstairs" (408).

Musical interludes are not the only episodes in *Night and Day* that read like staged scenes. Full of theatrical spaces and tableaux, the novel's action moves by means of stage whispers and overheard conversations. The Hilberys' afternoon tea parties, the Denhams' dining room, and Mary Datchet's political meetings are all contrasting scenes of social performance for invited audiences. The Cheyne Walk residence is the ideal spectacle of upper-class life: "an orderly place, shapely, controlled – a place where life had been trained to show to the best advantage" (36). Areas within the house are partitioned off into staged spaces: Richard Alardyce's portrait is ritually unveiled; the "relic room" contains museum-like displays (the poet's slippers under his desk); even the telephone is in an alcove "screened for privacy by a curtain of purple velvet" as if to allow for quasi-theatrical asides (296). Any such privacy, of course, is illusory: as the only daughter of this household, Katharine is the reluctant performer of a series of circumscribed roles, from Kensington hostess to highbrow tour guide and biographer's assistant.

Her "years of training in a drawing-room" make it possible for her to divorce appearance from reality and "adopt a manner of composure" when performing "the ceremony of ancestor-worship" (280, 279, 305). To Cassandra, dinner guests' voices are "like the tuning up of the instruments of the orchestra" (331), an excitement that soon gives way to a "a more subdued desire merely to watch and to whisper" (336). And while Ralph feels jealous of "the actors in so great a drama as that of Katharine Hilbery's daily life" (279), Katharine mocks the notion of herself as dramatic heroine: "'At twelve my horses turn into rats and off I go. The illusion fades'" (340).

Such explicitly theatrical imagery reflects the novel's concern with social control: private life is figured as a spectacle constantly judged by real or imagined audiences. Katharine anticipates continual commentary on her actions from "a collection of voices in the air" (298), a kind of self-censoring Greek chorus: "If some one opened the door at this moment he would think that they were enjoying themselves," she thinks (1). Mrs. Hilbery watches Katharine and Ralph "as if a scene from the younger generation were being played for her benefit" (12), and after surprising Katharine and William talking, withdraws "as if she forced herself to draw the curtain upon a scene which she refused all temptation to interrupt" (309, 314). And in the theatrical denouement of the marriage plot, Cassandra overhears Katharine and William's conversation: "The curtains hanging at the door of the little room parted, and Cassandra herself stepped forth" (397). Quite literally waiting in the wings, she is Katharine's fortunate understudy, taking over her cousin's unwanted role as traditional romantic lead. Such recurring episodes of overhearing, eavesdropping, and spying in *Night and Day* can be read as a direct commentary on the stifling atmosphere of the Victorian family home. For Katharine, this sense of constant surveillance quashes private thought and the possibility of movement. Woolf paints traditional domestic interiors as repressing individual interiority, since the space of the home is marked by the performance of public roles.

Held up against such constraints is Woolf's description of the couples' expedition to a music hall performance. Just as Mary Datchet thinks of the music hall as a "dissipation" (432), a sense of slight risk is involved in this outing, neither a highbrow cultural event nor an exclusive domestic recital. Katharine joins the men to "instruct" her cousin in "the peculiar delights of an entertainment where Polar bears follow directly upon ladies in full evening dress, and the stage is alternately a garden of mystery, a milliner's band-box, and a fried-fish shop in the Mile End Road" (439). The local, specific, and familiar are fused with the exotic, general, and even ridiculous: the very idea of the music hall, with its idiosyncratic blend of registers, tones, classes, and contexts, already stands in for variety and mobility.

Although the narrator notes that for the two couples "the programme that night [. . .] fulfilled the highest purposes of dramatic art" (439), Woolf's own attitude to the music hall – as to popular culture more generally – was varied at best. She calls it "an unheard of dissipation," notes its "incredible, pathetic stupidity," but admits "you can't help feeling its the real thing" (D1: 19, 144). She takes on a consciously ambiguous subject position: "What a queer fate it is – always to be the spectator of the public, never part of it" (D1: 222). But the music hall scene is not fraught with such divisions of class and taste. In fact, it constitutes a rare moment of communal identification, so that the music hall is figured as a site of change and possibility. The scene is elaborately framed as a staged spectacle: "The reds and creams of the background, the lyres and harps and urns and skulls, the protuberances of plaster, the fringes of scarlet plush, the sinking and blazing of innumerable electric lights, could scarcely have been surpassed for decorative effect by any craftsman of the ancient or modern world" (ND 439). The performance itself is described only briefly, in terms of the music that accompanies it: "The hall resounded with brass and strings, alternately of enormous pomp and majesty, and then of sweetest lamentation" (439). Woolf turns her attention instead to the composition of the audience. Like that of "The Opera," it is divided spatially into social classes, whose respective appearances initially reflect those distinctions: "bare-shouldered, tufted and garlanded in the stalls, decorous but festal in the balconies, and frankly fit for daylight and street life in the gallery" (439). Yet as spectators, the entire audience becomes part of what they are watching:

> However they differed when looked at separately, they shared the same huge, lovable nature in the bulk, which murmured and swayed and quivered all the

time the dancing and juggling and love-making went on in front of it, slowly laughed and reluctantly left off laughing, and applauded with a helter-skelter generosity which sometimes became unanimous and overwhelming. (439)

The music hall audience undergoes a transformation from a set of hierarchically defined groups into a communally unified entity. Woolf's language effects the same kind of movement, from the previous sentence's tripartite comparison – stalls, balconies, galleries – to the long, expansive description of the audience's reaction to, and participation in, the spectacle. By extension, the performers' "dancing and juggling and love-making" seems also to include the spectators.[3] The changing subject matter of the program is thus mirrored in the "helter-skelter generosity" of the audience. The shared emotion demands no loss of individual interiority, but rather effects a kind of sublimation into the "huge, lovable nature" of the group, the collective identity of an urban collection of strangers. Neither the characters themselves nor the narrator attempt to translate the performances into an explainable extramusical meaning. The music hall thus functions as the kind of imaginative space figured in Katharine's daydreams, "where feelings were liberated from the constraint which the real world puts upon them" (131).[4]

In its plot trajectory, *Night and Day* moves in an arc from the confined setting of the Victorian family house to the mixed settings of the streets and urban life in London. The novel's treatment of music might also represent such movement – from the classical model of Mozart, a private, enclosed aesthetic world, to the music hall, representing popular culture, variety, and the modern. For the most part, music in *Night and Day* is depicted as an empty social convention, as Victorian and immovable as the bulky piano; yet Woolf's deployment of language drawn from music in the novel actually works to the opposite effect. Metaphors of music are used self-consciously to draw attention to questions of form and meaning and to problematize the relationship between the world of external reality and the interior world of the imagination. As an analogy, then, music provides a potential means for movement between these two worlds.

Within the drawing-room scene, both Woolf's narrator and her characters explicitly invoke the idea of harmony in terms that emphasize social convention. The Hilbery women's efforts to make the house "appear harmonious" (*ND* 36) are figured as an activity of defensive listening. Katharine wonders how she will be able to "keep this strange young man [Ralph] in harmony with the rest" (3); Mrs. Hilbery is sensitive to silence "as of a dumb note in a sonorous scale" (6); and voices on the telephone either "combine" or "strike a dissonance" with Katharine's surroundings (296). Such willed creation of harmony, however forced and artificial, highlights the older generation's unwillingness to respond to problematic ideas. When Mr. Hilbery avoids discussing his black-sheep nephew, for example, Katharine thinks, "How superficially he smoothed these events into a semblance of decency which harmonized with his own view of life!" (100). Likewise, when Katharine tells Mrs. Hilbery that she and Ralph are thinking of living together without marrying, Mrs. Hilbery "[runs] over these phrases as if she were trying chords that did not quite satisfy her ear" (463) and concludes that the idea, like Katharine's beloved mathematics, is "dreadfully ugly" (464). The concept of classical harmony thus stands in for the seamless surfaces of social performance.

Yet Woolf also uses musical imagery to foreground individual perception, making it a metaphor for mental transformation of the everyday: more than emotional expressiveness, music sets in process the movement of the imagination.[5] Ralph's voice makes "pleasant music" in Katharine's mind and wakens "echoes" in her (318); when Ralph sees Katharine unexpectedly, "the whole scene in the Strand wore that curious look of order and purpose which is imparted to the most heterogeneous things when music sounds" (120). Rather than carefully contrived social harmony, this is a chance moment suddenly imbued with significance. Its "order and purpose" is not premised on surface sameness, nor does it erase the "most heterogeneous things" that make up the scene. Ralph attributes the characteristic emotive and expressive powers of music to Katharine herself, making her a personification of music. Later, he finds himself "queerly out of tune for a domestic evening" (120), because his imaginative impression of her, at odds with the reality of mundane familial interaction, breaks the surface of social harmony.

The similes of echo and pattern employed here also invoke the idea of temporality. Ralph's idealized musical image of Katharine fades and cannot be recaptured: "Like a strain of music, the effect of Katharine's presence slowly died from the room [. . .] The music had ceased in the rapture of its melody. He strained to catch the faintest lingering echoes" (369). Music's immediacy can lend a temporary transcendence and emotional significance to even the most ordinary space, but because it moves over time, the transformation – like the sound itself – is always over as soon as it happens. The "lingering echoes" suggest the incompleteness of aural memory: you can never turn back to a moment and listen again. Woolf thus holds the classical metaphor of stable, controlled harmony (in a musical score, figured in vertical terms) in tension with Romantic notions of melody, temporality, and expressiveness (which moves horizontally on a score). Listening involves a struggle to hold on to the illusion of meaning; music presents a problem rather than a triumph of form. Such problems of communication are tempered by Woolf's borrowing of another nineteenth-century image, the Paterian flame, as a leitmotif suggesting interiority, immediacy, and connection. In figuring the interior lives of both Katharine and Ralph, especially Ralph's favorite mental picture of a dot surrounded by flame, Woolf draws directly on Pater's image of the "hard, gem-like flame" (Pater 218–19).[6]

Woolf extends the equation between music and thought to descriptions of Katharine's secret interests: mathematics and astronomy. In their shared emphases on proportion and harmony, both disciplines are inextricably tied to traditional theories of music: from classical geometry onward, the idea of the music of the spheres has represented music's abstract and intangible qualities. Katharine's interests thus represent the philosophical origins of music. Through the abstraction of intellectual work, she finds both escape from social performance and access to a world of Platonic ideals (ND 37), "a dream state" of direct sensations: "There dwelt the things one might have felt, had there been cause; the perfect happiness of which here we taste the fragment; the beauty seen here in flying glimpses only" (131). The "flying glimpses" and "fragments" are momentary reminders of a real, yet inaccessible "perfect happiness" that resembles the classical notion of divine harmony, an abstract contemplative music unable to be heard by the human ear.[7]

Literal movement provokes a similar "dream state" for Katharine. She finds productive space for private thought walking through the city, comes to moments of vision almost by accident, and has trouble "waking from the trance into which movement among moving things had thrown her" (84). These walks also let her transcend the particulars of her own situation and trace out a kind of pattern, "some kind of arrangement of life," within which she thinks of herself and her friends as "scattered among the crowd," part of a wider group (301).[8] Woolf uses metaphors of sound to bind together Katharine's physical movement with that of the imagination. The city's irregular and unpredictable movement is figured as a river, the noise of which is imbued with a paradoxical sense of purpose:

> The great torrent of vans and carts was sweeping down Kingsway; pedestrians were streaming in two currents along the pavements. [. . .] The deep roar filled her ears; the changing tumult had the inexpressible fascination of varied life pouring ceaselessly with a purpose which, as she looked, seemed to her, somehow, the normal purpose for which life was framed; its complete indifference to the individuals, whom it swallowed up and rolled onwards, filled her with at least a temporary exaltation. The blend of daylight and of lamplight made her an invisible spectator. (422–23)

Rendered invisible by the half-light, she is at once part of public life and somehow removed from it, standing beside the "stream" as if deciding whether or not to join it. As in the music hall scene, Woolf's focus moves away from the "domestic streets of Chelsea" (422) toward a specifically urban area of London. Identity is divested into a positive impersonality: individuals are "swallowed up" and "rolled onwards" by the currents of the city, becoming part of its fluid and anonymous community. The scene's emphasis on movement and variety again recalls the music hall: struck by the "inexpressible fascination of varied life pouring ceaselessly," Katharine stands "unobserved and absorbed" in the "deep roar" and "changing tumult" of the city itself.

In descriptions of Mary Datchet, Woolf explicitly invokes music to link the movement of the body with that of the mind. As Mary departs a difficult social interaction, she finds "her mind uncomfortably full of different trains of thought. She started one and then another. They seemed even to take their colour from the street she happened to be in" (160). Far from the "exaltation" Katharine's walks offer, Mary is overcome by confusion; ideas multiply and elude her control, directed by the external stimuli of the city. She is subject to the affective power of particular locations and of city sounds such as that of the "belated organ-grinder," which "[sets] her thoughts dancing incongruously" (160).[9] Later, music changes from an unwanted influence on thought into a welcome one. Turning to listening as a simile for walking in the city, Woolf draws a direct parallel in their shared effect of setting the imagination in motion:

> Strange thoughts are bred in passing through crowded streets should the passenger, by chance, have no exact destination in front of him, much as the mind shapes all kinds of forms, solutions, images when listening inattentively to music. From an acute consciousness of herself as an individual, Mary passed to a conception of the scheme of things in which, as a human being, she must have her share. She half held a vision; the vision shaped and dwindled. She wished she had a pencil and a piece of paper to help her to give a form to this conception which composed itself as she walked down the Charing Cross Road. But if she talked to any one, the conception might escape her. Her vision seemed to lay out the lines of her life until death in a way which satisfied her sense of harmony. It only needed a persistent effort of thought, stimulated in this strange way by the crowd and the noise, to climb the crest of existence and see it all laid out once and for ever. Already her suffering as an individual was left behind her. (246–47)

This associative process is "full of effort" for Mary, but exhilarating nevertheless. "The crowd and the noise" allow her, like Katharine, to escape the bounds of her individual life and become anonymous in relation to the city spectacle; likewise, her thoughts move from her own situation to a broader abstract pattern in a "curious transformation from the particular to the universal" (248). Woolf combines visual and aural references to stress motion: even as Mary's vision "compose[s] itself" and satisfies her "sense of harmony," it "shape[s]," "dwindle[s]," and threatens to "escape." In this way Woolf rewrites the ideas of "composure" and "harmony," previously figured as limiting and static, into the kinesthetic representation of Mary's interiority.

Such passages reflect the beginnings of the fictional project Woolf outlines in "Modern Fiction," also first published in 1919. *Night and Day*'s narrative style is far from impressionistic, yet from Mary's "trains of thought" to Ralph's "dot with flames around it" (474) and Katharine's "something about flames" (486), the novel constantly foregrounds the world of impressions. Like mathematics, astronomy, and walking in the city, music provokes the "flight of the mind" and provides glimpses of the world of the imagination and what Woolf would later term "moments of being." Of course, Woolf herself referred to *Night and Day* as a novel of "non-being," following as it does the structural lines of the conventional marriage plot,[10] but the novel's formal conventionality can also be seen as highly self-referential.[11] Woolf's narrative constantly draws attention to questions of form and appearance, to the relationship between exteriority and interiority. And as the characters discover, form does not always have a straightforward meaning or function; it can also be used strategically. After the confrontation between Katharine, William, and Cassandra, the three try to conceal their improper behavior with the comfortable performance of familiar daily structures. In particular, Cassandra's piano playing creates an effective formal distraction that "lull[s] Mrs and Mrs Hilbery into the belief that nothing unusual had taken place":

> At the sound of the first notes Katharine and Rodney both felt an enormous sense of relief at the licence which the music gave them to loosen their hold upon the mechanism of behaviour. They lapsed into the depths of thought. Mrs Hilbery was soon spirited away into a perfectly congenial mood, that was half reverie and half slumber, half delicious melancholy and half pure bliss. Mr Hilbery alone attended. He was extremely musical, and made Cassandra aware that he listened to every note. [. . .] [Rodney] stayed a moment longer by the window than was, perhaps, necessary, and having done what was needed, drew his chair a little closer than before to Katharine's side. Under cover of some exquisite run of melody, he leant towards her and whispered something. (400–401)

On one level, this performance has a pacifying, almost soporific, function; yet at the same time, her parents' absorption in the drawing-room recital screens off the private communication between Katherine and William, providing "cover" for him to let her know that Ralph is waiting outside.

Until this point, domestic scenes of musical performance have been part of the very "mechanism of behaviour" that constrains the characters, yet Cassandra's deceptively simple display now provides a curtain behind which such constraints can loosen. Rather than reaffirming the boundaries of domestic space, it enables the world outside to permeate them. Here music works to two distinct effects. For Mr. and Mrs. Hilbery, perhaps, music tempers threats to social propriety: as in melodrama or silent movies, the musical soundtrack informs the plot, creating – even exploiting – particular and predictable emotional effects. For Katharine and William, however, music is not soothing. It opens up a space for private thought and allows for the productive discords of argument and action. Katharine's feelings of alarm, mystery, and agitation oppose, rather than reflect, the form of the music (401–402). The focus of the scene shifts from the form of the performance to the thought and action of the audience. The theatrical imagery of the novel changes direction: instead of being compelled to perform in compliance with audience expectations, the characters become aware that "form" can also be used consciously and strategically to obscure unorthodox action and development.

While musical content in the novel stresses the emptiness of conventional formal display, the language of music works as a metaphor for thought and suggests the possibility for new kinds of narration. It provides an answer to Katharine's questioning of the "perpetual disparity between the thought and the action, between the life of solitude and the life of society, this astonishing precipice on one side of which the soul was active and in broad daylight, on the other side of which it was contemplative and dark as night? Was it not possible to step from one to the other, erect, and without essential change?" (325). Woolf's self-conscious deployment of musical imagery in *Night and Day* suggests that she saw in music the potential for such movement between the worlds of thought and action, external reality and interiority. The movement of music, therefore, provides her with an important analogy for the kind of mobility she goes on to create in language.

The radical change of style between her first two novels and the short stories collected in *Monday or Tuesday* reflects Woolf's concern with finding new ways to represent the life of the mind. As early as 1908 she wrote of her ambition to "re-form the novel and capture multitudes of things at present fugitive, enclose the whole, and shape infinite strange shapes" (L1: 356), and in 1920 she described a new novelistic form with "no scaffolding; scarcely a brick to be seen; all crepuscular, but the heart, the passion, humour, everything as bright as fire in the mist" (D2: 13). In "The String Quartet" the abstract and impressionistic nature of music offers Woolf not merely a useful analogy for the movement of the mind but also a potential form for depicting that movement. Where *The Voy-*

age Out and *Night and Day* explore music within largely conventional narratives, "The String Quartet" goes a step further, using music as a vehicle for a new kind of narration. The story's setting emphasizes the superficial social rituals surrounding musical performance. Its narrative style, however, makes music more than just a descriptive mechanism: Woolf takes us inside the head of an audience member, recording the flow of impressions through the mind. The narrative's fluid and allusive movement mimics that of music itself, which becomes both subject and structure of the story.

The story's experimental style recalls Walter Pater's oft-quoted dictum that "all art constantly aspires towards the condition of music" (156): for Pater, music was the ultimate art form because of its lack of materiality, its focus on the moment, and its fusion of form and content.[12] In "The String Quartet" Woolf rejects conventional devices of narrative framing in order to create such effects of immediacy. A rare example of first-person narrative in Woolf's fiction, it has neither a linear plot nor an anchoring omniscient narrator. With the title as its only contextual key, its structure follows the twists and turns of a listening mind, tracing the particularities of its responses to both inner and outer realities as they unfold. In exploring the relationship between these two realities, Woolf self-consciously exploits the very duality that limits music's role in her earlier novels. "The String Quartet," therefore, highlights the importance of Woolf's thinking about music to her development of new techniques for representing interiority.

Woolf's short stories, as Gillespie notes, are almost uniformly overlooked (116). Woolf herself describes them in a 1930 letter to Ethel Smyth, for example, as "little pieces" that were "the treats I allowed myself when I had done my exercise in the conventional style" (*L* 4: 231). While both Lytton Strachey and Roger Fry admired the story, and T. S. Eliot singled it out for particular praise, critics largely dismissed it as a light formal experiment (*D* 2: 106, 125). E. M. Forster described the *Monday or Tuesday* stories as all form and no content: "an inspired breathlessness, [. . .] a beautiful drowning or gasping which trusted to luck" (242). *Times Literary Supplement* reviewer Harold Child was less complimentary in his judgment: "Prose may 'aspire to the condition of music'; it cannot reach it" (Majumdar 88).

Among more recent critics, Woolf's short fiction has received increased attention. Some perhaps take her interest in Paterian aesthetics rather too literally, however.[13] While "The String Quartet" self-consciously foregrounds issues of form and narrative, it is more than merely a technical exercise imitating the music itself. Rather than trying to reproduce the music's form, Woolf transposes its indeterminacy of meaning into linguistic play while holding that indeterminacy in tension with the formal and controlled social setting of the concert. External descriptions and mundane social interchange are mingled with extravagantly romantic narrative and the fluid imagery and style of a prose poem, with the result that it is often difficult to distinguish between dialogue, interior monologue, and associative fragments of thought. Such constant shifts in perspective create a complex texture of meaning: Davenport describes it as "two-layered fiction" (166), and Gillespie's metaphor of counterpoint (141) emphasizes Woolf's creation of the fictional effects of overlapping voices, simultaneity of action, and continual movement.

The impetus for the story seems to have come directly from a private chamber music series Woolf attended from 1918 to 1920 (D1: 219). She explicitly describes one such concert in March 1920 as work for this story: "I went up to Campden Hill to hear the S[c]hubert quintet – to see George Booth's house – to take notes for my story – to rub shoulders with respectability" (D2: 24). As subscription concerts, these were held in private homes rather than public halls; for Woolf as a young woman, "rubbing shoulders with respectability" was a way to keep in tangential contact with the social milieu in which she had grown up. Woolf's diary over this period reads like a gossipy concordance to the story itself. Her descriptions of the concerts focus more often on the audience than the music, returning repeatedly to "the eternal, & insoluble question of clothes" (D1: 220). She describes "the company" of a February 1919 concert as "decorous & fur bearing as usual," equating outward markers of status and wealth with corresponding – if less tangible – codes of social behavior (245). Such self-conscious codes could create impediments to listening: the social obligations of small talk, for example, hindered individual engagement with the music. On a concert of Mozart and Beethoven, she writes, "I don't think I did hear very much of them, seated as I was between Katie & Elena, & pitched headforemost into outrageous banter of the usual kind with the Countess" (D2: 14). Woolf was a borderline member of this society and found its "amiability [...] disarming" (D1: 251). She records that old family acquaintances "expressed great surprise at seeing me, as if I were a strange bird joining a flock of the same species. I felt strange enough; but oddly familiar with their ways after the first" (220). Only a month later, she depicts herself as "less than ever in touch with the gathering – as dusky, fur-clad & discreet as ever" (251).[14]

In "The String Quartet" Woolf addresses the issues of community and identification raised in both her diary entries and her early novels. The narrator figure, who seems to occupy an ambiguous position in relation to the rest of the audience, wonders at how superficial aspects of the evening's entertainment interfere with individual listening: "If it's all the facts I mean, and the hats, the feather boas, the gentleman's swallow-tail coats, and pearl tip-pins that come to the surface – what chance is there?" (CSF 138). Clothing and propriety are again conflated in the audience's concern with external appearances: "Why fidget? Why so anxious about the sit of cloaks and gloves – whether to button or unbutton?" (130). As much as clothing confirms inclusion in a particular social class, it also cements divisions between audience members, "a hundred people sitting here well dressed, walled in, furred, replete" (139). Politeness rather than familiarity compels the narrator to speak with a relative: "the ties of blood require me, leaning forward, to accept cordially the hand which is perhaps offered hesitatingly – " (138). Like Woolf, the narrator is unwilling to identify with this group and reluctant to participate in the conversations around her.

Yet what unites the group is their shared anticipation of the activity of listening. Before the concert starts, the narrator expects an indefinable effect from the music: "I too sit passive on a gilt chair, only turning the earth above a buried memory, as we all do, for there are signs, if I'm not mistaken, that we're all recalling something, furtively seeking something" (CSF 139). As in *Night and Day*, music is figured as a stimulus to the imagination; the search for a recalled "buried memory" suggests the philosophical idea of music as something mystical, echoing the Platonic ideal of classical harmony, like Katharine's astronomy or Mary's "vision." The power to feel, attributed to the music hall audience in the previous novel, is now given to this homogenous, upper-class chamber music audience. The concert creates a temporary and provisional community of dispersed subjectivities: the audience members react to the same music in individual ways. Yet while the sense of shared emotion is liberating in the music hall scene, here even this common experience is figured as something "furtive" that remains hidden and must be inferred from "signs." "The String Quartet" highlights such contradictions: the narrative's constant combination of outward form and inner feeling calls into question the relationship between the two.

The forced stasis that characterizes the waiting audience is thrown into relief by the narrative's emphasis on movement. Moving between outer and inner realities, Woolf juxtaposes large-scale movement through the city with that within the individual mind. The story opens with a list of modes of transport: "Tubes and trams and omnibuses, private carriages not a few, even, I venture to believe, landaus with bays in them, have been busy at it, weaving threads from one end of London to the other" (CSF 138). These "threads" at once suggest literal movement, connections between people, and the work of the narrative itself. But the threads of narrative in "The String Quartet" are so constantly moving that they are hard for the reader to follow, just as the narrator herself struggles to keep track of her thoughts and experiences:

> If the mind's shot through by such little arrows, and – for human society compels it – no sooner is one launched than another presses forward; if this engenders heat and in addition they've turned on the electric light; if saying one thing does, in so many cases, leave behind it a need to improve and revise, stirring besides regrets, pleasures, vanities, and desires – if it's all the facts I mean, and the hats, the fur boas, the gentleman's swallow-tail coats, and pearl tie-pins that come to the surface – what chance is there?
>
> Of what? It becomes every minute more difficult to say why, in spite of everything, I sit here believing I can't now say what, or even remember the last time it happened. (CSF 138)

In both subject matter and syntax, this question conveys a sense of the unpredictable movement of the mind. Woolf's characteristic use of the word "if" and the dash illustrates the ways in which ideas are continually generated, interrupted, and left unfinished. Visual images jostle with abstract emotions and the vocabulary of contemporary physics in a dynamic narrative style recalling Mary Datchet's fugue-like interior monologue.

Woolf's kinesthetic narrative in "The String Quartet" extends her previous deployment of music as a figure for various kinds of movement. She creates a quasi-musical sense of motion to represent the associative process of thought:

> Flourish, spring, burgeon, burst! The pear tree on the top of the mountain. Fountains jet; drops descend. But the waters of the Rhone flow swift and deep, race under the arches, and sweep the trailing water leaves, washing shadows over the silver fish, the spotted fish rushed down by the swift waters, now swept into an eddy where – it's difficult this – conglomeration of fish all in a pool; leaping, splashing, scraping sharp fins; and such a boil of current that the yellow pebbles are churned round and round, round and round – free now, rushing downwards, or even somehow ascending in exquisite spirals into the air; curled like thin shavings from under a plane; up and up ... How lovely goodness is in those who, stepping lightly, go smiling through the world! Also in jolly old fishwives, squatting under arches, obscene old women, how deeply they laugh and shake and rollick, when they walk, from side to side, hum, hah! (CSF 139)

As in *The Voyage Out,* music is equated with the fluid movement of water; the narrative style combines incomplete sentences, ellipses, and exclamations. The list of infinitives (or imperatives) opening the paragraph; the strings of present participles; and the rhythmic repetition, alliteration, and internal rhyme create a sense of immediacy and dynamism. Woolf's figuration of thoughts as swimming fish anticipates her later development of this metaphor in *A Room of One's Own* and "Professions for Women"; the "jolly old fishwives, squatted under arches" also pick up on key imagery from scenes of Rachel's delirium in *The Voyage Out* (CSF 139). Chasing the fish of ideas, Woolf's narrator is herself a "fishwife," and the mid-sentence aside "it's difficult this" creates a self-conscious commentary on the process of catching and recording thoughts.

Such passages show Woolf's narrator turning her listening experience into language without clarifying meaning. Yet other audience members feel an uncomfortable urge to translate music into words: "But the tune, like all his tunes, makes one despair – I mean hope. What do I mean? That's the worst of music!" (CSF 138); "No, no. I noticed nothing. That's the worst of music – these silly dreams. The second violin was late, you say?" (140). Where meaning is not immediately legible, some focus on technicalities, and others struggle to express themselves at all: "'How – how – how!' Hush!" (140).[15] Here Woolf returns to the problem in "Impressions at Bayreuth" of "how little words can do to render music" (*E*1: 291). Music is figured as creating meaning independently of language – "the words are indistinguishable though the meaning is plain enough" (*CSF* 141) – and the narrator finds meaning in the immediacy of impressions: "The tongue is but a clapper. Simplicity itself. The feathers in the hat next me are bright and pleasing as a child's rattle. The leaf on the plane-tree flashes green through the chink in the curtain. Very strange, very exciting" (140). The narrator's use of language as a malleable, dynamic medium suggests the constant flow of thoughts through the listening mind. "The worst of music," its untranslatable appeal to the senses and direct experience, is thus perhaps its most attractive feature for Woolf in developing a new narrative style.

The immediacy of music in "The String Quartet" works as a catalyst for emotion and memory. The music's "melancholy river" becomes a medium of communication with an unidentified second person somehow present within it: "I see your face, I hear your voice and the bird singing as we pass the osier bed. What are you whispering? Sorrow, sorrow. Joy, joy" (*CSF* 140). Sorrow and joy are "woven together, inextricably commingled" in this inaudible speech until the ghostly voice of a "dusky wraith" seems to speak directly to the listener:

> For me it sings, unseals my sorrow, thaws compassion, floods with love the sunless world, nor, ceasing, abates its tenderness, but deftly, subtly, weaves in and out until this pattern, this consummation, the cleft ones unify; soar, sob, sink to rest, sorrow and joy. (140)

The disembodied voice of the music forces the listener to access emotion that has been locked away, embodying a sorrow that must be "unsealed," an echo of the "buried memory" shared by the audience as they await the music. As sorrow and joy "soar, sob, sink to rest," music both provokes the difficulty of memory and provides consolation. Given the story's date of composition, these references to "buried memory" and "unsealed" sorrow can be read as an oblique commentary on society's inability to mourn the collective losses of World War I. The only explicit reference to the war occurs during the pre-concert chitchat: "'But I knew you at once!' / 'Still, the war made a break – '" (138). In this fragment of conversation, the war is mentioned as if it is no more than a slight inconvenience to social life, yet as the defining event of the recent past, it is the one experience that the audience unquestionably has in common. The listener's grief, as it is given voice by the music, is deemed unnecessary in an imaginary dialogue that implies that "all" is over and resolved:

> Why then grieve? Ask what? Remain unsatisfied? I say all's been settled; yes; laid to rest under a coverlet of rose leaves, falling. Falling. Ah, but they cease. One rose leaf, falling from an enormous height, like a little parachute dropped from an invisible balloon, turns, flutters waveringly. It won't reach us. (140)

As the music fades, its cathartic effect is stalled. Social exchange smoothes over individual mourning, covering unanswered question with platitudes. The single rose leaf, which "won't reach us," implies only an incomplete resolution. Images of music in the story, moreover, suggest a soundtrack of war: "silver horns," "seneschals [. . .] saluting the dawn," "trumpets" and "clarions" build up to the final alliterative and rhythmic "Tramp and trumpeting. Clang and clangour. Firm establishment. Fast foundations. March of myriads. Confusion and chaos trod to earth" (141). Jacobs describes these phrases as echoing the music itself in "highly rhythmical, alliterative verse of a mock Tennysonian kind" (244). I would suggest an alternative poetic source, however. Woolf's language here might allude to the martial music of John Dryden's 1687 poem "A Song for St. Cecilia's Day," where "The trumpet's loud clangor / Excites us to arms" (ll. 25–26). Dryden's ode to the patron saint of music, like Woolf's story, pays respect to the overwhelming power of music and in fact ends with an apocalyptic scene: "So, when the last and dreadful hour / This crumbling pageant shall devour, / The trumpet shall be heard on high, / The dead shall live, the living die, / And Music shall untune the sky" (ll. 59–63). Such music stirs emotion rather than laying it to rest.

The "crumbling pageant" in "The String Quartet" is that of postwar London society. If human character changed in 1910, the years between 1914 and 1918 made irrevocable alterations to the city and its people. The aristocratic privilege of this audience was dwindling into empty social performance. In "The String Quartet," Woolf displaces the fading romance of aristocratic society into a romance narrative, conflating literary and social conventions in order to undermine them. In her diary, Woolf records conversations at Chelsea concerts with Katie, Lady Cromer, who bemoans the decline of aristocracy with such phrases as "The end is coming. A la lanterne!" and "Civilisation is at an end" (D1: 309). Woolf admits that she can't help liking the spectacle of aristocratic society – "I'm critical, intellectually, of the aristocrats but sensually they charm" – yet she is aware of the outdated irrelevance of that way of life. She describes Lady Cromer as "letting fall sentences of curious remote force, as though she were on top of a mountain, or lost in a mist, as I can't help feeling these aristocrats are" (245), and speaking with a "humorous resignation which foretells a gallant death on the scaffold" (309–310).

In "The String Quartet," Woolf mimics such tones, using highly wrought literary diction to create melodramatic scenes of courtly romance. She transposes the mannerisms of aristocratic society into formulaic literary clichés. The "lovers on the grass" speak in the stylized language of Renaissance drama, and the passage immediately following is the most conventionally legible in the story in terms of narrative style, not only outlining what happens, but paying considerable attention to the details of what everyone was wearing:

> "He followed me down the corridor, and, as we turned the corner, trod on the lace of my petticoat. What could I do but cry 'Ah!' and stop to finger it? At which he drew his sword, made passes as if he were stabbing something to death, and cried, 'Mad! Mad! Mad!' Whereupon I screamed, and the Prince, who was writing in the large vellum book in the oriel window, came out in his velvet skull-cap and furred slippers, snatched a rapier from the wall – the King of Spain's gift, you know – on which I escaped, flinging this cloak to hide the ravages to my skirt."
> (CSF 140)

Despite its subject matter, this is a narrative of external action rather than interiority or emotion: its emphasis on the material relics of romance, the vellum book, velvet skull-cap and furred slippers, calls to mind the contemporary audience's preoccupation with coat buttons. The juxtaposition of swashbuckling adventure with such banal concerns works in ironic opposition to the repeated refrain of Dryden's poem, "What passion cannot Music raise and quell!" (ll. 16, 24). In "The String Quartet," Woolf affectionately parodies the obsolete trappings of both narrative and social conventions, making the romance of aristocracy into nothing more than a daydream of the past.

In its self-conscious layering of these different levels of experience, therefore, "The String Quartet" must be read as considerably more than an impressionistic imitation of musical form. While its evocation of the world of interiority responds directly to the movement of the music, the story is also concerned with the social world in which the concert takes place. In representing the interplay between these worlds, Woolf does not simply shift her focus from outer to inner realities; rather, the extreme stream-of-consciousness style of "The String Quartet" not only moves between these two worlds but also collapses them into each other.[16] As the music draws to a close, distinctions between the two worlds remain blurred: "Back then I fall, eager no more, desiring only to go, find the street, mark the buildings" (CSF 141). This sentence is at once inside and outside the music: part of the imagined narrative the listener constructs as the music plays, it is also her self-conscious reaction to the moment the music ceases. The idea of "falling back" from music suggests music's momentary effect of the suspension of time, as well as the spatial movement of reluctant reentry into the social world. In a diary entry during this period, Woolf discusses Oliver Strachey's attitude to music: "She disapproves of abstract questions in a world where there are so many concrete ones [. . .] A strange life – to believe in that division between reality and unreality" (D2: 81). Music's simultaneous communal and individual nature offered Woolf an ideal point of departure in her exploration of the overlapping categories of "reality" and "unreality."

In a paragraph of "The String Quartet" subsequently deleted from a January 1921 draft, Woolf explicitly discusses music's paradoxical power to move between "reality and "unreality," bypassing social concerns and creating the momentary illusion of community:

> I draw on my gloves with a sense of drawing on my body. There's very little to be said after a slow movement by Mozart. Together we've been under; together when the last ripple laps to smoothness, wake up, remember, and greet each other. – But I don't know. It's simpler than that; more entire; more intense. Oh much more intense! Aren't all the nerves still thrilling as if the bow had played on them? Isn't one half out of body and mind, beckoned still to release, dance free, caught when the music stops, far from home? But there's only one movement more, so for Heaven's sake look at everything, faces, furniture, pictures on the wall, look through the chink in the curtain and see the branch in the lamp light. Collect every fragment in this lovely and exciting universe. Listen; communicate. (CSF 301)

The audience has undergone a shared experience of interiority, figured as the semiconscious workings of a dream. The listeners "wake up" after having "been under": music enacts a collective anesthesia, a trancelike sleep beneath the smooth surface of consciousness. As the narrator puts on her gloves, she feels she is "drawing on [her] body," reemphasizing somatic experience and thereby redrawing the boundaries of her social self. This is a necessary effort, given her feeling of being outside herself: the mind, not the body, dances "far from home" in the imaginative space of the music. Despite her claim that such music leaves "very little to be said," the narrator cannot resist an extensive – if silent – apostrophe to the other listeners. Echoing the list of imperatives opening the music, she urges her fellow audience members to pay attention to their impressions as they occur, to create moments of being. The closing words stress that listening itself, as a catalyst for the imagination, contains the potential for communication.

In the published version of "The String Quartet," the concert is followed by a mere two lines of dialogue, set apart from the body of the story: "'Good night, good night. You go this way?'/ 'Alas. I go that.'" (CSF 141). This brief final exchange – like *Night and Day*'s ending, a doorstep farewell – emphasizes the listener's wish to preserve her individual experience, setting herself apart from the group with her solitary movement. By choosing not to spell out the listener's experience, and leaving the narrative fragmentary, Woolf puts her reader in the position of the listener, who must "collect every fragment" in order to follow the story. Just as the listening mind shapes images and impressions and constructs threads of narrative, the reader must respond associatively to the style of "The String Quartet" in order to shape an individual version of the story. Listening thus becomes an analogy for both writing and reading as creative narrative processes.

As well as echoing the scenes of musical performance in both *The Voyage Out* and *Night and Day*, this story anticipates memorable scenes of listening in later works, such as Rhoda in *The Waves* or the pageant in *Between the Acts*. In tracing the development of Woolf's interest in music through her early fiction, we can see a marked shift of focus from the performance of music to its reception. This emphasis on the listening individual suggests that the creative power resides in the activity of listening rather than the recital of music. "The String Quartet" can thus be seen as the culmination of Woolf's changing deployment of the idea of music. In *The Voyage Out*, music is the subject matter for explicit social critique: initially suggesting the possibility of autonomous life, it is repeatedly cast into patterns of restricted mobility. In *Night and Day*, music is at once both tired social ritual and suggestive descriptive analogy: musical scenes emphasize the power of such normative patterns, yet listening to music is employed as a key simile for the free associative process of thought. "The String Quartet" expands on the metaphorical connections outlined in both novels, drawing on music's double nature in order to play with the convergences and contrasts between external action and interior thought. Simultaneously solitary and social, music plays an important part in Woolf's experimentation with narrative techniques for representing interiority and offers her new capabilities for language as an artistic medium.

NOTES

1. As Gillespie notes, this was a somewhat disingenuous tactic (1).

2. Hussey argues that after *The Voyage Out*, Woolf shifts her focus "from music to the literary canon" (68).

3. For analysis of the novel's deployment of triple structures of plot and narrative, see Marcus.

4. As Faulk points out, depictions of the music hall as oppositional were a common literary trope, but anachronistic, as the music hall was increasingly frequented by middle-class audiences (Booth 11); note that the decision to go is made by Ralph and William "taking counsel fraternally over an evening paper" (439).

5. Woolf relies on a well-known Romantic topos; see Coleridge's "Eolian Harp," for example.

6. In *Virginia Woolf and the Languages of Patriarchy*, Marcus reads this as a feminist reworking of the sacred flame of Sarastro's temple in *The Magic Flute* (29).

7. Unhearable music is another Romantic topos; see, for example, Keats's "Ode on a Grecian Urn."

8. Woolf develops this idea further in "Street Haunting" (1927) (E4: 480–91). See Bowlby, esp. "Women, Walking, and Writing"; Nord; and Squier.

9. Marcus (*Languages* 60) draws parallels with Ralph Vaughan Williams's "London Symphony," an auditory tour of the city that stresses the emotional effects of place.

10. The novel is criticized for its rigid adherence to nineteenth-century realism and social comedy. E. M. Forster called it "an exercise in classical realism" (241), and Katherine Mansfield found it oddly old-fashioned, "as if World War One never happened" (82). Briggs calls it "the most consistently neglected of Woolf's novels" (xii), noting Woolf's own dismissal of it as a therapeutic exercise in convention for its own sake. Most readings locate what

little critical interest the novel offers in questions of political content, placing it in direct contrast to the more experimental short stories of the same period.

11. As Briggs points out, "Woolf endows it with that self-consciousness peculiar to Shakespearian comedy or Mozart opera, so that the comic unwinding draws attention to its own artifice" (xviii).

12. For more detailed discussion of Pater's influence on Woolf, see Meisel.

13. Wolf judges it as an example of "musico-literary intermediality"; Fleishman calls it "an exercise in form per se" (66); Jacobs identifies a "straightforward bithematic A-B-A-B-A-B-A scheme" (244); Crapoulet argues that Schubert's "Trout" Quintet, rather than Mozart, is the "real piece behind the story" (207–208).

14. Cuddy-Keane points out that wireless technology later let Woolf avoid "'music mixed with peerage' [L6: 301]" (76).

15. See "Impressions at Bayreuth," where the audience members seek to "disburden" themselves of music's impressions in the intervals (E1: 289), as well as *Between the Acts*.

16. For more on stream-of-consciousness style, see Bowlby (7); Snaith (87).

WORKS CITED

Booth, Michael. *Theatre in the Victorian Age*. Cambridge: Cambridge University Press, 1991. Print.

Bowlby, Rachel. *Feminist Destinations and Further Essays on Virginia Woolf*. Edinburgh: Edinburgh University Press, 1997. Print.

Briggs, Julia. "Introduction." *Night and Day* by Virginia Woolf. Harmondsworth: Penguin, 1992. xxxvi–xxxviii. Print.

Clements, Patricia, and Isobel Grundy, eds. *Virginia Woolf: New Critical Essays*. Totowa: Barnes & Noble, 1983. Print.

Crapoulet, Emilie. "Beyond the Boundaries of Language: Music in Virginia Woolf's 'The String Quartet.'" *Journal of the Short Story in English* 50 (2008): 201–15. Print.

Cuddy-Keane, Melba. "Virginia Woolf, Sound Technologies, and the New Aurality." *Virginia Woolf in the Age of Mechanical Reproduction*. Ed. Pamela Caughie. New York: Garland, 2000. 69–96. Print.

Davenport, Tony. "The Life of Monday or Tuesday." Clements and Grundy 157–75. Print.

Dick, Susan. "The Tunnelling Process: Some Aspects of Virginia Woolf's Use of Memory and the Past." Clements and Grundy 176–99. Print.

Dryden, John. "A Song for St. Cecilia's Day." *The Norton Anthology of Poetry*. 4th ed. Ed. Margaret Ferguson, Mary Jo Salter, Jon Stallworthy. New York: Norton, 1997. 287–88. Print.

Faulk, Barry J. *Music Hall and Modernity: The Late-Victorian Discovery of Popular Culture*. Athens: Ohio University Press, 2004. Print.

Fleishman, Avrom. "Forms of the Woolfian Short Story." Freedman 44–70.

Freedman, Ralph, ed. *Virginia Woolf: Revaluation and Continuity*. Berkeley: University of California Press, 1980. Print.

Gillespie, Diane Filby. *The Multiple Muses of Virginia Woolf*. Columbia: University of Missouri Press, 1993. Print.

Hussey, Mark. *The Singing of the Real World: The Philosophy of Virginia Woolf's Fiction*. Columbus: Ohio State University Press, 1986. Print.

Jacobs, Peter. "'The Second Violin Tuning in the Ante-Room': Virginia Woolf and Music." Gillespie 227–60. Print.

Majumdar, Robin, and Allen McLaurin. *Virginia Woolf: The Critical Heritage*. London: Routledge, 1975. Print.

Marcus, Jane, ed. *Virginia Woolf: A Feminist Slant*. Lincoln: University of Nebraska Press, 1993. Print.

———, ed. *Virginia Woolf and the Languages of Patriarchy*. Bloomington: Indiana University Press, 1987. Print.

Meisel, Perry. *The Absent Father: Virginia Woolf and Walter Pater*. New Haven: Yale University Press, 1980. Print.

Nord, Deborah Epstein. *Walking the Victorian Streets: Women, Representation, and the City*. Ithaca: Cornell University Press, 1995. Print.

Pater, Walter. *The Renaissance: Studies in Art and Poetry. Walter Pater: Three Major Texts.* 1873. Ed. William E. Buckler. New York: New York University Press, 1986. 69–220. Print.

Snaith, Anna. *Virginia Woolf: Public and Private Negotiations*. Basingstoke: Palgrave, 2000. Print.

Squier, Susan Merrill. *Virginia Woolf and London: The Sexual Politics of the City*. Chapel Hill: University of North Carolina Press, 1985. Print.

Wolf, Werner. *The Musicalization of Fiction: A Study in the Theory and History of Intermediality*. Amsterdam: Rodopi, 1999. Print.

Woolf, Virginia. *The Complete Shorter Fiction of Virginia Woolf*. Ed. Susan Dick. San Diego: Harcourt, 1985. Print.

———. *The Diary of Virginia Woolf*. 5 vols. Ed. Anne Olivier Bell. New York: Harcourt, 1977–1984. Print.

———. *The Essays of Virginia Woolf*. 4 vols. Ed. Andrew McNeillie. London: Hogarth, 1986–1994. Print.

———. *The Letters of Virginia Woolf*. Ed. Nigel Nicolson and Joanne Trautmann. 6 vols. London: Hogarth, 1975–1980. Print.

———. 1919. *Night and Day*. London: Vintage, 2000. Print.

———. *A Passionate Apprentice: The Early Journals, 1897–1909*. Ed. Mitchell A. Leaska. London: Hogarth, 1990. Print.

There is nothing about which Wagner has thought more deeply than redemption: his opera is the opera of redemption. Somebody or other always wants to be redeemed in his work: sometimes a little male, sometimes a little female – this is *his* problem. – and how richly he varies his leitmotif! What rare, what profound dodges! Who if not Wagner would teach us that innocence prefers to redeem interesting sinners? (The case in *Tannhäuser*.) Or that even the Wandering Jew is redeemed, settles down, when he marries? (The case in *The Flying Dutchman*.) we stop our ears to music [...] ?

FRIEDRICH NIETZSCHE,
The Case of Wagner (Nietzsche's emphasis)

SIX

Flying Dutchmen, Wandering Jews

ROMANTIC OPERA, ANTI-SEMITISM, AND
JEWISH MOURNING IN *MRS. DALLOWAY*

Emma Sutton

IN APRIL 1921 VIRGINIA WOOLF MADE THE FOLLOWING ENTRY in her diary: "L.[eonard] explained the plan of his new book – a revised version of the Wandering Jew. Very original & solid, it seemed to me; & like a good business man, I pressed him to promise it for the press [...] a solid big book like L.'s is essential" (D2: 111–12). Woolf's admiration for the "originality" of Leonard's "essential" book leaves unspoken the fact that Leonard was not alone in planning a work on the Wandering Jew in the early 1920s; *Mrs. Dalloway* might equally be described as a "revised version" of this legend. Woolf's novel is haunted by Richard Wagner's Romantic opera *Der fliegende Holländer* (1843), and, as Wagner's description of his protagonist as "this Ahasuerus of the seas" reminds us, the figure of the Flying Dutchman was frequently equated with the Wandering Jew, his fate read as an allegory of Jewish "redemption" (*Prose Works* 1: 17).[1] It will come as no surprise to scholars of Woolf and music that Woolf's fiction should be informed by a Wagnerian intertext, although Wagner's influence on *Mrs. Dalloway* is far less conspicuous than on *The Voyage Out, Jacob's Room, The Years,* or *The Waves,* for instance. In these texts Woolf's diegetic allusions to, and the formal influence of, Wagner are extensive and more explicit.[2] *Mrs. Dalloway* has played a relatively small part in analyses of Woolf and music to date;[3] its debt to Wagner's opera is opaque and its references to music relatively few, but Woolf's commanding knowledge of Wagner's oeuvre and her lifelong engagement with it in her fiction invite us to consider the discreet parallels between the texts seriously. Wagner's version of the legend was one Woolf had ample opportunity to hear, and the Woolfs' record collection later included a recording of excerpts of the opera.[4] In the third volume of his autobiography, Leonard made the qualified observation that there was "more, perhaps, to be said for the early Wagner" than *Der Ring* (BA 50). *Mrs. Dalloway*'s intertextuality with Wagner's opera places the novel in a matrix of discourses about music and Jews that includes this specific text representing the archetypal "Jew" "redeemed" by woman's love, Wagner's other operatic representations of Jews and Jewishness, and his published essays and private comments on Jews and music. It also inevitably engages other anti- and philo-Semitic discourses about music in the nineteenth and early twentieth centuries, from fiction and poetry to popular caricature, racial theory, and academic musicology. This essay introduces Woolf's responses to discourses about Jews and music through a twofold focus. First, it traces the relationship between *Mrs. Dalloway* and *Der fliegende Holländer*, exploring the significance of Wagner's opera to Woolf's novel. In doing so, it proposes that Woolf's postwar interest in Wagner's text crystallized around the figure of the displaced wanderer and the sexual politics of female self-sacrifice that are essential to this Wagnerian model of tragedy. Second, it considers the role and representation of Jewish individuals and religious practice in the novel. It suggests that *Mrs. Dalloway*'s intertextuality with Wagner's opera is juxtaposed with its representations of displaced Jews in pre- and postwar England and with the novel's extensive debts to Jewish mourning practice, shivah.[5] As Leena Kore Schröder acknowledges, there "can be no straightforward account" of Woolf's attitudes toward Jews and Jewishness (298); we have, collectively, been rightly attentive to Woolf's anti-Semitism and that of her contemporaries, but this attention has arguably discouraged consideration of the possibility that such negative views of Jews coexisted with more sympathetic, informed, and creative responses to Judaism. Without wishing to act as an apologist for Woolf, I hope that this analysis of her knowledge and fictional use of Jewish theology might encourage further consideration of this underexplored subject.

FROM ROMANTIC OPERA TO MODERNIST NOVEL

First, a brief summary of Wagner's plot: The opera traces the fate of the Flying Dutchman, condemned by the devil to sail the world eternally unless redeemed by the love of a faithful woman. Permitted to land ashore every seven years to seek this devotee, the Dutchman travels with his ghostly ship and crew. The opera begins with a Norwegian sailor, Daland, sheltering from a storm in a cove near his home. Shortly afterward the Dutchman lands and Daland goes ashore to question him. The Dutchman offers Daland gold and jewels if he will allow him to visit his home and meet his only daughter, Senta; Daland agrees, presenting Senta as an ideal wife. In the second act, Senta is at her father's house, where her female sewing companions tease her for her preoccupation with a portrait of a man (the Dutchman). She sings a ballad about the legend of the Dutchman, addressed to the painting, proclaiming that she will save him. Erik, a young hunter, enters and restrains Senta, reiterating his love for her. Appalled by Senta's devotion to the Dutchman, he leaves, and her father and the Dutchman arrive at the house. Senta recognizes the Dutchman and pledges to redeem him through her unqualified love; their marriage is settled. The third act begins with the Norwegian sailors' song; they invite the Dutch crew to join their drinking but then taunt the silent crew. A storm arises and the Dutch crew sing an uncanny song, terrifying the Norwegians. At Daland's house, Erik rebukes Senta for encouraging his love; overhearing them, the Dutchman believes that Senta has broken her pledge and tells her of the curse that afflicts women who reneged on their promises to him. He leaves on his ship and Senta climbs on a rock on the shore, declaring her absolute love for him before jumping into the sea. The opera ends with a vision of the transfigured Dutchman and Senta ascending to heaven.

Throughout the novel, Peter Walsh is repeatedly associated with the Dutchman, the displaced eternal wanderer, and Clarissa with Senta. Clarissa reflects that her intimacy with Peter endures though "they might be parted for hundreds of years" (MD 7), and the morning Peter appears unexpectedly in Clarissa's drawing room, she "stopped to look at a Dutch picture" (10) in Bond Street, echoing Senta's "conjuration" of the Dutchman through her singing and absorption in the portrait (Dalhaus 15). Immediately before Peter rings the bell, Woolf writes, "Fear no more, says the heart, committing its burden to some sea" (MD 39). Peter's role as a traveler and sea voyager is reiterated: he married "the girl on the boat going out to India" (45) and has just sailed back from India. His initial impression of Clarissa is that "here she's been sitting all the time I've been in India; mending her dress," like Senta spinning (40). Later, as he dozes in the park next to the "spectral presence" of the nurse, his dreams are those of a "solitary traveller" (55–57); the phrase is repeated five times in this passage. Peter's status as an outsider is emphasized – his youthful socialism, his residence in India, his erratic career ("he had never done a thing that they talked of; his whole life had been a failure" [8]), and his domestic relations repeatedly invoked as evidence of his marginal position in the Establishment. Indeed, his surname, Walsh, itself suggests the archetypally "foreign," as did "Welsh" in Old English. My point is not to suggest that he is Jewish, but that Peter the traveler shares something of the exiled, displaced position figuratively exemplified by the Wandering Jew and by the actual experience of many (exiled) Jews in early twentieth-century Europe. Here we might recall Schröder's proposal, following Hannah Arendt and Zygmunt Bauman, that the "threat" represented by Jews "is not that of the foreigner or the outsider as the discrete Other but rather [...] the foreigner and the outsider as already *within*, implicated in the foundations of identity" (Schröder 300; emphasis in original). Woolf draws attention to the way in which Peter's politics, gender identity, and social status are marginalized by patriarchs such as Richard Dalloway. His marginalization is one means by which Woolf critiques the national, racial, gender, and class prejudices dominating postwar English society and through which English identity is constructed and regulated.

Peter is not the only character who is perceived as or imagines himself as a traveler, however. The frequency with which this image recurs in the novel suggests that Woolf – like Joyce and Eliot – found the image of the Wandering Jew an apposite one for postwar experience more widely. The early pages of the novel stress the pervasive sense of displacement and isolation – of Clarissa, who has "a perpetual sense [...] of being out, out, far out to sea and alone" (*MD* 8); of Septimus, "the scapegoat" who suffers "eternal loneliness" (25); of Rezia, who longs for her sisters in Milan, crying, "I am alone" (23); and even of minor characters like the Scot Maisie Johnson, who asks, "Why hadn't she stayed at home?" (26). (Carrie Dempster, on the other hand, longs to travel and recalls "always" going "on the sea at Margate" [27]). Like the opera, the novel alludes to real and uncanny voyages: Septimus and Clarissa are linked by their repeated identification with lonely travelers and by their sense of temporal displacement, as if they, like the Dutchman and his ghostly crew, have been wandering for generations and are neither alive nor dead. Clarissa feels "very young; at the same time unspeakably aged" (8), and Peter recalls her youthful fondness for "nautical metaphors" – "we are a doomed race, chained to a sinking ship" (76). As Septimus hears music in Regent's Park, he hallucinates, feeling "high on his rock, like a drowned sailor on a rock" who has "been dead, and yet [is] now alive" (67). The cacophonous mix of car horns, anthems, elegies, piping, and penny whistles "cannon[ing] from rock to rock" (67) may recall the contrasting songs of the Norwegian and the ghostly crews in act 3, scene 1 of the opera, in which the boisterous jeers of the Norwegians are eventually answered by the uncanny sounds of the dead crew. And it may recall too Wagner's own flight from Riga in 1839 and his stormy journey through the Norwegian fjords – the journey he claimed as the inspiration for *Der fliegende Holländer* (*Prose Works* 1: 13–14, 17). Septimus again imagines himself as "some colossal figure who has lamented the fate of man for ages in the desert alone" (MD 68), reflecting later that "even Holmes himself could not touch this last relic straying on the edge of the world, this outcast, who gazed back at the inhabited regions, who lay, like a drowned sailor, on the shore of the world" (90). This biblical, fatalistic vocabulary suggestive of a curse is echoed when Septimus reflects that "to be alone forever" was the "doom pronounced in Milan" (142). The permanently displaced, paradigmatically isolated figure of the Flying Dutchman or Wandering Jew reflects, it seems, the postwar psyche of many characters. Woolf's interest in Wagner's mid-nineteenth-century text, like Eliot's in Ahasuerus,[6] surely springs from recognition of the contemporary resonance of the displaced wanderer.

The other aspect of the opera by which the novel is most obviously shaped is Senta's suicide, reworked through Septimus's own jump to his death. Septimus's awareness of the theatrical quality of his action is emphasized immediately before he jumps: he reflects that "the tiresome, the troublesome, and rather melodramatic business of opening the window and throwing himself out" was "their idea of tragedy, not his or Rezia's [...] Holmes and Bradshaw liked that sort of thing" (MD

145–46). The allusions to melodrama and the doctors' idea of tragedy underscore Septimus's recognition of the performative, artificial elements of his method of suicide; they recall the "melodramatic gesture which he assumed mechanically and with complete consciousness of its insincerity" when Septimus "dropped his head on his hands" and allowed Dr. Holmes to be called (88). Implicitly, these theatrical allusions critique the Wagnerian model of tragedy to which Septimus's suicide responds. They juxtapose a Romantic operatic model of tragedy with Woolf's modernist representation of this event[7] – and, I shall argue, with Judaic mourning practice.

The critique of Wagner implicit in Septimus's references to melodrama is amplified by Woolf's extensive use of theatrical terms to describe emotional insincerity and "sentimentality" throughout the novel. Reflecting on their time at Bourton, Peter recalls the "absurd" "terrible scenes" that occurred between him and Clarissa before "[t]he final scene, the terrible scene" in which she rejected him (62). The young Sally Seton has a "melodramatic love of being the centre of everything and creating scenes," which Clarissa fears will lead to her "death" or "martyrdom" or "some awful tragedy" (177). Clarissa's apprehensions of this Wagnerian end are parodied when we see the mature Sally, pillar of the Establishment, who fears that Peter will think her "sentimental" if she describes her youthful feelings for Clarissa (187). "Sentimental" is a resonant term in the novel: Mr. Bowley's knee-jerk patriotism is parodied when he is "inappropriately, sentimentally" moved by thoughts of poor women and the war (19); Clarissa reflects (four times in one paragraph) that Peter repeatedly accused her of being "sentimental" (35); after meeting, Peter concludes that she has become "a trifle sentimental" (48); he describes his own pride in his family history as a "strange" "sentiment" (54); and Lady Bruton's eugenicist emigration plans are edited into "sentiments in alphabetical order of the highest nobility" (107). Woolf's vocabulary associates sentimentality with nationalism, imperialism, and family pride and also registers the term's derogatory application to women's emotions and experience. Her use of the term, that is, suggests affinities between the "superficial emotion" prompted by certain types of (music) drama and by glib political rhetoric.[8] The allusions to melodrama and sentiment implicitly undercut overly affecting, emotionally trite art works, of which *Der fliegende Holländer* may have seemed to Woolf, as it did to Nietzsche, a representative example. In *Der Fall Wagner*, the opera is a keystone of Nietzsche's attack on Wagner's aesthetics, gender politics, and commercialism: Nietzsche champions Bizet's "polite[ness]," "light[ness]," and "supple[ness]" over Wagner's "*lie* of the great style." Whether or not Woolf was recalling Nietzsche's vilification of the "Senta-sentimentality" of the opera, her use of the term suggests similar aesthetic concerns – and in 1913 it was the "bawling sentimentality" of *Der Ring* that repulsed her (L2: 26).⁹ As Steve Ellis notes, "sentimentality" was a crucial term in Woolf's assessment of the Victorians and in her own ambivalent relation to modern(ist) aesthetics (7–8, 81). The theatrical vocabulary used throughout the novel, and of Septimus's suicide in particular, thus critiques Wagner's opera; like Joyce's numerous allusions to the Flying Dutchman in *Dubliners, Portrait, Ulysses, Exiles,* and *Finnegan's Wake,* Woolf's novel illustrates her growing skepticism about the "Romantic archetype" of artists and heroism fundamental to this model of tragedy.¹⁰

Woolf's text also, of course, responds to the gender politics of "sentimental" Wagnerian tragedy. In the opera, Senta's suicide exemplifies her own and woman's capacity for unqualified, redemptive love. Senta is an "angel," "a path to salvation," moved by the Dutchman's "need" and by "obedience" to her father. She describes her love as "woman's sacred duty," concluding the ballad with reflections on the "glory" that will be hers by saving the Dutchman (Wagner, *Flying Dutchman* 61, 109, 161–62, 166, and 112). As Pearl Cleveland Wilson put it in her 1919 study *Wagner's Dramas and Greek Tragedy:* "Not the assertion, but the forgetting of self, not the arbitrary rule, but the voluntary service of others – these are the ideals Wagner's dramas uphold. It is not the defiant will of the Flying Dutchman, but the compassion of Senta that we are led to admire" (8). Carl Dalhaus's proposal that Wagner's opera is a "martyr play" rather than a tragedy similarly emphasizes the centrality of (female) self-sacrifice to the opera (12). Woolf's reworking effaces the notion of self-sacrifice, making Septimus's death an act of affirmation, as Clarissa recognizes (MD 180). Woolf also reverses the gender roles: Septimus takes on the role that is gendered feminine in the opera while his female counterpart, Clarissa, survives. The opera's sexual politics are undercut, too, by Peter's recurrent fantasies of female devotion; like the Dutchman, he idealizes woman's love yet is "always in love with the wrong woman" (119). As he dozes, his "visions" of "womanhood" comprise a catalog of love objects and devoted matrons: "sirens lolloping away on the green sea waves"; a "figure" who will "shower down from her magnificent hands compassion, comprehension, absolution"; "the figure of the mother whose sons have been killed in the battles of the world"; "women [who] stand knitting," and the "landlady" (56–57). Peter's reflections on women's "faithfulness and audacity and greatness in loving which though it had its drawbacks seemed to him [...] so wholly admirable" expose his possessiveness and the transferability of the emotion: he would "tire very easily of mute devotion and [...] want variety in love, though it would make him furious if Daisy loved anybody else" (155). The sexual politics of Wagner's plot are resisted once again when Clarissa reflects on her marriage during the reunion with Peter; the images of mortality, sea voyages, and theater again invoke *Der fliegende Holländer:*

> If I had married [Peter], this gaiety would have been mine all day!
> It was all over for her [...] Lunching with Lady Bruton, it came back to her. [Richard] has left me; I am alone for ever, she thought [...]
> Take me with you, Clarissa thought impulsively, as if he were starting directly upon some great voyage; and then, next moment, it was as if the five acts of a play that had been very exciting and moving were now over and she had lived a lifetime in them and had run away, had lived with Peter, and it was now over.
> Now it was time to move, and, as a woman gathers her things together, her cloak, her gloves, her opera-glasses, and gets up to go out of the theatre into the street, she rose from the sofa and went to Peter. (MD 46)

Clarissa, it seems, momentarily puts herself in the role of Senta at the end of the opera, tempted to follow Peter/the Dutchman at any cost; instead, she draws back from the theatrical intensity, remaining instead with the conventional lover Richard/Erik. Once again, Wagner's "very exciting and moving" work is undercut, the Romantic plot bathetically countered by one determined by social caution and respectability. Woolf's use of the Flying Dutchman legend to reject the sexual politics of Wagner's text recalls instead texts such as Heine's 1834 *Memoiren des Herrn von Schnabelewopski* (Wagner's principal source), which ironizes the ideal of female love by juxtaposing the narrative of "Mrs. Flying Dutchman" with that of "a Dutch Messalina" (Dalhaus 7–8).

"JUDAISM IN MUSIC" AND MUSICAL JEWS

Sexual and ethnic politics are inextricable in *Der fliegende Holländer*: Senta's suicide simultaneously "redeems" the Flying Dutchman and the Jews. Wagner was unequivocal on this point, repeatedly comparing the Dutchman to Ahasuerus, the Jew of medieval legend condemned to perpetual wandering after taunting Christ on the way to Calvary. In *Eine Mittheilung an meine Freunde* (1851), for instance, Wagner described the Dutchman as "a remarkable mixture" of Ulysses and the Wandering Jew, while the last paragraph of *Das Judentum in der Musik* (1850), inviting Ludwig Börne to seek "redemption" by relinquishing his identity as a Jew, also explicitly identifies the legend of the Dutchman with that of Ahasuerus: "one only thing can redeem you from the burden of your curse: the redemption of Ahasuerus – *Going under!*" (Wagner, Prose Works 1: 307 and 3: 100; emphasis in original). Wagner's examples are among many anti- and philo-Semitic narratives that, from the mid-nineteenth century, associated Ahasuerus with "the fate of the Jewish people" (Borchmeyer 175). Whether or not Woolf had read these essays, she would undoubtedly have been familiar with the anti-Semitic arguments of a text as notorious as *Das Judentum in der Musik*; furthermore, she had repeatedly (sometimes with Leonard) seen *Die Meistersinger* and *Der Ring*, controversial even during Wagner's lifetime for their caricatures of stereotypically Jewish voices, physiognomy and character traits.[11] Woolf's familiarity with fictional and other discourses about Jews and music ranged from Eliot's sympathetic portraits of Jewish musicians in *Daniel Deronda* (which Woolf was reading in 1919) to du Maurier's *Trilby*, with its overdetermined caricature of the conductor and impresario Svengali, the "Oriental Isrealite Hebrew Jew" (du Maurier 194).[12]

Woolf's own remarks about Jewish musicians reflect a spectrum of contemporary opinions and stereotypes, liberal and derogatory, from perceptions of the "innate" musicality of Jews to their association with vulgar, commercial music making. In letters of 1909 she notes her "happy recollections" – but also the numerous "boots" and "objects" – of the "sumptuous" Jewess Miss Schreiner, who played Brahms or Schumann (L1: 394, 412). In another letter of the same year she again associates Jewish women with music (opera, this time) and ostentatious fashionable dressing – "There is a Jewess who spends 50 guineas on a hat" (L1: 398); and she notes the important collection of operatic photographs compiled by "that furtive Jew," "the great" Sydney J. Loeb (L1: 398, D3: 26).[13] Her diaries and letters include a number of observations on the musical accomplishments of Leonard's family in which admiration is tempered by distaste and unease. In 1915 she lists singing among the accomplishments of his youngest sister, Flora, for whom "there is something to be said" though she dislikes "the Jewish voice" and "the Jewish laugh" (D1: 6); in 1916 she describes Leonard as "a strict Jew as a small boy, and he can still sing in Hebrew" (L2: 85); and in 1928 his mother Marie's ignorance of *Scheherazade* and her recollections of the Schubert songs she received as a wedding present form a barbed account of Jewish music making (L3: 524–25). We can only speculate on the degree to which Woolf's attention to her relatives' musical skills intersected with her interest in the Flying Dutchman: Leonard's maternal grandparents were Dutch Jews who came to London in the 1860s; his mother's first husband was "such a charming man, a Dutchman" (S 16; L3: 525); and in his autobiography Leonard described his ancient "Semitic ancestors" in imagery strikingly reminiscent of the Wandering Jew – they were "already prisoners of war, displaced persons, refugees, having begun that unending pilgrimage as the world's official fugitives and scapegoats" (S 13). Similarly, in his autobiographical *The Wise Virgins* (1914), Harry Davis calls himself "the wandering Jew, the everlasting Jew" (L. Woolf, *Wise Virgins* 223). And in a 1930 letter written after a visit to her mother in law "aged 80," Woolf follows her recognition of her own "snob[bish]" dislike of marrying a Jew and her perception of the Jews' "immense vitality," a "quality" "I think I like [. . .] best of all," with images linking them to Ahasuerus or the Dutchman, cursed to eternal life: "They cant die – they exist on a handful of rice and a thimble of water – their flesh dries on their bones but still they pullulate, copulate, and amass" (L4: 195–96). Even as she acknowledges her own prejudice Woolf's vocabulary evokes, with revulsion as well as something closer to admiration and awe, the image of the Dutchman.

There are no explicit references to Jewish individuals or Judaism in *Mrs. Dalloway*, but Woolf, I would suggest, invites us to consider the possibility that at least two displaced characters in the novel – Joseph Breitkopf and Miss Kilman – may be Jewish. Clarissa recalls (as does Peter [*MD* 150] and Clarissa again [*MD* 177–78]) that Joseph Breitkopf "came every summer, poor old man, for weeks and weeks, and pretended to read German with her, but really played the piano and sang Brahms without any voice" (34). Presumably, he visits Bourton to act as a language tutor; we can conclude that he is a native German speaker, but must ask why he is repeatedly described as a "poor old man." Clarissa's vocabulary invites the speculation that Breitkopf has experienced, or is fleeing, the widespread continental European anti-Semitic persecution and legislation of the 1880s and 1890s, such as the Dreyfuss case of 1894 and the explosion of Russian and Eastern European anti-Semitism between 1881 and the war. Estimates place the number of displaced Jews in this period at 250,000, and between 1883 and 1905 the Jewish population in London grew to 150,000.[14] Is Joseph Breitkopf an annual exile from continental anti-Semitism, a figure to whom Clarissa's family offer refuge despite his limitations as a tutor? "Joseph" is, of course, a common Jewish forename and Miss Kilman's name, too, invites further consideration, since through her textual presence Woolf records the widespread British xenophobia, and perhaps more explicitly British anti-Semitism, around the war. We are told that she is of German descent (her family "spelt the name Kiehlman in the eighteenth century") and that British prejudice against the Germans "when the war came" led to her dismissal from her teaching job (120). But "Kiehlman" resembles a German transliteration of a Russian (Jewish?) name rather than an ethnic German name, and we are told that she "would do anything for the Russians, starved herself for the Austrians" (11). Miss Kilman's national and political sympathies obviously spring from her awareness of hardship in these regions during the Russian civil war and after the war, but they may also recall the particular plight of Jews in these areas.[15] The Woolfs' awareness of the persecution of Russian Jews at the time they were planning and working on their respective "versions" of the Wandering Jew was sharpened by their friendship, which Leonard dated from about 1920, with the Russian Jewish translator S. S. Koteliansky. In *Beginning Again*, Leonard alluded to the contemporary rise of pogroms – "[a]fter 1914 families like the Kotelianskys were ruthlessly wiped off the face of the earth" – and noted that the Kotelianskys' home, a ghetto village in the Ukraine, had suffered "more than three conquests," including fighting between the Austrians and the Russians. He described "Kot" as an archetypal, ageless representative of the Jews; he resembled "a major Hebrew prophet" of three thousand years ago who, "though [his] ancestors have lived for centuries in European ghettos, [was] born with certain characteristics which the sun and sand of the desert beat into the bodies and minds of Semites" (BA 248–50). Virginia Woolf, in a different register, also noted the plight of, and the prejudice against, Russian Jews; after attending a private concert in 1919 at which members of the aristocratic British audience expressed the fear that they would be shot by such an individual, she noted, "I almost proclaimed myself a Russian Jew" (L2: 334–35).[16] Both Joseph (who plays and sings Brahms and discusses Wagner with Peter [MD 34–35]) and Miss Kilman (an unskilled amateur violinist [121]) are musicians – details that may draw on Jewish stereotypes, although susceptibility to music is also a trait shared noticeably by Septimus and Clarissa, arguably intended as a textual device conveying their sympathetic affinity with others. If we conclude that Joseph and Miss Kilman may be Jewish or of Jewish descent, then Woolf's critique of the Wagnerian intertext is augmented: the novel responds to Wagner's representation of the archetypal Wandering Jew with reminders of the displacement of thousands of contemporary Jews as a result of real, historically specific anti-Semitism in continental Europe and in doing so resists the opera's ideology of "redemption" and conversion.[17]

THE JEWISH WAY IN DEATH AND MOURNING

Woolf's critique of Wagnerian tragedy and her sympathetic portraits of Jews in the novel conjoin in *Mrs. Dalloway*'s extensive allusions to the mourning customs of shivah.[18] These allusions counter Wagner's attacks on what he called in *Das Judentum in der Musik* the Jews' "travesty" of religious music (and, by implication, devotional practice more generally), and they provide a counterpart, too, to the representation of sacrificial death in the opera (*Prose Works* 3: 91). Woolf's most intimate knowledge of Jewish religious and social practices, and of shivah specifically, must have come through Leonard's family. Leonard described his father as a "believing, but not an orthodox, Jew" (S 21); he was a warden in the liberal Reformed synagogue based in Upper Berkeley Street, London, and though the family was liberal to the extent that they marked Jewish and Christian festivals in their observance, Leonard attended synagogue regularly until his teens, learned a "smattering" of Hebrew, and would certainly have learned practices including the mourning customs of shivah (Glendinning 9, 17; S 42). Indeed, in his autobiography, Leonard emphasizes Marie Woolf's reverence for her dead husband and her demanding expectation that her children would also "rever[e] the memory of their deceased father" (S 33). And he recalled, too, the devastating event that would again have exposed him – and Virginia – to shivah: the death of his brother Cecil during the war. Cecil Woolf was killed in action in 1917 by the shell that "severely wounded" his brother Philip, and in 1918 the Hogarth Press published a collection of his poems for private circulation (BA 181; Levenback 29n16). In *Beginning Again,* Leonard wrote: "The war brought tragedy to Cecil and Philip. Occasionally there grows up between brothers a David and Jonathan affection [. . .] they were inseparable." He judged that Philip never fully recovered from his brother's death and that it was partly responsible for his suicide in his seventies (BA 181–83).[19] Whether or not Woolf's portrait of the relationship between Septimus and his deceased officer Evans was shaped by the fraternal devotion of Cecil and Philip, shivah surely informs *Mrs. Dalloway* and its response to Wagner.

The novel repeatedly draws on the customs and language of shivah, using the mourning protocols derived from biblical and rabbinical authority to depict literal and symbolic deaths in the text. "Shivah" (שבעה; "seven") is the term given to the weeklong period of formalized grief and mourning observed by seven categories of relatives (including brothers and spouses) immediately following the burial of the deceased. Mourners manifest their grief by sitting on low stools or the floor – hence the term "sitting shivah" – and by tearing a garment (*keri'ah*): Clarissa's evening dress is torn, and just before Peter enters the house, she begins mending it "sitting down on the sofa" (MD 38). During the seven days of mourning, family members gather and receive visitors who may offer comfort through sharing stories about the deceased.[20] It is possible, then, to read Clarissa's party, for all its differences in tone and purpose, as partly shaped by the protocols of shivah: the occasion is not only a celebration that Clarissa conceives as an act of faith – an "offering" "to life" (118) – but also an episode in which she withdraws into a small room to mourn Septimus's death and in which others, too, discuss the deceased veteran. Rabbinical literature similarly identifies parallels between celebrations and mourning: the length of the principal feasts, Passover and Sukkot, is echoed in that of shivah, recalling Amos 8:10 – "I will turn your feasts into mourning." Furthermore, the *Zohar*, a foundational text in Jewish mysticism (*kaballah*), attributes the length of the mourning period to the belief that "for seven days the soul goes to and fro between the house and the grave, mourning for the body," a belief echoed perhaps in the arrival of Septimus's soul at the party (represented by the billowing curtain and "flight of wings" into the room [*MD* 164, 166]).[21] Certainly, Clarissa's perception that she is mourning a lost if unknown brother – she "felt somehow very like" Septimus (182) – is another instance of the novel's formal and diegetic endorsement of empathy that transcends national, religious, political, and gender differences. The "activity of the novel," as Gillian Beer has observed, supports Clarissa's sense of connection to Septimus (55).

The occurrence of the homophone "shiver" – as non–Hebrew speakers would pronounce it – at two points in the novel is further evidence of Woolf's discreet but informed evocations of Jewish mourning practice.[22] The word first appears when Clarissa learns that Richard is lunching with the eugenicist (anti-Semite?) Lady Bruton and again when Elizabeth hears the band playing "military music" near St. Paul's. The first allusion to shivah evokes a metaphorical, private death; the second calls to mind the real, mass losses of the war. Clarissa reflects: "the shock of Lady Bruton asking Richard to lunch without her made the moment in which she had stood shiver, as a plant on the river-bed feels the shock of a passing oar and shivers: so she rocked: so she shivered" (*MD* 29). The moment elicits Clarissa's fear of "time itself" and of the "dwindling of life"; she feels "suddenly shrivelled, aged, breastless." This acute premonition of mortality marks a metaphorical death of the self, and of the Dalloways' marriage – she compares herself to a "nun," retiring to a "narrower and narrower" bed (29–30), just as marital relations are forbidden for the duration of shivah. Secondly, when Elizabeth hears the trumpets of the "unemployed" penetrating the "uproar" of the city, "as if people were marching; yet they had been dying," the "consolatory" indifference of the music is stressed: "There was no recognition in it of one's fortune, or fate, and for that very reason even for those dazed with watching for the last shivers of consciousness on the faces of the dying, consoling" (135). This reflection is unspecific, generic, alluding to the death of an unnamed woman but also evoking, through the military context, the unnumbered war dead lost on the field, in hospitals and elsewhere. The two episodes referring to "shivers"/shivah use the term to link the domestic and the public, the civilian and combatant experiences of war. The number seven – evoked in Hebrew and Latin (shivah and Septimus) as well as in the seven years punctuating the Dutchman's landings, the seven miles he lands from Senta's home (Wagner, *Flying Dutchman* 19, 30), and shivah's seven days of mourning for the seven categories of relatives – is thus another device through which Woolf integrates the novel's structure and plots.

Finally, the allusions to shivah amplify Woolf's critique of the Wagnerian intertext: the elegiac dignity of shivah evoked at Clarissa's party contrasts sharply, for example, with the "melodramatic" – Wagnerian – moment of Septimus's death. Furthermore, Septimus's musical hallucinations that allude to and function as an elegy for Evans and the war dead more widely not only recall Wagner's ghostly sailors' chorus but also may allude to the prominence of chanted lamentations (*mekonenot; meqonenot*) in Judaic mourning traditions. Was Woolf also mindful of the aural proximity between the opening cry of Wagner's ghostly sailors – "*Hoe! Hoe!*" – and the biblical exclamation of grief ("*ho-ho*" or "*hoi*") employed, for instance, in the books of Amos, I Kings, and Jeremiah (Roth 487)? If so, this knowledge surely undercuts the theatricality of Wagner's sinister chorus – the novel answers Wagner's chilling (melodramatic?) music with the sounds of profound Jewish lamentation. Woolf thus responds to Wagner's opera about the "redemption" of Jews through woman's love with a text that draws on, rather than symbolically expunges, Jewish theology and practice. Her use of shivah to represent Septimus's suicide, the war dead, and the "death" of Clarissa's marriage counters Wagner's Romantic model of tragedy with one derived in part from Judaic mourning. The inevitable conclusion of Wagner's Romantic opera – Senta's death – is critiqued in Woolf's work, as are

Wagner's sexual and ethno-religious politics more widely. *Mrs. Dalloway* is arguably both a response to contemporary anti-Semitic discourse and to Wagner specifically, and to an operatic model of tragedy to which she, like a number of modernist contemporaries, was both indebted and resistant.

NOTES

1. I would like to thank Jocelyn Slovak, who first suggested the relevance of the opera to me in a personal communication on July 16, 2004.

2. See, for example, Blissett; DiGaetani; Furness; Phillips; and Sherard.

3. Exceptions include Slovak; Sutton, "Shell Shock"; and Sutton, *Virginia Woolf and Classical Music*.

4. It was the first of Wagner's operas to be staged in London (in 1870); see Loewenberg. I thank Sussex University Library for permission to consult Leonard Woolf's "Card Index of Gramophone Recordings" (LWP Ad.28). Leonard Woolf reused some cards, presumably as he updated, reclassified, or otherwise altered his collection. The erased holograph entry on the reverse of card 412 lists the following excerpts played by the Royal Philharmonic Orchestra, conducted by Bruno Walter: "Overture," "Senta's Ballad & Spinning Chorus," and "Steersman's Song & Erik's Song."

5. I am very grateful to the discussants at the London Modernism Seminar, May 2008, who first brought the relevance of shivah to my attention.

6. See Julius 71.

7. *Pace* Wagner's rejection of the term "romantic opera" in "A Communication to my Friends," Wagner, *Prose Works*, 1: 306.

8. "Sentimental," 1, OED. For further suggestive uses of this term, see Woolf's *Diary* of 1922, "Am I growing old & sentimental?" (D2: 217); "Sketch of the Past" on Leslie Stephen and sentiment (MB 123); and indeed Harry's statement in *The Wise Virgins* that "the only thing that a Jew is sentimental about is Judaism" (L. Woolf, *Wise Virgins* 127).

9. *The Case of Wagner*, in Nietzsche 158, 157 (Nietzsche's emphasis). I have not been able to establish if Woolf had read this essay by the 1920s, but she appears to have known *Beyond Good and Evil* and *Zarathustra* by the late 1920s or early 1930s; see Woolf, *The Waves* 329, 392–93, 395. Compare with Lara Trubowitz's argument that, for Woolf, anti-Semitism is "a matter of style," a modernist "technique." She proposes that in works including "The Duchess and the Jeweller," Woolf's transformation of "explicit antisemitism" into "genteel stylistic mannerism, a form that I would call civil antisemitism," is an ambivalent response to Victorian aesthetics and social decorum – a modernist validation of stylistic obliquity, suaveness and manners – and also a response to what Woolf perceived as a distinctly Jewish "category of style" (Trubowitz 273–306).

10. Martin 76–77. See also 54–77 and 237n1.

11. Here, I follow Marc A. Weiner, who proposes that the music dramas employ musical and dramatic caricatures of Jews, rather than, say, Borchmeyer, who argues that Wagner's anti-Semitism is largely irrelevant to the dramatic works (184).

12. L2: 321. The first of two essays on *Daniel Deronda* appeared in the *Times*

Literary Supplement on November 20, 1919 (L2: 385n), and the second in the *Daily Herald* in January 1921 (L2: 455). Neither essay comments on Eliot's representation of Jewish musicians, and the latter states of *Daniel Deronda* that Eliot had "lost much of her vigour and directness" (E3: 294). The first essay was reprinted in *The Common Reader* three months before the publication of *Mrs. Dalloway*.

13. For further information on Woolf and Loeb's musical knowledge, see Woolf, *Carlyle's House* 38–45.

14. See Glendinning 10.

15. For an illuminating alternative account of German-Russian relations in the novel, see Froula.

16. See also D1: 245.

17. Miss Kilman is, in fact, a convert to Anglicanism (MD 121) (from what we are not told), but, contra Wagner, Clarissa's numerous hostile reflections on the tyranny of religious faith undercut this act.

18. The heading for this section, "The Jewish Way in Death and Mourning," comes from the title of a monograph by Maurice Lamm.

19. On p. 182 of *Beginning Again* Leonard dates the battle to 1916; cf. p. 197 and LLW 219.

20. For shivah, see Roth 12: 485–92 and Wigoder.

21. Zohar, *Va-Yehi* 226a, quoted in Roth 12: 490.

22. Cf. Kermode on modernist shudders rather than shivers.

WORKS CITED

Beer, Gillian. *Virginia Woolf: The Common Ground*. Edinburgh: Edinburgh University Press, 1996. Print.

Blissett, William. "Wagnerian Fiction in English." *Criticism* 5.3 (1963): 239–60. Print.

Borchmeyer, Dieter. "The Question of Anti-Semitism." *Wagner Handbook*. Ed. Ulrich Müller and Peter Wapnewski. Cambridge: Harvard University Press, 1992. 166–85. Print.

Dalhaus, Carl. *Richard Wagner's Music Dramas*. Cambridge: Cambridge University Press, 1979. Print.

DiGaetani, John Louis. *Richard Wagner and the Modern British Novel*. Rutherford: Fairleigh Dickinson University Press, 1978. Print.

Ellis, Steve. *Virginia Woolf and the Victorians*. Cambridge: Cambridge University Press, 2007. Print.

Froula, Christine. "Mrs. Dalloway's Postwar Elegy: Women, War, and the Art of Mourning." *Modernism/modernity* 9.1 (2002): 125–63. Print.

Furness, Raymond. *Wagner and Literature*. Manchester: Manchester University Press, 1982. Print.

Glendinning, Victoria. *Leonard Woolf: A Biography*. New York: Free Press, 2006. Print.

Julius, Anthony. *T. S. Eliot, Anti-Semitism, and Literary Form*. Rev. ed. London: Thames & Hudson, 2003. Print.

Kermode, Frank. "Eliot and the Shudder." *London Review of Books* 32.9 (2010): 13–16. Print.

Lamm, Maurice. *The Jewish Way in Death and Mourning*. New York: Jonathan David, 2000. Print.

Levenback, Karen L. *Virginia Woolf and the Great War*. Syracuse: Syracuse University Press, 1999. Print.

Loewenberg, Alfred. *Annals of Opera, 1597–1940*. 3rd ed. London: John Calder, 1978. Print.

Martin, Timothy. *Joyce and Wagner: A Study of Influence*. Cambridge: Cambridge University Press, 1991. Print.

Maurier, George du. *Trilby*. Ed. Elaine Showalter. Oxford: Oxford University Press, 1995. Print.

Nietzsche, Friedrich. *The Birth of Tragedy and The Case of Wagner*. Trans. Walter Kaufmann. New York: Vintage, 1967. Print.

Phillips, Gyllian. "Re(de)composing in the Novel: *The Waves*, Wagnerian Opera, and Percival/Parsifal." *Genre: Forms of Discourse and Culture* 28.1–2 (1995): 119–44. Print.

Roth, Cecil, gen. ed. *Encyclopaedia Judaica*. 16 vols. Jerusalem: Keter, 1971. Print.

Schröder, Leena Kore. "Tales of Abjection and Miscegenation: Virginia Woolf's and Leonard Woolf's 'Jewish' Stories." *Twentieth-Century Literature* 49.3 (2003): 298–327. Print.

Sherard, Tracey. "'Parcival in the Forest of Gender': Wagner, Homosexuality, and *The Waves*." *Virginia Woolf: Turning the Centuries: Selected Papers from the Ninth Annual Conference on Virginia Woolf*. Ed. Ann Ardis and Bonnie Kime Scott. New York: Pace University Press, 2000, 62–69. Print.

Slovak, Jocelyn. "Mrs. Dalloway and Fugue: 'Songs without words, always the best. . . .'" Web. Feb. 15, 2010. http://www.unsaidmagazine.com/magazine/issue2/Slovak.html/.

Sutton, Emma. "Shell Shock and Hysterical Fugue, or Why Mrs. Dalloway Likes Bach." *Literature and Music of the First World War*. Spec. issue of *First World War Studies* 2.1 (2011). Ed. Kate Kennedy and Trudi Tate. 17–26. Print.

———. *Virginia Woolf and Classical Music: Politics, Aesthetics, Form*. Edinburgh: Edinburgh University Press, 2013. Print.

Trubowitz, Lara. "Concealing Leonard's Nose: Virginia Woolf, Modernist Antisemitism, and 'The Duchess and the Jeweller.'" *Twentieth-Century Literature* 54.3 (2008): 273–306. Print.

Wagner, Richard. *The Flying Dutchman: Romantic Opera in 3 Acts*. Complete vocal score by Otto Singer. English translation by Ernest Newman. The German text revised by Professor W. Golther. London: Breitkopf & Härtel, 1912. Print.

———. *Richard Wagner's Prose Works*. Trans. William Ashton Ellis. 8 vols. 1895–1899. London: Kegan Paul. Rpt. Lincoln: Nebraska University Press, 1993. Print.

Weiner, Marc A. *Richard Wagner and the Anti-Semitic Imagination*. Lincoln: Nebraska University Press, 1995. Print.

Wigoder, Geoffrey, ed. *The New Encyclopedia of Judaism*. New York: New York University Press, 2002. Print.

Wilson, Peal Cleveland. *Wagner's Dramas and Greek Tragedy*. New York: Columbia University Press, 1919. Print.

Woolf, Leonard. *Beginning Again: An Autobiography of the Years 1911 to 1918*. 1963. Orlando: Harvest, 1975. Print.

———. *Letters of Leonard Woolf*. Ed. Frederic Spotts. 1989. London: Bloomsbury, 1992. Print.

———. *Sowing: An Autobiography of the Years 1880 to 1904*. Orlando: Harvest, 1960. Print.

———. *The Wise Virgins: A Story of Words, Opinions, and a Few Emotions*. London: Persephone, 2003. Print.

Woolf, Virginia. *Carlyle's House and Other Sketches*. Ed. David Bradshaw. London: Hesperus, 2003. Print.

———. *The Diary of Virginia Woolf*. Ed. Anne Olivier Bell. 5 vols. Harmondsworth: Penguin, 1977–1984. Print.

———. *The Essays of Virginia Woolf*. Vol. 3: 1919–1924. Ed. Andrew McNeillie. London: Hogarth, 1988. Print.

———. *The Letters of Virginia Woolf*. Ed. Nigel Nicolson and Joanne Trautmann.

6 vols. New York: Harcourt, 1975–1980. Print.

———. *Moments of Being: Autobiographical Writings*. 2nd edition. Ed. Jeanne Schulkind. London: Hogarth, 1985.

———. *Mrs. Dalloway*. Gen. ed. Mark Hussey. Annot. Bonnie Kime Scott. Orlando: Harcourt, 2005. Print.

———. *The Waves*. Ed. Michael Herbert and Susan Sellers. Cambridge: Cambridge University Press, 2011. Print.

The Germans were over this house last night and the night before that. Here they are again. It is a queer experience, lying in the dark and listening to the zoom of a hornet, which may at any moment sting you to death. It is a sound that interrupts cool and consecutive thinking about peace. Yet it is sound – far more than prayers and anthems – that should compel one to think about peace. [...] But there is another way of fighting for freedom without arms; we can fight with the mind. We can make ideas that will help the young Englishman who is fighting up in the sky to defeat the enemy.

But to make ideas effective, we must be able to fire them off. We must put them into action. And the hornet in the sky rouses another hornet in the mind.

VIRGINIA WOOLF,
"Thoughts on Peace in an Air Raid"

SEVEN

The Efficacy of Performance

MUSICAL EVENTS IN *THE YEARS*

Elicia Clements

THE YEARS (1937) IS WOOLF'S MOST OVERTLY POLITICAL NOVEL; it reveals her growing concern in the 1930s to illuminate the social cost of what she will call "subconscious Hitlerism" in her 1940 essay "Thoughts on Peace in an Air Raid." Simultaneously, the novel "turns up the volume," so to speak, by foregrounding aurality in new and ubiquitous ways. In this essay, I argue that the two foci converge in the subject matter of *The Years*. In the thirties, Woolf searched for new ways not just to comment on social and political issues but also to produce writings that might break down the art/life dichotomy and actively engage in political critique. As Jessica Berman reminds us concerning *Orlando* and *The Waves*, "Woolf creates an alternative discourse of feminist action and power, one which seeks to intervene directly in the political life of Britain [during the period from 1929 to 1931]" (116). I would suggest further, for different but related reasons, that Woolf was equally concerned with generating "real" change through efficacious methods and means in *The Years* (especially as Hitler's voice thundered over the wireless). By analyzing representations of musical performance in the novel, I demonstrate that Woolf deftly integrates aspects from the art forms of music, drama, and literature to elaborate practices of aesthetic efficacy.

CULTURAL ANALYSIS

In her most recent study of the humanities, Mieke Bal argues for a concept-based approach to interdisciplinarity. Ideas *travel* across disciplines and fields, she contends; exploring these crossovers is a more productive way to perform cultural analysis (as distinct from cultural studies) than creating new methodological frameworks. I concur with Bal that a change in the way "we 'think' methodology within the different disciplines" (7) is needed. She details her reasons for proposing a new approach by enumerating three concerns she has with the interdiscipline of cultural studies. The first issue is one of coverage. Although cultural studies has been successful in presenting new objects for study by unsettling boundaries between different disciplines, "it has not been successful (enough) in developing a methodology to counter the exclusionary methods of the separate disciplines" (6–7). The other two issues Bal explicates include the deepening of a "divide between *les anciens* and *les modernes*" (7) and the fallout in academe in times of economic crisis when the first two issues seem to prevent stability (7). Bal's solution is to shift the object of analysis: "The counterpart of any given concept is the cultural text or work or 'thing' that constitutes the object of analysis. No concept is meaningful for cultural analysis unless it helps us to understand the object better *on its* – the object's – *own terms*" (8; emphasis in original). New means must be devised, therefore, to cope with the critical issues Bal delineates; her proposal to shift to a comparative analysis of the concept-object provides a potential solution.

Woolf's understanding of music, I would suggest, develops in tandem with her aesthetic methods and ideas. It is not a coincidence that music (and indeed sound more generally, as evidenced by the many critics who have explored aurality in *The Years*[1]) becomes a central component of her most political novel, not to mention her final, pointedly antifascist work as well, *Between the Acts*. Thus, a writer can be antididactic but still socialist and pacifist through effective tools of indirection. In fact, the oblique yet active capacity of musical performance, as I argue here, is precisely the point of it for Woolf. I would like to continue the conceptual debate about music in Woolf's work by using "performance" as a traveling concept to examine what it might have meant to Woolf from both a musical perspective and a theatrical standpoint.[2] I believe her understanding of performance is fundamentally informed by "classical" Western music but also by Greek drama. These two art traditions converge in scenes of musical performance in *The Years*. Lastly, I am not proposing a definitive reading by any means. Like Bal, I think that concepts should be "elastic" – "both an unbreakable stability and a near-unlimited extendability" (18) – "not because they mean the same thing for everyone, but because they do not" (17).

MUSICAL PERFORMANCE

Musical performance, as a skill or craft, has a very different history from that of dramatic performance and contemporary notions of performativity (which intersects with language (J. L. Austen) and subjectivity (Judith Butler) to unsettle our assumptions about how we act in our daily lives). Woolf, obviously, would not have been familiar with the notion of performativity, at least in its more congealed, current usage, even though her work and ideas (along with other modernists, especially James Joyce) enabled such postmodern concepts to emerge in the first place. Instead, Woolf would have been more familiar with a notion of performance that travels across the dynamic arts of music and theater.

According to the *Oxford English Dictionary,* the most common definition of "performance" is the accomplishment or carrying out of something commanded or undertaken; the doing of an action or operation. To perform, therefore, denotes a subject's active participation in a process. The study of musical performance has an identifiable history. It comes from the nineteenth-century German theory of *Aufführungspraxis,* typically translated as "performance practice," which focuses on the mechanics of musical enactments: the ways music is or has been performed, especially as it concerns issues of authenticity or appropriateness of style in the performance of music from a particular repertoire or date (OED). Notions of purity and essence abound in the tradition (which carries on today in North American musical training), as the chief goal is to get back to the presumed originary moment of the composer; this practice only gained momentum in the second half of the twentieth century.[3] Although Woolf might have encountered the results of this tradition variously in the many performances of the Western "classical" canon that she regularly attended or listened to on the Algraphone, it is doubtful she would have spent much time learning it (despite taking piano and voice lessons when she was young).

It is still useful, however, to examine what is involved in musical performance more generally in an effort to explore what Woolf might have gleaned as an audience member and an avid listener to myriad concerts and recordings. The music philosopher Stan Godlovitch enumerates a model of musical performance and concludes there are three primary components. First, the "significance of performance is strongly emphasized [...] performance rises from prominence to pre-eminence in the musical enterprise" (49–50). Second, "performances can fail both by misrepresenting the work and by disaffecting the listener" (50). The result is that, in general, the "performer-listener axis" carries more weight than the "composer-performer pair" (50). Put another way, "the occasion of performance is incomplete without an audience. Performance is relational" (29). And lastly, "performance is action-centred" (50). This last point is especially significant for my purposes because it not only suggests the active capacity of this art form found in Woolf's novels, but it also shifts the focus from a composer-centered view, traditionally ascribed to music making, to the performer as agent. As Godlovitch contends:

> notated works [...] have no direct bearing upon performance. They are instead constituents of larger, more diffuse, regulative composites. The performance model thus stands on its head the view that performance is a means to the end of making the work manifest. Instead, the work, in action-centred conceptions, becomes one means of organizing and marshalling various skills eager, so to speak, to issue forth in acoustic gifts to receptive beneficiaries. (51)

Significantly, therefore, music making is a complex and dynamic act that can engender agency in the performer and necessitates reaching out to perceivers. These two issues – a subject's ability to engage in creative acts and the need for an audience – were two of Woolf's major concerns by the mid-1930s. Thus, as Vladimir Jankélévitch suggests, music is not a cipher waiting to be decoded. It is, instead, tangled in networks of human experience, and with the physical, material reality of music in performance: "Music, like the divine nightingales, answers with the deed, by Doing" (84). Jankélévitch's understanding of music is remarkably similar to Woolf's. Time and time again, she utilizes the sonorous art to intervene into socially condoned modes of behavior precisely because music is "an act of Doing" (Jankélévitch 77) rather than saying.

According to the performance studies theorist Richard Schechner, the boundaries between life and art are often at issue in performances. As he has maintained, efficacy and entertainment, albeit not merely binary oppositions or a continuum, represent two ends of a performance scale. Schechner characterizes ritual, a type of performance, as being imbued with material circumstances and functionality. Theatrical performance, on the other hand, is said to be closer to entertainment or play.[4] Correspondingly, as Godlovitch outlines, where music is concerned, the act of performance can be closely aligned with ritual as opposed to entertainment. The performer's agency and the necessity of an audience both stress the efficacious side of the continuum – the functionality of musical enactment.

Unlike reading or writing, therefore, music making is commonly a communal endeavor. Even if a person plays or sings a solo without accompaniment, the soloist still typically performs for a group, for an audience of some sort (even the a cappella singing of the old street woman in *Mrs. Dalloway* is heard by an audience of passersby). Given Woolf's questioning of collective hierarchies and the role of the leader, particularly in the 1930s, it follows that in music she found an art form that could produce in the material world the collaborative and multifarious possibilities of community that she envisioned. Several critics have made this important claim.[5] But music is not only a metaphor for new forms of communal relations; it is also a model for them in its praxis – at least as Woolf conceived of it.[6] This is important because it speaks to the reason why she consistently employed the art form in her novels: life and art are inextricably commingled for Woolf. A proto-interdisciplinary thinker, she developed concepts about the relationships among the arts because "we are the words; we are the music; we are the thing itself" (*MB* 72).

GREEK THEATRICAL CORRELATIONS

The concept of performance in the theater carries with it another linked but largely separate tradition from the music-making one, with its own history and set of conventions. Although in the latter half of the twentieth century a shift in focus to performativity occurred, Woolf's understanding of theatrical performance would obviously not carry the same postmodern inflection (even though one finds prescient notions of the performative nature of language, for one example, in her writings); however, she would be familiar with Greek drama, as she made a lifelong study of Greek cultural material.[7] The word "theater" is derived from the Greek *theatron,* "a place of seeing" (Britannica), and in the West, as is well known, the Greeks are commonly credited with the development of the art form itself. Significantly, from its Western beginnings, theatrical performance is inextricably linked to ritual – of or relating to the performance of rites (a custom, habit, or practice). In Knossos in Crete, for example, anthropological studies have shown that some ancient architectural structures were purposely ceremonial in design, initially used as places of assembly at which a priestly caste would attempt to communicate with supernatural forces. Although when exactly and how strictly the shift in purpose to entertainment or art occurs is blurry at best, a transition from ritual involving mass participation to something approaching drama occurred in ancient Greece (circa fifth and fourth centuries BCE). But from the outset, the functional nature of ritual has been fundamental to what becomes the art form. This is the tradition about which Woolf was very knowledgeable: her acquaintance with Greek history (social and political) was extensive, as was her fluency with the language itself and the corpus of its dramatic texts, especially those of Aeschylus, Sophocles, and Euripides.

Yet, Schechner suggests that the opposition between the notions of ritual and theater is not the best way to examine the issues involved in performance, nor is the binary an accurate distinction to make in the first place. Instead, he explains:

> The basic polarity is between efficacy and entertainment, not between ritual and theater. Whether one calls a specific performance "ritual" or "theater" depends mostly on context and function. A performance is called theater or ritual because of where it is performed, by whom, and under what circumstances. If the performance's purpose is to effect transformations – to be efficacious – then the other qualities listed under the heading "efficacy" [results, link to an absent Other, symbolic time, performer possessed, in trance, audience participates, audience believes] will most probably also be present, and the performance is a ritual. And vice versa regarding the qualities listed under "entertainment" [fun, only for those here, emphasis now, performer knows what s/he's doing, audience watches, audience appreciates]. (130)

Thus, although there are two ends of a spectrum, they should not be thought of as exclusive binaries, but instead as a matter of degree: "No performance is pure efficacy or pure entertainment" (130). Moreover, Schechner argues for perceptible shifts throughout the history of theater that emphasize one side or the other. In the 1960s and 1970s, for example, there was an effort to "ritualize performance, to make theater yield efficacious acts" (131), which gained precedence over entertainment. Thus, the history of theater can be seen, according to Schechner, in terms of an efficacy/entertainment braid. At the start of the twentieth century, modern theater signals the beginning of a shift to the political theater of the 1960s.[8] I would argue, therefore, that Woolf is an example of a writer who was seeking out ways to integrate the efficaciousness of theatrical performance in her novels by utilizing concepts and methods from the Greek tradition in conjunction with ideas about music.

Woolf's affinity for Greek history and culture is well known. In *The Years* a direct connection is made to its drama, not only through the allusions to Sophocles's *Antigone* but also through the pidgin Greek sounds that come from the caretaker's children's chorus in the final chapter. As I will demonstrate, comparing the concept of performance in both musical and theatrical traditions illuminates Woolf's particular treatment of it and reveals commonalities between the two such as activity, correlation, and efficacy. Consequently, we can better understand why she deploys musical performance in her novels on such a crucial level: the emphasis on functionality is linked not only to thought (and language) as action but also to art's intersection with life.

THE "ETERNAL WALTZ" THAT IS *THE YEARS*

In the 1930s Woolf's concerns about the social cost of war intensify, becoming more urgent. Although Woolf's Bloomsbury-inflected pacifist stance is animate in earlier antiwar novels such as *Jacob's Room* and *Mrs. Dalloway*, it becomes more focused in both *The Years* and *Three Guineas*, the latter especially after the death of Julian Bell in the Spanish Civil War (July 18, 1937) and with the growing threat of Hitler's tyranny. As is well known, the two separate texts began conceptually as one work titled *The Pargiters* in October 1932.[9] From its inception, Woolf unassumingly yet elatedly exclaimed it would be an "important" book. In November of the same year, Woolf observed in her diary, "I think I shall have thus a very reasonable happy winter, writing The Pargiters, but for Gods sake, I must be careful, & go quietly, & order my litter of excitements ... feeling as I do for the first time that this book is important. Why do I feel this, & I never felt it in the least about the others?" (D4: 129–30). Although finishing *The Years* would become one of her most disheartening and self-deprecating experiences as a novelist, the weight she attaches to the arguments of both the eventual novel and the polemical essay suggests she hoped her new ideas about the interconnections between violence and gender might create some change in her readers through deliberate reflection.

"Thoughts on Peace in an Air Raid," written after the two works were completed but a text that brings together many of their most cogent and pressing ideas, summarizes Woolf's late form of pacifism, which attempts to be assertive yet simultaneously encourages antiviolence.[10] The epigraph to the present chapter details an interchange between thought and action, between fighting with the mind and political or social usefulness. Woolf searched for a way to speak out artistically and philosophically (indeed, *The Pargiters* is a prime example of her effort to combine these two seemingly disparate domains of cultural knowledge, suggesting she did not privilege one over the other). But she desired to do so without recourse to physical violence or didacticism. The strengthening of her conviction that tyranny must be opposed in material terms should not be underestimated. Correspondingly, as I have shown, an effective combination of thought and action is always at play when one performs music.[11] In Woolf's figuration, contemplation is not simply turned into deeds; it is superimposed on them and vice versa. Thought *is* activity. Music making is the realization of this relationship in artistic form.

But Woolf's active reflection is different from René Descartes's infamous dictum *Cogito ergo sum*, which privileges the intellectual capacity of humankind over the experiences of the body. Alternatively, Woolf works to dissolve oppositions rather than reinscribe them or "take sides." The later novels especially reveal that thinking and acting are equally important: what seems static – thought and contemplation – is vital for social change; what seems to be kinetic – the physical, material condition of the body and the senses – is inseparable from ideas and aesthetic value. Thus Woolf does not call for a simple reversal of age-old dualities, such as mind versus body, stasis versus movement, or even tyranny versus slavery. As she maintains in her essay on air raids, "What is it that prevents us [from being free]? 'Hitler!' the loudspeakers cry with one voice. Who is Hitler? What is he? Aggressiveness, tyranny, the insane love of power made manifest, they reply. Destroy that, and you will be free" (E6: 242). For Woolf this reversal is an illusion. In its place, she insists, "If we could free ourselves from slavery we should free men from tyranny. Hitlers are bred by slaves" (242). As she summarizes in the spirit of William Blake, "Mental fight means thinking against the current, not with it" (242).

Therefore, Woolf's employment of musical performance does not enact a withdrawal from corporeality. On the contrary, it marks the physically bound nature of sound and its intersection with subjectivity and insists on the interrelation of the two. As Jane Goldman has argued about Woolf's visual palette and her concept of "moments of being" as they are often linked to Henri Bergson, "Woolf's writing does more than record subjective impressions, or represent the Bergsonian flow of life: it seeks to intervene in life, and change it" (6). The concept of music is part of Woolf's interventionist strategies to reveal how the conditions of everyday life shape, govern, and, at times, liberate both individual subjects and communal relations. But the important aesthetic difference with music is that its very existence is particularly contingent on the physiological circumstances of the body (whether playing an instrument or singing, although there are different degrees of engagement involved).

In the introduction to the "1907" chapter of *The Years*, the narrator describes an "eternal waltz" produced by the noise and music of the Covent Garden Market and its "celestial laundry" of "cabbages, cherries and carnations" (Y 120).

> All the windows were open. Music sounded. From behind crimson curtains, rendered semi-transparent and sometimes blowing wide came the sound of the eternal waltz – After the ball is over, after the dance is done – like a serpent that swallowed its own tail, since the ring was complete from Hammersmith to Shoreditch. Over and over again it was repeated by trombones outside public houses; errand boys whistled it; bands inside private rooms where people were dancing played it. (120–21)

The waltz is both actual and intangible at the same time: "rendered semi-transparent" yet marking the atmosphere with the lingering resonance of musical sound. It is also perpetual (suggested by the reference to the Ouroboros), rhythmic, and easily integrated and performed – polytextural,[12] as heterogeneous bodies carry it, but somehow also tonally bound and therefore associated with the Western tradition of music.[13]

The life-affirming ambiance of this opening scene is reestablished in the events that follow, particularly when three female characters – Sara, Maggie, and their mother, Eugénie – partake in listening to a waltz. They become an unacknowledged, almost surreptitious audience. The segment begins with Sara overhearing the music from a party outside her bedroom window. Immediately, an association with the waltz is evoked: "One of the houses was brilliantly lit and from the long open windows came dance music. They were waltzing" (Y 124). Sara's circumstance as a furtive, even involuntary, auditor destabilizes the typical performer-listener relationship. Not only are the musicians unaware of this listener, but also, in turn, Sara cannot see the performers; she only hears them and observes the effect of their rhythms in the dancing guests, partly because sound can travel places that sight cannot. Although the musicians are deemphasized, therefore, the scene proceeds to document Sara's growing active participation as a performer in her own right. Unconstrained by the customs of the entertainment side of the performance spectrum, Sara is alone in her room, both enjoying and attempting to escape the sounds.[14] She can behave in whatever way she chooses, unlike an audience member or a partnered dancer at the fête, who would be inhibited by either performance and dance conventions or social codes of behavior.

Despite her attempts to fall asleep, the music keeps Sara awake. Music and street noises interrupt her purposefully; they instigate many of the significant moments in the chapter and provide the backdrop for her experience. The musical sounds, especially, help to produce new realizations and associational thoughts. Sara, a pianist and singer, has the ear to hear such an "eternal waltz." Links with energy and movement are also reiterated, "and though it was late, the whole world seemed to be alive; the rush of traffic sounded distant but incessant" (Y 124). The pulse of the city recalls the circular metaphor of the Ouroboros employed in the introduction to the chapter. Aurality interrupts Sara's sleep and instigates a series of ideas about thought and action.

In Sara's effort to become sleepy, she reads a "faded brown book" (Y 124) that Woolf does not name. The subsequent issues Woolf explores in the passage anticipate contemplations that occur to the speaker in "Thoughts on Peace in an Air Raid." In both the novel and the essay, the sleeper lies awake at night, considering the importance of "free" thought, for "if we were free we should be out in the open, dancing, at the play, or sitting at the window talking together" (E 6: 243). The scene with Sara in her bedroom presages and enacts precisely such freedoms, but buffets the life-affirming qualities of music with allusions to being buried alive and tyranny.

First Sara ponders the interchange between thought and action. In fact, she attempts to envision thought *as* activity:

> "And he says," she murmured, "the world is nothing but . . ." She paused. What did he say? Nothing but thought, was it? She asked herself as if she had already forgotten. Well, since it was impossible to read and impossible to sleep, she would let herself *be* thought. It was easier to act things than to think them. Legs, body, hands, the whole of her must be laid out passively to take part in this universal process of thinking which the man said was the world living. She stretched herself out. Where did thought begin?
> In the feet? she asked. There they were, jutting out under the single sheet. They seemed separated, very far away. She closed her eyes. Then against her will something in her hardened. It was impossible to act thought. She became something; a root; lying sunk in the earth; veins seemed to thread the cold mass; the tree put forth branches; the branches had leaves. (Y 125)

Sara's attempts to *be* thought are difficult for her; her body seems to get in the way. Action and imitation are easier. Indeed, she repeats the words and actions of others almost to the point of absurdity throughout the text. Later, when her mother comes into the room, for just one example she mimics what her mother says verbatim as well as some of her movements. Nonetheless, she envisions herself as "something; a root," a tangible entity, but not one that denotes fixed singularity or solidity. Rather, the root is described as containing a multitude of veins threading through it, and the tree trunk is only a vehicle for its branches and leaves. Thus, the scene emphasizes Sara's act of becoming, despite her frustration, the material body she imagines.

Subsequently, however, Sara opens her eyes and is disappointed to find the vision of the tree that she had imagined is not the same in the "real" world:

> " – the sun shines through the leaves," she said, waggling her finger. She opened her eyes in order to verify the sun on the leaves and saw the actual tree standing out there in the garden. Far from being dappled with sunlight, it had no leaves at all. She felt for a moment as if she had been contradicted. For the tree was black, dead black. (Y 125)

Woolf's comment on the present moment, of the emaciated tree that contains "no leaves at all" and does not benefit from sunlight, suggests a stark contrast between the human capacity to imagine new possibilities and the lack of such realization in actual material conditions – particularly for someone such as Sara, who will eventually become a socially discarded spinster in the text. The chapter, and the novel, reveals that people do not value the necessary exchange between thought and action, which Woolf indicates is essential for subjective and social transformation. If society is not allowed to imagine new possibilities – the freedom of thought or the creation of cultural material – life is "black, dead black."

Sara seems almost unwilling to listen to the eternal waltz at this point, although she does attempt to utilize its rhythm to compose a song about broken hearts and broken glass that will echo throughout the chapter.[15] As she takes down another book from the shelf – this time the intertext is named, Sophocles's *Antigone,* translated by one of her cousins, Edward – something else catches her attention as well: a couple talking in the garden. In the segment that follows, Sara "hum[s] the words" (notably, obscuring their precision) "in time to the melancholy waltz music" (Y 126). Repeatedly, as she turns the pages of the book, the narrative shifts back and forth between Sara's thoughts as detailed by the third-person narratorial voice (free indirect discourse) and her own words/thoughts (as direct or reported speech). Simultaneously, her ideas are also described as being tied rhythmically to the music. These narratorial techniques are intermingled with Sara's reading of *Antigone* and contemplations about the couple. The heterogeneous and mobile processes of thought, therefore, are foregrounded and performed in language as exceptionally active:

"The Antigone of Sophocles, done into English verse by Edward Pargiter," she read again. He had given it [to] her in Oxford; one hot afternoon when they had been trailing through chapels and libraries. "Trailing and wailing," she hummed, turning over the pages, "and he said to me, getting up from the low armchair, and brushing his hand through his hair" – she glanced out of the window – "'my wasted youth, my wasted youth.'" The waltz was now at its most intense, its most melancholy. "Taking in his hand," she hummed in time to it, "this broken glass, this faded heart, he said to me . . ." Here the music stopped; there was a sound of clapping; the dancers once more came out into the garden. (Y 127)

The undulating musical backdrop is significant in the passage. When music is performed (bound to "real" time as it is), both the music maker and the listener experience combined thought and action. Like an athlete but unlike a reader, the performer's body is enlisted by the mind to produce action, but unlike the athlete yet much like the reader, a musician also expresses cultural material. Sara's commingled experience of several different perceptions – reading the book, her memories of Edward, her audition of the waltz and party noises, her creation of "hummed" words (which would ultimately sound like a rhythmic melody as opposed to language), and her ideas about the couple she sees in the garden – enact the very interchange between thought and action she seemingly has just given up due to frustration and disappointment. Out of the combination of these elements, but facilitated and instigated by the music, she composes and performs her fragments for herself. These three activities – composing, listening, performing – comprise the act of musical labor (Godlovitch 3). Sara enacts all three, creating a paradoxical community of one. As Godlovitch contends, "One person busy in all three enterprises conceivably constitutes a self-sufficient (albeit minimal) musical community, but no musical community lacks any one of these factors" (3).

But so far, although remarkably active and even participatory, Sara's physical movement has been limited. This changes as she continues to read *Antigone*. After the segment above, Sara falls into a meditative state, simultaneously witnessing and experiencing (according to the way the narrative portrays the scene) Antigone's life in the process. Yet again the music in the background enables the reverie. The following quotations are long, but the interspersed nature of the elements – music, movement, narrative – lengthen the episode in the text:

> The unburied body of a murdered man lay like a fallen tree-trunk, like a statue, with one foot stark in the air. Vultures gathered. Down they flopped on the silver sand. [...] Then in a yellow cloud came whirling – who? She turned the page quickly. Antigone? (Y 127–28)

But the party intrudes.

> There was a roar of laughter from the garden. She looked up. Where did they take her? she asked. The garden was full of people. She could not hear a word that they were saying. The figures were moving in and out.
> "To the estimable courts of the respected ruler?" she murmured, picking up a word or two at random, for she was still looking out into the garden. The man's name was Creon. He buried her. [...] She was buried alive. The tomb was a brick mound. There was just room for her to lie straight out. Straight out in a brick tomb, she said. (128)

Subsequently, Sara reenacts the burial. With the repetition yet subtle shift into active voice of the words "lie straight out":

> She laid herself out, under the cold smooth sheets, and pulled the pillow over her ears. [...] The sound of the dance music became dulled. Her body dropped suddenly; then reached ground. A dark wing brushed her mind, leaving a pause; a blank space. Everything – the music, the voices – became stretched and generalized. The book fell on the floor. She was asleep. (128)

After this the narrative returns to the couple outside and a thwarted courtship that is potentially taking place at the party. Taken together, the scene reveals that Sara ritualizes her reading of *Antigone*. Similar to a minister or a priest presiding over a ceremony, Sara reads a line, then descends into a trancelike state in which she becomes the character she reads about. The lines between the physical world and the mental one are blurred. First she reads and intones a sentence or two from the Greek play; she watches the couple, hears the music (which pushes, pulls, and contributes to the experience); she contemplates and assesses the actions of the play and then enacts the physical state of the central character in her bed. Although Sara is her own audience, the active and participatory nature of what one might think would be simple bedtime reading is closer to efficaciousness in Schechner's terms: a link to an absent Other (Antigone), symbolic time (the present and the past are commingled), the performer is in a meditative state, and the audience (also Sara) participates by emulating the burial ritual. The only questionable component for the features of ritual enumerated by Schechner is a clear result from the process, but Woolf, strikingly so in this novel, is ambivalent about fixed outcomes. Transparent achievements are not the point. Indeed, this ritual is a lamentable one in which women are buried alive for speaking their minds or resisting tyrannical control. Thus, ultimately, the juxtaposed association to Sara's predicament, gleaned only by the reader of Woolf's text, is the crucial transformative component of the performance.

In case this juxtaposition is missed, however, the point is brought home, so to speak, when Maggie returns from the party and then Eugénie comes into their room to say good night. The sisters' mother is another musical character, so much so that she seems to exude rhythm (she is also a dancer). As she speaks to her daughters, "her words were stressed so that they seemed to rise and fall. She emphasized the rhythm still further by tapping with her fingers on Sally's bare arm" (*Y* 133). Despite her attempt to reinscribe the "proper" social behavior for ladies after Maggie questions such roles by unabashedly talking with her cousin Martin at the party – "'But you don't go to parties, my dear Maggie, to talk to your own cousins. You go to parties to – '" (133) – the waltz once again interrupts the scene, putting the listener into another trance-like state:

> Here the dance music crashed out. The first chords seemed possessed of frantic energy, as if they were summoning the dancers imperiously to return. Lady Pargiter stopped in the middle of her sentence. She sighed; her body seemed to become indolent and suave. The heavy lids lowered themselves slightly over her large dark eyes. She swayed her head slowly in time to the music.
> "What's that they're playing?" she murmured. She hummed the tune, beating time with her hand. "Something I used to dance to." (133–34)

Eugénie imagines a partner, at the urging of Sara, and "twirled round and round in the space which Maggie had cleared. She moved with extraordinary stateliness. All her limbs seemed to bend and flow in the lilt and the curve of the music; which became louder and clearer as she danced to it" (134). When she finishes they beg her to tell them the story that accompanies this movement and memory. Eugénie resists, however, and is cut short again, but this time by the sound of the abbey bells marking time and by her husband's voice. The content of Eugénie's memory is left unspoken, but the music and its capacity to produce bodily kinesis has made its impact. The scene demonstrates the interchange between thought and body, ideas and material conditions; once again, music enables reflection, action, and transformation. And, in effect, it prevents Eugénie, with "frantic energy," from burying both of her daughters alive with social obligations – a tyranny Woolf links directly to the public sphere in *Three Guineas*.

Last but not least, but briefly, as many have discussed the segment at length,[16] I would submit that the final chapter, which includes the singing of the caretaker's children, is highly pertinent given the focus on efficacy in musical and theatrical performance I have elaborated. The final (although certainly not definitive) performance in the novel is a chorus sung to inscrutable words that evoke the Greek language but at the same time resist denotation. The effect is a transformative event, inundated with the efficacious nature of musical performance.

Just before the children sing, Edward's life work is recalled, and with it the reader might remember *Antigone*, which Sara read and ritualized in 1907. Indeed, North even asks Edward to tell him about Aeschylus, Sophocles, Pindar, "'And the chorus,... The chorus –' North repeated" (Y 405). The Greek association is also evoked by the trochaic rhythm of the children's song:[17]

> [The children] swept their eyes over the grown-up people for a moment, then, each giving the other a little nudge, they burst into song:
>
> Etho Passo tanno hai,
> Fai donk to tu do,
> Mai to, kai to, lai to see
> Toh dom to tuh do –
>
> That was what is sounded like. Not a word was recognizable. The distorted sounds rose and sank as if they followed a tune. They stopped.
>
> They stood with their hands behind their backs. Then with one impulse they attacked the next verse:
>
> Fanno to par, etto to mar,
> Timin tudo, tido,
> Foll to gar in, mitno to par,
> Eido, teido, meido –
>
> They sang the second verse more fiercely than the first. The rhythm seemed to rock and the unintelligible words ran themselves together almost into a shriek. The grown-up people did not know whether to laugh or to cry. Their voices were so harsh; the accent was so hideous. (Y 407–408)

The Greek connection implies the choric function of commentary, even though, as Woolf acknowledges in "On Not Knowing Greek," this does not minimize its functional significance in the least. For Woolf, the chorus combines comment and action (either in isolation are ineffective). "It is this that the choruses supply; the old men or women who take no active part in the drama, the undifferentiated voices who sing like birds in the pauses of the wind; who can comment, or sum up, or allow the poet to speak himself or supply, by contrast, another side to his conception" (E4: 43). Moreover, in "imaginative literature," the kind she composes and within which, she states, the author is excised and the characters seem to speak for themselves, "the need of that voice is making itself felt" (43).

Additionally, the active, participatory/relational, and functional nature of musical performance compounds the efficacy of the moment. Ultimately, the event is a musical performance, not the simple recitation of a poem or a rhetorical, even dramatic, peroration. Working-class children reluctantly perform a song, not on a stage, but at an upper-middle-class get-together, impromptu, as it were. Dissolving the usual performer-listener boundaries established in staged performance on the entertainment end of the spectrum, this chorus is imbricated in the everyday social milieu of a family party – crossing (whether successfully or not) class-bound scripts that a legitimized performance would not, but also blurring the border between art and life. The "audience," for example, interacts with the performance of the music in a reciprocal manner, not unlike the call and answer of the music and nightingales alluded to in the 1907 chapter. "Old Patrick," Martin, Hugh Gibbs, Maggie, and Eleanor each make their choric comments and interpret the singing in their own terms. Eleanor and Maggie provide astute yet appreciative observations:

> "But it was..." Eleanor began. She stopped. What was it? As they stood there they had looked so dignified; yet they had made this hideous noise. The contrast between their faces and their voices was astonishing; it was impossible to find one word for the whole. "Beautiful?" she said, with a note of interrogation, turning to Maggie.
> "Extraordinarily," said Maggie.
> But Eleanor was not sure that they were thinking of the same thing.
> (Y 408–409)

But there is no summing up the event. As Margaret Comstock and others have shown, any finality in the scene is tentative at best: "No one will sum up the party or *The Years*; not Nicholas, not Peggy, who is asked to speak 'for the younger generation' but who refuses; not even the caretaker's children, who sing their song for sixpence" (Comstock 262). As Nicholas declares, "'There is going to be no peroration – no peroration!' he exclaimed, throwing his arm out, 'because there was no speech.'" (*Y* 409). The auditors of the song in the text and the reader of the novel, however, are left with an ineffable yet transformative experience. As Victor Turner has argued in reference to ritual as a rite of passage, the participants are not the same after the performance as they are before it. Thus, whatever is signified or declaimed in the song is not the point, for music making, as noted earlier, "answers with the deed, by Doing" (Jankélévitch 84).

The active capacity of musical performance is called upon at important moments in *The Years* to represent the issues discussed above: not as a vehicle for the actions of "great men," but as an artistic practice that is imbricated in daily life and capable, at the very least, of maintaining a productive tension between being and doing. Music is also an instigator – a sort of jump start, or "shock," to use Woolf's word in "A Sketch of the Past" to describe her notion of a "moment of being" (72), inducing characters not only to listen but often to act thoughtfully. As well, rhythm and movement become ways to dislodge the limits of social modes of behavior. By exploring the concept of performance and comparing musical and theatrical versions of it, we can better understand why Woolf deploys musical events in her novels on such a crucial level: the emphasis on functionality is linked not only to thought as action but also to art's intersection with life. Woolf is certainly a writer dedicated to disclosing the processes of *being*, but she is equally concerned with elaborating the conditions of *doing*. Music making helps her to articulate and instantiate such issues in her novels. In the process, she also politicizes artistic practices.

NOTES

1. The highly aural nature of the novel is evidenced by the number of critics who have explored urban sound in the text. Margaret Comstock's contribution to the 1977 *Bulletin of the New York Public Library*, "The Loudspeaker and the Human

Voice: Politics and the Form of *The Years*," is a case in point. More recently (2002), Rishona Zimring has argued that "Woolf uses sounds to insist upon the alienating noise of a modern, urban existence (and its ideologies of progress)" (129). Melba Cuddy-Keane considers the novel in her exploration of modernist aurality (2005), and Angela Frattarola (2005) includes *The Years* in her analysis of "found sound" sampling in Woolf's works. Anna Snaith explored the novel's sonics in her keynote lecture at the 2009 Woolf conference at Fordham University, New York City. See also Clements, "Reconfigured Terrain: Aural Architecture in *Jacob's Room* and *The Years*," in *Woolf and the City: Selected Papers from the Nineteenth Annual Conference on Virginia Woolf*, 2010.

2. Emilie Crapoulet deploys Bal's concept-based approach by surveying some of Woolf's musical tropes from the major novels. She uses the term "musicality" to argue that it is an example of one of Bal's travelling concepts: "'Musicality' is a 'travelling concept' par excellence ... but its nomadic nature is rarely taken into account" (Crapoulet 80). Yet, Crapoulet eventually reiterates a version of Woolf and her "musicality" that depoliticizes both Woolf's understanding of art and the concept of musicality itself. Referring to Woolf's 1906 essay "Street Music," Crapoulet concludes her paper: "Precisely because the material of [a musician's] art, cannot 'argue a cause,' as such, it becomes for Virginia Woolf, the model for the ideal art form, one which is both impersonal and apolitical" (85). I would suggest that Woolf's particular brand of "musicality" changes considerably from the time of the 1906 reference to the novel of 1937 (*The Years*) and I disagree that music is an ideal art for Woolf (even though it is acutely esteemed in her writing), impersonal, or apolitical.

3. Musical performance practice was pioneered in England by Arnold Dolmetsch (1858–1940). For more on this seminal figure in the revival of early music, see Margaret Campbell's *Dolmetsch: The Man and His Work* (London: Hamilton, 1975).

4. For a discussion of the terms of the debate and a critique of Schechner's theory, see Stephen J. Bottoms, "The Efficacy/Effeminacy Braid: Unpicking the Performance Studies/Theater Studies Dichotomy," *Theater Topics* 13.2 (2003): 173–87.

5. For at least twenty years in Woolf studies, there has been a concerted effort to explore the novels and essays for their political nuances rather than assuming the high modernist narrative of aesthetics in isolation. Several critics have explored the relationship between the conceptual notion of music and Woolf's social project. Robin Gail Schulze posits that Woolf's dissatisfaction with the form of the novel, famously detailed in her 1924 essay "Modern Fiction," leads Woolf to music rather than painting, "for a compact, nonchronological, simultaneous expression of 'life going on'" (10). Schulze proposes that Woolf decentralized the narrative drive of writing to critique "the world in a new way without becoming a new dictator" (19). For additional essays that explore the links between music and ideology in Woolf's novels, see Sonita Sarker and Arianne Burford. Rishona Zimring also examines the social ramifications of sound in Woolf's late work, particularly *The Years*. Melba Cuddy-Keane, in her study of the function of the chorus in *Between the Acts*, contends that Woolf's employment of musical tropes illuminates a pluralistic and inclusive model for communal relations. More precisely, Cuddy-Keane maintains that for Woolf, "conventional meaning, because it attempts to *impose* unity, becomes exclusive and partial; only meaning that, like music, lacks definite articulation is fully inclusive

and therefore truly unifying" ("Politics" 282). Music, therefore, is representative of a new model for social organization. See also Angela Frattarola and Michelle Pridmore-Brown, who both focus on *Between the Acts*. Additionally, for the complexity of Woolf's political ideas as well as her husband's, see Natalia Rosenfeld's *Outsiders Together*.

6. Woolf's understanding of music's communal capacities tends to focus on ensembles, such as the string quartet (which rarely has a conductor, although the first violin usually counts the players in) or female piano players and their audiences. The potentially authoritarian role of a conductor, or music director, is also critiqued in her final novel with the figure of Miss La Trobe (a character I have argued elsewhere is modeled on the composer/conductor Ethel Smyth; see my article "Virginia Woolf, Ethel Smyth, and Music: Listening as a Productive Mode of Social Interaction," *College Literature* 32.3 [2005]: 51–71). Yet ultimately one could read the Western tradition of music in very different and constricting terms. For a discussion of music's imbrication in the hierarchical codings of Western thought, see Susan McClary's *Feminine Endings*.

7. For an excellent summary and analysis of Woolf's admiration of Grecian history, language, and art, and its significance for her writing, see Rowena Fowler, "Moments of Metamorphoses: Virginia Woolf's Greece" (*Comparative Literature* 51:3 [1999]: 217–42). Woolf's decisive essay on language, "On Not Knowing Greek," reveals her comprehensive, yet humble, knowledge of the cultural significance of the country's traditions. In addition to two trips to Greece (one in 1906 and the other in 1932, which she and Leonard took with Roger and Margery Fry just before *The Pargiters* project began), she was taught Greek by Clara Pater (Walter Pater's sister) and Janet Case. Woolf was capable of reading in Greek, although her grammatical skills were said to be less than Case had hoped for. We know, for example, that she read Sophocles's *Antigone* in Greek (Fowler 221).

8. The two ends of the spectrum are quite far apart at the beginning of the twentieth century. They converge, for Schechner, in the 1960s. I am suggesting that Woolf was developing such ideas in the 1930s.

9. For a discussion of the project's genesis and a reproduction of the holographs of the earlier "novel-essay," see Mitchell Leaska's *The Pargiters*.

10. The pressing tone of the essay owes much to its date of composition: August 1940, squarely in the midst of the Battle of Britain (July to October 1940), Hitler's effort to wipe out the Royal Air Force (and annex the British Isles) with the *Luftwaffe*.

11. I would argue that "absolute" music and music with words (vocal and programmatic) both incorporate this capacity, albeit at different semantic levels.

12. Cuddy-Keane explores the notion of Woolf's polytextural aurality by widening the scope of what constitutes "music" ("New Aurality" 88, 90).

13. By the Western tradition I mean "classical" art music that relies on the Western major-minor, equal-tempered harmonic system with which Woolf was familiar.

14. Sara's circumstance in her room enables a type of solitary freedom that would not be lost on any reader of *A Room of One's Own*.

15. As Sue Asbee notes, "Sara's speech characteristically falls into rhythmic and/or rhyming patterns, very similar to vw's character Isa in *Between the Acts* (1941); Sara's words have distinct literary echoes, but are difficult to trace, as she has usually, in some way, made them her own" (470). The connection to *Between the Acts*

is also significant; as depicted in that novel, "Music wakes us. Music makes us see the hidden, join the broken" (BA 108). Additionally, the highly performative moment in that novel (Cuddy-Keane reads it as Cagean) also details shards of glass (mirrors). Moreover, Rishona Zimring suggests that Sara "composes the city" in this and other scenes, "an isolated, strange figure constantly warding off noise from her world of private reverie" (133, 142). Unlike Zimring, I am suggesting it is significant not only that music (not just fragments of city noise) is incorporated in the scene but also that Sara actively integrates sounds and thoughts into her own efficacious performance.

16. Critics interpret the final party and the scene with the caretaker's children in both positive and negative terms. Jane Marcus, for example, understands the moment as signifying a chorus of freedom: "Our ears cringe at the accent, Latin words and Cockney English mixed with echoes of Greek. But Eleanor, Woolf's Brunnhilde, has faith in the working classes' song of freedom. No false note of nostalgia intrudes; no utopian pretense of class comradeship mars the clarity of vision" (*Languages* 50). Alternatively, Zimring argues, "The sounds of *The Years* are so aggressively intrusive, and felt as such by several characters, that they cannot simply be taken straightforwardly as redemptive signals of mobility or expansion, the embrace of new or other worlds" (132).

17. According to Thomas Drew-Bear, although not commonplace, the meter of trochaic tetrameter was sometimes employed in Greek drama to heighten the intensity or excitement of the final scene. The chorus was often the carrier of this particular rhythm. See "The Trochaic Tetrameter in Greek Tragedy," *American Journal of Philology* 89.4 (1968): 385–405.

WORKS CITED

Asbee, Sue. Explanatory notes. *The Years*. By Virginia Woolf. Ed. Hermione Lee. Oxford: Oxford World's Classics, 2009.

Bal, Mieke. *Travelling Concepts in the Humanities: A Rough Guide*. Toronto: University of Toronto Press, 2002. Print.

Berman, Jessica. *Modernist Fiction, Cosmopolitanism, and the Politics of Community*. New York: Cambridge University Press, 2001. Print.

Bottoms, Stephen J. "The Efficacy/Effeminacy Braid: Unpicking the Performance Studies/Theater Studies Dichotomy." *Theater Topics* 13.2 (2003): 173–87.

Burford, Arianne. "Communities of Silence and Music in Virginia Woolf's *The Waves* and Dorothy Richardson's *Pilgrimage*." *Virginia Woolf and Communities: Selected Papers from the Eighth Annual Conference on Virginia Woolf*. Ed. Jeanette McVicker and Laura Davis. New York: Pace University Press, 1999. 269–75. Print.

Clements, Elicia. "Reconfigured Terrain: Aural Architecture in *Jacob's Room* and *The Years*." *Woolf and the City: Selected Papers from the Nineteenth Annual Conference on Virginia Woolf*. Ed. Elizabeth F. Evans and Sarah E. Cornish. Clemson: Clemson University Digital Press, 2010. 71–76. Print.

———. "Virginia Woolf, Ethel Smyth, and Music: Listening as a Productive Mode of Social Interaction." *College Literature* 32.3 (2005): 51–71. Print.

Comstock, Margaret: "The Loudspeaker and the Human Voice: Politics and the Form of *The Years*." *Bulletin of the New York Public Library* 80 (1977): 252–75. Print.

Cuddy-Keane, Melba. "Modernist Soundscapes and the Intelligent Ear: An Approach to Narrative through Auditory Perception." *A Companion to Narrative Theory*. Ed. James Phelan and Peter J. Rabinowitz. Oxford: Blackwell, 2005. 382–98. Print.

———. "The Politics of Comic Modes in Virginia Woolf's *Between the Acts*." *PMLA* 105.2 (1990): 273–85. Print.

———. "Virginia Woolf, Sound Technologies, and the New Aurality." *Virginia Woolf in the Age of Mechanical Reproduction*. Ed. Pamela L. Caughie. New York: Garland, 2000. 69–96. Print.

Drew-Bear, Thomas. "The Trochaic Tetrameter in Greek Tragedy." *American Journal of Philology* 89.4 (1968): 385–405.

Fowler, Rowena. "Moments of Metamorphoses: Virginia Woolf's Greece." *Comparative Literature* 51:3 (1999): 217–42.

Frattarola, Angela. "Listening for 'Found Sound' Samples in the Novels of Virginia Woolf." *Woolf Studies Annual* 11 (2005): 133–59. Print.

Godlovitch, Stan. *Musical Performance: A Philosophical Study*. London: Routledge, 1998. Print.

Goldman, Jane. *The Feminist Aesthetics of Virginia Woolf: Modernism, Post-Impressionism, and the Politics of the Visual*. Cambridge: Cambridge University Press, 1998. Print.

Jankélévitch, Vladimir. *Music and the Ineffable*. Trans. Carolyn Abbate. Princeton: Princeton University Press, 2003. Print.

Leaska, Mitchell A., ed. and intro. *The Pargiters by Virginia Woolf: The Novel-Essay Portion of* The Years. New York: New York Public Library, 1977. Print.

Little, Judy. *The Experimental Self: Dialogic Subjectivity in Woolf, Pym, and Brooke-Rose*. Carbondale: Southern Illinois University Press, 1996. Print.

Marcus, Jane. "*The Years* as Greek Drama, Domestic Novel, and Gotterdammerung." *Bulletin of the New York Public Library* 80 (1977): 276–301. Print.

McClary, Susan. *Feminine Endings*. Minneapolis: University of Minnesota Press, 1991. Print.

Monson, Tamlyn. "'A Trick of the Mind': Alterity, Ontology, and Representation in Virginia Woolf's *The Waves*." *Modern Fiction Studies* 50.1 (2004): 173–96. Print.

Pridmore-Brown, Michelle. "1939–40: Of Virginia Woolf, Gramophones, and Fascism." *PMLA* 113.3 (1998): 408–21. Print.

Rosenfeld, Natania. *Outsiders Together: Virginia and Leonard Woolf*. Princeton: Princeton University Press, 2000. Print.

Sarker, Sonita. "An Unharmonious Trio? Georg Lukács, Music, and Virginia Woolf's *Between the Acts*." *Virginia Woolf and the Arts*. Ed. Diane F. Gillespie and Leslie K. Hankins. New York: Pace University Press, 1996. 158–65. Print.

Schechner, Richard. *Performance Theory*. New York: Routledge, 2003. Print.

Schulze, Robin Gail. "Design in Motion: Words, Music, and the Search for Coherence in the Works of Virginia Woolf and Arnold Schoenberg." *Studies in the Literary Imagination* 25.2 (1992): 5–22. Print.

Turner, Victor. "Liminality and Communitas." *The Performance Studies Reader*. Ed. Henry Bial. New York: Routledge, 2003. Print.

Vandivere, Julie. "Waves and Fragments: Linguistic Construction as Subject Formation in Virginia Woolf." *Twentieth-Century Literature* 42.2 (1996): 221–33. Print.

Wallace, Miriam L. "Theorizing Relational Subjects: Metonymic Narrative in *The Waves*." *Narrative* 8.3 (2000): 294–323. Print.

Woolf, Virginia. *Between the Acts*. 1941. Oxford: Oxford University Press, 1992. Print.

———. *Between the Acts*. 1941. New York: Harcourt, 2008. Print.

———. *The Diary of Virginia Woolf*. Ed. Anne Olivier Bell. Vol. 4. New York: Harcourt Brace Jovanovich, 1982. Print.

———. *The Essays of Virginia Woolf*. Vol. 4. Ed. Andrew McNeillie. Orlando: Harcourt, 1994. Print.

———. *The Essays of Virginia Woolf*. Vol. 6. Ed. Stuart N. Clarke. London: Hogarth Press, 2011. Print.

———. *Moments of Being*. 2nd ed. Ed. Jeanne Schulkind. San Diego: Harcourt Brace & Company, 1985. Print.

———. *The Years*. 1937. New York: Harcourt, 2008. Print.

Zimring, Rishona. "Suggestions of Other Worlds: The Art of Sound in *The Years*." *Woolf Studies Annual* 8 (2002): 127–56. Print.

I

Turning back among the many leaves which the past had folded in him, peering into the heart of that forest where light and shade so chequer each other that all shape is distorted, and one blunders, now with the sun in one's eyes, now with a dark shadow, he sought an image to cool and detach and round off his feeling in a concrete shape.

VIRGINIA WOOLF,
To the Lighthouse

EIGHT

Sounding the Past

THE MUSIC IN *BETWEEN THE ACTS*

Trina Thompson

VIRGINIA WOOLF'S LAST NOVEL, *BETWEEN THE ACTS*, WAS FIRST published in 1941, the year of her death. Begun before Britain's engagement in World War II, the novel retains the imprint of the time of its historical inception. Although fictional, this work seems to follow Roland Barthes's dictum on the writing of history and the effect of historical time. In his essay "The Discourse of History," Barthes postulates that "the nearer we are to the historian's own time, the more strongly the pressure of the uttering makes itself felt, and the slower the history becomes. There is no such thing as isochrony – and to say this, is to attack implicitly the linearity of the discourse" (9). Thus, while Woolf must suffer the war, the residents and guests of fictional Pointz Hall remain poised before the violence. This temporal bifurcation plays an important role in constructing the complex texture of the novel.

In fact, the mere act of prying apart the strands of history – the creation of *space* – is a sonic act, one that allows for echoes, for the noisy layering of sounds. Judith Greenberg notes that the novel "is full of echoes – repeated words and noises, fragmented music and phrases, and disembodied voices" (52). And, as we shall see, Woolf's preoccupation with music and aural imagery is an especially arresting aspect of this work. Indeed, as Avrom Fleishman explains, the provisionally "solid world of Pointz Hall" is splintered into multiple, simultaneous narratives, a "juggling of illusion and reality" (247) that is engendered by conflicting, vertiginous mise-en-abîme framing. The most obvious of these frames is the novel's equivocal division between real(istic) life and an unfolding pageant, a play within a play. Understanding both of these aspects as novelistic fictions, what are we to make of the real-life voices that encroach on the integrity of the pageant? This duality is complicated again by the novel's final line, which suggests that the entire novel has itself been an "entr'acte" in yet another play (247). These "mutually framed and framing visions of the novel and the play" (McWhirter 799) emphasize the importance of the interval, of that which comes to life in between.

The author's early formulations of what was to become her final novel posit a supersaturated wholeness of experience, a genre incorporating both life and art, both facts and inspiration. Midway through its composition, Woolf notes that "P. H. [*Pointz Hall*, Woolf's working title] is to be a series of contrasts. Will it come off? Am I in earnest?" (*D*5: 159). At the same time, the unusual texture of the work would dissolve the isolation of the individual. In her initial speculation, she writes:

> But to amuse myself, let me note: why not Poyntzet Hall: a centre: all lit. discussed in connection with real little incongruous living humour; & anything that comes into my head; but "I" rejected: 'We' substituted: to whom at the end there shall be an invocation? "We" ... composed of many different things ... we all life, all art, all waifs & strays – a rambling capricious but somehow unified whole – the present state of my mind? And English country; [...] & a perpetual variety & change from intensity to prose. & facts – & notes; & – but eno'. (*D*5: 135)

In a sense, then, the community created by the mode of this novel was also intended to collapse the traditional boundary between fact and fiction, a boundary Woolf often remarks. Again, in her diary she asks, "But what are the interesting things? I'm thinking of what I should like to read here in 10 years time. And I'm all at sea. Perhaps literal facts. The annal, not the novel (*D*5: 216–17).

As the epigraph passage from *To the Lighthouse* suggests, Woolf had been continually interested in the blending of fact and fiction inherent in efforts of memoir, in "reading" the pages of one's own life. The period of the composition of *Between the Acts* is no exception. "I was thinking of my memoirs," she explains in her diary, "The platform of time. How I see father from the 2 angles. As a child condemning; as a woman of 58 understanding – I shd say tolerating. Both views true?" (*D*5: 281). The interlacing of contrasts in *Between the Acts* occasions the multiplication of perspectives, and the lacunae, particular to memory. During the lengthy process of writing *The Years* (the novel that preceded *Between the Acts*), Woolf eventually decided *not* to reread earlier chapters of her writing in preparation for new sections. John Whittier-Ferguson explains that Woolf intended *The Years* "to register compositional time, to record the history of its own making in its incompletely realized echoes, its slightly misrecalled allusions to preceding chapters, as well as its triumphant instances of perfect retrieval" (298).

In *Between the Acts* the texture of memory is evoked through a conscious procedure of erasure and broken connections. In *Orlando*, Woolf had written, "Memory is a seamstress, and a capricious one at that. [. . .] We know not what comes next, or what follows after. Thus the most ordinary movement in the world [. . .] may agitate a thousand odd, disconnected fragments" (*O* 58). As Whittier-Ferguson suggests in his study of the drafts of this final novel, "The three versions of *Between the Acts*, when read in order of their composition, reveal a text in the process of forgetting itself: a novel that grows more elliptical, less discursive, less explanatory with each revision" (301). Near the end of the process, the author herself writes, "I am a little triumphant about the book. I think its an interesting attempt at a new method. I think its more quintessential than the others" (*D5*: 340). Woolf understands this process of fictional culling as a way to the heart of things, a means to trace the concrete shape of feeling. Thus, in *Between the Acts* memory and forgetting are no longer merely described (as in *Orlando*) or permitted as hallmarks of time's passage (as in *The Years*). Instead, they participate in the construction of Woolf's "new method" – a method that invokes music as both symbol and process.

II

> It was a miserable machine, an inefficient machine, she thought, the human apparatus for painting or for feeling; it always broke down at the critical moment; heroically, one must force it on.
>
> Virginia Woolf, *To the Lighthouse*

Music scholars have addressed the question of the relationship between text and music from the following standpoints:

1. Language: How is music like language?[1] And how does music convey meaning, broadly construed? Ethnomusicological studies have highlighted the fact that many non-Western cultures do not distinguish radically between language and music. For example, Kofi Agawu explores the fusion between language and music in many African cultures, insisting that "to the West African, the idea that an instrumental genre exists outside the functional domain of words and their meanings is simply absurd" ("Rhythmic Structure" 415). Recent studies in music psychology suggest that while "language and music have distinct and domain-specific syntactic representations [. . .] activating these representations as part of online processing draws on a common pool of limited neural resources" (Patel 213). Even so, this standpoint is necessarily fraught; as Daniel Albright concludes, "the more we try to understand music as a language, the more strongly it resists that understanding; and the more we try to understand music as the opposite of language, the more sweetly, strongly, plainly it speaks to the ear" (19).

Scholarship from this standpoint often focuses on a particular dimension of language and its musical parallels. As Harold Powers states, "The metaphor of music as language has three principal aspects, depending upon whether the focus is on semantics, on phonology, or on syntax and grammar" (1). Fred Lerdahl and Ray Jackendoff's 1983 *A Generative Theory of Tonal Music* theorizes ways tonal music may be parsed and understood as a linguistic system, complete with well-formedness rules and so forth. The work of music semioticians including Jean-Jacques Nattiez, Robert Hatten, Raymond Monelle, and Agawu explores the issue of sign and meaning in music. This line of questioning addresses music not necessarily as "literature," but rather as "language." But Hatten's musical "expressive genres" certainly parallel archetypal literary plots (*Musical Meaning in Beethoven: Markedness, Correlation, and Interpretation*, 1994). And Agawu's *Playing with Signs: A Semiotic Interpretation of Classic Music* invokes the art of rhetoric, as does Mark Evan Bonds's *Wordless Rhetoric: Musical Form and the Metaphor of the Oration* (both published in 1991).

2. Multimedia: How do/can text and music relate within a work such as an art song or opera? Multimedia genres have inspired analytical frameworks that attempt to grapple with the artwork's component media as well as the "third thing" – the multimedia artwork itself. Notable

here are the models for lied analysis described by Agawu ("Theory and Practice") and refined by Suzanne Lodato ("Recent Approaches"). In his 1998 *Analysing Musical Multimedia,* Nicholas Cook describes possible interactions between media that have been forced into contact within a single, multimedia artwork: the media may function as synonyms for one another, as complements of one another, or as antagonists. Lawrence Kramer evokes a similar sense of struggle between media in an art song: "The music appropriates the poem by contending with it, phonetically, dramatically, and semantically, and this contest is what most drives and shapes the song" ("On Deconstructive Text-Music Relationships" 173).

3. Ekphrasis: How can a work of art in one media be "translated" into another media? What is it about the artwork that can only be "said" or "expressed" in its home media, and what (content? form? cognitive experience?) can be effectively translated into another media? Kramer refers to "shared structural rhythms" – deep similarities between art of different media (*Music and Poetry* 10), Werner Wolf's 2002 article frames this concept as transmedial characteristics ("Intermediality Revisited"). In Siglind Bruhn's writing, the focus is on trying to understand how intermedial translations or "transmedialization[s]" often cause restructuring of the receiving medium (*Musical Ekphrasis* 51). David Urrows remarks on the rise of adaptation studies (for example, studying a play that has been turned into an opera). He observes that such criticism previously gave attention to the adaptation's "perceived 'fidelity'" to the original, but that more recently scholars have called such arguments into question, leading to a "revaluing" of adaptation genres per se (x–xi). Ekphrastic approaches are often theories of violent or transformative change; neutral translation is understood as both impossible and aesthetically undesirable. Eric Prieto insists that "as a general rule, it is during periods of stylistic flux and innovation that we find the highest concentration of appeals to the other arts" (64). It is the tracing of ekphrasis that is most pertinent to Woolf's approach to *Between the Acts.*

This novel becomes "musical" in several meanings of the word. Woolf's attention to aural imagery in general, and to music in particular, pervades the work. Not only is music delivered by the gramophone an important actor in the pageant, but sound and music also frequently appear in service as metaphors or symbols. In order to create the distinctive textures of her prose, Woolf moves more deeply into ekphrastic territory, employing two idiomatically musical techniques: (1) motivic repetition and development and (2) the creation of compound melody, a relative of counterpoint. Finally, the unique structures of this novel show similarities to the development of opera, a musical genre that solders text to music.

In *Between the Acts* Woolf's characters experience history as an audible resonance. On the morning of the pageant, the residents of Pointz Hall reenact conversations that had been rehearsed for years: the elderly siblings, Lucy and Bart, converse according to a kind of anticipated echo. The narrator explains that "the words were like the first peal of a chime of bells. As the first peals, you hear the second; as the second peals, you hear the third" (BTA 12). The gramophone's familiar music also calls up the expectation of continuity: "Like quicksilver sliding, filings magnetized, the distracted united. The tune began: the first note meant the second; the second a third" (113). Similarly, at one bleak moment in the pageant – the amateur performers faltering in their parts – nature intervenes with a voice that carries the emotion of the moment and communicates the persistence of prehistory: "Then suddenly, as the illusion petered out, the cows took up the burden. [...] From cow after cow came the same yearning bellow. The whole world was filled with dumb yearning. It was the primeval voice sounding loud in the ear of the present moment" (83). Woolf also addresses the aural quality of empty spaces, acknowledging silence as a part of the music of experience: "Empty, empty, empty; silent, silent, silent. The room was a shell, singing of what was before time was" (21). Indeed, the verbal repetitions that characterize this quote enact their own echoic patterns. Repeatedly, then, the intersections and conflations of past and present are suggested through aural connections that bridge disparate moments.

In addition to evoking the resonance of history, music also serves as a metaphor for and catalyst of harmonious security. This is true both of Woolf's diegetic music – the gramophone that figures so prominently throughout the novel's pageant – and of her musical imagery. In the experience of the pageant's audience, only music can heal the raw gap of the present – music redolent of the past: "For I hear music, they were saying. Music wakes us. Music makes us see the hidden, join the broken" (BTA

71). Palpable, audible music emerges as an antidote to confusion and anxiety. It constitutes an intelligible voice: "Was it Bach, Handel, Beethoven, Mozart or nobody famous, but merely a traditional tune? Anyhow, thank heaven, it was somebody speaking after the anonymous bray of the infernal megaphone" (113). Then, too, musical imagery achieves an instance of sublime coherence between art, nature, and humanity:

> The gramophone, while the scene was removed, gently stated certain facts which everybody knows to be perfectly true. [...]
> The view repeated in its own way what the tune was saying. [...]
> The cows, making a step forward, then standing still, were saying the same thing to perfection.
> Folded in this triple melody, the audience sat gazing. (80)

In this scene the music of the gramophone, the view at sunset, and the cows themselves are experienced by the audience as "saying the same thing," as belonging to a "triple melody" whose multiple sources nevertheless sing the same, inalienable tune. Woolf uses literal music (the gramophone recordings) as merely a part of a larger metaphorical harmony. At another point in the novel, the pageant again seems on the edge of failure: "But she [Miss La Trobe] had nothing. She had forbidden music. [...] This is death, death, death, she noted in the margin of her mind; when illusion fails" (108). Here the music of nature replaces the gramophone: it begins to rain. The "sudden, profuse" shower is interpreted by the audience as "weeping for all people," and Woolf writes it as percussive music – "Tears. Tears. Tears" (108). The sense of community achieved elsewhere via the gramophone is here accomplished by the musical, "universal" rain (108).

In Woolf's nuanced use of music as symbol, its connotations are not always positive. At times the feeling of harmonious union may exclude those beyond its circle. This is the case, for instance, with the attraction Isa feels for Rupert Haines: "Mrs. Haines was aware of the emotion circling them [Isa and Rupert], excluding her. She waited, as one waits for the strain of an organ to die out before leaving church" (2). Another dysphoric resonance arises from Woolf's use of the gramophone to effect social control: "The audience was assembling. The music was summoning them" (70), and again, "The tick, tick, tick seemed to hold them together, tranced" (48). Here the novel's music acts as a mechanism of unification;

Woolf uses sound to stand for the power of the collective, its comforting reassurance and its terrifying control.[2] Music is therefore not only the metaphor for historical resonance and community, but it also figures as the voice of exclusion and a potentially dangerous manipulation.

Yet, without music, "all their nerves were on edge. They sat exposed. The machine ticked. There was no music. [...] They were neither one thing nor the other; neither Victorians nor themselves" (106). In fact, this confusion of identity is the artistic result of the pageant. Miss La Trobe shows them vignettes of England's history, only to end with a literal reflection of their own time: the actors confront the audience with mirrors. The audience cannot interpret this move. When they catch sight of their reflections in the mirrors, when the disembodied megaphone asks them to reflect on themselves, they respond, "Ourselves? But that's cruel. To snap us as we are, before we've had time to assume . . . And only, too, in parts. . . . That's what's so distorting and upsetting and utterly unfair" (110). The gramophone's music of social cohesion and historical retelling thus shatters against the resistant, obsidian anxiety of the present. If we are able to capture only fragments of ourselves, the audience seems to ask, how do we find coherence or community?

III

> No one need wonder that Orlando started, pressed her hand to her heart, and turned pale. For what more terrifying revelation can there be than that it is the present moment? That we survive the shock at all is only possible because the past shelters us on one side, the future on another.
>
> Virginia Woolf, *Orlando*

For Miss La Trobe – as for Woolf – the manipulation of auditory events is crucial to artistic endeavor. The artist "was one who seethes wandering bodies and floating voices in a cauldron, and makes rise up from its amorphous mass a re-created world" (BTA 91). Our experience of this world may be one of apparent violence. In *Between the Acts* its creative force is likened to jazz, to "the young, who can't make, but only break; shiver into splinters the old vision; smash to atoms what was whole" (110). To Woolf's narrator(s), this scene's music is almost indefinable, as was that of the previous scene: "The tune changed; snapped; broke; jagged. Foxtrot was it? Jazz?" (109). Thus the new universe results from an audible tessellation of the old. In *Between the Acts,* Woolf destabilizes the shelter of the past; the present cannot be absorbed, it fragments and echoes.

In this context, the experience of multiple aural strata – rather than rational teleology – is of particular importance. This is suggested by Isa's experience of the pageant, in which

> there was such a medley of things going on, what with the beldame's deafness, the bawling of the youths, and the confusion of the plot that she could make nothing of it. [...]
> Don't bother about the plot: the plot's nothing. (53–54)

Instead of focusing on plot, then, the novel employs surface fragmentation and motivic repetition. In celebrating the gap, Woolf allows the boundaries that used to isolate each individual character to become increasingly permeable, permitting the creation of new kinds of voices and communities. Woolf also recognizes that this artistic process can be both violent and alienating: instead of integral, we come to understand our lives and our selves as fragmentary. In musical composition, however, the fragment is an artistic blessing, as the act of fragmentation frees a motive from its initial context to become a different type of building block. A motive can be more subtle and more flexible than a musical theme. It can be used to create connections between otherwise contrasting passages. The musical motive, while itself fragmentary, generates the expectation of continuity.

The saturation of the novel's texture with repeated motivic images is one means by which musical, aural rhetoric is imported to the literary genre.[3] Here my analysis turns from music as metaphor or theme to ways that Woolf treats the construction of the novel as a musical composition. Specifically, she uses indivisible verbal images (motives) to create far-ranging coherence across large spans. These repetitions help unify the soundscape of *Between the Acts,* simultaneously making connections between characters whose experiences seem disparate.

The swallows, emerging from Lucinda Swithin's conversation, constitute one of these recurring motifs:

> The swallows "come every year," she [Mrs. Swithin] said, "the same birds." Mrs. Manresa smiled benevolently, humouring the old lady's whimsy. It was unlikely, she thought, that the birds were the same. (BTA 60)

> "They come every year," said Mrs. Swithin, ignoring the fact that she spoke to the empty air. "From Africa." As they had come, she supposed, when the Barn was a swamp. (61)
>
> "Swallows," said Lucy, holding her cup, looking at the birds. [. . .] Across Africa, across France they had come to nest here. Year after year they came. Before there was a channel, [. . .] they had come. (64)

And as Bartholomew goes to catch the pageant's second act, we hear him take up the thread: "'Swallow, my sister, O sister swallow,' he muttered, feeling for his cigar case, following his son" (65). We then accompany other characters, only to return later to Mr. Oliver, who's still "murmuring" and "muttering" the same refrain (68, 69). Still later in the pageant, Etty Springett observes the scenery for the next segment: "'Look Minnie!' she exclaimed. 'Those are real swallows!'" (98). After this segment, Mrs. Lynn Jones remains oblivious to the next scene change, savoring the evocation of *home*, which she sees in her imagination even as "real swallows were skimming over real grass" (103). Yet again, "real swallows" appear to dance to the gramophone's music (109). The echoing of these motivic swallows throughout the novel constitutes another type of historical echo, another pealing of the bell.

The splintering of the novel's surface is apparent from its punctuation. As James Naremore asserts, "There is, in fact, no other novel by Mrs. Woolf that uses the ellipses so freely. In *Between the Acts* it appears everywhere, as if to emphasize the tenuous and fragmentary quality of life" (223). This punctuation choice recreates an aural experience: we hear only some discourse in full. Much of the time, however, we overhear fragments; our attention is momentarily diverted – even from conversations in which we participate. Woolf's fractured and repeating evocation of memory and echo is also implied in the novel's frequent use of recalled quotations, both literary and musical. Declaring that "this peppering of fragmentary quotations throughout the scenes is perhaps the most distinctive attribute of the novel," Naremore interprets the use of quotation as a symptom of Woolf's interest in "orts and fragments" (128).

In her evocation of multiple aural layers in *Between the Acts*, Woolf allows us to listen to her characters in anonymous contrapuntal fragments. As William Freedman suggests, passages of literary counterpoint may not mimic the simultaneity of a polyphonic composition, but instead actually recreate the compound melody found in music for solo melodic instruments. In such compositions, a single voice leaps between multiple vocal parts, conveying a sense of the full, harmonic texture.[4] While the audience's experience of jazz in the pageant as an almost violent art (109) is opposed to the calming effect of Bach, Handel, Beethoven, and Mozart (113), the contrapuntal, multivoiced *literary* effect I describe here could derive from either music. However, the disruption it presents to traditional literary modes certainly allies it with the ethos – in this context – of jazz.

This type of literary compound melody emerges clearly as the audience leaves the pageant and we hear their unattributed remarks, punctuated by Woolf's ellipses: "I do think," someone was saying, "Miss Whatshername should have come forward and not left it to the rector... After all, she wrote it.... I thought it brilliantly clever... O my dear, I thought it utter bosh" (BTA 118). The contrapuntal, communal surfaces of *Between the Acts* further a trajectory prefigured in *Orlando:* the increasingly porous nature of subjective experience. Naremore notes that in this later work, the individual is no longer strictly isolated, even within the ostensibly hermetic space of the internal monologue (191–92).

Erich Auerbach's notion of the "'multipersonal representation of consciousness'" (536) is instructive here. Along similar lines, Naremore writes that "Woolf's characters always tend to merge with the narrator and become slightly disembodied" (216). Auerbach develops this idea in response to a passage from Woolf's *To the Lighthouse*. In this work, rather than focusing on the explication of a single mind's experience, Woolf presents the reader with glimpses of multiple consciousnesses, shuttling quickly back and forth between individuals, thereby diminishing the sense of the subject's boundaries and, crucially, attempting to depict an "objective reality" (Auerbach 536). In *Between the Acts*, the characters *themselves* (and not merely the reader) experience this collective consciousness. During preparations for the pageant, for instance, Miss La Trobe hears the audience talking: "Over the tops of the bushes came stray voices, voices without bodies, symbolical voices they seemed to her, half hearing, seeing nothing, but still, over the bushes, feeling invisible threads connecting the bodiless voices" (BTA 90). Woolf thus fractures the normative boundaries of character and dialogue, and the disembodied voices become a vehicle of emotional power, a new means of community.

IV

> It's odd that science, so they tell me, is making things (so to speak) more spiritual ... The very latest notion, so I'm told is, nothing's solid.
>
> Virginia Woolf, *Between the Acts*

Viewed through the chronologically prior lens of Woolf's *Orlando* (1928), *Between the Acts* emerges as a new way of understanding historical narrative. While the "biography" of Orlando traces a single life over fantastical temporal spans, this final novel embodies multiple historical chronologies. Although *Between the Acts* observes the tempus and locus of the classical unities,[5] the pageant within the novel is a montage rendering of England's growth from "a child new born" (45) through the "'Present time. Ourselves'" (105). Again, although the novel was completed during Britain's involvement in World War II, it is set in the "demilitarized zone" of the previous decade: the impending conflict still hovers in the wings.[6] In a sense Woolf applies the new material physics – itself remarked by a member of the pageant's audience – to the temporal continuum.

Between the Acts is set only a heartbeat behind Woolf's own time. Nevertheless, its structuring event – the village pageant – replicates an authentic aspect of the period.[7] Further, the novel's preoccupation with the interpretation and experience of the past marks it as a kind of historical fiction, one that both questions and reifies the boundaries of historical experience. Kristina Busse writes, "Neither a traditional historical novel, nor a text completely divorced from history, *Between the Acts* problematizes historiography and our ability to (re)construct historical events" (90). As an experiment with historically infused genres, *Between the Acts* recapitulates Woolf's long-standing engagement with the past as well as her exploration of alternatives to traditional historiography.

The 1930s saw the rise of fascism throughout Europe (with Franco's victory in March of 1939 coterminous with Woolf's final draft of *Between the Acts*). More pointedly, Woolf lived under the shadow of England's impending involvement in World War II; this final novel was composed during the early months of Britain's entrance into armed conflict. Her diary entries of these years are permeated by the timbre of war. She writes, "But theres a vast calm cold gloom. And the strain. Like waiting a doctors verdict. And the young – young men smashed up" (*D*5: 231). A year later she records the emotional oppression of war, "Now we are in the war. England is being attacked. I got this feeling for the first time completely yesterday. The feeling of pressure, danger horror" (313). Woolf's passionate artistic address of political issues – her pacifism and coeval critique of masculine hegemony – reflects contexts both private and public.

The traumas of her personal life, including the deaths of several family members and the experience of sexual abuse, gave terrible resonance to contemporaneous European events. Further, Leonard Woolf's Jewishness, as well as the couple's socialist politics, confirmed their sense of immediate danger. In May 1940 so personal was the threat in the case of a Nazi invasion that Leonard and Virginia planned to commit suicide by poison should the event arrive.[8] Woolf's resistance to the real events of history is manifested in her rephrasing of the grand narrative of the past. Thus, in *Between the Acts,* Woolf deliberately creates a parallel historical record, one orchestrated by a woman (Miss La Trobe) and devoid of armed conflict. This pageant is contained within the novel's historical environment, in which war is already audible: imminent. The strains of history multiply, for in addition to this twinned strand, Woolf interjects the selves of the audience, the selves that do not constitute either record, although they may "play" as historical types (the villagers are cast in various historical roles).

Between the Acts makes explicit use of the embedded pageant to complicate the novel's engagement with history. On the one hand, the chronicle of the British Empire is replayed, excerpted, and edited in artistic revision by Miss La Trobe (herself "othered" by way of her gender, sexual orientation, nationality, and profession). Simultaneously, Woolf gives us the audience, a community placed in juxtaposition to their own fragmented history – an audience struggling to synthesize a coherent narrative that might connect their past to their present, and themselves to one another.

Woolf's splintered narrative style is a function of her double-edged historiography: in *Between the Acts,* she leaves aside fictional biography (which she had previously explored in *Orlando*), creating instead a fictive microhistory.[9] As Jill Lepore explains, in contrast to biography, "Microhistory will always draw the writer's, and the reader's, attention away from the subject and toward the culture" (142). It is precisely this shift of focus that is operative in *Between the Acts;* here is the "we" Woolf had imagined in her diary sketch of April 1938.

The use of multiple foci in *Between the Acts* – that is, the book's *dissociation* from any single character – has been explained as a result of Woolf's modernist emulation of the comic pose in literature of the Elizabethan period, or of the eighteenth century. For instance, David McWhirter observes that Woolf's "status as an exemplary modernist is also confirmed by her fascination with literary modes and figures – Elizabethan and Restoration drama, comic opera, Austen, Pope, and Congreve – that reflect an alternative impulse towards comic distance and formal perfection" (788). Alternately, Melba Cuddy-Keane suggests that the formulation of community in this novel constitutes a kind of Grecian chorus (275–76). Woolf likely also understood this less romanticized inhabitation of conflicting consciousnesses as part of a necessary Georgian escape from Edwardian literary modes. As she declares in her 1924 essay "Character in Fiction," "The sound of breaking and falling, crashing and destruction [...] is the prevailing sound of the Georgian age" (51). The monolithic, seamless approach of the previous era could not deliver a true character study; new methods must smash the old, much like the jazz music in *Between the Acts,* whose innovation sounds as a kind of violence.

Rather than a definitive study of a central character (perhaps she might have chosen Miss La Trobe or Isa Oliver), or a historical chronicle of war – the grand narrative – this last novel reflects a kind of community, an assortment of people collected temporarily at Pointz Hall. As such, *Between the Acts* records a historical truth, for as Woolf's diary shows, the author struggled with a personal negotiation between the grand narrative of World War II and the events of her daily life. This relationship is felt as one of distance, a disconnect that Woolf describes in both spatial and temporal terms. Only three months before finishing this novel she writes:

I have only five minutes [...] to say that the war – yes I have left only 5 minutes to fill in that omission – the war goes on; [...] But it dribbles out in such little drops. One cant always catch them. The war slowly enacts itself on a great scene: round our little scene. We spend 59 minutes here; one minute there. (D5: 343)

The war's scale cannot be fully absorbed or experienced by a single individual; neither does its narrative fully articulate the lives of those it touches. Woolf's diary entry expresses this fact as a kind of shuttling of experience between intervals of the "great scene" and the "little scene." Historical truth in *Between the Acts* also resides in the gap; it describes lives encompassed by "history" – by the great events of history – but not voiced in the chronicle.

Throughout the novel, the permeability of temporal and personal experience infuses the present with a layering of historical chronologies. For the community in *Between the Acts*, history must be a negotiation of private pasts, shared historical narratives and the sense of the gap between the individual (further, the present) and the intelligible past. The reader senses that the official history inflicts a kind of order. Analogically, "the trees, O the trees, how gravely and sedately like senators in council, or the spaced pillars of some cathedral church. . . . Yes, they barred the music, and massed and hoarded; and prevented what was fluid from overflowing" (109). Opposed to, or contending with, the grand narrative, this small community finds its voices in between the recorded events.

V

But he paused.
    As this pause was of extreme significance in his history, more so, indeed, than many acts which bring men to their knees and make rivers run with blood, it behoves [sic] us to ask why he paused.

Virginia Woolf, *Orlando*

In this final novel, Woolf creates space for an alternative historical narrative. As I have said, this has aural consequences. *Between the Acts* invokes music as metaphor, uses motivic saturation as a means to continuity, and splinters its textures as it recreates multiple contrapuntal layers. Woolf's use of the pageant – specifically the way in which she fractures its performance – also has musical import.

The "seamless" narrative of the national historical record problematized in the pageant is also opened to the world and experience of the audience. In performance, the historical gaps are translated as temporal intervals, the intermission:

> Here was her [Miss La Trobe's] downfall; here was the Interval. Writing this skimble-skamble stuff in her cottage, she had agreed to cut the play here; a slave to her audience – to Mrs. Sands' grumble – about tea; about dinner – she had gashed the scene here. Just as she had brewed emotion, she spilt it. (BTA 56)

In this chronological space, people speak, adding resonance and interference to the sounds of the collective. We hear voices both bodied and disembodied, as conversation is exchanged between the main characters or excerpted in overheard fragments from the anonymous attendees. Further, it is during these intervals that the personal dramas of the characters unfold. As I have suggested, these are the conversations and interactions that constitute yet another kind of interstice, as Giles and Isa Oliver negotiate their emotional estrangement before the evening's inevitable fight and embrace. Indeed, Woolf ends the novel with the narrator speaking:

> But first they must fight, [...] in the heart of darkness, in the fields of night. [...]
> Then the curtain rose. They spoke. (131)

Turning analytical attention to what Kramer might call "shared structural rhythms" (*Music and Poetry* 10), it is worth comparing the structural conceit of *Between the Acts* to the pattern of formal evolution, amalgamation, and experimentation that gave rise to opera.[10] At the royal courts of Renaissance Italy, improvised musical entertainments (*intermedi*) were performed during the intermissions of the primary theatrical piece. These entertainments initially served to indicate the passage of time within the drama, to mark the interval, or simply to divert the audience's attention from any necessary changes of scene. Toward the latter part of the sixteenth century, the incorporation of increasingly sophisticated music and spectacle (including dancing and mechanical apparatus) underscored the political might of the courts that produced these events. As Thomas Walker describes:

> "The Medici court at Florence was particularly lavish with this kind of entertainment. The *intermedi* for Bargagli's comedy *La pellegrina*, organized by

Giovanni de' Bardi as part of the festivities celebrating the wedding of Grand
Duke Ferdinando de' Medici and Christine of Lorraine (1589) exemplify the
powers of music." (15)

Eventually, the hierarchy between principal drama and *intermedi* was overturned: the musical power and spectacle on display during the intermissions came to overshadow what was nominally the main event.[11] As Antonfrancesco Grazzini, a Florentine writer active in the latter half of the sixteenth century, observes, "'Once intermedi were made to serve the comedy, but now comedies are made to serve the intermedi'" (qtd. in Carter, "Seventeenth Century" 3). More than three hundred years later, Piero Weiss asserts, "Opera was born in Florence at the end of the sixteenth century. It derived almost seamlessly from its immediate precursor, the intermedio, or lavish between-the-acts spectacle presented in conjunction with a play on festive occasions" (1).

As this new genre coalesced, musicians became increasingly self-conscious about its rhetorical heritage and possibilities. Apologists for the new Baroque style explained their aesthetics in humanist terms, as a recapturing of classical Greek practice. Claude Palisca describes Girolamo Mei (1519–1594) as an "Italian humanist, editor of Greek texts and historian of Greek music." Palisca goes on to note that Mei's "pioneering research into Greek music was of fundamental importance and a decisive influence on the emergence of monody and music drama." One of Mei's most influential ideas was that the classical Greek dramas were *sung* from beginning to end (Palisca). Another important focus was on the power of ancient Greek music to affect the listener. Not only did Mei write about Greek musical systems, as described by Aristoxenus, Ptolemy, and Aristides Quintilianus, among others – but he also discussed the place of these musical structures and materials "in education, moral conduct and therapeutics" (Palisca).

In a critique of the previously established style of music, Vicenzo Gailei, a close correspondent of Mei (Palisca) avows that "'the end of music today is nothing but the delight and pleasure of the senses. Among the ancients it was to move and dispose the soul to virtue'" (trans. Claude Palisca, *Beginnings of Baroque Music*; qtd. in Carter, *Music in Italy* 186). In 1634 Pietro de' Bardi, son of the Giovanni de' Bardi mentioned in conjunction with the 1589 *intermedi,* explains that, driven by the desire to recapture the expressive power of ancient music, composers of the musico-dramatic *intermedi* developed the recitative-like *stile rappresentativo*, in which declamatory speech was given melodic scaffolding (523–25). The humanists believed that it was the expressive *fusion* of text and music that had given the ancient Greeks their supposed power to move and influence the audience.

Beyond shared structural rhythms, there are shared affinities between Woolf and the community that invented opera. First, like these early Baroque musicians and humanists, Woolf returned repeatedly to the idea of music's power to shape or influence an audience. What concerns her is not merely the ability to manipulate feelings, but to affect deeply, perhaps even on the moral or societal level. Cuddy-Keane writes that "for Woolf, music has a greater unifying power than discursive prose, since music is capable of containing and sustaining personal associations while still being something the listeners share" (281). In fact, the many references to the powerful, even controlling, effect of music on the audience in *Between the Acts* are a return to an earlier theme.[12] In *The Voyage Out*, the narrator describes an audience listening to Rachel at the piano: "Then they began to see themselves and their lives, and the whole of human life advancing very nobly under the direction of the music. They felt themselves ennobled" (179).[13]

Second, as did the apologists of the new monodic style, Woolf had an abiding interest in Greek drama. Rowena Fowler explains Woolf's encounter with the Greek language as akin to an encounter with music: "The Greek language held out the possibility of absolute clarity, and yet offered Woolf the alternative eloquence of pure, pre-verbal, non-verbal sound" (218). Woolf herself describes the choruses of Sophocles's *Ajax* as "hav[ing] a rough kind of beauty & pathos ... a music of words – transcending meaning." (Monks House Papers, A21; qtd. in Fowler 228). Cuddy-Keane argues for the antifascist political shift effected by the emergence of the "communal chorus" in *Between the Acts* (275) – a chorus descended from, and evocative of, Greek comedies. Similarly, Fowler identifies "three formal conventions from ancient Greek literature" that "enjoy a radical renewal in Woolf's novels: the reporting of action, the Socratic dialogue, and, most memorably, the chorus" (226).

As we have seen, opera – powerful, emotionally expressive music bound inextricably to dramatic text – evolved between the acts. Similarly, the conflicted social collective gathered at Pointz Hall finds its voice between historical events: Woolf's narration of their lives constitutes an opposing historical genre, one spliced with events of the historical record, corralled by the music (itself also recorded), yet still heterophonic. I do not, of course, intend to imply that the structure of *Between the Acts* resulted from an intentional mimicking of opera's developmental trajectory. It is rather that Woolf's novel functions – just as opera evolved – as a fiction of the interlude, a powerful historiography of the lacuna. It gives voice to what happens *between*, between vignettes in the pageant, between wars, between individuals.

The fictional microhistory of *Between the Acts* gives precedence to the voice – to voices echoing scripts from their past, to the recorded music that orders and interprets, to the speaking voices that splinter and falter. The novel's essential crises arise as problems of interpretation or integration, moments in which characters cannot satisfactorily draft the events of their own lives. This disorientation is sounded by metaphors of reverberation and interference, aural experiences that may be understood to underlie Woolf's uses of symbolic music and ekphrastic musical processes. *Between the Acts* opens resonant historical space for the lives of ordinary people whose defining moments do not coincide with the events of the grand narrative, but happen, propositionally – between.

NOTES

1. John Williamson discusses this perspective in his introduction to the 2005 anthology *Words and Music* (6).

2. On this topic, see Michele Pridmore-Brown.

3. As William Freedman asserts, "No formal principle is more fundamental to music than repetition" (167). Working with linguistic units below the level of conscious semantic, Kathleen McCluskey explores phonemic motives in the writings of Virginia Woolf, albeit not in *Between the Acts* (*Reverberations*). Stella McNichol addresses the development of thematic ideas in *Between the Acts*, concurrently discussing the role of "recurrent theme words" (163).

4. "This rapid alternation and juxtaposition for contrapuntal effect may certainly be viewed as an imperfect imitation of musical counterpoint, the illusion of simultaneity masking as simultaneity. It may also be read as a quite comfortable literary adaptation and counterpart of an actual

contrapuntal procedure. [. . .] I am speaking of the unilinear polyphony of Bach's unaccompanied suites for violoncello" (Freedman 64).

5. The day is here stretched to twenty-four hours. This classical organization is also remarked by Howard Harper (291–92).

6. One of the attendees complains, "Also, why leave out the Army, as my husband was saying, if it's history?" (BTA 118).

7. In "*Between the Acts* and Louis Napoleon Parker – The Creator of the Modern English Pageant," Ayako Yoshino explains that the pageant was "an art form explicitly associated with local pride, patriotism, charity, and on occasion the war effort" (53). In their work, *The Long Week End: A Social History of Great Britain, 1918–1939*, Robert Graves and Alan Hodge remark on the rise of the News Cinemas, a similarly segmented genre. "The programme," they explain, "consisted usually of two short news reels giving pictures of parades, disasters, sporting events and so on; a Walt Disney film for the comic strip; [. . .] often an interview; musical interludes" (407).

8. According to Quentin Bell, "Even if one were optimistic enough to believe that there might be a grain of pity [. . .] in the heart of such an enemy, it was quite certain that there would be none for a Jewish socialist and his wife; for them the gas chamber would be an unlooked-for mercy" (216).

9. The project of biography haunted her differently during this period. While working on *Between the Acts*, Woolf was also writing her (nonfictional) biography of the painter Roger Fry. In her September 20, 1938, diary entry, she writes, "Note: fiction is far more a strain than biography – thats the excitement" (D 5: 172).

10. Tim Carter's *Music in Late Renaissance and Early Baroque Italy* provides a nuanced account of the various musical strands from which opera coalesced.

11. Cuddy-Keane writes similarly of the hierarchical shift that takes place within *Between the Acts*: "The dramatic form inverts itself. What was background shifts to foreground; what was foreground appears merely as surface agitation" (281).

12. Despite the authoritarian acts Miss La Trobe undertakes, Cuddy-Keane counters that Miss La Trobe's "dedication to process rather than to control becomes her way of overcoming defeat" (279).

13. I am grateful to Adriana Varga for suggesting this connection.

WORKS CITED

Agawu, Kofi. *Playing with Signs: A Semiotic Interpretation of Classic Music*. Princeton: Princeton University Press, 1991. Print.

———. "The Rhythmic Structure of West African Music." *Journal of Musicology* 5.3 (1987): 400–418. Print.

———. "Theory and Practice in the Analysis of the Nineteenth-Century 'Lied.'" *Music Analysis* 11.1 (1992): 3–36. Web. Aug. 7, 2013. http://www.jstor.org/stable/854301.

Albright, Daniel. "Stances towards Music as a Language." *Phrase and Subject: Studies in Literature and Music*. Ed. Delia da Sousa Correa. London: Legenda, 2006. 12–20. Print.

Auerbach, Erich. *Mimesis: The Representation of Reality in Western Literature*. Trans. Willard R. Trask. Princeton: Princeton University Press, 1953. Print.

De' Bardi, Pietro. "Letter to Giovanni Battista Doni (1634)." *Strunk's Source*

Readings in Music History. Ed. Leo Treitler. New York: Norton, 1998. 523–25. Print.

Barthes, Roland. "The Discourse of History." *Comparative Criticism: A Yearbook*. Ed. E. S. Schaffer. Cambridge: Cambridge University Press, 1981. 3–20. Print.

Bell, Quentin. *Virginia Woolf: A Biography*. Vol. 2. London: Hogarth, 1972. Print.

Bonds, Mark Evan. *Wordless Rhetoric: Musical Form and the Metaphor of the Oration*. Cambridge: Harvard University Press, 1991. Print.

Bruhn, Siglind. *Musical Ekphrasis: Composers Responding to Poetry and Painting*. Hillsdale: Pendragon Press, 2000. Print.

Busse, Kristina. "Reflecting the Subject in History: The Return of the Real in *Between the Acts*." *Woolf Studies Annual* 7 (2001): 75–101. Print.

Carter, Tim. *Music in Late Renaissance and Early Baroque Italy*. Portland: Amadeus, 1992. Print.

———. "The Seventeenth Century." *The Oxford Illustrated History of Opera*. Ed. Roger Parker. Oxford: Oxford University Press, 1994. 1–46. Print.

Cook, Nicholas. *Analysing Musical Multimedia*. Oxford: Clarendon, 1998. Print.

Cuddy-Keane, Melba. "The Politics of Comic Modes in Virginia Woolf's *Between the Acts*." *Publications of the Modern Language Association of America* 105.2 (1990): 273–85. Print.

Fleishman, Avrom. *The English Historical Novel: Walter Scott to Virginia Woolf*. Baltimore: Johns Hopkins University Press, 1971. Print.

Fowler, Rowena. "Moments and Metamorphoses: Virginia Woolf's Greece." *Comparative Literature* 51.3 (1999): 217–42. Print.

Freedman, William. *Laurence Sterne and the Origins of the Musical Novel*. Athens: University of Georgia Press, 1978. Print.

Graves, Robert, and Alan Hodge. *The Long Week End: A Social History of Great Britain, 1918–1939*. New York: Macmillan, 1941. Print.

Greenberg, Judith. "'When Ears Are Deaf and the Heart Is Dry': Traumatic Reverberations in *Between the Acts*." *Woolf Studies Annual* 7 (2001): 49–74. Print.

Harper, Howard. *Between Language and Silence: The Novels of Virginia Woolf*. Baton Rouge: Louisiana State University Press, 1982. Print.

Hatten, Robert S. *Musical Meaning in Beethoven: Markedness, Correlation, and Interpretation*. Bloomington: Indiana University Press, 1994. Print.

Kramer, Lawrence. *Music and Poetry: The Nineteenth Century and After*. Berkeley: University of California Press, 1984. Print.

———. "On Deconstructive Text-Music Relationships." *Music, Culture, and Society: A Reader*. Ed. Derek B. Scott. New York: Oxford University Press, 2000. 173–79. Print.

Lepore, Jill. "Historians Who Love Too Much: Reflections on Microhistory and Biography." *Journal of American History* 88.1 (2001): 129–44. Print. Also available online at http://historiasen construccion.wikispaces.com/file /view/lovetoomuch.pdf.

Lerdahl, Fred, and Ray Jackendoff. *A Generative Theory of Tonal Music*. Cambridge: MIT Press, 1983. Print.

Lodato, Suzanne. "Recent Approaches to Text/Music Analysis in the Lied." *Words and Music Studies: Defining the Field*. Ed. Walter Bernhard, Steven Paul Scher, and Werner Wolf. Atlanta: Rodopi, 1999. 95–112. Print.

McCluskey, Kathleen. *Reverberations: Sound and Structure in the Novels of Virginia Woolf*. Ann Arbor: UMI Research Press, 1986. Print.

McNichol, Stella. *Virginia Woolf and the Poetry of Fiction*. London: Routledge, 1990. Print.

McWhirter, David. "The Novel, the Play and the Book: *Between the Acts* and the Tragicomedy of History." *English Literary History* 60.3(1993): 787–812. Print.

Naremore, James. *The World without a Self: Virginia Woolf and the Novel*. New Haven: Yale University Press, 1973. Print.

Palisca, Claude V. "Mei, Girolamo." *Grove Music Online. Oxford Music Online.* Web. Aug. 22, 2012. http://www.oxfordmusiconline.com/subscriber/article/grove/music/18271.

Patel, Aniruddh D. "Music and the Brain: Three Links to Language." *The Oxford Handbook of Music Psychology*. Ed. Susan Hallam, Ian Cross, and Michael Thaut. Oxford: Oxford University Press, 2009. 208–16. Print.

Powers, Harold S. "Language Models and Musical Analysis." *Ethnomusicology* 24.1 (1980): 1–60. Print.

Pridmore-Brown, Michele. "1939–40: Of Virginia Woolf, Gramophones, and Fascism." *Publications of the Modern Language Association of America* 113.3 (1998): 408–21. Print.

Prieto, Eric. "Metaphor and Methodology in Word and Music Studies." *Word and Music Studies: Essays in Honor of Steven Paul Scher and on Cultural Identity and the Musical Stage*. Ed. Suzanne M. Lodato, Suzanne Aspden, and Walter Bernhart. New York: Rodopi, 2002. 49–68. Print.

Urrows, David Francis, intro. and ed. *Essays on Word/Music Adaptation and on Surveying the Field*. Word and Music Studies, vol. 9. Amsterdam: Rodopi, 2008. E-book.

Walker, Thomas. "I. Italy." *The History of Opera*. Ed. Stanley Sadie. Norton/Grove Handbooks in Music. New York: Norton, 1980. 15–26. Print.

Weiss, Piero, ed. *Opera: A History in Documents*. New York: Oxford University Press, 2002. Print.

Whittier-Ferguson, John. "The Burden of Drafts: Woolf's Revisions of *Between the Acts*." *Text* 10 (1997): 297–319. Print.

Williamson, John, ed. *Words and Music*. Liverpool: Liverpool University Press, 2005. E-book.

Wolf, Werner. "Intermediality Revisited: Reflections on Word and Music Relations in the Context of a General Typology of Intermediality." *Word and Music Studies: Essays in Honor of Steven Paul Scher and on Cultural Identity and the Musical Stage*. Ed. Suzanne M. Lodato, Suzanne Aspden, and Walter Bernhart. New York: Rodopi, 2002. 13–34. Print.

Woolf, Virginia. *Between the Acts*. Annot. and intro. Melba Cuddy-Keane. Ed. Mark Hussey. Orlando: Harcourt, 2008. E-book.

———. "Character in Fiction." *Virginia Woolf: Selected Essays*. Ed. David Bradshaw. Oxford: Oxford University Press, 2008. 37–54. Print.

———. *The Diary of Virginia Woolf*, Vol. 5: *1936–1941*. Ed. Anne Oliver Bell. London: Hogarth, 1984. Print.

———. *Orlando: A Biography*. Annot. and intro. Maria DiBattista. Mark Hussey, gen. ed. Orlando: Harcourt, 2006. Print.

———. *To the Lighthouse*. Annot. and intro. Mark Hussey. Mark Hussey, gen. ed. Orlando: Harcourt, 2005. E-book.

———. *The Voyage Out*. Intro. Louise DeSalvo. New York: Signet, 1991. Print.

Yoshino, Ayako. "*Between the Acts* and Louis Napoleon Parker – The Creator of the Modern English Pageant." *Critical Survey* 15.2(2003): 49–60. Print.

PART THREE

Music, Art, Film, and Virginia Woolf's Modernist Aesthetics

NINE

Broken Music, Broken History

SOUNDS AND SILENCE IN VIRGINIA
WOOLF'S *BETWEEN THE ACTS*

Sanja Bahun

IN HIS 1909 LETTER TO FERRUCCIO BUSONI, ARNOLD SCHOENBERG describes his objective in music composition as follows:

> And the results I wish for: no stylized and sterile protracted emotion. People are not like that: It is *impossible* for a person to have only one sensation at a time. One has *thousands* simultaneously. And these thousands can no more readily be added together than an apple and a pear. They go their own ways. And this variegation, this multifariousness, this illogicality presented by their interactions, set forth by some mounting rush of blood, by some reaction of the senses or the nerves, this I should like to have in my music. (Busoni 389; original emphasis)

These words find correspondence in Virginia Woolf's well-known proclamation in 1925:

> Look within and life, it seems, is very far from being "like this." Examine for a moment an ordinary mind on an ordinary day. The mind receives a myriad impressions – trivial, fantastic, evanescent, or engraved with the sharpness of steel. From all sides they come, an incessant shower of innumerable atoms; and as they fall, as they shape themselves into the life of Monday or Tuesday, the accent falls differently from of old; the moment of importance came not here but there [...] Life is not a series of gig lamps symmetrically arranged; life is a luminous halo. ("Modern Fiction," CR1: 150)

Both statements emphasize the variegation and simultaneity of impressions received by "an ordinary mind" and call for a novel mode of expressing the corollary rearrangement of the inner landscape. This new aesthetics aims to articulate the very border of exteriority and interiority – a boundary that serves as a coalescing point for diverse sensations that continuously reshape the subject – and the "discord in accord" that informs the subject and its relationship with others. A result of this artistic practice would be a non-hegemonic rendition of a "rambling capricious but somehow unified whole" (D5: 135). The latter is the phrase by which Woolf has described her last novel, *Between the Acts*.[1]

The objective to articulate a "discordant unity" connects not only (seemingly disparate) aesthetic practices of Woolf and Schoenberg but also Woolf's mature art and modernist music in general. This cross-artistic allegiance has acquired a palpable shape in *Between the Acts:* the novel is a complex sound-and-silence piece, replete with fragments, unusual caesuras, halting repetition, cathartic basses, subdued explosions, and anticlimaxes. At the structural and thematic heart of this "rambling whole," there lies a somewhat hesitant belief in the procreative quality of music, its ability to summon the "scattered, shattered, hither, thither" and then to assimilate, reunite, make a whole out of "fragments" and "disparity" "compelled" by contemporary history (BTA 74, 114). To capture heterogeneity – or, if one wills, isolation – of these fragments and yet present them as a "unified whole" becomes a common mission of modernist music and literature.

Despite the commensurability of artistic tasks and the analogous means of expression, Woolf and contemporary classical music (Schoenberg in particular) are strange bedfellows. Woolf's admiration for music is well documented,[2] but we have few traces of her interest in modernist classical music. Still, a sketch could be attempted. Woolf was apparently enthralled by the potentials of the "new music" to "reach a place not yet visited by sound" (E1: 289). Following Richard Wagner's conceptualization of the *Gesamtkunstwerk,* she seems to have had preference for art-form mixtures.[3] In addition to her well-recorded "affair" with Wagner's music, she also enjoyed Claude Debussy's and Richard Strauss's pieces, and she greeted enthusiastically the complex musical scores brought to London by the Ballets Russes (E1: 289; L1: 410). Her frequent presence at the performances of the Ballets Russes, especially during their London season 1918–1919, indubitably contributed to Woolf's appreciation of Igor Stravinsky's music.[4] In her 1928 notice on a performance of Stravinsky and Ramuz's *L'Histoire du Soldat,* Woolf acknowledged the radical nature and cross-artistic relevance of Stravinsky's music: "Like all highly original work [Stravinsky's music] begins by destroying one's conceptions, and only by degrees builds them up again."[5] It is likely that Woolf had already reflected on Stravinsky's music, and *L'Histoire du Soldat* in particular, a year before. The London premiere of this piece, which Leonard Woolf attended and Virginia Woolf regretted missing (D3: 147), caused a public controversy in 1927. The role of Stravinsky advocate was played by Sacheverell Sitwell – Edith Sitwell's brother and Woolf's acquaintance since 1918 – who wrote the explanatory notes for *L'Histoire du Soldat* in the *Radio Times* (July 8, 1927).[6]

It appears that Woolf's interest in modernist music increased in the late 1920s and the 1930s. Two factors contributed to this development. First, as her friendship with the British composer Ethel Smyth intensified, Woolf found herself more consistently exposed to contemporary classical music. As recorded in Louise Collis's biography of Smyth, Woolf attended the latter's rehearsals, and the two discussed musical theory and compositional practice (123). Robin Gail Schulze highlights that Smyth was well conversant with, if principally inimical to, Schoenberg's music (10) and suggests another possible point of intersection: we know that Woolf was an ardent radio listener and that the BBC happened to be a major promoter of modernist music. Jennifer Doctor's recent study of the BBC's programming politics similarly dispels the myth of the modernist Britain's unawareness of the developments in contemporary continental music. Doctor emphasizes the assiduous efforts of the BBC music cadre (Percy Pitt, Adrian Boult, Edward Clark, and Kenneth Wright) to disseminate modernist music in the years 1922–1936. The BBC programs abounded with works by Schoenberg, Stravinsky, Anton Webern, and Béla Bartók, and these were frequently commented on in radio talks and the *Radio Times*. The rapidly increasing British radio audience was particularly well acquainted with, if not unanimously sympathetic to, the repertoire of the Second Viennese School. Doctor's findings indicate the noteworthy popularity of Schoenberg (who even came to London to conduct his *Five Pieces for Orchestra,* op. 16, in January 1914), an early presentation of his work (the first British performance of Schoenberg music – *Three Piano Pieces*, op. 11 – took place in January 1912, and the atonal *Second String Quartet* premiered in Britain on June 10, 1914), and the frequent coupling of Schoenberg's pieces with Beethoven's *Late String Quartets* – Woolf's favorite piece of music – in the BBC broadcasts and concerts.[7] To these records one may add Woolf's professional engagement with the BBC precisely during the period when its commitment to contemporary music peaked, namely, from 1933 to 1935.[8]

While this recent scholarship suggests some level of contact between Woolf and what was then called "ultramodern music," the actual evidence of her involvement in contemporary music is lacking and may well remain beyond our reach forever. The lack of conclusive documentary evidence on direct influence, however, should not prevent us from considering Woolf's writing and contemporary classical music as mutually illuminating phenomena or phenomena that are most productively understood in parallax. Indeed, the correlation between Woolf's and Schoenberg's statements on art that I have used to begin this essay underscores the need for one such comparative perspective. The justification for this type of comparison should be sought in the modernist aesthetic practice itself, in its predilection for generic intertwines and mixed-media ventures, but also in its status as an expression wrought by history. The modified status of music in Woolf's mature work witnesses to this inflection. Coincident with her promulgation of their "ahistoricity," the arts (among them music and especially music-in-performance) acquired a vigorous sociohistorical role in Woolf's last writings. To critically face this contradiction in Woolf's stance means to understand a crucial line of development not only in Woolf's novelistic art but also in classical music itself, namely, their simultaneous move from lyric abstraction (open to historical abuse) to the no less poetic, but historically specified, refiguration of conventional structures.

One of Woolf's early excurses in music criticism highlights precisely the importance of understanding art in relation to historical vicissitudes. In her note on the fifth volume of *The Oxford History of Music* (*Guardian*, June 14, 1905), Woolf expresses her regrets that the history of music is still largely a history of universal form. "What we should all like to see," she suggests, "is a history rather of music expression, of the sources, and conditions which render possible the 'inspiration' of a noble melody or striking progression" (E1: 374). As Woolf wonders about Beethoven's ability to render each of the nine symphonies in a different mood and through a different expression, all the time keeping in mind his historical and personal context, we may ask ourselves a similar question with respect to her own art. One may advance further, Woolf advises us, by exploring what "conditions" such transformations (374). In this light, the curious parallelism between Woolf's mature fiction and contemporary developments in classical music may be seen to reflect the sociohistorical and artistic position in which modernist artists found themselves in the late 1930s. While the agglomeration of violence instilled a sense of historical paralysis in Woolf and her contemporaries ("There is no retreating or advancing," a character comments in *Between the Acts* [114]), this sentiment simultaneously provoked vigorous aesthetic interrogation, a belligerent trust in regenerative powers of art in the face of annihilating work of history.

The modernist composer is "rarely a crusader," Daniel Albright notes (3). Rather, she or he effects a change by probing technical boundaries, by investigating the possibilities of "aesthetic liberation" so as to foreground the potential for advancement not only in the arts but also in material history. Such indirect commitment is conditioned by one conviction that Woolf shared with modernist composers: that the prefigurative forces that drive content (historical and social context and one's engagement with it) also drive form. For Woolf and modernist composers, the only authentic response to the bloodbath of history is to try to capture and instantiate – rather than merely describe – the dissonant rhythms of this "new music." The contemporary music experimentation, then, not only appealed to Woolf's interest in composition but also spoke to the writer's historically specific concerns: like many modernist compositions of the late 1930s, the "broken" music of *Between the Acts* articulates the writer's cogitation on the (im)possibility of human agency at the beginning of the Second World War. But the discoveries of new music also served Woolf's search for a pattern that could make history intelligible. For one, the sighting of tones abiding in the interstices of the scale provided Woolf with a formal stencil for her lifelong interest in the representation of unrecorded histories.

My reading of *Between the Acts* engages this set of questions as I argue that the semi-ironic, agonistic, "bared" and "barred" expression of history in Woolf's last novel is coterminous with the modernist formal experimentation in classical music. This inquiry embraces Albright's proposition to emancipate a theory of comparative arts so as to disclose mutually illuminating conjunctions of the modernist arts. By focusing on Woolf's *Between the Acts* as a unique formal articulation of the moment of its production, I intend to highlight the cross-sections between the sociohistorical content and artistic practice in modernism. With modernist experimenters such as Woolf, Stravinsky, Schoenberg, and others, history became not only a subject for expressive interrogation but also the very form of artwork. To address this shift, my essay takes on a music criticism robe suggested by Woolf, that of an inquiry in the modes and conditions of expression.

COMPOSITION: A COMPLETE WHOLE AND THE UNREST PROBLEM (WOOLF AND SCHOENBERG, PRIME SERIES)

Woolf's last artistic efforts engendered a work of a uniquely indefinable style, lyrical but sarcastic, intimately agonistic and significantly meta-narrative. Compressed within the course of twenty-four hours, *Between the Acts* records the events of a June day in 1939. Against the background of the early days of the *Sitzkrieg* and the anticipated "gun slayers, bomb droppers" (BTA 187) of the Second World War, a village pageant is performed, aspiring to present the entire English history as well as the history of English literature; a family goes through a subtly intoned crisis; a house reaches mythic proportions; and some correspondences are established between private life and history. The composition comprises four movements: the evening (Elizabethan-drama preamble), the morning (curtain up), the day (preparations, the pageant itself), and the evening/night (curtain down). The novel unfolds spatially, through layers of analogies (history–story–theater play), mirroring stories (war, private war), and respondent casts (the three sets of characters). It builds its "melody" on vertical rather than horizontal accumulation of tones and tonal fragments, a composition that, I would argue, shows structural affinities to the chromatic extensions of tonality in Wagner and Schoenberg (see, in particular, the latter's expressionist period, from *Gurrelieder* to *Pierrot Lunaire*). Presenting in this "vertical" fashion the links between art and history, fiction and facts, the modernist "I" and the communal "we," *Between the Acts* both endorses and revokes each of these binaries. Integral to the novel, these opposites witness to Woolf's effort to represent them as simultaneously irretrievably separate and eventually bridgeable.

The paradoxical nature of this project is reflected in the contradictory interpretative potential of *Between the Acts:* a memento to Woolf's disillusioned view of history and her idiosyncratic conflation of art and death, the novel is – without canceling its opposite – an astonishing affirmation of life and creativity.[9] Accordingly, the narrative modes are baffling: *Between the Acts* advances a realistic-ironic representation while maintaining the poetic-music tenor throughout. As if this hybridity were not enough, the novel is also inflected by the modalities of the most social of arts, drama. Thus *Between the Acts* presents itself as a composite instantiation of what Woolf termed "a complete whole."[10] While the novel's modal, generic, and art-form crossings testify to Wagner's influence noted above, the concept of "complete whole" also gestures another musical interlocutor, presumably unknown to Woolf: Schoenberg's mysterious project of presenting a "single complete thought," of relating everything in a composition to one notion – *der musikalische Gedanke* (the Musical Idea). For, although her last comment on *Between the Acts* was a complaint about its sketchiness (L6: 482), Woolf's manipulation of compositional elements to render a "complete thought" is nowhere more sophisticated than in this novel of "dispersion" and "unification." On a micro-structural level, *Between the Acts* bounds its multiple leitmotifs by strong internal relations while the triple analogical link "history–story–theater play" constellates the novel as a whole. The juxtaposition of these two planes makes the novel's complex structure and its purpose graspable as a "single complete thought" or a "complete whole."

No wonder, then, that the thirty-seven sections or "movements" of *Between the Acts* unfold in a manner typical of a musical piece – the work develops from an opening "statement" and progresses by means of augmentation, substitution, and variation. Woolf appropriates Wagner's practice of employing music motifs to indicate characters, mythic objects, and emotional states. As the novel's structure relies heavily on leitmotifs, the readers of *Between the Acts* are invited to become the "Wagnerians detecting motives" (E1: 271). The opening statement of *Between the Acts* – the summer night scene in the Oliver household – plays out all the prominent motifs of the piece to follow: the cesspool, horse, perambulator, graves, birds, cows, butterflies. These are specifically linked to their later symbolic-expressive values: the cesspool marks the ironic mode of narration, the horse symbolizes force and aggressiveness, birds assure the link to nature and the "supra-natural" world of music, and the motif of the beak is "sounded" as the signal for a violent action. Thereafter the novel's "movements" are scrupulously linked by motif development: each section opens with a subtle reinforcement of a motif introduced in the previous episode. This "reinforcement" may take the form of simple repetition (the phrase "The laughter died away" begins sections 14 and 15 [BTA 58, 65]), contraposition (Isa's "outer" and "inner" love in sections 3–4), development (the motif of the fish in sections 7–8), metaphorical extension (the cluster around the motif of the lily pond), or shifting perspectives (Lucy's looking out of the window onto the garden in section 2 is reversed as a view *from* the garden in section 3).

This motivic "working out" may easily situate the "music" of *Between the Acts* in the Wagnerian score or, equally convincingly, in the context of harmonic motif use in Beethoven's *Late String Quartets*.[11] Yet, it may also be illuminating to consider this practice in the light of Schoenberg's serial composition, which would retrospectively give an additional importance to the measures of the first step, the first row, or, in terms of Woolf's novel, the first section. A dodecaphonic piece, such as Schoenberg's *Piano Suite*, op. 25, usually opens with a short stretch of music – the twelve tones sounded equally – which represents the *prime series*. This densely chromatic row is the seed (*Grundgestalt*) out of which the piece grows: composition consists of the transformations of the measures/relations in the prime series. These variations usually include transpositions up or down, retrograde arrangement, inversion of intervals (reversal in pitch), and combinations of these techniques (*Style and Idea*, 214–49). In Schoenbergean light, then, the seemingly traditional composition of *Between the Acts* reveals itself as surprisingly radical. Indeed, Woolf's compositional practice as presented above is not solely (or primarily) based upon the development of melodic motifs, but on the growth of *relations* and *formal measures* between them. Accordingly, the first movement of *Between the Acts* enacts all the relationships/measures that are to comprise the fabric of the novel. Woolf is astonishingly specific in her adumbration of the restless dynamics to follow: a set of emotional relations (love, jealousy, hatred), communal and individual attitudes toward the "history of scars" (the site for the cesspool), remembrance and forgetting (Bart's memories), and the relationship between the animal and the human (the portrayal of Mrs. Haines). Most important, the first movement stages what for Woolf, as much as for Schoenberg, was the major latent dynamics of human life and history: the perpetual "unrest," or agonic structuring, within a unity.

In his 1934 note, Schoenberg explains composition as a development of the "Musical Idea" through this "unrest problem":

> The furtherance of the musical idea [...] may ensue only if the *unrest-problem* – present in the *Grundgestalt* or in the motive [...] is shown in all its *consequences*. These consequences are presented through the destinies of the *motive* or the *Grundgestalt*. Just how the *Grundgestalt* is altered under the influence of the *forces struggling* within it, how this *motion* to which the unrest leads, how the forces attain a state of *rest* – this is the *realization of the idea*, this is its *presentation*. (*Musical Idea* 227; emphasis Schoenberg's)

The compositional problem that Schoenberg faces here is equivalent to that experienced by Miss La Trobe, as recorded in the holograph notes of *Between the Acts:* "But the next problem was on her. And a damned ticklish one it was: [...] they had to hear a discord; yet it must not break the harmony" (PH 521). The problem was not new for Woolf. Already in 1908 she had defined her artistic project as aiming at the kind of literary discourse that could "achieve a symmetry by means of infinite discords, showing all the traces of the minds passage through the world; & achieve in the end, some kind of whole made of shivering fragments" (PA 393). The comparable philosophy of composition yielded a similar artistic organization: in both Schoenberg's music and Woolf's late novel the presentation of imbalance, discordance, and tension unfolds through a series of agons that are linked by analogy or motif repetition rather than by direct contentual connections. With both Woolf and Schoenberg, this series of agons (tensions) is often interrupted by abrupt "paralyses" of action/sound (unconceivable in the previous music or writing) and closed by a restoration of balance (release) upon whose ambivalent final value Schoenberg and Woolf might have agreed. For both artists, this structure of "unrest" presented a formal way to express their increasing concerns with contemporary history.

The much discussed library scene provides us with a representative demonstration of this agonic composition. In the Oliver library, Isa listens to the music of a familiar exchange: "Every summer, for seven summers now, Isa had heard the same words [...]. The same chime followed the same chime" (BTA 22). The small agon between Bart the separatist and Lucy the unifier (who took a hammer without asking leave) is innocuous, for the mental opposition does not change their mutual affection (26). Yet, earlier that morning Isa read an article about a military rape,[12] and, as the known melody unfolds, she now hears an additional sound: "The same chime followed the same chime, only this year beneath the chime she heard: 'The girl screamed and hit him about the face with a hammer'" (22). The music has become ominous, and then it halts. Anchored in the eternal agonistic pattern, the two phrases fuse into a concocted match of the past action ("hitting") and the present means ("a hammer"). Like Schoenberg's inversion of the tonal qualities of the prime series and his superimposition of music and speech in *A Survivor from Warsaw*, op. 46, Woolf's narrative inflection formally renders what the text implies: the absurd brutality of history.[13]

This agonic interchange corresponds to the dynamics of confrontation, with the examples of which history furnished Woolf and her contemporaries. The "fight" is a primordial and everlasting state of history, Woolf argues as she closes *Between the Acts*: "first they must fight, as the dog fox fights with the vixen, in the heart of darkness, in the fields of night" (219). However, rather than confining this exchange to the notions of aggression and destruction, Woolf presents agon as a primal (historical and personal) compositional pattern to which different emotional values can be attached, a pattern that makes the entire history, that "of warrior and lover, the fighter, the singer" (84), metaphorically congeal in the moment of Isa and Giles's fight. For Woolf, as much as for Schoenberg, the self-reproductive way in which history unfolds is a continuous recurrence of agons between conjoined opposites – a structure of unrest that may take form of historical games, struggles between the sexes, chords in tension, verbal juxtapositions, and epistemic or harmonic "unresolves." It is in the paradoxical status of repeated measure/sound of agon that Schoenberg and Woolf find a responsible artistic reaction to contemporary history and a compositional pattern fit to express its melody of discordant unity. Positioning their respective artistic projects as a battle against a "sterilized" representation of human experience, both Schoenberg and Woolf realized the necessity of addressing the inherently agonic nature of existence. The "unrest" composition discloses that the major continuity between Schoenberg's studies in dissonance and Woolf's mature agonistic novel – and, generally, that between contemporary classical music and Woolf's art of fiction – lies in the concept of a world where everything contains its opposite, where tension and contradiction are inevitable (but not ineliminable) modes of existence.

SOUNDS AND RHYTHMS: WOOLF AND STRAVINSKY

That music plays an important role in *Between the Acts* is hard to miss: the novel is saturated with songs and tunes. All songs – especially those included in the pageant, such as "The Valiant Rhoderick's Song" (BTA 79) – mimic the vocabulary, style, and compositional patterning of the historical era they represent. In addition, Woolf playfully revisits the "sounds" of her previous work, indulging in a complex series of auto-citations (cf. the bell chiming in BTA 7). However, songs, tunes, and scales practicing comprise just the "surface sound" that guides the reader to a more intricate musical patterning. Natural or mechanical sounds such as "mooing," "whizzing," and "jingling" are accorded a more significant narrative function: they guide, modulate, symbolize, or contrapuntally modify the events in the novel. *Between the Acts* is a study in the emancipation of sounds, similar to that carried out in the "ultramodern" music.

This hidden project is first indicated by the prominence of the verbs denoting musical functions with which Woolf endows animate and inanimate objects. In this way a great number of previously "unrecorded" sounds is made audible: the room-as-a shell "sings" (BTA 36); the plane "whizzes," "whirs," and "buzzes" (15); the cows "moo" (84); the breeze "rustles" (98); the wheels of the cars "purr" (73); the gramophone "chuffs." Emotions and interactions are also rendered in terms of music: the feeling encircling Isa and Mr. Haines is compared to a stroke of the organ (6), and the library exchange between Lucy and Bart is sounded as peals of chimes (22). More traditionally, Woolf attaches groups of sounds to the speech of each character. Isa is always associated with a subdued continuous sound of nature (she murmurs and hums), whereas Bart's sonorous voice reverberates into contorted barking. As these examples indicate, such sounds often intertwine human and animal voicing: the distinction between the animal and the human worlds is blurred through repeated murmuring, humming, mumbling, groaning, bawling, and chirruping. As in any good piece of music, these vocalizations make unexpected pairs that alternate and unfurl into endless interpretative paths: murmuring (Lucy–Isa); humming (Isa–Dodge); chirruping (Lucy–birds); bowling (Bart–the Afghan hound); muttering (Giles–Bart); keeping beat (Mrs. Manresa–Bart). The ambiguity of human voicing is further explored in the experiments with the spoken and the sung in Miss La Trobe's pageant, where many utterances take form of animate-inanimate recitatives: the young England, Phyllis Jones, "pipes" (BTA 76); Mrs. Clark/Queen Elizabeth "bawls" (84); Albert, the village idiot, "titters" and "whistles"; Mrs. Otter of the End House "croaks out" (89); and so on. Heeding Woolf's description, one could imagine the vocal quality of these connectives as a version of Schoenberg's *Sprechstimme*. This innovative recitative device, most famously deployed in Schoenberg's *Pierrot lunaire* (1912), combines speech and song: keeping the indicated rhythm, the vocalist performs in such a way that the pitch is sounded (recited) but never held (sung). Even though Miss La Trobe's actors rarely aspire to the emotional duress of the Schoenbergean *Sprechstimme,* they remain in this ambivalent speech-song vocal space throughout the pageant. Similarly to *Pierrot lunaire*, these vocalizations appear in counterpoint, here with the villagers' song of "digging and delving."

Yet the foremost feature of the sounds in *Between the Acts* is their separation from their poetic-metric utility (which they nonetheless serve). An early episode in the novel provides one with a good insight into this dynamic. The voices of the main characters, "wimpling and warbling" as they come into the hall, are specifically differentiated through their musical expression value ("gruff–Bart's voice; quavering–Lucy's voice; middle-toned–Isa's voice," BTA 37). Through this process of personification, the sounds and voices acquire a curiously autonomous status: the characters' "voices impetuously, impatiently, protestingly [come] across the hall" (37); the music "wails" at the dispersion of the audience

(97–98); and a "pompous popular tune" "brays" and "blares" of its own accord (79). This relegation of sounds from the perspective of a human auditor into the realm of autonomous functioning eventually singles out a whole plethora of voices, assigning them a life of their own.

Importantly, the meaning of these autonomized sounds is rooted in contemporary history. The sounding of the megaphone in *Between the Acts* is revelatory of the dynamics described above: "the anonymous bray of the infernal megaphone" (188) conjoins the animate and the inanimate in complex and disturbing ways. Alienated and alienating, this ambiguous polychord disjoints the melody of the backdrop narration with an omnipresence whose power to "compel disparity" is both affirmed and questioned. As Mitchell Leaska notices, this metal sound is a reference to a real historical voice. In her 1940 diary entries Woolf frequently records an anonymous radio voice "urging Londoners to be fitted to gas masks, ordering them to take cover during the raids" (*PH* 239). Correspondingly, the sound of the megaphone in the novel asserts its history-endowed presence: punctuating the narration, it produces a disquieting effect similar to, for instance, the speaker's shouts against a jarring orchestral backdrop in Schoenberg's *A Survivor from Warsaw*. In both instances the sound functions as a stark reminder of contemporary history that recontextualizes the surrounding harmony. But Schoenberg's percussive shouts representing German police find an even better correlative in the zooming sound of war planes that severs the reverend's fund-raising verbiage in *Between the Acts*: "'So that each of us who has enjoyed this pageant has still an opp . . . 'The word was cut in two. A zoom severed it" (*BTA* 193). The zoom-drone that fractures the prefigured melody of the campaign tensely reminds the audience that "mechanical birds" have become an instrument of war (cf. Beer 288). With both Woolf and Schoenberg, then, the intrusions of history refigure the composition by introducing dissonance and orchestral fragmentation.

This autonomization of sounds and their symbolic association with history has many correspondences in modernist music. For the purpose of understanding Woolf's treatment of sounds, it is illuminating to square Woolf's writing practice with another contemporary, whose work – we have at least that association confirmed – Woolf actually knew: Igor Stravinsky. While the famous bassoon opening of Stravinsky's *The*

Example 9.1. Igor Stravinsky, *Le Sacre du printemps* (1913), movement 13, opening. © 1912, 1921 by Hawkes & Son (London) Ltd. Reproduced by permission of Boosey & Hawkes Music Publishers Ltd.

Rite of Spring may be the most conspicuous example of the strategy of autonomization of sounds, I would like to propose a melodically less expected accompaniment to Woolf's novel – the repetition of a dissonant polychord at the beginning of the "Augurs of Spring" (see example 9.1). The assertive entrance of strings via E-flat dominant seventh over F-flat major, irregularly accentuated, autonomizes sound and generates an impression of its "primordiality." Here I would like to suggest that this influential stampede is also a good analogue of Woolf's experimentation in rhythm.

The exploration of rhythms is an old interest of Woolf's. Detecting in rhythm a subversiveness at which the customary tune-oriented study bridles, she finds "the beat of rhythm in the mind akin to the beat of the pulse of the body" (E1: 30). It was Stravinsky's discovery of jagged rhythm and displaced accents, as in the example above, that might have influenced Woolf in her appraisal of innovative rhythmic structuring. She herself professes a dread of the "tune with its feet always on the same spot," which inevitably "[becomes] sugared, insipid; [bores] a hole with its perpetual invocation to perpetual adoration" (BTA 118).

This dissatisfaction with the conventional rhythmic organization propels Woolf's experimentation. The variegation of syntactic rhythms in *Between the Acts* may be seen as corresponding to the use of rhythm in *The Rite of Spring*, where the cross-rhythms and polyrhythms capture the various "pulses" of the modern era, but also record cultural inheritance, including pagan "primordiality," as it interacts with the present. Miss La Trobe's pageant is a superb instance of this rhythmic interrelating – the brisk staccato of the Elizabethan age is different from the repetitious tendrils of the Victorians, and both of them are opposed to the broken but steadfast rhythm of the villagers' song. These historically and mythically endowed rhythms are further inflected by the displacement of accents within each section – the product as much of Miss La Trobe's vision as of chance encounters (for instance, the meeting of a Shakespeare song and the bellow of cows).

Like in Stravinsky's piece, the rhythms in the novel are motivically attached to characters and their actions. This strategy generates individualized rhythmic patterns for different actions by different people; once personalized, rhythms interrelate in constant variation. A nice example of the interaction of rhythms and tempos may be found in the underdiscussed yet stimulating scene in which Lucy and Mrs. Sands prepare sandwiches for the pageant:

> Mrs. Sands fetched the bread; Mrs. Swithin fetched ham. It was soothing, it was consolidating, this handwork together. The cook's hands cut, cut, cut. Whereas Lucy, holding the loaf, held the knife up. Why's stale bread, she mused, easier to cut than fresh? And so skipped, sidelong, from yeast to alcohol; so to fermentation; so to inebriation; so to Bacchus; and lay under purple lamps in a vineyard in Italy, as she had done, often; while Sands heard the clock tick; saw the cat; noted a fly buzz; and registered, as her lips showed, a grudge she mustn't speak against people making work in the kitchen while they had a high old time hanging paper roses in the Barn. (BTA 34)

The strong regular beat of Mrs. Sands's action and the lingering tendrils characteristic of Lucy's mental processes are comically juxtaposed here. They are metatextually overlaid by a blend of nursery rhyme (primary narrative rhythm) and an elaborate "writerly" rhythm. This rhythmic interplay is chiefly intended for comic effects and character designation, but it is also class-inflected: it instantiates different temporalities of the cook and her mistress, presenting the sides in relation as dissonant yet still functioning in unison (the work together is "consolidating," Woolf announces). This interlacing of rhythms draws the reader's attention to the general polyrhythmic organization of the novel and, analogously, a polyrhythmic organization of our world. The syncopated series at the end of Miss La Trobe's pageant is a case in point:

> The tune changed; snapped; broke; jagged. Foxtrot, was it? Jazz? Anyhow the rhythms kicked, reared, snapped short. What a jangle and jingle! [...] What a cackle, a cacophony! Nothing ended. So abrupt. And corrupt. Such an outrage; such an insult; And not plain. Very up to date, all the same. What is her game? To disrupt? Jog and trot? Jerk and smirk? Put the finger to the nose? Squint and pry? Peak and spy? O the irreverence of the generation which is only momentarily – thanks be – "the young." The young, who can't make, but only break; shiver into splinters the old vision; smash to atoms what was whole. What a cackle, what a rattle, what a yaffle – (BTA 183)

This is a modern rhythm, high pitched, fragmentary, and broken. Sudden contortions and irregular intervals are linked to contemporary history and positioned over against the conventional, steady beat of the elders – "the old vision" – while the frequent shifts of rhythm and unorthodox accentuation introduce contradiction, or "unrest." This is the microscopic image of the irregular beat of Woolf's novel itself, the capable management of which allies her with the masters of syncopation such as Stravinsky or jazz musicians. As the above excerpt also suggests, this rhythm is sometimes so compelling that it leads its own creator into un-referential play; thus "the ivy mocks tap-tap-tapping on the pane" (85) and Lucy walks "tottering yet tripping" (67). While these rhythmic excursions might look like chance rhymes, I interpret them as integral to Woolf's novel: they are both Woolf's glosses on the art of "composition" and the audio indicators of the skewed semantics of contemporary history. They vocalize a world of displaced accents.

To advance this unusual rhythmic orchestration, Woolf utilizes her customary set of poetic strategies: rhymes and alliteration. The use of assonance, so prominent in *The Waves*, now yields the floor to consonant alliteration; the novel's melody displays a heavy reliance on fricatives and plosives, as well as the exploitation of "r"(olling) sounds ("ground corn," "brayed and blared," "her words peppered the audience as with a shower of hard little stones" – I randomly list examples appearing in BTA

78–79). The reverberation of the present participle is another device that Woolf habitually utilizes for rhythmic purposes ("Digging and delving, ploughing and sowing, they were singing" [124]), as is her repetition of a word with grammar variants ("She advanced, sliding, as if the floor were fluid under her shabby garden shoes, and, advancing, pursed her lips and smiled, sidelong, at her brother" [49]). The last sentence is also informative of the way Woolf builds rhythm in her last novel: the polyrhythmic organization is achieved through a metrically proficient repetition of prolonged active verbs/actions that lead to or are interrupted by sudden caesuras.

It is in this way that what I term "broken music" is built in *Between the Acts*. Emotionally pitched fragments alternate with anticlimactic clauses and displaced caesuras, and the functional harmony breaks down: Woolf's iridescent sentences are frequently governed by their own chromatic contortions rather than by a fixed center, the subject or the semantic object. This is what happens in the description of the Barn:

> The roof was weathered red-orange; and inside it was a hollow hall, sun-shafted, brown, smelling of corn, dark when the doors were shut, but splendidly illuminated when the doors at the end stood open, as they did to let the wagons in – the long low wagons, like ships of the sea, breasting the corn, not the sea, returning in the evening shagged with hay. The lanes caught tufts where the wagons had passed. (BTA 26)

In this asymmetrical sketch, the subject and the object slide away under the import of expression, producing a singularly "keyless" melody. The chromatic contortion of the central sentence is suddenly broken, as if the convoluted affective description had exhausted itself; but then the chromatic expression unexpectedly resumes, as a surge of the last wave, only to finish with an anticlimactic, differently rhythmically organized, fade out.

The unusual syntax of this passage is representative of the novel as a whole: contortions, inflections, and anticlimaxes are its signature devices. This "composition" owes its melodic distinction to Woolf's specific use of semicolons to articulate a half stop, or a caesura. The relation between fragments installed thereby is that of the grammatical function called *deletion transformation* (PH 20). In this variant of parataxis, the second part of the sentence alternates while the first part is assumed to be repeated in subsequent transformations; witness, for example, Bart's remembrances of his mother ("Of his mother he remembered that she was very stout; kept her tea-caddy locked; yet had given him in that very room a copy of Byron" [BTA 5]), where the pointed use of deletion transformation relays, rhythmically, the character's difficulties in not so much remembering as articulating an emotionally significant event. This use is related to Woolf's more general experimentation with polyrhythm in parataxes with semantic accretion. Lucy's dreamy vision of the history of humankind is a good example here:

> She had stretched for her favorite reading – an Outline of History – and had spent the hours between three and five thinking of rhododendron forests in Piccadilly; when the entire continent, not then, she understood, divided by a channel, was all one; populated, she understood, by elephant-bodied, seal-necked, heaving, surging, slowly writhing, and, she supposed, barking monsters; the iguanodon, the mammoth, and the mastodon; from whom presumably, she thought, jerking the window open, we descend. (BTA 9)

The semicolons in this polyrhythmic passage take on the function of dashes and commas (with which this passage also abounds). In this sentence of semantic superfluity a prominent role is given to the anticipated and unanticipated caesuras. While the accretion of words and sounds develops a "melody," caesuras convolute and break the sequence, recasting it into a series of disjointed patterns. The shifts in accents repeatedly deceive our rhythmic expectations, establishing an emotional polyrhythm of fragments in action. This fractured melody is pointedly accompanied by the gradual diminishing of Lucy's semantic authority: "she understood"/"she supposed"/"she thought." The last process reminds us that the broken music of *Between the Acts* is inextricably bound to the questions of knowing and unknowing, that the novel acoustically represents a history of gaps and fissures.

THE LANGUAGE OF THE UNRECORDED: WOOLF AND SCHOENBERG, #2

As early as in 1905 Woolf complained about the state in music in which "the whole of rhythm and harmony have been pressed, like dried flowers, into the neatly divided scales, the tones and semitones of the pianoforte"

(E1: 30). What lurks behind this statement is not only Woolf's suspicion of the "recorded," "approved" art but also her dissatisfaction with the recorded history itself. Here Woolf's historical aesthetics is commensurate with the search into the "forbidden" gaps in the scale that lies at the heart of modernist revolution in music.

The most radical articulation of this search, Schoenberg's twelve-tone technique, could be described as an expansion of the known (seven-note scale) into the previously unknown/unheard (twelve-note scale). Schoenberg's formal experimentation connotes philosophical-cum-political shift of emphasis: instead of lingering on the notes customarily deemed significant (the tonic or the dominant), Schoenberg's serial music attributes equal value to all twelve semitones of the chromatic scale. The egalitarian nature of this technique becomes audible particularly in the instances of inversion of the prime series, wherein the reversal in pitch redistributes the "power" in the scale. The lack of a keynote or the tonal center engenders a sense of the absence of an organizing viewpoint, comparable to the effect of Woolf's syntactic experiments discussed above. The subversive potential of Schoenberg's technique is obvious: with the proposition that no tone should lead or tend toward the other, Schoenberg moves beyond the major versus minor key musical meta-narrative into what may be called "democratic" music. Schoenberg's serial method may be thus viewed as coextensive with Woolf's lifelong project to capture the histories of the socially "unrecorded," to depict the "Lives of the Obscure" (D3: 37).

In this light, the individuation of (previously "unheard") sounds that I addressed above may be seen as sharing the social impetus with Schoenberg's innovative technique. The same pertains to the inflection of Woolf's text by multiple "outsider narratives." From the story of "silent and sardonic" Bond (BTA 28) to the sketch of Mrs. Sand or that of assiduous gardener Cobbet of the Cobbs Corner, *Between the Acts* abounds in minor (hi)stories competing for our attention. People, animals, and even some inanimate objects manifestly assert the right to their own voice, their own narrative/score. The novel is punctuated by different "obscure" voices – chirruping, creaking, and other sounds belonging to nature or domestic space. In a markedly "written" sentence at the beginning of the novel, the reader's attention is directed to an alternative history, incidents of which remain mostly "inaudible, invisible" to us (14), that of a daylight bird "chuckling over the substance and succulence of the day, over worms, snails, grit, even in sleep" (3). These textual individuations have a vital function in the novel: they instate a radical play of politico-historical possibilities. The readers find themselves immersed in a set of disquieting questions: to whose story one should attend? who has been given a voice? whose voice has been subdued? But the egalitarian treatment of minor "tones" is deceptive: no story develops into a "pitch," however picturesque and full of narrative potentials it may be. One after another, the characters relate their (hi)stories, but none of these is accorded the motivational value; they "make sense" only when polyphonically sung together.

This multifarious melody is, furthermore, punctuated by intoned silence. If one wants to present history truthfully, Woolf suggests, one needs to render its occlusions, too. Although she frequently tried to vocalize the absence of sound, Woolf had never previously assigned such textual importance to this phenomenon. In *Between the Acts*, however, Woolf represents silence vocally (descriptions), visually (elisions), metrically (caesuras), and rhythmically (stases). She also appears to distinguish between its two modes – the absence of sound as a product of silencing (presentable through caesuras and elisions) and silence, which is a constitutive, fundamental aspect of life/score. This treatment of silence likens Woolf's art to the empowering of silence in modernist music. Composers as different as Schoenberg, Stravinsky, Erik Satie, Charles Ives, and, later, John Cage, created music in which the expressively and semantically emancipated silence "competes" with sounds, disrupting them, correcting them, restructuring them. Schoenberg's *Six Little Piano Pieces*, op. 19, II, reproduced in example 9.2, presents one of the most famous utilizations of the dialectics of silence in this context. In Schoenberg's piece silence is no longer treated as an unstructured rest, but as a dynamic and meaningful interactor with the sound. In this articulation of the "unrest problem" through the contrasting of the staccato thirds in the left hand and the sustained melody of the right hand, silence/rest emerges as the sound's "competitor."

This strategy finds its correspondent in Woolf's use of ellipses to explore the dynamics of "silencing." By a deliberate artistic move, the

Example 9.2. Arnold Schönberg "6 kleine Klavierstücke für Klavier op. 19/II."
© Copyright 1913, 1940 by Universal Edition A.G., Wien/UE 5069.

writer frequently cuts off minor stories/attempts at voicing an alternative history, the endeavor that she herself advertised throughout her life. These forceful occlusions are most poignant precisely where the ostensible polyphony peaks – in Miss La Trobe's pageant. The petering away of the villagers' voices in the song of "digging and delving" is the most memorable example of Woolf's tactical use of silence. As they pass in and out of the stage, the villagers chant monotonously: "Cutting the roads ... up to the hill top ... we climbed. Down in the valley ... sow, wild boar, hog, rhinoceros, reindeer ... Dug ourselves in to the hill top ... Ground roots between stones ... Ground corn ... till we too ... lay under g-r-o-u-n-d" (BTA 78). The song purports to record the peasants' toil and historical position, but the bands of silence signal "gaps" in personal and group memory. The contrapuntal choir finally hears its own words dying away: "The wind rose, and in the rustle of the leaves even the great words became inaudible; and the audience sat staring at the villagers, whose mouths opened, but no sound came" (140). It is not difficult to identify the social correspondences of this silencing. The peasants' "making of history" has long vanished from the official score, Woolf suggests by presenting the tonally "occluded" and the historically "obscured" as isomorphic. In the place of a potential record, then, there is a marked silence which re-accentuates the surrounding phrases. Now the craggy sonorities of Lucy's Outline of History also appear in a novel light. Formally exteriorizing the gaps and fissures of history, both

Lucy's musing and the peasants' song are structurally opposed to the content (historical record) they purport to convey. Breaking the music into unequally measured fragments, they disperse the chimera of unity, or wholeness, of history.

Out of this recognition of the selective nature of the historical score, a profound emancipation of the non-recorded arises. For the function of silence in modernist works such as Schoenberg's *Six Little Piano Pieces* or Woolf's *Between the Acts* extends beyond a mere representation of "silencing." Here I would like to remind the reader that Schoenberg's piece relies equally upon the tones as on their absence. Exalting the inaudible, Woolf and Schoenberg simultaneously empower those whose voices have remained out of history's earshot. Silence binds history and *possible history*. This is the reason why, when the gendered "histories" are juxtaposed through the presence and absence of sound in a well-known episode in the novel, the aim is not a lament. We learn that while the male ancestor in a painting in the Olivers' dining room masters sound and genealogy ("he had a name [. . .] he was a talk producer" [BTA 36]), the lady in the adjacent painting has neither a name nor a narrative/history of her own. A being without social life, she is also an imaginary construct. This circumstance relates her silence to a realm beyond history: "silent, silent, silent," this feminine emblem of art still sings – "of what was before time was" (36–37). This "qualitative silence" ushers us into the dominion of timeless time world of timelessness, art, and peace. Silence, of course, is the hidden face of music, its core against which sound develops. To "hear silence," then, means to approach the potent space of blank bars, the white space between the hands of a clock (the realm in which Rhoda in *The Waves* abides), the very site of Woolf's super-historical art. It also means to invert the hierarchies of the non-manifest and the manifest, to redefine the relationship between art-as-timelessness and history-as-time-record.

"THE TREES WITH THEIR MANY-TONGUED MUCH SYLLABLING": THE FORGING OF THE PRIMEVAL VOICE

To the agons of love and hate in *Between the Acts*, Woolf adds a third condition: "peace." ("Peace was the third emotion. Love. Hate. Peace."

[BTA 92].) The last word read "death" in the early typescripts of *Pointz Hall* (PH 442). Much as we may admire the aesthetically emancipatory nature of silence/stasis, it is only through its interaction with voices that personal and general histories keep moving, this constellation of emotions/states suggests.

The following description of the silent library is quintessential for understanding of this dynamic: "The fire greyed, then glowed, and the tortoiseshell butterfly beat on the lower pane of the window; beat, beat, beat; repeating that if no human being ever came, never, never, never, the books would be mouldy, the fire out and the tortoiseshell butterfly dead on the pane" (BTA 17). The rhythm of this chromatically contorted sentence relies upon the butterfly's abortive attempts to come closer to the light, an occurrence to which Woolf returned almost compulsively in her diary and correspondence. The reiteration of "beat, beat, beat," although generative of this sad melody, leads the reader down the paths of silence-as-death, Freudianly marked by repetitive phrases. Like the repetitious chuffing of the gramophone needle in Miss La Trobe's pageant,[14] the butterfly's futile beating on the entrance to the storehouse of knowledge connotes death. But while the passage speaks poetically about life and death, its impetus is, in fact, sociohistorical: it intimates the dangers of the non-sound, non-existence. As the speechless Giles observes a snake choked with a toad in its mouth during an intermission of the pageant, the reader becomes aware of another face of silence: the moment of silent stasis may be empowering, but it also transfixes historical agents in negativity, *death,* divesting them of interrelation and language, that is, sound (or, as Giles puts it, depriving them of "metaphor" [53]).

One similar instance in Miss La Trobe's pageant deserves particular attention of an interpreter concerned with Woolf's sounds and silences. As the contrapuntal choir's song becomes inaudible, the stage is left empty and silent; terrified, Miss La Trobe whispers: "This is death [...] death." Silence is broken by a curious aid. One of the cows grazing around lifts "her great moon-eyed head" and starts bellowing in attempt to summon her lost calf. As the bellow spreads to other cows, "the whole world [gets] filled with dumb yearning." This bellow, the narrator comments, has "annihilated the gap; bridged the distance; filled the emptiness and continued the emotion." Linking this welcome sound to the creative activity of Eros, Woolf describes the bellow as "the primeval voice sounding loud in the ear of the present moment" (BTA 140). Melodically unsophisticated, this sound is the zero degree of music, its forgotten core, suffused with nothing but desire for the Other. Only as such can it reactivate the series of agons, and, like the stamping dissonant polychords in the "Augurs of Spring," revitalize the score. Indeed, when Woolf exalts rhythm as a vibrant force still audible only as a "vast pulsation" in "forests and solitary places" (E1: 30–31), her words invoke Stravinsky's constellation of the modern and the pagan. And, like Stravinsky, Woolf grounds her expressive primitivism in the search for what she believes to be the authentic core of music: its capacity to be a unifying force in history:

> Music wakes us. Music makes us see the hidden, join the broken. Look and listen. See the flowers, how they ray their redness, whiteness, silverness and blue. And the trees with their many-tongued much syllabling, their green and yellow leaves hustle us and shuffle us, and bid us, like the starlings, and the rocks, come together, crowd together. (BTA 120)

What Woolf seeks in musical experimentation, therefore, is not only a means to render the chaos of contemporary history and the brutal paralysis in which our "civilization" has found itself, but also a tool to recover some "primeval" voices that might break this stasis and reactivate history.

This theme figures prominently in her coextensively written manuscript *Anon*. In the melodic prose of the latter piece, Woolf plunges into mythic time to forge an image of the primary creator, the singer whose "voice [. . .] broke the silence of the forests." The voice was singing for community, but was also its part – it was "the common voice singing out of doors" (E6: 581–82). Anon, she or he, stands at the beginning of an alternative history, that of creative work. Here, literature (oral and written), the act of uttering, the bellowing of cows, and music in its diverse manifestations coalesce under the concept of primordial voice. It is this voice that springs forth into contemporary history, "sounding loud in the ear of the present moment" (BTA 140). How socially radical this primal sound may be is what Theodor Adorno has failed to recognize in Stravinsky's music and what I imagine he would have missed in Woolf's writing.[15]

CODA: ART AND THE SOCIUM

By opening the psychological and formal space of the primordial voice, Woolf and Stravinsky made a compelling statement on the necessity to interrelate art and the socium. While the autonomy of art is unquestionable for Woolf, the "Anon" fragment also suggests that the history of art *is* part of general history; indeed, it is its most important, creative-productive part. The voice of the primal singer that resonates through the ages and that of the unknown peasants whose song peters away each time they start it are one and the same. Behind the broken chords and the raucous rhythms of the late 1930s, there still lies the inner harmony of music, Woolf suggests; for "how can we deny that this brave music [...] is expressive of some inner harmony?" (BTA 36) It is in the light of this singular conjunction of historical melancholia and imperative of social action that we should read Woolf's mature interest in the liberating potentials of music and her belief that music informs the "hidden pattern" that makes us all not only creators but also "parts of the work of art" (MB 119).

It is for this reason that the finale of Miss La Trobe's pageant houses a range of music modes. It begins with a Brechtian exercise, a band of silence that fixates historical time (BTA 179). As the experiment fails, the nature helps: a sudden shower, sonorous, profuse, and purificatory, comes to aid. An optimistic tune ensues ("Each of us a free man; plates washed by machinery; not an aeroplane to vex us; all liberated; made whole" [182]), but it suddenly transmogrifies into a modern rhythm, jagged and cacophonous – "Foxtrot, was it? jazz?" (183). While the audience listens to this discordant music, the actors come in with mirrors, performing the fragmentation of experience that is modern life. The megaphone announces what the mirror images suggest: all we can ever fathom of ourselves is "scraps, orts, and fragments" (188). Yet, bearing in mind the problematic figuration of the "megaphone," the reader understands this fragmentation and contortion of rhythms as only one aspect of Woolf's "Musical Idea." Indeed, another change of music is pending, this one leading into premodernist era, binding the primordial, the classic, and the contemporary together. The pageant closes with an unnamed piece of music, "Bach, Handel, Beethoven, Mozart or [...] merely a traditional tune" (188):

> The tune began; the first note meant a second; the second a third. Then down beneath a force was born in opposition; then another. On different levels they diverged. On different levels ourselves went forward; flower gathering some on the surface; others descending top wrestle with the meaning; but all comprehending; all enlisted. The whole population of the mind's immeasurable profundity came flocking; from the unprotected, the unskinned; and dawn rose; and azure; from chaos and cacophony measure; but not the melody of surface sound alone controlled it; but also the warring battle-plumed warriors straining asunder: To part? No. Compelled from the ends of horizon; recalled from the edge of appalling crevasses; they crashed; solved; united. (189)

Gaining force in tension in a Schoenberg manner, this passage unites the world of art and that of social life in a measure of opposition. While they may be irreconcilable, art and history are not unbridgeable, since "*we* are the words, *we* are the music, *we* are the pattern itself" (MB 72) – the pattern that is dissonant yet integrated since the dawn of the times. When the "triumphant yet valedictory" gramophone gurgles "Unity-Dispersity" at the end of the novel (BTA 201), it has its needle on the right spot. In order to join what has been broken, make a whole of what has been historically smashed, we, the incongruous fragments, need to *perform* ourselves as a "rambling capricious but somehow unified whole" (D 5: 135), a secreted modernist music pattern.

Oriented by this indirect relationship between art and the socium, the final chords of *Between the Acts* bridge the primordial and the present yet again and leave the reader, like Woolf and her contemporaries, with mixed feelings. When Giles and Isa are left alone in the evening, tense silence covers Pointz Hall, a silence before history, "before roads were made, or houses" (BTA 219). Yet the last word in the novel – at the point where its own "silence" begins – is a sound: "They spoke" (219). The latter repeats the sound heard by Miss La Trobe at about the same (fictional) time: that of the first words of her new play (212). The outcome of both will be another series of agons, and, perhaps, "another life" (219). The last chimes, one realizes, open space for a new composition.

NOTES

This chapter relies on, and features parts of, my rather different discussion of Woolf's novel in *Modernism and Melancholia: Writing as Countermourning*. See

154–94. I am grateful to Oxford University Press for allowing me to reproduce parts of that discussion.

1. Cf. "to whom at the end there shall be an invocation? 'We'... composed of many different things... we all life, all art, all waifs & strays – a rambling capricious but somehow unified whole" (D5: 135).

2. Woolf relished music with the ardor of an amateur, Nietzscheanly passionate about its ontological potentials. Versatile in taste, Woolf was devoted to performance; she attended concerts and ballet and opera performances not only in London but across Europe as well (for instance, according to Adrian Stephen's diary, in the period of just six weeks in the summer of 1909, Woolf went twice to performances of W. A. Mozart's *Don Giovanni*, twice to that of Gustave Charpentier's *Louise*, to the premiere of Ethel Smyth's *The Wreckers*, to Giuseppe Verdi's *Aida*, Giacomo Puccini's *Madame Butterfly*, Charles Gounod's *Faust*, C. W. Gluck's *Orpheus and Eurydice*, several performances of the Ballets Russes, and concerts of instrumental music [Bell 149]). She also wrote a few articles about opera ("The Opera," "Impressions at Bayreuth") and ballet ("Plays and Pictures"). At the same time, her knowledge of music appears to have been limited: she did not play any instrument, and, as Quentin Bell somewhat dismissingly points out, it is dubitable that "she could follow a score with any deep comprehension" (149).

3. The term *Gesamtkunstwerk*, denoting a synthesis of various artistic disciplines in the formation of an artistic whole, was first used by Richard Wagner in his 1849 paper "The Artwork of the Future." By the detour of Wassily Kandinsky's art, the concept also critically influenced the composers of the Second Viennese School. See Schoenberg's correspondence with Kandinsky.

4. The 1918–1919 season starred Lydia Lopokova, the future spouse of John Maynard Keynes. On the Bloomsbury Group's involvement with the Ballets Russes, see Garafola 316, passim.

5. E4: 564. The Woolfs attended the production of Stravinsky and Ramuz's *L'Histoire du Soldat* (at Cambridge University's ADC Theatre) on November 10, 1928. Woolf's review appeared in the *Nation and Athenaeum* on November 17, 1928.

6. The London premiere of the Stravinsky/Ramuz piece in English translation happened on July 12, 1927. For the Stravinsky controversy, see Doctor 122–23. Woolf's acquaintance with Sacheverell Sitwell is well recorded in her diary; see entries from D1: 201 onward.

7. See, for one, the evening broadcast on January 7, 1931 (Doctor 349). On Beethoven's *Late String Quartets* as Woolf's favorite piece of music, see Bell 149.

8. For the scope, modes, and ethics of the BBC engagement with contemporary music, see Avery, esp. 33–74. Woolf broadcast three times, two of these broadcasts being solo talks. In 1933 Logan Pearsall Smith invited Woolf to become a member of the BBC Advisory Committee on Spoken English, and she accepted the proposal with some hesitation. She withdrew in 1934 (D4: 204). In November 1935 Woolf received an unusually lavish offer for her own program at the BBC – "a soliloquy [...] with all the resources of the BBC behind one: real railway trains; real orchestras; noises; waves, lions & tigers &tc." (D4: 351).

9. Cf. Mitchell Leaska, introduction, PH 15. The novel has attracted widely different interpretations, the range of which the reader may sample in the following representative pieces of scholarship: Beer; Cuddy-Keane; Smythe; Ames; Esty; Kahane.

10. Woolf's first allusion to *Between the Acts* appears in her diary on April 11, 1938: "Last night I began making up again: Summers night (sic!): a complete whole: that's my idea" (*D*5: 133).

11. See, for example, the descending of melody in pitch by a semitone, a minor third, and another semitone in the final movement of Beethoven's String Quartet in C-sharp minor and the same motif inverted in the opening of his String Quartet in A minor.

12. Stuart Clarke has traced this story to an actual rape that occurred on April 27, 1938, and was recorded in the *Times* (June 28–30, 1938); see Clarke.

13. Schoenberg both composed and wrote the text for *A Survivor from Warsaw*, op. 46 (1947). Recognized as one of the masterpieces of modern classical music, this short twelve-tone piece for the narrator, chorus, and orchestra is based on the Warsaw Ghetto survivors' story about a group of prisoners who began singing the Jewish prayer song *Shema Yisrael* (Deuteronomy 6: 4–9) as they were being deported to a death camp. Schoenberg's piece consists of two sections, played without pause. The first part contains a *Sprechstimme* account of the narrator-survivor positioned both against and in symbolic unison with the raucous orchestral backdrop; the second part features the male chorus bursting into prayer against the orchestral variation of the tonalities of the prime series.

14. For different readings of the gramophone in *Between the Acts*, see Pridmore-Brown; Scott, esp. 104–13.

15. In *Philosophy of Modern Music*, Theodor Adorno criticizes Stravinsky for his alleged subscription to "restoration" and pandering to populism and exalts Schoenberg as a "progressive" devotee to pure form.

WORKS CITED

Adorno, Theodor W. *Philosophy of Modern Music*. Trans. Anne G. Mitchell and Wesley V. Blomster. New York: Continuum, 2003. Print.

Albright, Daniel. *Modernism and Music: An Anthology of Sources*. Chicago: University of Chicago Press, 2004. Print.

Ames, Christopher. "Carnivalesque Comedy in Virginia Woolf's *Between the Acts*." *Twentieth-Century Literature* 44.4 (1998): 394–408. Print.

Avery, Todd. *Radio Modernism: Literature, Ethics, and the BBC, 1922–1938*. London: Ashgate, 2006. Print.

Bahun, Sanja. *Modernism and Melancholia: Writing as Countermourning*. Oxford University Press, 2013. Print.

Beer, Gillian. "The Island and the Aeroplane: The Case of Virginia Woolf." *Nation and Narration*. Ed. Homi K. Bhabha. London: Routledge, 1990. 265–90. Print.

Bell, Quentin. *Virginia Woolf: A Biography*. San Diego: Harcourt, 1974. Print.

Briggs, Asa. *The Golden Age of Wireless*. Oxford: Oxford University Press, 1965. Print.

Busoni, Ferruccio. *Selected Letters*. Trans. and ed. Antony Beaumont. London: Faber, 1987. Print.

Clarke, Stuart. "The Horse with a Green Tail." *Virginia Woolf Miscellany* 34 (Spring 1990): 3–4. Print.

Collis, Louise. *Impetuous Heart: The Story of Ethel Smyth*. London: Kilber, 1984. Print.

Cuddy-Keane, Melba. "The Politics of Comic Modes in Virginia Woolf's

Between the Acts." *PMLA* 105.2 (1990): 273–85. Print.
Doctor, Jennifer. *The BBC and Ultramodern Music*. Cambridge: Cambridge University Press, 1999. Print.
Esty, Joshua D. "Amnesia in the Fields: Late Modernism, Late Imperialism, and the English Pageant-Play." *English Literary History* 69 (2002): 245–76. Print.
Garafola, Lynn. *Diaghilev's Ballets Russes*. Oxford: Oxford University Press, 1989. Print.
Hillis Miller, Joseph. *Fiction and Repetition: Seven English Novels*. Cambridge: Harvard University Press, 1982. Print.
Kahane, Claire. "Of Snakes, Toads, and Duckweed: Traumatic Acts and Historical Actions in *Between the Acts*." *Virginia Woolf and Trauma: Embodied Texts*. Ed. Suzette Henke and David Eberly. New York: Pace University Press, 2008. 205–22. Print.
Pridmore-Brown, Michele. "1939–40: Of Virginia Woolf, Gramophones, and Fascism." *PMLA* 113.3 (1998): 408–21. Print.
Schoenberg, Arnold. *The Musical Idea and the Logic, Technique, and Art of Its Presentation*. Ed. and trans. Patricia Carpenter and Severine Neff. New York: Columbia University Press, 1995. Print.
———. *Style and Idea*. Ed. Leonard Stein. Trans. Leo Black. Berkeley: University of California Press, 1984. Print.
Schoenberg, Arnold, and Wassily Kandinsky. Correspondence. *The Arnold Schönberg Center*. Archive. Web. Sept. 15, 2012. http://81.223.24.109/letters/search_result.php?UID=f3a3b4e73e83c609672b42e5f2db9d1c&max_result_reached=.
Schulze, Robin Gail. "Design in Motion: Words, Music, and the Search for Coherence in the Works of Virginia Woolf and Arnold Schoenberg." *Studies in the Literary Imagination* 25.2 (1992): 5–22. Print.

Scott, Bonnie Kime. "The Subversive Mechanics of Woolf's Gramophone in *Between the Acts*." *Virginia Woolf in the Age of Mechanical Reproduction*. Ed. Pamela Caughie. New York: Garland, 2000. 97–113. Print.
Sears, Sallie. "Theater of War: Virginia Woolf's *Between the Acts*." *Virginia Woolf: A Feminist Slant*. Ed. Jane Marcus. Lincoln: University of Nebraska Press, 1983. 212–35. Print.
Smythe, Karen. "Virginia Woolf's Elegiac Enterprise." *NOVEL: A Forum on Fiction* 26.1 (1992): 64–79. Print.
Wagner, Richard. *The Art-Work of the Future and Other Works*. Trans. William Ashton Ellis. Lincoln: University of Nebraska Press, 1994. Print.
Woolf, Virginia. "Anon": typescript with the author's ms. corrections (Nov. 24, 1940). Berg Collection, New York Public Library. Print.
———. *Between the Acts*. San Diego: Harvest, 1970. Print.
———. *The Diary of Virginia Woolf*. Ed. Anne Oliver Bell. San Diego: Harcourt, 1977–1984. Print.
———. *The Essays of Virginia Woolf*. Ed. Andrew McNeillie. 4 vols. London: Hogarth, 1986. Print.
———. *The Essays of Virginia Woolf*. Vol. VI: *1933–1941 and Additional Essays 1906–1926*. Ed. Stuart N. Clarke. London: Hogarth, 2011. Print.
———. *The First Common Reader*. Ed. and intro. Andrew McNeillie. San Diego: Harcourt, 1984. Print.
———. *The Letters of Virginia Woolf*. Ed. Nigel Nicolson and Joanne Trautmann. 6 vols. London: Hogarth, 1975–1980. Print.
———. *Moments of Being: Unpublished Autobiographical Writings*. Ed. Jeanne Schulkind. London: Chatto & Windus, 1976. Print.

———. *A Passionate Apprentice: The Early Journals, 1897–1909.* Ed. Mitchell A. Leaska. New York: Harcourt, 1990. Print.

———. *Pointz Hall: The Earlier and Later Typescripts of "Between the Acts."* Ed. and annot. Mitchell A. Leaska. New York: John Jay, 1983. Print.

———. *The Second Common Reader.* Ed. and intro. Andrew McNeillie. San Diego: Harvest, 1986. Print.

———. *Virginia Woolf's Reading Notebooks.* Ed. Brenda Silver. Princeton: Princeton University Press, 1983. Print.

I attain a different kind of beauty, achieve a symmetry by means of infinite discords, showing all traces of the minds passage through the world; & achieve in the end, some kind of whole made of shivering fragments; to me this seems the natural process; the flight of the mind.

VIRGINIA WOOLF,
A Passionate Apprentice:
The Early Journals, 1897–1909

TEN

"Shivering Fragments"

MUSIC, ART, AND DANCE IN
VIRGINIA WOOLF'S WRITING

Evelyn Haller

THE AURALITY OF WOOLF'S NOVELS

From her vantage of a later century Angela Frattarola rightly cites "the often-overlooked aurality of the twentieth-century novel" and examines Woolf as a major exemplar (133n2). "Music" in relation to Woolf, is of particular importance. To take a congeries of instances: the rhythmic sound of "the sea" she intended to be heard "all through" *The Waves* (1931) (*D* 3: 34); the sound of the skywriting aeroplane in her war-haunted novel, with its implied cacophony of the battlefield in Septimus's memory in *Mrs. Dalloway* (1925); and the harsh, unmelodic singing of the caretaker's children in *The Years* (1937). In her posthumously published novel, *Between the Acts* (1941), the flamboyant and uninhibited Mrs. Manresa "was afloat on the stream of the melody," that of a "pompous popular tune" that "brayed and blared" (96–97). Machines, not unlike people, can disappoint: "Chuff, chuff, chuff [. . .] It was the noise a machine makes when something has gone wrong" (93). Three and a half decades earlier the young Virginia had written, "Music perhaps because it is not human is the only thing made by men that can never be mean or ugly" (*E*1: 31). She was to hear many kinds of sounds, but not all were to be understood as music without the intervention of a Stravinsky. Still, sounds – stated and implied – of various kinds as well as music would be major tools of her craft. Her multifaceted evocation of Kew Gardens, for example, alludes in its conclusion to the metronomic rhythm of machinery outside its walls: "But there was no silence; all the time the motor omnibuses were turning their wheels and shifting their gears." Moreover, London itself is recognized as an enormous machine: "like a vast nest of Chinese boxes all of wrought steel turning ceaselessly one within another the city murmured" (CSF 95).

Providing a historical frame of the period immediately before the outbreak of the Great War, Richard Shone writes:

> In late 1913 and the first half of 1914 several exhibitions, ballets, and operas contributed to the increasing excitement and novelty of a London becoming caught up in the general artistic ferment in Europe . . . the summer impact of the Russian Ballet, the opening of one of the city's first cabaret night-clubs, the visits of the Futurists, culminating in Marinetti's talk at the Rebel Art Centre. (125)

Virginia Woolf lived at a time when not only was the composition of music changing radically but also when, as Vanessa Bell recalled, such new sounds of music "excited ecstasy rage and disdain" (Spalding 131). Hence, in response to the predictable question of how and whether "noise" in modernist texts can be thought of as "music," consider that T. S. Eliot recognized such an equation when he wrote after attending a ballet performance of *The Rite of Spring* on June 27, 1921, that Stravinsky's music seemed to "transform the rhythm of the steppes into the scream of the motor horn, the rattle of machinery, the grind of wheels, the beating of iron and steel, the roar of the underground railway, and the other barbaric cries of modern life; and to transform these despairing noises into music" ("London Letter for the *Dial*, September 1921," in Rainey 189). Of the ballet itself, Eliot recognized that "the Vegetation Rite upon which the ballet is founded remained, in spite of the music, a pageant of primitive culture. . . . In everything in the *Sacre du Printemps*, except in the music, one missed the sense of the present" (189).

Eliot made use of the rhythms of jazz in *The Waste Land* (1922), for the agitated music provided a dimension to which one could move consciously or unconsciously. One's thoughts could fall into its syncopated patterns, and therewith one might compose poetry. When Woolf walked between Futurist paintings of dancing couples painted by Vanessa Bell and Duncan Grant on either side of the entrance to the Omega Workshops at 33 Fitzroy Square, she no longer moved to the melodies of Victorian verse as she speculated had been experienced by previous generations in *A Room of One's Own*. Thus, one can rejoice in jazz as Sally finds her poetic voice accompanied by a stranger's trombone in a squalid London neighborhood in *The Years*. Sally's repetitions as well as her flights of fancy oddly fit her domestic setting better than when she is seated with her cousin North in a restaurant. Sally, in her developmentally challenged way, is an exponent of jazz while her wealthy cousin Kitty is a consumer of exponentially higher Wagnerian volume.

In 1909 when the young Virginia wrote an extended essay about opera that included classification of Wagnerian fans, she had recourse in the conclusion to a painterly description of the opera house and, by way of synecdoche, the people within it – a description not unlike Walter Sickert's paintings of music halls with their popular entertainments. Sickert was an older painter whose works she admired and about whom she composed the essay "Walter Sickert: A Conversation."

> The words "The Opera" alone call up a complex vision. We see the immense house, with its vast curved sides, its soft depths of rose colour and cream, the laces hanging down in loops from the boxes, and the twinkle of diamonds within. We think of this: of the hum and animation when the pyramid of light blazes out and all the colours move; and of the strange hush and dimness when the vistas of the stage are revealed and the voices mingle with the violins. (E1: 271–72)

Recognizing a merging of the muses, Daniel Albright observes that "the twentieth century reaches out to the freakish circumferences of art. The extremes of the aesthetic experience tend to converge" (ix). In her foreword to *Catalogue of Recent Paintings by Vanessa Bell* (1934), Woolf resorts to synesthesia to encompass such a convergence: "People's minds have split out of their bodies and become part of their surroundings. Where does the man end and Buddha begin? Character is colour, and colour is china, and china is music." Nor is a still life entirely still: "The onions and the eggs perform together a solemn music" (E6: 29–30).

Her articulated responses to music are not surprising, for the young Virginia had already experienced an intimation of her own modernist technique during travel in Italy. What James Joyce, her precise contemporary (1882–1941), building on a medieval Italian theologian, Thomas Aquinas, wrote about beauty and, hence, great art through Stephen Dedalus in *Portrait of the Artist as a Young Man* applies to each of our foreshortened lives: potentially at least, we possess "wholeness, harmony, and radiance" (Joyce 479), but with the insights of modernist praxis, we know our subjective experience of reality to be one of "shivering fragments."

PERUGIA 1908

The twenty-six-year-old Virginia Stephen's analysis of her own aesthetic while she was in Perugia with her artist sister, Vanessa Bell, and her art critic brother-in-law, Clive Bell, has parallels with emerging modernist movements in the arts, including music. Although she was drawn to the stasis of Pietro Vanucci's [Perugino's] mural, probably *The Almighty with Prophets and Sibyls* (c. 1500), one can observe how its self-contained sublimity jarred her into recognition of a different mode of art she was compelled to explore. Thus we can situate her desire to "achieve a symmetry by means of infinite discords, showing all traces of the minds passage through the world & achieve [. . .] some kind of whole made of shivering fragments [. . .] the flight of the mind" (PA 393).

The young Virginia reacted against the stasis of beatitude and a fixed worldview, for while she recognized the instability of "some kind of whole made of shivering fragments" into which sound and rhythm figure, she also had mental and emotional roots in a more distant tradition of thought, as when Hesiod envisioned the nine muses – not only Terpsichore – stamping their feet in dance. In *The Waves*, which Woolf says she wrote "to a rhythm and not to a plot" (L4: 204), Louis says, "Every day I unbury – I dig up" (W 92). From early in the novel, Louis hears "something stamping," "it stamps and stamps and stamps" (4). As I have argued, Woolf is likely to have composed the soundscape of her masterpiece, *The Waves*, "from the physiologically imperative pulsations of Stravinsky's music," which had been emphasized by the choreography of Nijinsky for *The Rite of Spring* (1913) and of his sister, Bronislava Nijinska, for *The Village Wedding* (1923) (Haller 205).

Woolf's conception of the essence of music – its ultimate value – was not conventional. Moreover, it was far-reaching in its import. For clarity I would like to expand the quoted passage below:

> The voices of friends are discordant after listening to beautiful music because they disturb the echo of rhythmic harmony, which for the moment makes of life

a united and musical whole; and it seems probable [. . .] that there is a music in the air for which we are always straining our ears and which is only partially made audible to us by the transcripts which the great musicians are able to preserve. In forests and solitary places an attentive ear can detect something very like a vast pulsation, and if our ears were educated we might hear the music also which accompanies this (E1: 31).

Virginia expresses it best.

NIJINSKY

While Woolf wrote of Lydia Lopokova in her essays (E4: 247, 248n2, n3, 564&n3), diaries (D3: 18, 38, 43–44, 70, 76, 147&n, 164, 181), and letters (L3: 120, 149, 198n, 277, 289, 349, 376–77, 521, 560n), she named Nijinsky in her novel *The Years* (1937). A young woman speaks: "'And when he gives that leap!' she exclaimed – she raised her hand with a lovely gesture in the air – 'and then comes down!' she let her hand fall in her lap" (254).

As a *danseur noble* Nijinsky was unparalleled, but as a choreographer he angered dancers of the Diaghilev company by demanding postures and movements that were counter to classical ballet. The stomping of *Le Sacre* as well as distorted counter-positions did not come easily to them, and they resented him deeply. But as T. S. Eliot heard "the present" in Stravinsky's music, he also recognized prehistoric myth in the ballet itself.

In her essay "Street Music" (1905), wherein her defense of street musicians is the starting point, the young Virginia invokes a god of music who sounds more like Pan or Dionysius than Apollo, for he is not a god of reason and order: when he returns, he "will breathe madness into our brains, crack the walls of our temples, and drive us in loathing of our rhythmless lives to dance and circle forever in obedience to his voice" (E1: 29–30). The music of Dionysian frenzy we encounter in classical literature was loud and unnerving – not unlike the "noise" of revolutionary twentieth-century music. Stravinsky's music, however, often had rhythm expressed in relentless movement not unlike Virginia Stephen's "shivering fragments." Moreover, that Stravinsky's rhythms could be counted to reluctant dancers is evidenced by the choreographer Nijinsky's shouting from offstage over the pandemonium of opening night in 1913. Similarly, Lydia Sokolova, who danced the role of the Chosen Virgin (as she named it) in the production choreographed by Léonid Massine in 1920, recalled that a colleague "prompted" her during a performance "by counting aloud up to thirteen." Sokolova described herself in 1968 as "the only living person who knows, and remembers, the original version of the *Danse Sacre* in its entirety." She said, "It is generally agreed that the *Sacre du Printemps* contains the longest, the most exhausting, and the most difficult solo dance of all ballets" (Gottlieb 1061). The intensity of Stravinsky's revolutionary music for *Le Sacre du Printemps* and for *Les Noces* (*The Village Wedding*), choreographed by Nijinsky's sister, Bronislava Nijinska, restored – albeit violently – the rhythm whose loss the young Virginia had deplored when she wrote: "The safest and easiest attribute of music – its tune – is taught, but rhythm, which is its soul, is allowed to escape like the winged creature it is" (E1: 30). In her essay on cinema Woolf hypothesized savages knocking two iron bars together as a primeval attempt to make music, and thus she provided instrumentation for rhythm (E4: 348, 352).

A statue by Umberto Boccioni, *Forme uniche della continuità nello spazio* (*Unique Forms of Continuity in Space*) (1913) provides a visual counterpart to Nijinsky, who embodied a unique form of continuity in space through the force of his corporeal presence. Particularly noteworthy are the bronze statue's massive thighs – resembling Nijinsky's in proportion to the figure as a whole – which appear to provide propulsion more than the nearly vestigial wings at the calves, which in turn recall the winged heels of Hermes/Mercury while intimating a headwind of what would later be referred to as g-forces. The continued presence of the statue as opposed to the brief span of Nijinsky's time to perform and to choreograph ballets underscores the place of Nijinsky in the balletomane's imagination, for we have only photographs and no motion pictures from which to infer his command of space. While Nijinsky's command of space as a *danseur noble* was unparalleled, "his preoccupation was with the design of dancing rather than with his effect in the dance" (Kirstein 897). Through opportunities offered him by Diaghilev, and by building on Marius Petipa's and Michel Fokine's work as well as by scores composed by Tchaikovsky and Stravinsky, Nijinsky contributed to raising choreography "as equal in depth and expressiveness to the other arts" (896). Lincoln Kirstein writes of Nijinsky as "a sculptor" who "seems primarily to have been inspired by plasticity – the projection of forms activated in high relief. He worked in three dimensions linked to a fourth – the musico-temporal – by new and arbitrary movement" (897). The latter is apparent in his choreography for Debussy's *The Afternoon of a Faun,* with its geometric positions of the arms of the nymphs as they move across the stage in nearly two dimensions, evoking the flattened patterns of Greek vases Nijinsky had seen in the British Museum. His legacy is ongoing, for "instinctively, or however, Nijinsky (with Rodin, Cézanne, Picasso, and Brancusi) for his generation murdered beauty" and "established an entire field theory that ensuing decades have not begun to exhaust" (899).

The epitomizing mechanical invention not only for the contested claims of Futurism but also for modernism itself is the aeroplane, for it enables earthbound mortals to accomplish what ballet dancers can only aspire to. As Kirstein frames his essay on Nijinsky, "Dancers glide, spin, leap, almost fly; yet they have only two arms and two legs" (895–96). Indeed Boccioni's *Forme uniche della continuità a nello spazio* (1913; bronze 117.5 x 87.6 x 36.8 cm) resembles a bird man – ironically armless – who is held to earth and restrained from flying only by dual massive plinths of the same brazen substance as himself. It also bears a faint resemblance to a man wearing knightly armor, with archaic restrictions on movement overcome as a prodigious headwind blows against him. And while it may be argued that it celebrates the physical attributes of male muscular strength (as in Boccioni's earlier statues: *Synthesis of Human Dynamism* [1912], *Speeding Muscles* [1913], and *Spiral Expansion of Speeding Muscles* [1913]), a more multifaceted dimension than virility is present in Boccioni's "monumental" statue, for it also relates to the outer reaches of mathematical speculation, as its title, "Forms of Continuity in Space," suggests. As Herbert Read concluded in 1964:

> His monumental *Unique Forms of Continuity in Space* succeeds in conveying the striding advance of a human figure – one is tempted to add "through space," but since we have been told that "space no longer exists" the intention is presumably to suggest "a bridge between the exterior plastic infinite and the interior plastic infinite." ... Boccioni had in mind the idea that "objects never end," and "intersect with infinite combinations of sympathetic harmonies and clashing aversions." The infinity is one of movement and not of space (133–34).

A less theoretical kind of movement that increased exponentially was enabled by "the motor" as the car was often called during Woolf's lifetime. As Jan Morris observes, "The car became in her mind a very engine of release, like travel itself perhaps" (7). Filippo Tommaso Marinetti, the arch Futurist, favored large and fast cars – an aspect of his persona manifesting "the sinister abandon of Borgiac Italy" (see Lowenthal 380n91); Woolf herself became enamored of access to mechanized movement through space after repeatedly enjoying the rapid movement of mechanized descent at "The Chute" at the annual Earls Court exhibition. In 1903 she wrote of the Water-Chute: "The first thing we made for was the Chute [. . .] The Chute is unfailing: I tremble to think what my state of mind will be when I cease to appreciate the Chute. And yet last year I made six descents running without any hesitation, & this year I didn't mind stopping after the third" (PA 179–80). Although Virginia Woolf's choice of "on or about December 1910" (E3: 421) for change in "human character" might have seemed arbitrary, the accelerated movement of the subsequent century has validated her generalization. Our present understanding of human character – as in Read's commentary on Boccioni's statue and his ideas – suggests that human character "intersects with infinite combinations of sympathetic harmonies and clashing aversions." We all are engaged in an infinity of movement merged with the past as well as the present and future. Boccioni's bronze statue reifies what each life epitomizes in its instance of human character, albeit of limited duration.

THE "MUSIC" OF FRAGMENTATION AND ACCELERATION

In her fragmentary "The Telephone," with its evocation of London, Woolf wrote, "Innumerable houses, points of light [. . .] float sprinkled in millions of particles" (CSF 315). Vanessa Bell's original cover design for *To the Lighthouse* also conveys "shivering fragments" in points emanating from the lighthouse and descending to the waves below, which are also in "shivering fragments." Woolf was eager to collapse artistic conventions of time and space. As is well known, she was impatient with the novelist's burden of pedestrian detail. Although she succeeded in capturing "an ordinary mind on an ordinary day," she also experienced life as "being blown through the Tube at fifty miles an hour ... With one's hair flying back like the tail of a race-horse" (E2: 106; CSF 84). Giacomo Balla's painting *The Car Has Passed* (1913) conveys a similar sensation of speed. Not only does Balla's surname mean "he dances," but also he prevailed upon the brothers Bruno and Arnaldo Ginanni-Corradini, who made films, to change their names to Bruno Corra (run) and Arnaldo Ginna, with its "suggestion of gymnastics" (Rawson 257n7). Consider further that Woolf's declaration that "Life is not a series of gig lamps symmetrically arranged but a halo that surrounds us from the beginning of consciousness to the end" corresponds to another painting by Balla, his *Street Light* (1909), a large oil on canvas measuring 174.7 cm × 114.5 cm (68 ¾ in × 45 ¼ cm). Herbert Read's summary of Futurist art in his *Concise History of Modern Sculpture* as one that "sought to realize movement and 'states of mind'" (135–36) corresponds to Woolf's own writing.

Since I refer to the Futurists, clarity demands that I address the tension between their English exponents and Woolf. She was not friends with Wyndham Lewis (1882–1957), who was hailed by Seamus Cooney as "the founder of Vorticism, the only original movement in twentieth-century English painting" (329). Indeed he set her up as the target to attack in chapter 5, "Virginia Woolf: 'Mind' and 'Matter' on the Plane of a Literary Controversy," of his book *Men without Art* (1934). Lewis chose as epigraph to the chapter: "We must reconcile ourselves to a season of failures and fragments" from her essay "Mr. Bennett and Mrs. Brown," which is the focus of his vituperation. Acidly expressed anger was Lewis's major key, however, as he had demonstrated toward Roger Fry two decades earlier after his break with the Omega Workshops. Nor was she friends with Ezra Pound, who made a disadvantageous comparison of her with Henry Miller in a letter to T. S. Eliot in 1935: "Hen. Miller having done presumably the only book a man cd. read for pleasure and if not out Ulyssesing Joyce at least being infinitely more part of permanent literature than such ½ masted slime as the weakminded, Woolf female" (*Pound Letters* 272). Personality clashes aside, Woolf was keenly aware of what was happening in the arts beyond literature through Vanessa Bell, Roger Fry, and Duncan Grant, not to mention arts coverage in the *Nation and Athenaeum*. A case in point is the rapidity with which Futurist painting was disseminated. An exhibition was held at the Sackville Gallery in London in 1912. "Within two years, Futurist painting had been seen in cities as far apart as Moscow and San Francisco" (Todoli 17). In June 1914, "Duncan sent two abstracts to the Vorticist exhibition organized by Wyndham Lewis" (Spalding 141–42), and in June 1915 he exhibited "three pictures by invitation at the Vorticist Exhibition at the Doré Galleries, London" (Shone 263). More to the musical point, in 1914 at the outbreak of the Great War, at Asheham House in Sussex, which Virginia and Vanessa had leased (Whitworth xiii), "Duncan busied himself with an abstract scroll which he intended should be viewed through an aperture as it wound past to musical accompaniment" (Spalding 132). *Abstract Kinetic Collage Painting with Sound,* which is now at the Tate Gallery, "was nearly 15 feet long" (Turnbaugh, plate 21, fig. 48 and caption). Of that bountiful time Vanessa Bell wrote in a memoir:

> It must now be almost incredible how unaware we were of the disaster so soon to come [...] when beauty was springing up under one's feet so vividly that violent abuse was hurled at it and genius generally considered to be insanity [...] when music joined in the general chorus with sounds which excited ecstasy rage and disdain: a great new freedom seemed about to come and perhaps would have come, if it had not been for motives and ambitions of which we knew nothing. (Spalding 131)

In July 1917 Clive Bell "lambasted contemporary English painting as provincial, inveterately suburban, and completely adrift from European currents" (Shone 172). Beyond French painters he expressed approval of "Larionov, Goncharova, the Italian Futurists, Kandinsky, and the Munich School." "Fry and the Omega circle were exempted," which was not surprising as Fry was editor of the *Burlington Magazine,* where Bell's article appeared (173).

MOTOR CARS AND AEROPLANES

Viewed from a long perspective, Woolf's work can be heard as a congeries of motorcars and aeroplanes as well as less euphonious noises cited by T. S. Eliot as conveying "the sense of the present." Their "music" like a drone accompanies rhythm and movement, divides sound from silence, and invites classification beyond such a reductive word as "noise."

Although other painters were interested in the relationship of art and music, including an older painter, Walter Sickert, whose work Woolf admired, by 1914 a Futurist music score for *intonarumori* (noise intoners) titled *Convegno d'aeroplani e d'automobili (The Meeting of Aeroplanes and Automobiles)* had been published. The noise intoners, conceived as superseding orchestral instruments of passé-ism, were a serious undertaking constructed by a Futurist painter, Luigi Russolo. Indeed concert performances were given in urban settings including Milan and London. If one imagines oneself in Woolf's London, one is surrounded by a variety of traffic noise, be it the iron-shod hooves of horses or iron wheels of carts on cobblestones; the cacophony of the Underground; or the darting movement of motorcars, lorries, and omnibuses with their shifting gears as she suggests in an aerial view over Kew Gardens. One doesn't have to like noise to recognize in it a defining aspect of the twentieth century as T. S. Eliot suggested. In the fragments she later titled "Cracked Fiddles," having canceled the title "ILLUSIONS. Written to the tune of a street violin," Woolf heard such "music" as when she wrote in the fragmentary "A Death in the Newspaper": "So from an express train I have seen the man with a scythe look up from the hedge as we flew past, and the lovers lying in the long grass stared – stared. Wheels and cries sound now low, now high; all in harmony" (CSF 314–15).

Although Virginia Stephen had double glazing placed on her first rooms in Bloomsbury, she was alert to the auditory possibilities of her beloved city whether they grated upon her inner ear or not by way of "infinite discords . . . & achieve in the end some kind of whole made of shivering fragments" (PA 393). Such is the exterior experience of urban life. But with the opening of the Omega Workshops, Ltd., at 33 Fitzroy Square on July 8, 1913, modernist interior design heightened by fabrics, objects, and decorated furniture were available to Woolf, her family, and her friends, as well as to members of the discerning public. Not everyone was pleased, however. To provide a description of an "unmistakably Omega" room, Richard Shone quotes from a 1918 novel by Arnold Bennett: "The place resembled a gigantic and glittering kaleidoscope deranged and arrested." (Recall that Woolf contrasted Bennett's work as a novelist with her efforts to capture the soul of the hypothetical "Mrs. Brown" in her essay on the writing of fiction.) Bennett details the elements of the "unmistakably Omega" room in geometric terms: "The walls were irregularly covered with rhombuses, rhomboids, lozenges, diamonds, triangles, and parallelograms; the carpet was treated likewise, and also the upholstery and the cushions" (Shone 97). Much of Omega style throughout its products was rhythmic in design, especially large figures used on screens or in murals. As Shone notes, the influence of the Russian Ballet was evident. A particular example is a decorative panel by Duncan Grant titled *Dancers* (1917) showing significantly distorted nude figures in a round dance. Grant often painted bodies in motion but not always dancers. *Bathing* (1911), a mural for the dining room of the Borough Polytechnic, has swimmers in motion among rhythmically moving waves. In the adjacent mural, *Football*, male bodies leap diagonally. "These murals brought Grant his first public success" (Turnbaugh, plate 15, fig. 41 and caption).

The "shivering fragments" to denote the collapse of space and time that Virginia Stephen recognized in Italy as a vital aspect of her own writing also occurred in various forms among the men violently dedicated to the future at the expense of the past. Why did such a movement arise in Italy, a country to which the Stephen sisters and Clive Bell traveled more than once? As David Lowenthal observes in *The Past Is a Foreign Country:* "The Futurist ideology... first arose in northern Italian cities – Turin, Genoa, Milan – transformed by industrialization over a few short years. The bizarre survival of antique and Renaissance forms in a landscape of radical technological change may help to explain Futurist manifestos against the past" (see 380n91). C. R. W. Nevinson, the major though temporary British adherent of Futurism, writes of Marinetti: "His idea was to make Italy a country with a future as well as a country with a past, and to attack the malady of passé-ism, which was the way he defined the intellectual curse of Europe and America" (*Paint* 57).

BLOOMSBURY AND VORTICISM

Christine Froula argues that "Bloomsbury's aesthetic formalism resonates with other London movements such as Vorticism" (365n29). Diane Gillespie denies a connection: "Woolf was not associated with the Vorticists; when she allied herself briefly with the suffrage movement, it was with the nonmilitants, some of whom she presents none too favorably in *Night and Day*" (*Sisters'Arts* 319n44). In the first issue of *BLAST*, with its strident pink cover, Vorticists offered in capital letters "TO SUFFRAGETTES / A WORD OF ADVICE": that the women "LEAVE WORKS OF ART ALONE" lest they "DESTROY A / GOOD PICTURE BY ACCIDENT." Still, they commended the suffragettes for their bravery and assured them of their votes (qtd. from "Our Vortex," *BLAST* 1: 151). Miranda B. Hickman, however, includes references to Woolf in her important study *The Geometry of Modernism: The Vorticist Idiom in Lewis, Pound, H. D., and Yeats,* wherein she "addresses how a fascination with geometric forms [. . .] provided many modern writers with a language through which to imagine and articulate their ideals: a language, in Ezra Pound's words, both to 'think in' and to 'use'" (*Literary Essays* 194, qtd. on p. xiii). Hickman notes, "By 1927, when Virginia Woolf had a puzzled Mr. Bankes in [. . .] *To the Lighthouse* tap painter Lily Briscoe's canvas with his penknife and ask her to explain the 'triangular purple shape – just there,' she was clearly using this inquisitive gesture to evoke a moment twenty years before" (3). Hickman also mentions Woolf's drawing "a geometric figure of three fused rectangles in her notebooks to capture the structure" of that novel (255). "Three fused rectangles" bespeaks the "aesthetic formalism" cited by Froula. By organizing *To the Lighthouse* within three subtitles – "The Window," "Time Passes," and "The Lighthouse" – Woolf contains the "shivering fragments" of actions both inside and outside the French window of the summer residence; the passage of ten years, during which Mrs. Ramsay, Andrew, and Prue die in company with the dead of the Great War; and the finally completed journey to the lighthouse as well as Lily's completion of the portrait of Mrs. Ramsay and James. Woolf thereby employs "a language through which to imagine and articulate" her ideals. Similarly, Mrs. Ramsay's personal descent into "a wedge-shaped core of darkness" wherein she loses "personality" is accompanied by the triple sweep of beams from the lighthouse as she waits for "the long steady stroke, the last of the three, which was her stroke," as in a duet with a violin bowed beside a wedge-shaped piano (TL 62–63).

The poet Ezra Pound, who was a music critic as well as a composer, set a geometric form in motion: "a radiant node or cluster; . . . what I can, and must perforce, call a VORTEX, from which, and through which, and into which, ideas are constantly rushing," in his memoir of the sculptor Henri Gaudier-Brzeska (92), which Woolf read (D1: 90, Dec. 10, 1917). She was therefore likely to have been aware of Pound's statement that Gaudier-Brzeska "chose to call himself a 'vorticist'" (18). The French sculptor's participation in the Omega Workshops (1913–1919) founded by Roger Fry with the collaboration of Woolf's sister, Vanessa Bell, brief though it was before his death in France (1915), had resulted in significant contributions to the enterprise. Among the objects he designed or made was a tray that Roger Fry called "The Wrestlers" in his article on the sculptor. Evelyn Silber, however, observes that "the composition chosen also evokes a dance." In sum, "The dance motif can be linked to the fascination at the Omega (and in London generally) with the Ballets Russes" (qtd. in *Beyond Bloomsbury* 66). Woolf visited the shops at 33 Fitzroy Square (Nov. 10, 1917; D1: 72–73), thereby passing between "the large dancing couples in evening dress painted into the recesses of the façade in an exuberant Futurist style," one designed by Vanessa Bell (*Beyond Bloomsbury* 83, 62) and the other by Duncan Grant.

Richard Shone acknowledges the impact of the Russian Ballet on the productions of the Omega Workshop, especially in the massive figures that appear on screens and murals. In the painted rhythm of large figures, their distortion conveys past and present movement much as one experiences music, with its present instance containing its past and anticipating its future. While he was at the Omega Workshops wearing his white-and-black-checked cap, Wyndham Lewis painted a screen titled *Acrobats* or *Circus*. In their distortion, Roger Fry had remarked, "Art is significant deformity."

SPEED CONTAINED IN FORM AND RELEASED IN EXPLOSIVE FORCE

Woolf was exasperated with "this appalling narrative business of the realist: getting on from lunch to dinner: it is false, unreal, merely conventional" (D3: 209). She therefore set for herself an accelerated pace. The urban sensibility of modernist art, however, absorbs not only a glorification of speed but also the heightening of experience that technology makes possible. For his ballet *Jeux* (*Games*), "Nijinsky proposed the harsh artificial glare of electric arc lights in early evening, as screened through chestnut trees in a city park," while two women and a man, dressed for tennis, engage in flirtation. Bare electric bulbs when they were introduced also cast a new light. Indeed the liturgical sense of magnification – giving glory – applies. In "Moments of Being: 'Slater's Pins Have No Points,'" first published in *Forum* in 1928, Woolf collapses the life history of a frugal piano teacher, Miss Julia Craye, into the seconds that her pupil, Fanny Wilmot, searches for the pin that has let a flower fall from her dress. As Miss Craye's life history becomes known to the reader (as it will later to Fanny), so, too, does her desire "to break the spell that had fallen on the house; to break the pane of glass which separated them [her deceased brother as well as herself] from other people" (CSF 216). Miss Julia Craye, having played a Bach fugue "as a reward to a favourite pupil," is still, but her stillness contains explosive force as it breaks "the glassy surface" (or becomes "shivering fragments") propelled into the London night. The apotheosis is seen by Fanny Wilmot, for whom Miss Julia Craye explodes out of her precisely crafted existence of modulated pleasures into the scale and visual devices of a modernist painting accompanied by the implicit *sound* of shattering glass and *rhythmic pulsations* of a fountain:

> Fanny had surprised her in a moment of ecstasy. She sat there, half turned away from the piano, with her hands clasped in her lap holding the carnation upright, while behind her was the sharp square of the window, uncurtained, purple in the evening, intensely purple after the brilliant electric lights which burned unshaded in the bare music room. Julia Craye, sitting hunched and compact holding her flower seemed to emerge out of the London night, seemed to fling it like a cloak behind her. It seemed, in its bareness and intensity the effluence of her spirit, something she had made which surrounded her, which was her. Fanny stared. (CSF 220)

As she stared, "as if looking through Miss Craye she saw the very fountain of her being spurt up in pure, silver drops. She saw back and back into the past behind her. [...] She saw Julia." The apotheosis witnessed by Fanny – "Out of the night she burnt like a dead white star" – is followed by Julia's kiss (220). For a moment the pane of glass has been broken. The apotheosis of the older woman – indeed a spinster – witnessed by the young Fanny Wilmot gives her an experience to ponder in her heart as well as an intimation of what dedication to music and aesthetic pleasure can bestow on her own life. As Herbert Read understood of Boccioni's statue *Unique Forms of Continuity in Space*, "a bridge" is suggested "between the exterior plastic infinite and the interior plastic infinite . . . The infinity is one of movement and not of space" (133–34). Miss Julia Craye is not merely her confined self; rather, her essential being or "soul," as Woolf discovered in Russian novels and failed to find in those by Arnold Bennett, H. G. Wells, and John Galsworthy, is extended by "infinite combinations of sympathetic harmonies and clashing aversions" with which they intersect, to continue to apply Read's commentary on Boccioni's bronze statue.

Russolo, the painter who intuited the experience of the pianist in an enormous painting titled *Music* (1911–1912), said, "I am able to divine the great renewal of music by means of the Art of Noises." He was not to be satisfied with the percussive resources of the piano, however, for he was to construct new machines to make new noises. Russolo, influenced by Francesco Balilla Pratella, stated that "noise is triumphant and reigns sovereign over the sensibility of man" (Hayward n.p.). Indeed Russolo exhorted urban dwellers to immerse themselves in their soundscape, echoing T. S. Eliot's recognition of the ability of art "to transform these despairing noises into music" in which he heard the raw material of "the present."

> Let us cross a great modern capital with our ears more than our eyes. We will delight in distinguishing the eddying of water, of air and gas in metal pipes, the muttering of motors that breathe and pulse with an indisputable animality, the throbbing of valves, the bustle of pistons, the shrieks of mechanical saws, the jolting of trams on the tracks, the cracking of whips, the flapping of awnings and flags. We will amuse ourselves in orchestrating together in our imagination the din of rolling shop shutters, slamming doors, the varied hubbub of train stations, iron works, thread mills, printing presses, electrical plants and subways. (Hayward n.p.)

To express similar sounds Russolo constructed noise intoners (intonarumori) in his Milan laboratory with the assistance of fellow painter Ugo Piatti. The instruments, too early for electrical amplification, consisted of "various motors and mechanisms and were operated by means of a protruding handle, while pitch was varied with a lever and a sliding scale" (Hayward n.p.). By spring of 1914 four noise intoners had been constructed: "a buster (*scoppiatore*), a crackler (*crepitatore*), a hummer (*ronzatore*), and a scraper (*scropiccatore*)." Scores for two "Networks of Noise" titled *Risvelglio di una Citta* (*The Awakening of a City*) and *Convegno d'aeroplani e d'automobili* (*The Meeting of Aeroplanes and Automobiles*) had been published. Francesco Canguillo, in his autobiography, *Le serate futuriste* (1930), describes the salon demonstration at the home of Marinetti, where Diaghilev, Stravinsky, and Nijinsky were also favorably impressed. It is not surprising that the impresario, the major composer, and the leading dancer of the Ballets Russes were attuned to challenging aural possibilities.

The impulse to make new noises before an audience could not be confined to Italy, however. Within a year of the riot-inducing performance of Stravinsky's *Rite of Spring* at the Théâtre Champs d'Elysée in Paris,[1] audiences were provoked at the far more extreme sounds of the intonarumori at London Coliseum on Monday, June 15, 1914. The audience limited their negative response to prolonged boos, thereby adding a drone to the crank-induced sounds of the noise intoners. Nevertheless, performances continued during the week, perhaps as many as twelve. To quote from the poster: Marinetti, described as "The Futurist Leader," spoke in Italian on the Art of Noises before a "Performance of Two Noise Spirals composed and conducted by the painter Luigi Russolo, Inventor of the Art of Noises." To someone who is not prepared to hear Italian Futurist music or to revisit it by choice, the sounds are likely to be disturbing if not agitating and without redemptive pleasure. Such music is, however, about concepts – particularly urban concepts – rather than the reassurances of euphonious harmony often associated with idealized pastoral scenes. Ezra Pound, the American poet, who also composed music, including operas, and wrote music criticism, spurned the performance as "a mimetic representation of dead cats in a fog horn" (Tisdall 104).

While Woolf disliked noise, she knew how to use it to advantage as a kind of background music, for "an ordinary mind on an ordinary day" is often besieged by such sound, especially in places of urban density (E2:106). In *The Years* (1937), for example, North has returned to England after a considerable time spent in Africa. "The noise of London still seemed to him deafening, and the speed at which people drove was terrifying" (Y 331). Vestiges of older modes of transportation remain, adding to the complexity of the danger inherent in traffic: "A man went to the horse's head, for it was a coal-cart, and the horse slowly plodded on" (334). Again, "the noise of London still bothered him. Against the dull background of traffic noises, of wheels turning and brakes squeaking, there rose near at hand the cry of a woman suddenly alarmed for her child" (341), which parallels Walter Benjamin's remarks on "the heightened state of mortal peril that modern man must face" as well as "changes that at the level of private life are felt by every pedestrian in city traffic" (49). Yet again when North is indoors: "But a great lorry came crashing down the street. Something rattled on the table. The walls and floor seemed to tremble. She [Sally] parted the two glasses that were jingling together. The lorry passed; they heard it rumbling in the distance" (Y 343).

"THE STRING QUARTET" AND *LES NOCES*

In the wake of the Treaty of Versailles signed in Paris on June 28, 1919, to which she refers in the second paragraph, Woolf composed "The String Quartet" with instances of "shivering fragments." The Great War had ended or, more accurately, was in remission. Maynard Keynes's warnings about the economic consequences of "the peace" would go unheeded. At the concert the narrator resents social amenities and is impatient not only with strangers but also with her own agitation: "Why fidget, why so anxious about the sit of cloaks; and gloves – whether to button or unbutton?" is relieved when "the four black figures [...] seat themselves facing the white squares under the downpour of light" and begin to play. Bronislava Nijinska's choreography for *Les Noces* set to music by Stravinsky was realized following the Great War. Lydia Sokolova noted Natalya Goncharova's decision "to use the somber colors of autumn, black, brown and white" in contrast to her prewar plans for brightly embroidered dresses. Goncharova had written to Diaghilev: "There is a saying that Russians love their suffering. This is not a gay or happy marriage, there are many laments and sighs and the dominant tone is that of tragedy" (Chamot 74–77).

WORDS WRIT IN AIR

As the Vorticist painter C. R. W. Nevinson observed in support of an exhibition of Gino Severini's works (1913), "Aeroplanes flying above the heads of an excited throng satisfy our sense of the lyric and dramatic universe better than do two pears and an apple." "The flight of the mind" manifests itself more concretely than in metaphor in Woolf's use of the "aeroplane" with the whine of its vibrating engine. Indeed Woolf used skywriting to separate the shell-shocked Septimus from "an excited throng" in London in *Mrs. Dalloway*, suffused as it is with the ongoing suffering of the Great War. Consider further how in *Mrs. Dalloway* skywriting – albeit advertising – is a kind of Free Words, the poetry advocated and promoted by Marinetti. Around 1914, Futurists advocated "the free composition of words and letters (*parole in libertà*), evoking simultaneously sound, shape and meaning" (Licht 181).

An earlier manifesto of Marinetti's had been written and delivered with variations but always with blasts of oratory in Woolf's famously cited year of 1910. In the 1930s Woolf used this quintessentially Futurist genre to discharge her anger. As Jane Marcus states:

> *Three Guineas* is a manifesto, a polemic in the great age of polemics. It is peace propaganda written as Europe gears up for war, as Woolf's comrades in politics and intellectual debate who had been pacifists in the First World War called for artists to take arms in the struggle in Spain against Franco and fascism. (xlix–l)

Tullio Crali's *Nose-Diving on the City* (1939), which Jane Marcus specifically requested for the cover of the Harvest edition of *Three Guineas*, which she edited (Hussey n.p.), is destabilizing in its cinematic effects, for the city over which the dogfight takes place is represented vertiginously as the off-center pilot dives toward it. The fuselage and diagonally projecting struts partially obscure the leather-helmeted aviator as he fixes his goggled gaze upon his prey below. The effect is both glamorous and deadly. The *sound* of the nose-diving plane is implied. Crali's painting reinforces Jane Marcus's commentary on Woolf's extended essay wherein she iterates what was then a new military atrocity:

> The German and Italian bombing of Spain, photographs of which inspired *Three Guineas*, was the first modern bombing attack on cities and civilians. (Franz

Borkenau's 1937 eyewitness account of the Spanish Civil War is called *The Spanish Cockpit*.) (lxviii)

Both the painting and its title elicit an accompanying *sound* in one's auditory imagination. While Woolf was composing *Between the Acts*, the country village of Rodmell, where she and her husband, Leonard, lived in Monks House, became their only residence after their apartment at 52 Tavistock Square was made uninhabitable during an air raid. But their country retreat was only marginally safer than Bloomsbury, because Rodmell was on the flight pattern of Nazi bombers. Upon hearing the whine of aeroplane engines, they lay on the ground when they had no time to take cover.

Not only did the aeroplane, which once epitomized innovation and breaking with the past, become a demonic source of death from the sky, but it was also a source for metaphors related to erotic attraction. In *The Years* (1937), North, adjusting to the "deafening" noise and the "terrifying" speed at which people drove, analyzes his impression of the foreign Nicolas known as "Brown": "Yet he had liked him – he gave off an aroma; a whirr" (Y 347). An onomatopoetic passage in Woolf's posthumously published novel *Between the Acts* (1941) demonstrates her own ability to invoke/intone noise while Isa (sibilant in name) fancies herself in love with a country neighbor and is moved to compose poetry:

> Since the words he said [...] could so attach themselves to a certain spot in her; and thus lie between them like a wire, tingling, tangling, vibrating – she groped [...] for a word to fit the infinitely quick vibrations of the aeroplane propeller that she had seen once at dawn at Croydon. Faster, faster, it whizzed, whirred, buzzed, till all the flails became one flail and up soared the plane away and away. ... Flying, rushing through the ambient, incandescent, summer silent ... The rhyme was "air" (BTA 20–21).

During the first dinner at Hampton Court, Bernard "see[s] India" before Percival's departure and describes his friend establishing imperial order in righting a bullock cart "by using the violent language that is natural to him" (W 98). Louis, merging the Percival "sitting silent" at the dinner with a younger Percival "as he sat among the tickling grasses," observes "there is a chain whirling round, round, in a steel-blue circle beneath" (99). With its implicit auditory dimension, the spinning of the geometric metallic form signals future danger. Another layer of meaning and auditory dimension is present in the sentence, however. Recall that Woolf heard Jane Ellen Harrison speak on Greek art and religion at the British Museum when an element of her dramatic performance was the sound of a bullroarer, an ancient ritual musical instrument. As noted in the eleventh edition of the *Encyclopedia Britannica* in 1910: "There is no doubt that the rhombus ... which was whirled at the Greek mysteries was one [that is, a bullroarer]." The "booming, humming noise" of the bullroarer is uncanny. "Though treated as a toy by Europeans, the bullroarer has had the highest mystic significance and sanctity among primitive people" (4: 791). Woolf has again merged Ancient Greece with the twentieth century.

C. R. W. NEVINSON, PERCUSSIONIST AND PAINTER OF WAR

Among English painters Nevinson most eagerly embraced Futurism, maintaining allegiance to Marinetti after Wyndham Lewis's defection. He possessed an ability to render the aeroplanes of war with extraordinary immediacy. As General Sir Ian Hamilton wrote in a preface to an exhibition of Nevinson's war paintings at a one-man show at the Leicester Galleries: "The appeal made to a soldier by these works lies in their quality of truth. They bring him closer to the heart of his experiences than his own eyes could have carried him." He then waxes lyrical about Nevinson's rendering of aeroplanes:

> And yet we know it is a machine – a poor imitation of a grasshopper trying to look at a distance like a gilded butterfly. But war spiritualizes, magnifies, intensifies. The artist lets us glance a moment through his magic lens; we see what he sees: we see, instead of the Taube, Satan flying meteor-like from Paradise, chased by the swords of the Seraphim. Is this an illusion! No, it is a symbol (86).

Woolf recorded an unsuccessful meeting with "young Nevinson" (1889–1946) – he was six and a half years younger – after an introduction by Clive Bell at the exhibition of Walter Sickert's (1860–1942) works at the Eldar Gallery (Feb. 15, 1919; D1: 240). Had it not been for Clive Bell's rallying bonhomie, the introduction might have been more successful. Woolf wrote that he introduced her to "young Nevinson, with the Prince Albert whiskers – making allusion to our both being 'such celebrated figures," which Nevinson did not appreciate.[2] While Nevinson's health prevented him from enlisting in the army as a soldier, his ability to paint was such that after an initial effort to conform to conventional style, his superior urged him to follow his own unconventional technique, with notable results. His role resembled that of an embedded journalist during American wars in Afghanistan and Iraq.

Nevinson had had an earlier experience of war as artistic performance, for he had made percussive sounds upon drums during Marinetti's London performance of "The Battle of Adrianople." Marinetti moved about the auditorium pausing at blackboards to draw the action, thereby compelling members of the audience to pivot around. Although such a recitation might sound risible, to hear the partial recording of Marinetti's rendering of the sounds of battle – mostly through his voice – is to grasp that his assimilation of the noise means he was able to remain a conduit for the traumatic experience of war. Indeed, Nevinson's father, the celebrated war correspondent Henry Nevinson, wrote of Marinetti's performance in the *Newark Evening News*:

> Antiquity exploded. Tradition ceased to breathe ... I have heard many recitations and have tired to describe many battles. But listen to Marinetti's recitation of one of the battle scenes ... the noise, the confusion, the surprise of death, the terror and courage, the shouting, curses, blood and agony – all were recalled by that amazing succession of words, performed or enacted by the poet with such passion of abandonment that no one could escape the spell of listening. (Tisdall 104)

Still, Nevinson had his own domestic peace to make with a masculinist role model. "My father," he wrote in his memoir, "worshipped the Man of Action ... it is easier now for me to see ... that the most useless picture is better than the most useful bomb, and that contemplation is better than maneuver" (40). Despite recurrent bouts of rheumatic fever, Nevinson contributed to the war effort with extraordinary paintings that not only captured the experience of soldiers but also portrayed men drawn from the working class, as Woolf was to do with Septimus Smith in *Mrs. Dalloway*. Men of the working class, known as "Archies," did not conform to the near-Aryan stereotypes that war propaganda had favored. While Septimus is not precisely an "Archie," since he is "a border case; he might have been a clerk, but of the better sort." His description is not prepossessing, with "his angular, big-nosed, intelligent, sensitive profile," and his lips "were loose" (*MD* 82). Nevinson also painted images of *War Profiteers* – women as well as men. An example of the latter is titled *He Gained a Fortune but He Gave a Son*. Nevinson's work was published in 1918 in *The Great War Fourth Year* with an essay by J. E. Crawford Flitch, RFA. Flitch is described on the title page as author of *A Little Journey in Spain: Notes of a Goya Pilgrimage*. Goya's portrayal of human suffering may be said to anticipate the photographs of dead children that Woolf was unwilling to have reproduced in *Three Guineas* for fear of inciting further violence (Marcus lxiv–lxv). Among the paintings Nevinson chose for his memoir, *Paint and Prejudice* (1937), is one titled *A Taube*, depicting a dead French child clothed in a smock and lying on cobblestones. Of Nevinson's paintings in *The Great War Fourth Year*, which had been exhibited in autumn of 1916, Flitch observed that picture after picture "expresses the soldier's view of the war" (9). Similarly, Woolf's characterization of Septimus Smith delineates what would now be recognized as posttraumatic stress disorder. The term "shell shocked" as it was applied to veterans of the Great War contains the destabilizing noises of artillery to which soldiers were subjected: Septimus was victim to the cacophony of detonation, among other horrors.

Despite his early allegiance to Vorticism, by 1937 Nevinson declared, "I wish thoroughly to dissociate myself from all geometric mumbo-jumbo, mathematical metaphysics." Nevinson evidently scorned all of Bloomsbury, as had Wyndham Lewis, given his reference to "the pretentious Bloomsbury Belles," whom he scarcely understood. The misunderstanding between Nevinson and Woolf was mutual. The younger Nevinson was compelled to use the methods of Futurism and Vorticism to fulfill his vision as a painter, for, as he concluded, "Experimentation is the cause of all regeneracy in art; an endless repetition of tradition the cause of its decadence" (216). Virginia Woolf also achieved her vision as a writer while living the major portion of her life in the twentieth century: to "achieve in the end, some kind of whole made of shivering fragments," which was to her "the natural process; the flight of the mind" (*PA* 393). The music of "the present" – be it composed by Stravinsky; choreographed by Nijinsky or his sister, Bronislava Nijinska; made accidentally by machinery or intentionally by operators of motorized vehicles on land or in the air, or even by the ambitious but ill fatedly conceived intonarumori – is essential to an understanding of Woolf's achievement as a modernist as well as to her contribution to regeneracy in art.

NOTES

1. Joan Acocella cites the recent biography of Diaghilev by Sjeng Scheijen, in which he counters the received opinion that the riot "that has usually been explained as the response of fuddy-duddies to the arrival of brutality, of ugliness – that is, of modernism" was the opposite: "that the people who hissed were not conservatives but the avant-gardists – the 'snobs,' he calls them – who, on seeing this barbaric spectacle, felt that they had been pushed out of the vanguard by something larger than they" ("The Showman," *New Yorker* (Sept. 20, 2010), 12.

2. Anne Olivier Bell, who edited volume 1 of the *Diaries*, writes: "In 1917 young Nevinson had been appointed an official war artist and his semi-cubist paintings had attracted considerable attention" (D1: 240n5).

WORKS CITED

Acocella, Joan. "The Showman." *New Yorker* (Sept. 20, 2010). Print.

Albright, Daniel. "Border Crossings. Series Editor's Foreword." *Virginia Woolf in the Age of Mechanical Reproduction*. Ed. Pamela L. Caughie. New York: Garland, 2000. vii–xiv. Print.

Bell, Anne Olivier, ed. *Diaries*, Vol. 1: *1915–1919*. New York: Harcourt, 1977.

Bell, Quentin. Foreword. *The Omega Workshops*. By Judith Collins. Chicago: University of Chicago Press, 1984. vii–x. Print.

Benjamin, Walter. *The Work of Art in the Age of Mechanical Reproduction*. Trans. J. A. Underwood. 1936. Rpt. London: Penguin, 2008. Print.

Beyond Bloomsbury: Designs of the Omega Workshops, 1913–19. Ed. Alexandra Gerstein. An exhibition held at the Courtauld Gallery, Somerset House, London, June 18-Sept. 20, 2009. London: Fontana 2009. Print.

BLAST 1 Review of the Great English Vortex. Ed. Wyndham Lewis. 1914. Rpt. Santa Rosa: Black Sparrow, 1992. Print.

Borkenau, Franz. *The Spanish Cockpit: An Eyewitness Account of the Spanish Civil War*. London: Faber & Faber, 1937. Print.

Brockington, Grace. "The Omega and the End of Civilisation: Pacificism, Publishing, and Performance in the First World War." *Beyond Bloomsbury* 60–69. Print.

Chamot, Mary. *Goncharova*. Trans. Helen Gerebzow. Paris: La Bibliothèque des Arts, 1972. Print.

Collins, Judith. *The Omega Workshops*. Chicago: University of Chicago Press, 1984. Print.

Cooney, Seamus. Introduction. *Men without Art*. By Wyndham Lewis. Santa Rosa: Black Sparrow, 1987. Print.

Eliot, T. S. "London Letter for the *Dial*, September, 1921." *The Annotated Waste Land with Eliot's Contemporary Prose*. Ed. Lawrence Rainey. New Haven: Yale University Press, 2005. Print.

Encyclopedia Britannica: A Dictionary of Arts, Sciences, Literature, and General Information. 11th ed. New York: Encyclopedia Britannica, 1910. Print.

Flitch, J. E. Crawford. Introduction. *The Great War Fourth Year*. London: Grant Richards, 1918. Print.

Frattarola, Angela. "Listening for "Found Sound" Samples in the Novels of Virginia Woolf." *Woolf Studies Annual* 11 (2005): 133–59. Print.

Froula, Christine. *Virginia Woolf and the Bloomsbury Avant-garde: War, Civilization, Modernity*. New York: Columbia University Press, 2005. Print.

Gillespie, Diane F. *The Multiple Muses of Virginia Woolf*. Columbia: University of Missouri Press, 1993. Print.

———. *The Sisters' Arts: The Writing and Painting of Virginia Woolf and Vanessa Bell*. Syracuse: Syracuse University Press, 1988. Print.

Gottlieb, Robert. *Reading Dance: A Gathering of Memoirs, Reportage, Criticism, Profiles, Interviews, and Some Uncategorizable Extras*. New York: Pantheon, 2008. Print.

Haller, Evelyn. "Her Quill Drawn from the Firebird: Virginia Woolf and the Russian Dancers." *The Multiple Muses of Virginia Woolf*. Ed. Diane F. Gillespie. Columbia: University of Missouri Press, 1993. 180–226. Print.

Hamilton, Ian. Preface. *C. R. W. Nevinson's Paintings at the Leicester Galleries*. n.d. Print.

Hayward, James. Unpaginated liner notes for the CD *Musica Futurista: The Art of Noises*. Salon LTMCD 2401. 2004. Print.

Hickman, Miranda B. *The Geometry of Modernism: The Vorticist Idiom in Lewis, Pound, H. D., and Yeats*. Austin: University of Texas Press, 2005. Print.

Hite, Molly. Introduction and annotations. *The Waves*. 1931. Rpt. Gen. ed. Mark Hussey. Orlando: Harcourt Annotated Ed., 2006. Print.

Hussey, Mark. Message to the author. Dec. 27, 2012. E-mail.

Joyce, James. *The Portable James Joyce*. New York: Penguin, 1985. Print.

Kirstein, Lincoln. "Nijinsky" from "Nijinsky Dancing." 1975. Gottlieb, *Reading Dance*. 895–99. Print.

"La Battaglia di Adrianopoli" (1924 recording of Fillippo Tommasso Marinetti's performance). *Musica Furista: The Art of Noises*. 2004. CD.

Lewis, Wyndham. *Men without Art*. Ed. Seamus Cooney. Santa Rosa: Black Sparrow, 1987. Print.

Licht, Fred. "Carlo Carra, The Chase." Umberto Boccioni: Dinamismo di un cavallo in corsa +case, an exhibition 3 febbraio-19 maggio 1996. Venice: Peggy Guggenheim Collection, 1996. Print.

Lowenthal, David. *The Past Is a Foreign Country*. Cambridge: Cambridge University Press, 1985. Print.

Marcus, Jane. Introduction. *Three Guineas*. By Virginia Woolf. 1938. Rpt. Gen. ed. Mark Hussey. Orlando: Harvest, 2006. xxxv–lxxii. Print.

Marinetti, Filippo Tommaso. "Definizione di Futurismo" (1924 recording of Marinetti's speech). *Musica Furista: The Art of Noises*. 2004. CD.

Modernism 1890–1930. Pelican Guides to European Literature. Ed. Malcolm Bradbury and James McFarlane. Harmondsworth: Penguin, 1976. Print

Morris, Jan, ed. *Travels with Virginia Woolf*. London: Hogarth, 1993. Print.

Musica Futurista: The Art of Noises. Music and words from the Italian Futurist Movement, 1909–1935, including original recordings by Marinetti/Russolo/Pratella. Salon LTMCD 2401. 2004. CD.

Nevinson, C. R. W. *The Great War Fourth Year*. With an essay by J. E. Crawford Flitch, RFA. London: Richards, 1918. Print.

———. *Paint and Prejudice*. London: Methuen, 1937. Print.

Pound, Ezra. "Affirmations, IV." *New Age*, Jan. 28, 1915: 349. *Selected Prose, 1909–1965*. Ed. William Cookson. London: Faber & Faber, 1973. Print.

———. *Gaudier-Brzeska: A Memoir*. 1916. Rpt. New York: New Directions, 1970. Print.

———. *The Letters of Ezra Pound, 1907–1941*. Ed. D. D. Paige. New York: Harcourt, 1950. Print.

———. *Literary Essays*. Ed. T. S. Eliot. Norfolk: New Directions, 1954. Print.

Rainey, Lawrence. *The Annotated Wasteland with Eliot's Contemporary Prose*. New Haven: Yale University Press, 2005. Print.

Rawson, Judy. "Italian Futurism." *Modernism, 1890–1930*. Ed. Malcolm Bradbury and James McFarlane. 1976. Atlantic Highlands: Humanities Press, 1978. 243–58. Print.

Read, Herbert. *A Concise History of Modern Sculpture*. New York: Praeger, 1964. Print.

Reed, Christopher. *Bloomsbury Rooms: Modernism, Subculture, and Domesticity*. New Haven: Yale University Press, 2004. Print.

Russolo, Luigi. "Convegno d'aeroplani e d'automobili." (1977 recording of intonarumori.) *Musica Furista: The Art of Noises*. 2004, CD.

———. "Risvelglio di una Citta" (extract). (1977 recording of intonarumori.) *Musica Furista: The Art of Noises*. 2004. CD.

Shone, Richard. *Bloomsbury Portraits: Vanessa Bell, Duncan Grant, and Their Circle*. Oxford: Phaidon, 1976. Print.

Spalding, Frances. *Vanessa Bell*. New Haven: Ticknor & Fields, 1983. Print.

Tisdall, Caroline, and Angelo Bozzolla. *Futurism*. London: Thames and Hudson, 1977. Rpt 1993. Print.

Todoli, Vincente. Director's foreword. *Futurism*. London: Tate Publishing on the occasion of *Futurism* at Tate Modern, London, June 12-September 20, 2009. 15, 17. Print.

Turnbaugh, Douglas Blair. *Duncan Grant and the Bloomsbury Group*. Secaucus: Lyle Stuart, 1987. Print.

Whitworth, Michael. *Virginia Woolf*. Oxford World's Classics. New York: Oxford University Press, 2005. Print.

Wood, Jon. "Henri Gaudier-Brzeska: Artistic Identity and the Place of Sculpture in the Omega Workshops." *Beyond Bloomsbury* 34–43. Print.

Woolf, Virginia. *Between the Acts*. 1941. London: Hogarth, 1960. Print.

———. "Character in Fiction." *Essays* 3: 420–38. Print.

———. "The Cinema." *Essays* 4: 348–54. Print.

———. *The Complete Shorter Fiction*. New ed. Ed. Susan Dick. Orlando: Harvest, 1989. Print.

———. *Diary*. Vol. 1: *1915–1919*. Ed. Anne Olivier Bell. New York: Hogarth, 1977. Print.

———. *Diary*. Vol. 3: *1925–1930*. Ed. Anne Olivier Bell and Andrew McNeillie. London: Hogarth, 1980. Print.

———. *Essays*. Vol. 1: *1904–1912*. Ed. Andrew McNeillie. London: Hogarth, 1986. Print.

———. *Essays*. Vol. 2: *1912–1918*. Ed. Andrew McNeillie. London: Hogarth, 1987. Print.

———. *Essays*. Vol. 3: *1919–1924*. Ed. Andrew McNeillie. London: Hogarth, 1988. Print.

———. *Essays*. Vol. 4: *1925–1928*. Ed. Andrew McNeillie. London: Hogarth, 1994. Print.

———. *Essays*. Vol. 6: *1933–1941*. Ed. Stuart N. Clarke. London: Hogarth, 2011. Print.

———. Foreword. *Catalogue of Recent Paintings by Vanessa Bell*. *Essays* 6: 29–30. Print.

———. "Kew Gardens." *Complete Shorter Fiction*. 90–96. Print.

———. *Letters*. Vol. 4: *1929–1931*. Ed. Nigel Nicolson and Joanne Trautmann. New York: Hogarth, 1978.

———. "Modern Fiction." *Essays* 4: 157–65. Print.

———. "Moments of Being: 'Slater's Pins Have No Points.'" *Forum,* Jan. 1928. Rpt. *A Haunted House and Other Short Stories.* London: Hogarth, 1944. Print.

———. *A Passionate Apprentice: The Early Journals, 1897–1909.* Ed. Mitchell A. Leaska. New York: Harcourt, 1990. Print.

———. *Three Guineas.* 1938. Ed. Jane Marcus. Orlando: Harvest, 2006. Print.

———. *To the Lighthouse.* 1927. Orlando: Harvest, 2005. Print.

———. *The Waves.* 1931. Ed. Molly Hite. Orlando: Harvest, 2006. Print.

———. *A Writer's Diary.* Ed. Leonard Woolf. London: Hogarth, 1959. Print.

———. *The Years.* 1937. Rpt. London: Hogarth, 1958. Print.

ELEVEN

Chiming the Hours

A PHILIP GLASS SOUNDTRACK

Roger Hillman and Deborah Crisp

MUSIC ACCOMPANYING THE PROCESS OF ARTISTIC CREATION IS to be found in many films, primarily, of course, in those whose stories concern the composition of music. This can most straightforwardly involve a great composer (Mozart in Milos Forman's *Amadeus*);[1] a fictitious composer figure whose work nonetheless has cultural resonances (the "Concerto for the Unification of Europe" in Krzysztof Kieslowski's *Three Colours: Blue* [Hillman 325]); or a fusion of the two (Luchino Visconti's character Aschenbach, based closely on Gustav Mahler, composing a contemplative section from the Third Symphony, very different from the lush Adagietto from the Fifth Symphony, which so dominates this film). In this last example, Visconti provides a musical parallel to the page and a half of perfect prose produced by the writer Aschenbach in Thomas Mann's novella. The transposition of a writer into a composer is a wise choice in seeking cinematic equivalents for a literary text, and therein lies the rub. Via the convention of music accompanying the action, a given in all but the most experimental films, it is dramatically more convincing for a viewer to feel privy to the evolving of a musical creation rather than a literary one. The gestation process behind the written word is more akin to prose (unless exposed to the vagaries of voice-over in film) and hence more at home in prose. The soundtrack, by contrast, is unique to film and transcends direct equivalences in adapting a novel into a film. Films about leading composers can naturalistically feature their music and the formative stages of its composition. A comparable biopic subgenre of prominent writers and their creative processes is likely to be sparse, even with a director who uses rich soundtracks, such as Jane Campion (*Sweetie, The Piano*). When engaging with the biography of a writer (Janet Frame, in *An Angel at My Table*), she reduces the narrative presence of creative writing in favor of other details that are less related to the inner life and hence more readily realizable in a medium with images as concrete as those of film.

The 2002 film *The Hours,* directed by Stephen Daldry, with a screenplay by David Hare, closely follows Michael Cunningham's 1998 novel of the same name. Cunningham's novel in turn bears a productive relationship to Virginia Woolf's novel *Mrs. Dalloway* (1925), so that a brief account of all three works is called for to clarify what the film embeds. *Mrs. Dalloway* recounts a day in the life of Clarissa Dalloway as she prepares for a fashionable evening party. Her thoughts and actions are counterpointed against those of Septimus Warren Smith, a shell-shocked and delusional war veteran, whose day ends in his suicide. Cunningham's Pulitzer Prize–winning novel, *The Hours,* takes the original working title of Woolf's novel and uses Woolf herself as one of the characters. The screenplay of the film version depicts the intertwined lives of three women of different times and places. Woolf's life (England, 1923) is paralleled with the suburban domesticity of Laura Brown (California, 1951) and with the busy city life of Clarissa Vaughan (a New York publisher, 2001). All three are dealing with depression and thoughts of suicide (though Laura is unsuccessful, and in Clarissa's case it is her friend Richard, dying of AIDS, who suicides). At the end of both novel and film two of the lives coalesce: in the meeting of Laura Brown, the estranged mother of Richard, with Clarissa.

The film relates music to three main female figures, the first of whom is a fictionalized Virginia Woolf.[2] Nicole Kidman plays Mrs. Woolf, while a musical soundtrack by Philip Glass permeates the film. Our analysis locates this nonprogressive music as an apt vehicle for conveying the time patterning of the film. The nonlinearity, even circularity, of the music matches the film's dramatic constellation, which moves like the crystals of a kaleidoscope. Beyond surface-level thematic overlap across the three narrative strands, it is the music that creates an underlying connection ("Music of *The Hours*"). It is uniquely equipped to do this, since for all the visual links across the stories, the mise-en-scène for Mrs. Woolf's Richmond has to be more dated than Clarissa Vaughan's New York, whereas the music can consistently remain oblivious to jumps across time frames.³ In this it functions far more like associative memory itself, like "another stream of consciousness, another character," as Daldry himself puts it ("Music of *The Hours*"). The aesthetic and philosophical content of the film is thus informed by music whose achievement is remote from conventional Hollywood soundtracks and more akin to a literary role or that of visual editing.⁴

The prominence of the Glass soundtrack in no way reflects or materializes comments on music by Mrs. Woolf – there are none. What of music in the two novels that underpin the film? In *Mrs. Dalloway* there is a single mention of Peter's interest in Wagner (MD 7), while one senses the narrator's skepticism when reporting of Clarissa as hostess that "she said she loved Bach" (172). Clarissa is spared any elaboration. The two most prominent musical effects are as part of Septimus's delirium (matching Richard's "voices" in *The Hours*) and the bells of Big Ben and other London clocks. Septimus imagines he hears "Evans . . . singing behind the screen" (MD 137; for Daldry's viewer, the music of Glass has the same dramatic but not thematic function, "singing" behind the cinema screen). The chimes that are such an integral part of a London soundscape provide an outer, socially anchored regulator of time, order, and mortality that is missing in Cunningham's novel (another price paid for isolation from London: Richmond features "clocks striking the hours in empty rooms" [Cunningham 83]). Otherwise occasional scenes involve music – the song of a female beggar (MD 78–80), music as part of Miss Kilman's conversion (121), and military music on Fleet Street are foremost among Elizabeth's impressions of the big city.

Music is foregrounded more in Cunningham's novel than in Virginia Woolf's. Sound is present from the outset, and in a work to which writing is so central the prism of memory lends music supreme value. Clarissa muses upon an image of a branch knocking against a window as a catalyst of music inside her childhood house: "The branch and the music matter more to her than do all the books in the store window" (Cunningham 23). When Clarissa first visits Richard, he is heard offstage, and then the initial visual impression is of him with "eyes closed, as if listening to music" (Cunningham 57). In the film, music keeps suggesting this inner realm, almost a poetic spirit, particularly on the "bad days" against which Mrs. Woolf and Richard both struggle. Historically and dramatically porous, music operates like a stream of consciousness, with transitions between levels of consciousness matched by that between identities. In the second half of Cunningham's novel, music is far less prominent in the text. It is as if his work's architecture corresponded to Virginia Woolf's accents in a passage about the onset of Big Ben's chime that Laura Brown lingers over: "First a musical warning; then the hour, irrevocable" (Cunningham 41). The strong presence of music in the first half of Cunningham's novel gives way to the irrevocability of the hours, and to the relative absence of music, in the second half. Glass's film music operates in less linear fashion, consistent with its minimalism: it, too, functions as a warning, as a reminder and anticipation of the hours, as a millennial memento mori.

Glass's music for the film is in no sense constrained by textual references to music. His soundtrack plays a structural role, functioning not unlike the editing of visual material, as it relates the three separate stories to each other. It is a film (soundtrack's) equivalent for the literary intertwining of characters, such as in *Mrs. Dalloway*. This film then yields insights into a retrospective view of the historic Virginia Woolf and her legacy as well as into the patterning of narratives across literary, visual, and musical forms. Cunningham's novel, with its homage to Woolf's, is something of a reworking of the latter at two (generational) historical removes. This reflects Glass's relationship to Virginia Woolf, too. His "orchestration" of David Hare's screenplay parallels the relationship of Clarissa Vaughan to her forebear in *Mrs. Dalloway*. Beyond the creative process foregrounded in the Virginia Woolf episodes in both Cunningham's novel and Daldry's film, there is the implicit creative task facing Cunningham, Hare, and Glass.

Already in the adaptation of Cunningham's novel to a screenplay, Hare has reverted to a less linear narrative structure. With Cunningham the narratives are delineated by chapters; Hare rearranges the narratives so that they are closely intertwined – indeed at times almost simultaneous, so rapid are the shifts from one time and place to another. This technique of seamlessly intertwined narratives is much closer to Woolf's own practice in *Mrs. Dalloway,* where the frequent shifts of first-person narrator are not always marked by division into chapters or even sections – frequently they occur mid-scene. The substantial rearrangement of Cunningham's novel was a bold step on Hare's part, and it is one that must have required a considerable leap of faith on the part of the director and the actors. Certainly it placed very complex demands on the provider of the musical score.

The time structure of Cunningham's novel, to which the film conforms, focuses on the years 1923 and 1941 in the life of Virginia Woolf, including the poetic process of conceiving *Mrs. Dalloway*; the early fifties in Los Angeles suburbia (centered on Laura Brown, overwhelmed by her roles as mother and wife); and end-of-the-millennium New York (Clarissa Vaughan, addressed with affectionate irony as "Mrs. Dalloway" by her ex-lover Richard). As part of her inner emigration from the pressures of a domesticity she is unable to relate to, Laura Brown reads *Mrs. Dalloway*, so the triptych of women represents three links to this particular novel by Virginia Woolf, itself the dramatic centerpiece of Cunningham's novel. Those links are respectively the creation, the reception, and an enactment of *Mrs. Dalloway*. The creating author, with actress Nicole Kidman clearly visible through the persona, is of course anything but an attempt at documentary recreation, however much the story line of the script intersects with known biography. The reader Laura Brown, experiencing a different constellation of male expectations and female identity from that of the historical Virginia Woolf, nonetheless finds in the latter's work resonant echoes of her own confusion, not least a temptation to suicide. The namesake Clarissa does far more than enact Mrs. Dalloway; she does organize an elaborate party as the core of her day's activities and takes special delight in flowers. But she also relates very differently to the issues felt as oppressive by the first two figures, having a confident lesbian relationship (though she is still moved by the romantic reveries of Richard) and a daughter conceived by artificial insemination. Note, too, that she is an editor, having in this sense taken over the role of Leonard Woolf in the first section, one of a number of mirror images (e.g., her fussing over whether Richard has eaten his breakfast, an echo of Leonard Woolf's solicitude toward his wife). But this detail also shows that both in career and motherhood, the advances for which the historical Virginia Woolf strove have led to unexpected outcomes at the end of her century.

Undoubtedly, the means of Clarissa's motherhood primarily show the endpoint of women's liberation from dependence on males in the course of the century. But they also make explicit the life-giving process of artistic creation. The spirit of Virginia Woolf, who gives birth to *Mrs. Dalloway* but is without biological children, lives on in Clarissa in New York. Something of a mise-en-abîme of the creative process is provided by the fate of Richard. At the end of a life whose peak was clearly his love for Clarissa, dying of a disease contracted from his male lover, he writes a novel that is to be celebrated at Clarissa's party, even though it seems to have satirized her social set and Clarissa herself. Many scenes of the film combine a latter-day embodiment of the Mrs. Dalloway figure, burgeoning with flowers and life but devoid of creativity (biological or artistic) in a traditional sense, with a male whose literary creation has different repercussions, whose reunions with his mother and his former lover Louis are frustrated, and whose hourglass is fast emptying. A further mirroring, or vortex inversion, is provided when his death fulfills Mrs. Woolf's realization that "the poet will die, the visionary." This in turn applies both to the figure Septimus in *Mrs. Dalloway* and to Virginia Woolf, as is known by the film's audience. Cunningham's novel and Daldry's film are about characters in (fictionalized) life and in books. Mrs. Dalloway – both the figure created by Virginia Woolf and the figure of Clarissa Vaughan – features in both realms, while Mrs. Brown is in a sense confined to their reception, as bewildered observer of life and implicated reader of Virginia Woolf. An early shot shows her lying in a bed vacated by her husband and shared by a copy of *Mrs. Dalloway*. The intricacy of the many meshed time levels, and of overlapping identities across figures who simultaneously retain a strong sense of individuality, creates an architectural challenge to a filmmaker molding a story through images and sound.

Linked by their shades of the soul of Virginia Woolf, the two American women unexpectedly meet toward the end, as Richard proves to be the son of Laura Brown. But as a sign of the ongoing passing of the baton across generations of women, Clarissa's daughter is the one who responds with more warmth and charity to the fate of Laura. The social and historical vicissitudes of being male are in turn registered, though far less foregrounded. The Septimus figure in the 1920s setting of Virginia Woolf's novel defenestrates and impales himself, a victim of belated shell shock from his service in World War I. The Richard whom Clarissa tends to dies in similar fashion, a victim of one of millennial society's great bogies, a fault line through its technological and medical advances. All these inflections to *Mrs. Dalloway,* both evoking its origins and transposing it to new social contexts while retaining a continuous emotional lode, pose challenge enough to the novelist Cunningham. In a film that retains so much of the novel, what might be an adequate music, and could any music capture the sense of a cyclical substratum?

ANALYSIS OF THE OPENING SCENES

Perhaps the most striking aspect of Philip Glass's music for this film is that despite the three parallel narratives of quite distinct characters, time, and place, he does not attempt to distinguish these different characters and scenarios by any kind of leitmotif or distinct musical style. As Glass himself has acknowledged, the music serves as an underlying connection between the narratives, aided (according to Glass) by the use of the piano, which he describes as "a personal instrument, which can cross periods easily" ("Music of *The Hours*"). While there are, of course, shifts in the musical character, these mostly occur mid-scene, as a means of dovetailing, rather than at the points of dramatic change from one narrative to another. Thus the score creates a continuity of narrative, beneath the frequent visual shifts across the three narratives.

The overall style of the musical score enhances this capacity for blending and suggesting connections between scenes. There are few "melodies" as such; rather, the thematic material tends to be triadic in repeating patterns, or scalic. Harmonic patterns are mostly cyclic rather than developmental. Rhythms, too, fall into repeating patterns. The meter is predominantly quadruple, though it is triple meter for Woolf's suicide, and shifts between the two at points of crisis (Laura's near-suicide, Richard's suicide). On a micro level the small changes that occur within the melodic/harmonic/rhythmic/metric patterns are of most interest; on a larger level the overriding interest and most notable change is the texture. Susan McClary has noted the "piano concerto" texture of the score and the significance of this choice.[5] This in itself provides quite dramatic textural change (for instance, the first entry of the piano with the beginning of the opening titles of the film after the scene of Woolf's suicide). Shifts of register are also widely used (for instance, low strings accompany Woolf's suicide; a high violin melody is heard as Dan looks in on the sleeping Laura), as is a cyclical thickening and thinning of texture.

The minimalist patterning of melody, rhythm, and harmony seems not to demand closure, therefore lending itself either to fading out midstream or to the superimposition – or subtraction – of another melodic layer. Both tactics are frequently used, and "cadence" in the usual sense is avoided, either by overlapping (for instance, the link between the first two scenes – Los Angeles/London – analyzed below), or by the dramatic intervention of diegetic sound (the second and third scene, where the cadence of the scene in London is subverted by the deafening roar of the New York subway), or by delay (in its final appearance, the "Bell" theme dramatically reaches its penultimate note, then there is silence through rapid cuts from Clarissa to Virginia, and then the final chord is heard *piano* with the image of Virginia alone in her drawing room). As McClary has pointed out, the musical resolution that accompanies the kiss between Clarissa and Sally (toward the end of the film, after Richard's death) is accompanied by a rare moment of musical "repose" (61–62).

The film begins with two sequences of quite rapid crosscuts between scenes with little if any dialogue. Philip Glass's music plays a crucial role in maintaining continuity through these sequences, the first of which is Woolf's suicide in 1941. This is a complex series of cuts backward and forward (not in chronological order) of Mrs. Woolf in her study writing to Leonard and her sister, Vanessa; hurrying through the garden down to the riverbank; and wading out into the water and drowning. Interspersed are shots of Leonard Woolf arriving home, finding the letters, and rushing to the river. The final shot is of Mrs. Woolf's drowned body being carried along under water by the current, and this is followed by the film's title and opening credits. The music that accompanies this introductory scene begins with the first voice-over (Woolf's voice reading the content of the letter she is writing to Leonard); up to this point we have heard the diegetic sounds of footsteps, birdsong, the river, and so on. The music is characterized by an underlying accompaniment figure (strings only) of oscillating thirds in triple meter, and two melodies, both played by cello. The music of this scene resembles the ostinati used in the opening of the third movement of Glass's Third Symphony (1995); however, the soaring violin melody that is overlaid in the symphony is here replaced with a more somber cello melody.

More virtuosic still, both in its music and its cinematography, is the second sequence, which is overlaid by the film's title and opening credits. The technique of rapid cuts established in the introductory scene is continued in this sequence of about six minutes, and indeed throughout the film. This sequence is more complex than the first and introduces the three narrative threads of the film: Los Angeles in 1951 (Laura Brown), London in 1923 (Virginia Woolf), and New York in 2001 (Clarissa Vaughan). Our initial introduction to each time, place, and set of characters is relatively long, with roughly a minute each devoted to Laura and Dan Brown, Virginia and Leonard Woolf, and Clarissa Vaughan and Sally Lester (in that order). This is followed by a series of rapid crosscuts from narrative to narrative, some as short as two seconds, others quite a bit longer. We see the three principal female characters in their homes, with their partners, waking up, preparing to face the day. The whole sequence is underpinned by continuous music that ends as one of the principal characters (Mrs. Woolf) speaks for the first time: having prepared herself for the day ahead, she comes downstairs and converses with Leonard.

This opening scene mimics the strategy used by Woolf in the first section of *Mrs. Dalloway*. In the novel the London morning is seen first through the eyes of the principal character, Clarissa Dalloway. Through her musings we also meet Hugh and Evelyn Whitbread; Peter Walsh; Clarissa's daughter, Elizabeth; and her companion, Miss Kilman. At the arrival of a VIP car outside the florist's (the onlookers speculate on who it might be: the queen, the prime minister, the prince of Wales?), the first-person narrative suddenly and seamlessly switches to Septimus Warren Smith; then to his wife, Lucrezia; then back to Mrs. Dalloway. For the rest of this scene the narrative oscillates between these three and various people in the street.

In the film Philip Glass's music plays a crucial role in establishing and maintaining continuity throughout the first sequence. The very first shot after the title (a modern suburban street) signals a complete shift

Example 11.1a-d. Thematic Material.

of time and place, from 1941 rural England to postwar Los Angeles. This shift is supported by a marked change in musical texture and style, from the low strings and triple meter of the introductory scene to the mid-register piano in quadruple meter (designated in tables 1–3 as theme A). There is only one brief exchange of dialogue throughout this sequence (between Leonard Woolf and the doctor); despite the rapid shifts of time and place, the music is continuous throughout and ends with a distinct cadence as all three characters commence the day's action. In this sense the sequence is a "closed" structure, with the disparate narratives bound together by one musical structure. The principal events and their musical accompaniment are summarized in tables 1–3.

The first part of this musical structure (shown in table 1) introduces the characters and might be seen as variations on the distinctive piano theme that opens the sequence (theme A, shown in example 11.1a[6]). In its first appearance (Dan and Laura), the theme is in eighth notes; in its second (Leonard and Virginia) it is in eighth-note triplets; in its third

Table 1. The Characters Are Introduced

0:00	Dan Brown arrives home; he looks into the bedroom where Laura is still sleeping	piano solo – theme A alternates with oscillating 3rd accompaniment (8th notes); theme B in high strings (¾); theme A (¼) leads into scale passage in piano
1:06	Leonard Woolf walks home from the railway station; talks with the doctor; camera pans upstairs; Virginia is lying awake in bed	(overlaps with scale passage); a fragment of theme A in triplets alternates with oscillating 3rds (duplets) – strings only; theme B (fragment) in piano with strings; triplet pattern (piano); theme A leads into descending scale passage (in 16th-note broken octaves – piano)
2:07	Sally Lester walks home along the New York streets; undresses, gets into the bed where Clarissa is sleeping	(descending scale cut off by noise of subway); triplet/duplet polyrhythm in strings alternates with repeated piano broken chord pattern in 16th notes (theme A); theme A (piano in triplets) leads into descending scale passage (in 16th-note broken octaves)

appearance (Sally and Clarissa) it is in sixteenth-note quadruplets. The narrative parallels of the three scenes are also marked by musical variations. In each case it is the woman's partner we see first, coming down the street, arriving home. For each of these images the theme is initially tentative – it stops and starts again. When the camera shows the women in bed, the melody becomes more continuous, and the rhythmic pace slows in each case: for Laura there is a switch from eighth notes to quarter notes for a high string countermelody; for Virginia triplets change to duplets; for Clarissa the sixteenth-note quadruplets slow to triplets as Sally gets into bed. Each scene ends with a variant of theme A that merges into a cadential scale, which in turn provides a link with the following scene.

The use of variation techniques here seems to be a clever solution to the problem of at once connecting the scenarios yet clearly distinguishing one from another for the sake of the audience – particularly important given the rapid shifts that are to come. In each case the musical breaks between the scenes are sufficiently distinctive to separate them yet nevertheless make the parallelisms clear from the start. In the case of the first switch (Los Angeles to London), there is a degree of overlap as the piano scale is continued as the shot changes from Laura to Leon-

Table 2. The Characters Awake

2:46	Clarissa starts to wake up and looks at the clock	theme A (piano) and theme B (high strings) over oscillating 3rd string accompaniment (duplets) in unstable meter (quadruple/triple); high piano trill throughout, and successive sounds of mechanical alarm clock, grandfather clock, and digital clock. The segment ends with an ascending scale (in 16th-note broken octaves)
2:53	Laura's alarm clock sounds	
2:58	Virginia's clock chimes	
3:02	Clarissa's alarm clock sounds	

ard Woolf, but then the piano drops out, leaving only strings. The piano theme resumes as Leonard arrives at Hogarth House and opens the gate. The second change (from London to New York) is far more dramatic and immediate: we see Virginia lying awake in bed, a falling scale in the piano in broken octaves cadences with the change in scene, and the final note of the scale is replaced by the roar of the New York subway. Noteworthy throughout this opening sequence is the increasing rhythmic and textural complexity, from solo piano (mid-register) in eighth notes (Dan arrives home), to polyrhythms and the contrast between low strings and upper-register piano (Sally hurries along the New York street).

The following sequence (see table 2) appears to be a musical, as well as narrative, transition: their various alarm clocks go off, and the three women begin to stir. In the previous sequence the visuals established the individuality of the characters and their circumstances, while the music subtly emphasized some of the parallels. Here the women are drawn together visually as the camera cuts from one to the other, and the musical materials, too, are drawn together, restated more or less simultaneously under the unifying continuous high trill of the piano. This brief, aurally static interlude prepares us for the virtuosic visual interplay that is to come.

Table 3 shows the pace of the action being dramatically stepped up with rapid scene shifts – some last only a few seconds – and a series of "match cuts" (Virginia bends over the basin to wash her face, but it is Clarissa's face that we see coming up from the basin; Clarissa goes to pick up the vase of flowers, Dan puts the vase down, Nellie rearranges the flowers).[7] Despite the increase in tempo (from measure 108 to 120), musically the parallel actions are bound together by a much slower rate of change than that of the visuals. Indeed, the visual cuts are masked to an extent by the continuity of the musical texture, with the onset of action or change of scene only rarely corresponding with musical change. Thematic and textural changes occur for the most part in the middle of scenes rather than at the shifts from one scene to the other.

The three significant musical events in this sequence are all thematic and all the more noticeable for the generally non-thematic nature of Glass's minimalist textures. Theme C (which seems to be an elaboration of A; see example 11.1c) emerges in a series of rapid crosscuts from Clarissa to Virginia – it is difficult to pinpoint the precise image it matches. Theme D (example 11.1d) – by far the most energetic of the themes – coincides precisely and dramatically with Clarissa opening the curtains but is retained for the following five scene changes (across seventeen seconds in all). Theme C reappears as Clarissa notices the vase of flowers but is retained as Dan and Nellie in turn deal with the flowers. Here, as before, the music binds the actions together, draws parallels between the three locations, and serves to mask the effect of the rapid pace of visual change. The final minute or so of the sequence focuses on the Woolf household: Virginia pauses at her bedroom door, Leonard works at the table downstairs. As in the first sequence, closure is marked by a piano scale passage (as Virginia walks down the stairs); they speak, the texture thins, and the dynamics drop through *piano* to *pianississimo*. The understated cadence effects the transition between the musical soundtrack and the extended section of dialogue that follows. It also marks the end of this extended musical structure that has introduced the principal characters, underlined the parallels in their circumstances, and effectively bound their actions together in a way that the camera alone never could.

This sequence is unique in the film for the length of the musical structure and for the almost complete absence of dialogue. Nevertheless, the approach taken here – the dovetailing of music and scene changes, the use of variation techniques, and the carrying of one musical theme across different scenarios – operates to varying degrees throughout the film.

An interesting example of thematic recurrence is the strikingly distinctive theme that appears first as Dan Brown goes off to work, leaving

Table 3. The Characters Prepare for the Day

3:07	Clarissa gets up and walks out into the hallway	tempo increases from 104 to 120 (quarter note) oscillating thirds in 8th notes (strings only);
3:22	Virginia does her hair in front of the mirror	(continued)
3.26	Clarissa looks in the mirror, bends down to the basin	theme C (derived from theme A) in piano over piano accompaniment;
3:30	Virginia goes to the dresser, pours water, washes hands, bends down to basin	(continued)
3:49	Clarissa lifts her head from the basin, having washed her face	oscillating thirds and theme C replaced by triadic pattern in triplets (piano)
3:51	Laura picks up *Mrs. Dalloway* from the pile of books by the bed, sits up . . .	(continued)
3:59	. . . listens to sounds of Dan looking for something in the kitchen (shots from bedroom to kitchen)	piano drops out, triadic pattern in strings in duplet/triplet polyrhythm
4:13	Clarissa opens the curtains	theme D (syncopated) in piano over triplet pattern in strings;
4:15	Laura sits up straighter, still listening to Dan	(continued)
4:17	Clarissa stands by the window, thinking)	(continued)
4:19	Virginia stands in front of the full-length mirror, then walks to the door	(continued)
4:26	Laura sits in bed, listening	(continued)
4:30	Virginia pauses before the door	(continued)
4:33	Clarissa stands by the window, notices a vase of dead flowers, and goes to pick them up	theme C returns (piano) above triplets in strings

Table 3. The Characters Prepare for the Day (*cont.*)

4:42	Dan picks up the vase of roses and takes it to the bench	(continued)
4:46	Nellie adjusts the cornflowers in the vase and walks out to the kitchen	(continued)
4:55	Virginia comes downstairs; begins conversation with Leonard	dynamic level drops to *p*, descending piano scale in triplets, then texture thins to broken octave accompaniment (strings) and high countermelody in strings (theme B); understated cadence in low strings (*ppp*)

Laura and Richie alone in the house. Like the other themes, this one is more a repeating melodic pattern than a conventional melody, but while the other themes tend to be rhythmically active, triadic in nature, and of limited range, this one is rhythmically static, has a much larger span, and, in its extended form, covers as many as four octaves (see example 11.2).

Given the film's title and content, the theme's resemblance to a chime is surely intentional – in fact, there is more than a passing resemblance to the "quarters" chimes of Big Ben, which in turn inevitably recalls the striking of Big Ben throughout Woolf's novel. One of the most poetic images of the novel, the recurring sentence "The leaden circles dissolved in the air" aptly captures the resonating of the metallic sounds of the bells. It first appears on the second page of the novel (*MD* 4) and is subsequently used as a device to link the various characters – for example, roughly midway through the novel (92), the striking of midday links the actions of Mrs. Dalloway and the Warren Smiths ("twelve o'clock struck as Clarissa Dalloway laid her green dress on her bed, and the Warren Smiths walked down Harley Street").

In the film this recurring musical motive – the "Bell" theme (see example 11.2) – appears four times in all. We hear it first in a truncated version as Dan Brown leaves for work; second as Clarissa leaves Richard's flat for the first time, continuing through the following scene of Virginia at work in her study before she is interrupted by Nelly. The theme's third appearance is at the end of Kitty's visit to Laura (again she and Richie are

Example 11.2. The Bell Theme.

left alone in the house). In its final appearance it again cuts across two scenes: Vanessa and her children leaving Hogarth House and Louis leaving Clarissa's apartment. In all four scenes the theme marks a departure that – except perhaps for the first case – follows some sort of emotional disruption. In nearly every case the departure is preceded by a kiss – not a casual, habitual kiss, but one that is lent deliberate significance. Laura kisses Dan as a rather awkward "happy birthday," perhaps aware that she may not see him again; Clarissa kisses Richard after their heated exchange; Laura kisses Kitty on the mouth; and Virginia passionately kisses Vanessa. The emotional turmoil that precedes each of these kisses and their deliberate nature also suggest a change in the dynamic of the various relationships. It might be argued that each of these events has a significant bearing on the outcome of the plots. Laura is aware of her awkwardness with her husband, and Kitty's visit opens her eyes both to her inadequacy as a housewife and to the fact that even someone as apparently successful in the role as Kitty is, at bottom, miserable. Richard has told a shocked Clarissa that he is staying alive only for her and has indirectly warned her that he intends to die soon. For Mrs. Woolf, seeing her sister from London has brought home to her the nature of her imprisoned existence: she asks, "You think I may one day escape?" Each woman is suddenly aware of the perceived limitations of her current existence.

Related to this theme, perhaps, is another with connotations of a bell (see example 11.3). This theme first appears in the florist's shop, where Clarissa buys her flowers. It emerges under the conversation with the florist, when the florist confesses that she has tried to read Richard's novel and then says, rather abruptly, "It's you, isn't it" (meaning the principal character in the novel is a thinly disguised Clarissa). The recurring theme is itself recycled Glass, having appeared in the composer's score for the Errol Morris film *The Thin Blue Line* (1986). But the quality of his music is such that this quotation is not remotely intrusive, even if registered by the viewer. It is as amorphous and as suggestive as "existential

Example 11.3. Further "Bell" Connotations.

dread," Errol Morris's description of what Glass can convey better than anyone else.[8]

The theme remains as the visuals shift backward and forward from the florist's shop to Woolf's study, where she is writing, to Laura and Richie in their kitchen, preparing to make the cake. With the first scene change to Woolf's study there is a voice-over ("Just one day. And in that day, her whole life"). This is presumably what Woolf is thinking as she plans her novel, but it carries over into the following scene shift to the Browns' kitchen – like the music, it binds the characters together while showing the disparity in their lives and circumstances. The theme is still there as Clarissa leaves the shop, walks along the street to Richard's flat, is greeted by him ("Mrs. Dalloway!"), and ends with Clarissa opening the curtains, letting more light into the room ("It's still morning?" Richard asks).

The above analyses are intended to demonstrate the ways Philip Glass's score subtly marks both the similarities and differences among the three narratives. Glass's music binds them together in a way that reinforces their commonalities yet, paradoxically, in no way detracts from the individuality of each of the narratives and the characters involved. There can be no question in the viewer's mind that Laura Brown, Clarissa Vaughan, and Mrs. Woolf are highly distinctive characters in their external circumstances and in their personalities. Indeed the scene in which Clarissa Vaughan and Laura Brown actually meet is quite uncomfortable and hardly a meeting of kindred spirits – at least on the surface. Rather, it shows two very different women, who seem surprised to find a common, circumstantial thread to their lives, and perhaps neither recognizes the psychological level of this connection. The planned sixty guests for the dinner Clarissa has been preparing do not materialize, and the guest of honor has absented himself definitively; Richard's mother, the person never contemplated as guest, and in her fictitious embodiment "killed" in the novel to be celebrated, alone sits opposite Clarissa in a kitchen cluttered with empty chairs. The details of their individual stories somehow remain distinct from one another, while the cyclical nature of the underlying tensions of their lives is laid bare to the audience.

To express the cyclical, the choice of Philip Glass was of course inspired. In a DVD featurette on the advent of the music ("Music of *The Hours*"), director Stephen Daldry speaks of how the "temp track" (see Sadoff) referred to Glass in elaborate attempts to find an appropriate score. While the film's "layered, subtextual emotions" resisted most music, Daldry was delighted when Glass took on the assignment and feels that what he produced provided "another stream of consciousness in the film" (Daldry). Glass's music for this film thus reflects one of the defining characteristics of the writer (and her afterlives, so to speak: both the characters in Cunningham's novel and Cunningham's novel itself), in a different artistic medium and in a very different era, where the points of convergence are nonetheless what prevail.

Formalistically, the Glass music can correspond to the contemplative, generally creative process in appropriate sections of the film – the very first entry of the music is synchronized with a close-up of Mrs. Woolf's hand, writing her suicide note to Leonard. It can imply the presence of this process even when the figure is not writing or thinking creatively. It does this through being non-diegetic, not related to any identifiable source in the image. This does not apply to the only other musical presence, a brief appearance of "Beim Schlafengehen" from Richard Strauss's *Four Last Songs*, as the early arrival of a guest (Louis) distracts Clarissa from her party preparations. While this music initially fills the screen space with a surge of color akin to Andrei Tarkovsky's use of Bach,[9] it is ultimately seen to emanate from Clarissa's CD player when she switches it off. The Strauss functions tellingly as Romantic aspiration of the heroine, grounded by the incursion both of everyday reality and of the past. Its counterpoint effect against the Glass music presents a Janus face on contemplating death and on recalling the Indian summer of Clarissa and Richard, when she was eighteen and he nineteen, disturbed by the intrusion of Louis. The music's transcendent view of mortality means it will be a constant companion, the viewer senses, once Clarissa comes to terms with Richard's death. The reception of this music outside Daldry's film brings a further context of a flux of time, a resplendent late flowering of Romanticism in the immediate postwar period. It also possibly implies its companion piece in Strauss's cycle "September," where sadness at the departure of summer parallels the passing of that youthful summer that remains indelibly etched in the memories of Richard and Clarissa. And the cycle indirectly pays tribute to the four deaths registered in *The Hours:* Mrs. Woolf, Richard, and the offstage deaths of Richie's father and sister. The use of "Beim Schlafengehen" in this film is far more effective than the similar dramatic weighting of the 1999 Marlene Gorris film *Mrs. Dalloway*. In the latter, the sole classical music within a largely original soundtrack is the *Traviata* death scene immediately before Septimus plunges to his doom, robbing his shell shock of its social moorings and rendering him a figure of melodramatic excess.

The Strauss excerpt is the sole exception to the otherwise dominant Glass soundtrack (alongside often long stretches without music). Glass's music seems to guide the every movement of the onscreen characters as if they were aware of it, not simply as the doubling effect of mood music, but almost as a *spiritus loci et tempi*. This choreographic function is equally remote from classical Hollywood notions of an "invisible" soundtrack underpinning images as it is from Adorno/Eisler notions of film music as a conscious counterpoint to what the images convey. It defies such reduction partly because it relates not to images, but to the amorphous flux (of emotions, creativity, identity) behind the images. Such music certainly seems indispensable to the progression of the story and above all to the suturing of its joins. These it combines across time and space, and across characters, even as it implies and embodies the continuous spectrum between the players. It bonds three sisters with an elegiac quality akin to Chekhov.

It is telling that of the three, Clarissa Vaughan alone hears music, and then turns it off, in the course of the film. Richard upbraids her gently: "O Mrs. Dalloway, always giving parties to cover the silence" (creating a further link between Clarissa and Leonard, whom Mrs. Woolf advises: "You cannot find peace by avoiding life"). Richard's astute observations of her elsewhere mean we have to take this seriously rather than as his own projected approach to the void. Silence is what none of the three is accorded by the soundtrack; or rather (for of course we alone hear it) their scenes of aloneness, whether of isolation or self-sufficiency, are generally accompanied by music. At this level the Glass score seems to be a vindication of their stances rather than of Richard's assessment, either of life in general or of the woman he knows best. Elsewhere music links the three, from the acute sensitivity of Mrs. Woolf through to the superficially prosaic Clarissa (in this, too, reflecting Mrs. Dalloway in Virginia Woolf's novel). It endows them all with the potential, without the accompanying mental disintegration, of the first figure. The silences of Daldry's overall conception are also telling: note how the kiss between Laura and Kitty has no music at all, barely conceivable by standard Hollywood conventions.

Cunningham's novel, again an homage to its model, typically mixes inner musings of a character with an omniscient narrator presenting the inner life (see especially pp. 11–12). The film largely avoids voice-over. Much of the Clarissa-Richard relationship, for instance, emerges in their direct dialogue, in reminiscent vein. The dimension of interiority is then regained by a music score, in particular through the qualities of this Glass score. The book is far more rambling and panoramic than the film, as instanced by Clarissa's inner monologue of self-assessment on page 23. In the film her vulnerability is expressed more by body language, especially her collapse in tears when she slumps down in her kitchen, in the presence of Louis. So the visuals and the music, in combination, frequently translate the novelist's word when states of mind are foregrounded. Cunningham's book and Hare's film script quote their literary model liberally. But the process of these quotes also transmits: repetition of *Mrs. Dalloway* phrases in Cunningham's book acknowledges the stylistic quickening of Woolf's novel, so in a sense the style of the model inhabits the characters' perception of their world in Cunningham's homage.

At a more technical level, the music functions as a sound bridge across the three time realms, functioning like a match shot in the visual sphere (cf. the three vases of flowers) or creating transitions between characters. These are ruled out for the novelist (whether Woolf or Cunningham) by chapter breaks, even when the end of one section is repeated by the first words of the next (e.g., Mrs. Woolf penning the words

"*Mrs. Dalloway said she would buy the flowers herself*" [Cunningham 35], followed by one and a half blank pages, followed by the new section "Mrs. Brown" beginning with the same sentence, now read by Laura). In film, repetition of a phrase bridges the physical gap created by a chapter break in the act of reading. Via Hare's script, all three women are juxtaposed in rapid visual succession at this point. Mrs. Woolf speaks the sentence quoted above, Laura Brown reads it aloud, and then Clarissa/"Mrs. Dalloway" incarnates it with her version: "I think I'll buy the flowers myself." To return to the starting point of this paragraph, Glass's acoustic equivalent of match shots across edits creates ongoing links. Classical Hollywood attempted to hide editing by "seamless realism," creating an illusion of continuity of time and place. Glass's music reinforces that illusion at a more subliminal level: that of film music.

By the end of the novel *The Hours*, a paragraph like the following is characteristic: "Laura reads the moment as it passes. Here it is, she thinks; there it goes. The page is about to turn" (Cunningham 208). The whole process of reading is built in as an ongoing metaphor, totally appropriate to Cunningham's reflective and self-reflective book. In the film the multiple variations of the motifs of book, author, reader, and character are captured by Glass's circling score, generating its own ongoing metaphors. The historical Virginia Woolf and her contemporaries (e.g., Faulkner, Joyce) strove to privilege individual consciousness in the wake of the nineteenth-century omniscient narrator, however challenged that convention came to be in the course of the century and beyond. At the end of the millennium, Glass's score replaces the anachronism of an omniscient narrative viewpoint with omni-sentience.

The classical Hollywood score, with David Raksin's *Laura* at the peak, reinforced a unique individuality and utilized a leitmotif technique derived from Wagner to shore up that individuality dramatically. Glass's score here forsakes individuality, even that of the exceptional historical individual Virginia Woolf, in merging predispositions and blending states of consciousness across individuals and their places and times. The stream-of-consciousness technique here becomes a stream (very much the effect of Glass's minimalism) of a broader consciousness, beyond any one individual, yet without the hubris of some latter-day *Weltgeist*. With two of the three female figures coming from the New

World, the class-ridden society that further marginalizes Virginia/Mrs. Woolf is in turn a phenomenon of the past. In addition, the hierarchy of an intellectual elitism has been usurped, and that, too, is one of the achievements of Glass's score.

Mrs. Woolf, Laura Brown, and Clarissa Vaughan are far from being pale figures. But their cross-linkages and dramatic weighting ensure that *The Hours* does not compress three female leads into a single, overwrought work. Philip Glass's score is crucial to the intricacies of that structure, while its submerging of more individual musical identities enhances the panoramic, millennial perspective of Cunningham's reader and Daldry's viewer: a perspective that contrasts strikingly with Strauss's "Beim Schlafengehen," a last, brief afterglow of Romantic self-transcendence.

NOTES

Our thanks to Jeongwon Joe of the College-Conservatory of Music, University of Cincinnati, for helpful comments and encouragement. For feedback on an earlier version, thanks to Australian National University colleague Lucy Neave. For release of their rights to an earlier version of this chapter, our thanks to the journal *Music and the Moving Image*.

1. On this "genre," see Tibbetts.

2. Except in tables 1–3, "(Virginia) Woolf" will be used for the historical personage, and "Mrs. Woolf" will be used for Cunningham's fictitious rendering of her. In some places, characteristic for the film, the distinction blurs. On issues of transposition from the Virginia Woolf original, to Cunningham, to Daldry, see Lee.

3. Susan McClary observes how the "flat-line procedures of minimalism frequently seem to have pulled the plug not only on that particular outmoded language [the symphonic tradition of Max Steiner and other Hollywood composers], but also on the very notion of signification in music" (52).

4. Michael LeBlanc notes how "the motifs of Glass's score are able to loosen themselves from identificatory bonds so that they might take on the dreamwork function of condensing and displacing interconnections between character subjectivities, visual metaphors, and thematic content" (117).

5. "As did Nyman, Glass opted for the luxuriant orchestra of classic cinema, along with the piano in a concerto texture that pits the heroic, slightly alienated solo instrument against the social group" (McClary 57). In the same article McClary gives a detailed analysis of the interaction between music and dialogue in one scene of *The Hours* to demonstrate the affective potency of Glass's music.

6. The music examples included in this chapter are the authors' own transcriptions of the soundtrack.

7. LeBlanc has noted also the interesting use of camera angles here – in particular, the clever alternation of left and right views – and observes, "There is a musicality in the rhythmic intercutting

of the characters in this waking-up sequence, a lyricism that intermediates across historical periods through a sort of dream logic" (115).

8. In Scott Hicks's film *Glass: A Portrait of Philip in Twelve Parts* (2007), the director interviews both Glass and Morris in the wake of a clip from *The Thin Blue Line* that employs this particular music.

9. One instance is the return of "Erbarme dich, mein Gott" from the *St. Matthew Passion*, at the end of *The Sacrifice* (1986). But the prime example is the flood of sound (rising volume) and golden light transfiguring the final sequence of *The Mirror* (1974), with "Herr, unser Herrscher, dessen Ruhm" from the *St. John Passion* carrying all before it. Altogether the fusion of past and present in this remarkable ending bears comparison with the challenges faced by representing the triptych of women in *The Hours*.

WORKS CITED

Cunningham, Michael. *The Hours*. London: Fourth Estate, 1999. Print.

Hillman, Roger. "Cultural Memory on Film Soundtracks." *Journal of European Studies* 33.3/4 (2003): 323–32. Print.

LeBlanc, Michael. "Melancholic Arrangements: Music, Queer Melodrama, and the Seeds of Transformation in *The Hours*." *Camera Obscura* 61, 21.1 (2006): 105–45. Print.

Lee, Hermione. *Virginia Woolf's Nose: Essays in Biography*. Princeton: Princeton University Press, 2005. 37–62. Print.

McClary, Susan. "Minima Romantica." *Beyond the Soundtrack: Representing Music in Cinema*. Ed. Daniel Goldmark, Richard Leppert, and Lawrence Kramer. Berkeley: University of California Press, 2007. 48–65. Print.

Sadoff, Ron. "The Role of Music Editor and the 'Temp Track' as Blueprint for the Score, Source Music, and Scource Music of Films." *Popular Music* 25.2 (2006): 165–83. Print.

"The Music of *The Hours*." (Additional material on) *The Hours*. Dir. Stephen Daldry. 2002. Paramount Pictures and Miramax Films, 2003. DVD.

Tibbetts, John C. *Composers in the Movies: Studies in Musical Biography*. New Haven: Yale University Press, 2005. Print.

Woolf, Virginia. *Mrs. Dalloway*. London: Harcourt, 2005. Print.

Contributors

SANJA BAHUN is Associate Professor in the Department of Literature, Film, and Theatre Studies, the University of Essex. She is the author of *Modernism and Melancholia: Writing as Countermourning* (2013) and co-editor of *The Avant-garde and the Margin: New Territories of Modernism* (2006); *Violence and Gender in the Globalized World: The Intimate and the Extimate* (2008); *From Word to Canvas: Appropriations of Myth in Women's Aesthetic Production* (2009); *Myth and Violence in the Contemporary Female Text: New Cassandras* (2011); and *Language, Ideology, and the Human: New Interventions* (2012).

ELICIA CLEMENTS is Associate Professor in the Departments of English and Humanities at York University, Toronto. She has published on the musical connections between Virginia Woolf and Ethel Smyth, as well as the links between Ludwig van Beethoven's late compositions and Woolf's narrative method in *The Waves*. Additionally, with the assistance of a Social Sciences and Humanities Research Council of Canada Standard Research Grant, she has finished a book-length study on Woolf's treatment of language, music, and sound in her novels. She has also co-edited a collection of essays with Lesley J. Higgins titled *Victorian Aesthetic Conditions: Pater across the Arts*, which was published in 2010.

DEBORAH CRISP was Senior Lecturer in Musicology at the Australian National University until her recent retirement. Alongside her research collaboration with Dr. Roger Hillman on music and film, other research interests are connections between music and the other arts in nineteenth-century Europe, as well as music in nineteenth-century Australia.

EVELYN HALLER is Professor of English and Chair of the Fine Arts/ Humanities Division at Doane College. Among her publications are essays on Virginia Woolf and dance in *The Edinburg Companion to Virginia Woolf and the Arts* (2010) and on Woolf, E. M. Forster, and Alexandria in *Woolf Studies Annual* (2003). She has also published essays on Octavia Wilberforce, Woolf's third cousin and last physician; Ezra Pound; Willa Cather and Flaubert; Cather and Leon Bakst; and landscapes and soundscapes of Ireland in the poetry of Yeats. Haller was a contributing editor for *The Feminist Companion to Literature in English* (1990).

ROGER HILLMAN teaches Film Studies and German Studies at the Australian National University, Canberra, Australia. Publications cover the areas of film and history, European Cinema movements, and film and music – in particular, the monograph *Unsettling Scores: German Film, Music, and Ideology* (2005).

ROSEMARY LLOYD was educated at the Universities of Adelaide and Cambridge and taught at Cambridge University and Indiana University. She has published books on Baudelaire, Mallarmé, and Flaubert and on both childhood and jealousy in French literature, as well as a study of the written still life. Among her translations are the letters of Baudelaire and Mallarmé, Baudelaire's prose poems, George Sand's *Les Maîtres Sonneurs*, and poems by various contemporary poets. She is Rudy Professor emeritus of French at Indiana University; Fellow emerita, Murray Edwards College, Cambridge; and Adjunct Professor of French, University of Adelaide.

VANESSA MANHIRE is a writer and editor based in Dunedin, New Zealand. She completed her PhD at Rutgers University. Her doctoral dissertation explores the changing importance of music in the work of Virginia Woolf. Her research interests are modernist fiction and the relationship between music and literature.

JIM STEWART teaches English literature at the University of Dundee, Scotland. He is on the advisory board of the Cambridge Edition of the Works of Virginia Woolf and was AHRC Research Assistant to Jane Goldman, one of the edition's general editors, in her work on *To the Lighthouse*. He contributed incidentally to the edition's *The Waves* and

Between the Acts (2011) and provided editorial assistance for *The Years*. His current co-editing of *The Voyage Out* includes the tracing of Woolf's classical and biblical allusions in her first novel. He co-teaches creative writing at the University of Dundee with the novelist Kirsty Gunn.

EMMA SUTTON is Senior Lecturer in English at the University of St Andrews, Scotland. She has broadcast and published widely on music and literature, and is co-editing *The Voyage Out* for Cambridge University Press. Her publications include *Aubrey Beardsley and British Wagnerism in the 1890s* (2002), *Opera and the Novel* (co-edited, 2012) and *Virginia Woolf and Classical Music: Politics, Aesthetics, Form* (2013).

MIHÁLY SZEGEDY-MASZÁK is Professor of Comparative Literature and Cultural Studies at Eötvös Loránd University, Professor Emeritus of Central Eurasian Studies at Indiana University, and a member of Academia Europaea (London) and the Hungarian Academy of Sciences. He is the author of *Literary Canons: National and International* (2001), sixteen books in Hungarian (among them monographs on the authors Zsigmond Kemény, Sándor Márai, Géza Ottlik, and Dezső Kosztolányi); editor in chief of a three-volume history of Hungarian literature (2007) and the journal *Hungarian Studies*; and co-author of *Théorie littéraire* (1989), *Epoche – Text – Modalität* (1999), *A Companion to Hungarian Studies* (1999), *Angezogen und abgestoßen: Juden in der ungarischen Literatur* (1999), *The Phoney Peace: Power and Culture in Central Europe 1945–49* (2000), *National Heritage – National Canon* (2001), and *Der lange, dunkle Schatten: Studien zum Werk von Imre Kertész* (2004).

TRINA THOMPSON teaches music theory and piano at Andrews University and is a PhD candidate in Music Theory at the Indiana University Jacobs School of Music. She taught written and aural theory on both the undergraduate and graduate levels at IU and previously served as a member of the music faculty at Walla Walla University. Thompson is the editor of two double issues of the *Indiana Theory Review*, one on general topics in music theory and one on the interaction of text and music. Her dissertation focuses on the solo songs of Debussy.

ADRIANA VARGA teaches English and Global and Historical Studies at Butler University, Indianapolis. She earned her PhD in Comparative

Literature at Indiana University–Bloomington. She is currently working on a comparative study of the modernist novel in the interwar period as well as conducting research for the critical edition of the modernist author Dezső Kosztolányi's translations of British and American poetry. Her research and publication interests include modernism, narrative theory, postcolonial theory, reception aesthetics, translation and translation theory, inter-art poetics, and diaspora and immigrant literatures.

Index

Italicized page numbers refer to musical examples.

absolute music, 5, 19n9, 200n11
acceleration, 267–70; form and, 274–78
adaptation studies, 209
aesthetic perspective, 11–12
aesthetics, 7–8, 19n11, 27–28, 87; Baroque, 221; Bloomsbury Group, 27–28, 30–34, 39–40, 42, 47, 272; Greek drama, 117–18; modernist, 229–30, 232–33, 251, 263–64, 273
Afternoon of a Faun, The (Debussy), 267
Agawu, Kofi, 208, 209
agon, 118, 125, 131, 233–34; as structure, 238–39
Ahasuerus, 161, 165, 169
Albright, Daniel, 13, 208, 233–34, 263
Algraphone. *See* gramophone
Allied String Quartet, 60
alliteration, 244–45
Almighty with Prophets and Sibyls, The (Vanucci), 264
Ambrose, Ridley (*The Voyage Out*), 112, 115, 131
Anacreontic Ode (Smyth), 61
Antigone (Sophocles), 111–13, 130, 187; "fast off the mark," 116–17; in *The Years*, 187, 192–94, 196
Apollinaire, Guillaume, 35
Apolline mode, 123–24, 126–27, 130
Apostles (secret society), 31
Arányi, Jelly, 63

Archies (working-class men), 282–83
Aristotle, 113–14, 115
Arnott, Peter, 116
art: Futurism, 262, 266–70; history of, 253–54; life interconnected with, 185, 197; socium linked with, 253–54; Vorticism, 272–74
art criticism, 8, 36–37
Asbee, Sue, 200n15
associative process of thought, 143, 147, 150, 156, 290
atonal music, 106n11, 233, 236, 238, 247, 256n13. *See also* Schoenberg, Arnold; Schoenberg, Arnold, works
audience, 15; in *Between the Acts*, 77–78, 96; British radio, 3, 231–32; communal aspect of, 77–78, 96, 127, 134, 138–39, 148–49, 200n6, 210–12, 222, 254; concerts as social experiences, 10, 15, 18n4, 33–34, 39–41, 146–47; historiography and, 217–18; indifference, 80; in *Night and Day*, 136; performer-listener axis, 184, 190; in *A Room with a View*, 80; self as, 193–95; social stratification, 138–39; upper middle-class, 147–49; in *The Voyage Out*, 77, 84–85, 87; Wagnerian, 122; Woolf as, 134, 138, 147–48; in *The Years*, 190. *See also* community; reader
Auerbach, Erich, 215
Aufführungspraxis (performance practice), 183
aulos (double pipe), 117

315

316   INDEX

aurality, x–xi, 16–17, 95, 143, 189; aural imagery, 205, 209; autonomization of sounds, 241–42; fragmentation and, 219–20; of history, 210–11; machinery, sounds of, 261–62; in *Mrs. Dalloway*, 261; multiple layers, 214–15; narrative function of sounds, 239–41; repetitions, 213–14; sounds of danger, 280–81; of Woolf's novels, 261–64; in *The Years*, 16, 182, 261, 263. *See also* noise

Bach, J. S., 35, 54, 60
Bakst, Leon, 35
Bal, Mieke, 181–82, 183, 199n2
Balla, Giacomo, 269
ballet, 29, 39, 56–58
Ballets Russes (Russian Ballet), 29, 57–58, 63, 230, 265, 272, 274, 277
Baroque style, 58, 221–22
Bart (*Between the Acts*), 96, 209, 210, 240, 246
Barthes, Roland, 205
Bartók, Bela, 7, 51, 64, 66, 231
Bayreuth, 4, 55
BBC, 3, 7, 231–32, 255n8
Beecham, Thomas, 29, 39–40, 43n4, 49, 54, 61, 62, 64
Beer, Gillian, 174
Beethoven, Ludwig van, ix, 14; Op. 111, 10, 54, 79–82, 85–86, 88, 104n3, 105n5, 105n6; Op. 130, 59; Op. 131, 64, 67, 87–89; *Pastoral Symphony*, 36; string quartets, 59–61, 66, 231–32, 236, 256n11; tragic-to-transcendent trajectory, 81–82; tragic-to-triumphant trajectory, 81
Beginning Again (L. Woolf), 28, 56, 59, 162, 170, 173
Bell, Clive, 7, 12, 129, 270, 281
Bell, Julian, 187
Bell, Michael, 121
Bell, Quentin, 2, 39, 57, 121, 224n8
Bell, Vanessa, 2, 18n2, 39, 61, 262; Omega Workshops and, 262, 274; Sydney-Turner, portrayal of, 32–33, 43n6
Benjamin, Walter, 278
Bennett, Arnold, 12, 271–72
Berg, Alban, 65

Bergson, Henri, 189
Bernard (*The Waves*), 66, 85, 88, 89, 91–92, 94, 102, 104, 280
Between the Acts (Woolf), 6, 10, 76, 82, 182; alliteration, 244–45; animate-inanimate recitatives, 239–41; aurality in, 205, 209–210, 261, 280–81; binary oppositions in, 234–35; bird imagery, 95–96; "broken music" in, 212, 233, 243–46, 254; caesuras, use of, 245, 246, 248; as composition, 234–39; continuity in, 210, 213–14, 219; ekphrasis in, 209–210; fragmentation in, 205, 207, 212–15, 217–20, 253; indeterminate spaces, 101–102; knowing and unknowing, questions of, 246, 247; language of the unrecorded, 246–50; leitmotifs, 235–36, 243; megaphone imagery, 211, 212, 241, 253; micro-structural level, 235; motivic repetition in, 210, 213–14; multiple voices in, 99–101, 205, 206–207, 217–18; music, language, and community in, 77–78, 94–102; music, language, and moments of being, 99–102; music as metaphor, 211–12, 219; music of the spheres, 97–99, 141; musical patterning, 239–46; noise in, 201n15, 205, 261–62, 280–81; operatic structure, 16, 210; *Outline of History*, 246, 249; pageant, 205–206, 210–12, 217, 219–20, 224n7, 234, 239; pageant, silence and, 249–50; parallel historical record, 217; poetic writing in, 99–100; as *Pointz Hall*, 67, 206, 251; polyphonic texture, 215, 248, 249; polyrhythmic organization, 67, 243–44; punctuation choice, 214; reader-oriented approach, 101–102; reality modeled on musical experience, 77–79, 84; relations and formal measures, 236–37; synesthetic perception, 77–78, 95, 101; temporal and spatial dilation in, 97–98; thirty-seven sections, 235–36; three versions of, 207; "triple melody," 77–78, 211; unrest problem, 237–39, 244, 248–49; villagers' song, 240, 243, 249–50, 253; voice sounds in, 239–41

biographical perspective, 14

birdsong imagery, 95–96
Birth of Tragedy from the Spirit of Music, The (Nietzsche), 15, 111, 120–23, 125
Bloomsbury Group, ix, 3; absence of music in interests of, 27–29, 38–40; ballet, interest in, 28–29, 41; Cambridge University friends, 31–32, 49; conservative tastes, 39–41; depictions of music in works of, 42; importance of music to, 13–14; influences on musical tastes of, 31–37; performances as social experiences, 10, 18n4, 15, 33–34, 39–41; visual-art criticism, 8; Vorticism and, 272–74
Boccioni, Umberto, 226, 266, 267, 276
bodily kinesis, 142–43, 188–89, 193, 195–96
Boulez, Pierre, 52
Brahms, Johannes, 33
Breitkopf, Joseph (*Mrs. Dalloway*), x, 170–71, 172
British musical life, 48–49; ballet, 56–58; radio audience, 3, 231–32; reception of modernist music, 7–9, 65
Brown, Cedric, 11, 19n16, 129–30
Brown, Dan (*The Hours*), 296, 300, 302
Brown, Laura (*The Hours*), 289, 291–93
Bruhn, Siglind, 78, 209
Burian, Peter, 121
Busch Quartet, 63–64
Busoni, Ferruccio, 229
Busse, Kristina, 216

Cameron, Julia Margaret, 28
Canguillo, Francesco, 277
Car Has Passed, The (Balla), 269
Carrington, Dora, 39
Case, Janet, 112
Case of Wagner, The (Nietzsche), 111, 122, 160, 176n9
Catalogue of Recent Paintings by Vanessa Bell, 263
Caughie, Pamela, 3, 67
Child, Harold, 146
chorus, 2, 187, 196–98. *See also* Greek chorus
city, 201n15; imagination equated with, 136, 142–43, 149

Clark, Kenneth, 35
classical style, 8
Collis, Louise, 231
comic genre, 96, 218
community: city as, 136, 142–43, 149; identification and, 147–48; individual responses and, 149, 154; longing for harmony, 97–99; moment of being and, 77–78, 94–95; multiple voices, 217–18; music as model for, 185, 193; music hall experience and, 138; shared experience, 148–49, 154–55; unified through music, 77–78, 96, 127, 134, 138–39, 148–49, 210–12, 222, 254. *See also* audience
comparative analysis, 182
comparative arts, 233–34
comparative perspective, 14, 232
composer-performer pair, 184
composition, 234–39
Comstock, Margaret, 198
Comus (Milton), 111, 116, 129
concerts: Greek music drama compared with, 119; instrumentalists, 63–64; recording industry reduces, 64–65; as social experiences, 10, 15, 18n4, 33–34, 39–41, 146–47; V. Woolf's attendance, 3, 14, 49–64, 119, 121, 230, 255n2
Concise History of Modern Sculpture (Read), 269
conductors, 64
consciousness, 86, 143; multipersonal representation of, 215–16; music similar to, 290–91; shared, 134, 154–55; as transcending time, 76–77; in twentieth-century literature, 308
contextual perspective, 14
continuity, 210, 213–14, 219; of narrative, 294–95
conversation, musical, 89–91
Cook, Nicholas, 209
Copland, Aaron, 8
Cortot, Alfred, 63, 65
counterpoint, literary, x, 65, 91, 147; in *Between the Acts*, 210, 214–15, 219, 223n4, 240; in *The Hours*, 289, 305–306
Covent Garden, 4, 28, 33, 38, 49
Crali, Tullio, 279

Crapoulet, Emilie, 2, 10, 199n2
Craye, Miss Julia ("Moments of Being: "Slater's Pins Have No Points"), x, 275–76
creation: as alternative history, 252; context, 101; jazz metaphor, 212–13, 218; listening as, 155; as moment of performance, 96; permanence of, 93–94; as sonic act, 205; violence of, 212–13
criticism: art, 8, 36–37; genetic, 8; music, 3, 4, 5, 30, 232–33, 246–47
Cross, Ian, 6, 19n9
Cuddy-Keane, Melba, 96, 199n5, 218, 222
cultural analysis, 181–83
cultural studies, 182
Cunningham, Michael, 17, 289, 290, 291–92, 307

Daldry, Stephen, 17, 289, 290, 305, 307; *The Hours*, 288–310
Dalhaus, Carl, 167
Dalloway, Clarissa (*Mrs. Dalloway*), 10, 53, 55; equated with Senta, 163–64; as model for Clarissa in *The Hours*, 291, 292, 293; music, susceptibility to, 172
Dalloway, Mrs. (*The Voyage Out*), 112
Dalloway, Richard (*Mrs. Dalloway*), 164, 168
dance, 17, 29, 127–28
Dancers (Grant), 272
Daniel Deronda (Eliot), 169, 176n12
Das Judentum in der Musik (Wagner), 169, 172
Datchet, Mary (*Night and Day*), 137, 142–43, 149
Davenport, Tony, 147
de' Bardi, Giovanni, 221
de' Bardi, Pietro, 221–22
De Quincey, Thomas, 83
Debussy, Claude, 35
deletion transformation, 245–46
democratic music, 247
Dempster, Carrie (*Mrs. Dalloway*), 164
denoted, level of, 78
Der fliegende Holländer (Wagner), 15, 161–65; inspiration for, 165; as martyr play, 167; plot summary, 162–63; sexual politics, 167–68, 169
Descartes, René, 188
Diaghilev, Sergei, 35, 41, 56–58, 277
Dionysiac mode, 111, 115–16, 123–24, 265; emergence of tragedy from, 128–29; fusion of Apolline with, 126–28; in music, 118–25
discordance, 97–98, 237–39, 260, 271; discordant unity, 229–30, 238–39, 264–65
dissonance, 6, 51, 233, 239, 241–44, 254
dithyramb, 115–16, 124
Doctor, Jennifer, 231
Doctor Faustus (Mann), 80
Dolmetsch, Arnold, 2
drama, 15, 100, 166; *intermedi*, 220–22; musical, 16, 119, 121, 137, 177, 221; Nietzsche's music drama, 124–25; as social art, 245; Wagner's neoclassical music drama, 111, 121, 123, 126. *See also* Greek drama
Dreyfuss case (1894), 171
Dryden, John, 152
du Maurier, George, 169
Duckworth, Stella, 2, 28, 58
Dukas, Paul, 54
Duke Bluebeard's Castle (Bartók), 51

Easterling, P. E., 113
efficacy, 16, 181, 186–87, 194–96
egalitarian technique, 247–48
ekphrasis, musical, 78, 209–210, 213
Eleanor (*The Years*), 197
Elgar, Edward, 37
Eliot, George, 169, 176n12
Eliot, T. S., 9, 165, 262, 272, 276
Elizabeth (*Mrs. Dalloway*), 174–75
ellipses, 248–49
emotion, musical, x, 5, 8, 84
entertainment, 16, 185–86, 197, 220–21; performance as, 16, 185–86, 197
Eugénie (*The Years*), 190, 195–96
excitement (*orgiastika*), 115, 116
expression-based approach, 11, 19n11
expressive genres, 208

fidelity, 209
First Viennese School, 7, 8

Fleishman, Avrom, 9, 204
Flitch, J. E. Crawford, 283
Flying Dutchman story, 161–64
Foley, Helene, 125
form, 7–8, 134, 139; acceleration and, 274–78; content and, 134–35, 144–47; history as, 234; in *Night and Day*, 134, 144, 145; representational, 63
Forme uniche della continuità nello spazio (Unique Forms of Continuity in Space) (Boccioni), 226, 267
Forster, E. M., 38–39, 66, 146; *A Room with a View*, 80, 104n3
Fowler, Rowena, 222
fragmentation: in *Between the Acts*, 205, 207, 212–15, 217–20, 253; music of, 268–70; "shivering fragments" image, 237, 260, 264, 265, 268, 271–73, 275, 278, 283; in "The String Quartet," 141, 147, 151–52, 154–55
Freedman, William, 214–15, 223n3
French Postimpressionists, 35
Fromm, Harold, 84
Froula, Christine, 272, 273
Fry, Roger, ix, xi, 7–8, 9, 14; on art as deformity, 274; influence on Bloomsbury Group, 28, 35–36, 38; Omega Workshops, 28, 262, 269, 271–72, 274; on rhythm, 67–68; theoretical writings, 37–38; view of "The String Quartet," 146; visual music, 36–37; Woolf's biography, 66;
Fry, Roger, works: "The Artist and Psycho-Analysis," 37; "Significant Form," 12
fugue, x, 56, 66, 83, 90, 124, 126, 128, 130, 149
Furness, Robert, 39
Futurism, 17, 35, 262, 266–70; Free Words (*parole in libertà*), 279; London, 281–83

Gailei, Vicenzo, 222
Garnett, David, 34
Gaudier-Brzeska, Henri, 274
gender: feminist discourse of action, 181; Greek chorus and, 125, 126, 130; history and silencing, 250; Jewish women, portrayals of, 169–70; Miltonic roles, 129; redemption allegory and, 161, 162, 167; sexual politics of female self-sacrifice, 162, 167–69, 175–76; social obligations, 195–96; violence, connections with, 188; Wagner's politics, 167; Woolf's critique of, 112, 164
Generative Theory of Tonal Music, A (Lerdahl and Jackendoff), 208
genetic criticism, 8
Genette, Gérard, 47
geometric forms, 273–74
Geometry of Modernism, The: The Vorticist Idiom in Lewis, Pound, H. D., and Yeats (Hickman), 273
Gerhardt, Elena, 63
Gesamtkunstwerk, 32, 101, 230, 255n3
gesture, literary, 83, 84, 86
Gier, Albert, 78
Gillespie, Diane Filby, 146, 147, 272–73
Glass, Philip, 17, 289–309; music for *The Thin Blue Line*, 303–304; thematic material for *The Hours*, 297; Third Symphony, 296
Gluck, Christoph Willibald, 5, 34, 43n8, 121
glyconic meter, 117
Godlovitch, Stan, 184, 193
Goldman, Jane, 100, 189
Goncharova, Natalya, 278
Gorris, Marlene, 306
gramophone, 3, 29, 64–65, 183, 211–12; in *Between the Acts*, 77, 210
Grant, Duncan, 34–35, 39, 262, 269, 270; Futurist paintings, 272, 274; memoir of Virginia Woolf, 42
Gray, Harry, 31–32, 49
Grazzini, Antonfrancesco, 221
Great War Fourth Year, The, 283
Greek chorus, 2, 15, 96, 100–101, 119, 218; as actor, 114; birdsong imagery, 114–15; bodily movement, 116; characters in role of, 197–98; choric song and its music, 111–18; gendered aspects, 125, 126, 130; standing songs, 113, 116–17, 130
Greek drama, 182–83, 185–87, 196–98; Renaissance research, 221–22

Greek language, 196, 222
Greek philosophical tradition, 6, 19n9
Greenberg, Judith, 205

Hafley, James, 105n3
Haines, Mr. (*Between the Acts*), 95, 211
Haines, Mrs. (*Between the Acts*), 95
Hare, David, 289, 291, 308
harmony, social, 139–40
Harrison, Jane Ellen, 281
Hatten, Robert S., 81, 208
Heckert, Deborah, 7–8
Heine, Heinrich, 168
Hewet, Terence (*The Voyage Out*), 84, 85, 128
Hewitt, Thomas J., 100–101
Hickman, Miranda B., 273
Hilbery, Katharine (*Night and Day*), 135–44
Hilbery, Mr. (*Night and Day*), 140, 144
Hilbery, Mrs. (*Night and Day*), 135, 137, 140, 144
Hirst, St. John (*The Voyage Out*), 33
historically infused genres, 16, 216–19
history: alternative, 16, 216, 219–20, 247–50, 252; aurality of, 210–11; as creation of space, 205; as form of artwork, 234; microhistory, 218, 223; modernist music's concerns with, 233–34; music as unifying force in, 252; occlusions, 248, 249; primordial world/prehistory, 105n7, 210, 238, 242, 243, 251–52, 253, 254, 262; rhythmic shifts associated with, 244; sounds associated with, 241–42
Hitler, Adolf, 181, 187, 189
Hogarth Essays, 4
Hogarth Press, 4, 18n6, 100, 173
Holroyd, Michael, 33, 34
Hours, The (Cunningham), 17, 290, 291–92, 307
Hours, The (Daldry), 17, 288; analysis of opening scenes, 294–309; crosscuts, 295–96, 300; Cunningham's novel and, 17, 290, 291–92; narrative strands, 289–90; nonlinear structure, 289, 291–92; parallel actions ("match cuts"), 299–300, 308; screenplay, 289, 291, 308; silence in, 306–307; stream-of-consciousness narrative, 290–91, 308; three narrative threads, 292, 294, 296, 304. See also *Mrs. Dalloway* (Woolf); soundtrack for *The Hours*)
Hussey, Mark, 13, 20n19, 104n2

identification, community and, 147–48
ideological positions, 68, 89, 199n5
imagination, 6, 15, 38, 103, 134; associative process, 143, 147, 150, 156; auditory, 280; city equated with, 136, 142–43, 149; dilation of time and space, 97–98; listening and, 155; moment of being and, 143–44; movement of, 135, 139–46; music and access to, 140–42; poetic, 95–96; of reader, 102; thought as activity, 188–89, 191–93, 198
immediacy of music, 141, 146, 150–51
"Impressions at Bayreuth" (Woolf), 4, 5, 8, 113, 123; on language-music relationship, 11; on music criticism, 29–30
indeterminacy: of meaning, 15, 147; spaces of, xi, 101–102
individual, listening and, 155–56
inter-art studies, x, 4, 13, 16, 314
interdisciplinarity, 181–82
interior design, 271
interiority: exteriority, bridging, 86, 144, 229–30, 267, 269–70, 276; multiple impressions, 229–30; music as model for representation of, 6, 134, 139, 141–44, 154–55
interludes, 136, 223, 299; operatic, 16, 223; in *The Waves*, 89–90, 93
intermedi, 220–22
intermissions, 219–20
intervals, 122, 206; "between the acts," 101–102, 122, 206; creation during, 96; historical gaps as, 220
Iolanthe (Gilbert and Sullivan), 34
Iser, Wolfgang, 76–77, 101

Jackendoff, Ray, 208
Jacobs, Peter, 9–10, 47, 48, 55, 68, 121–22, 152

Jankélévitch, Vladimir, 184, 198
jazz, 262–63; as creation metaphor, 212–13, 215, 218
Jews: anti- and philo-Semitic discourses about music, 162, 169; anti-Semitism of 1880s and 1890s, 171–72; displaced, in London, 171; portrayal of in *Mrs. Dalloway*, 161–79; redemption allegory, 160, 161, 162, 169; Russian, 171–72; shivah mourning custom, 15, 162, 166, 172–76; V. Woolf's view of, 169–73; Wandering Jew figure, 160, 162, 164–65, 169–72; women, 169–70
Jinny (*The Waves*), 91, 92, 93–94, 102–103, 166
Johnson, Maisie (*Mrs. Dalloway*), 164
Joyce, James, 263–64

Kelly, Joyce E., 2, 56
Keynes, John Maynard, 39–40, 278
Kidman, Nicole, 289, 292
Kilman, Miss (*Mrs. Dalloway*), 171, 172, 290
"Kinetic Scroll" (Grant), 35
Kirstein, Lincoln, 266–67
Kitto, H. D. F., 117
Knossos (Crete), 186
Knox, Bernard, 113, 117
Koteliansky, S. S., 171–72
Kramer, Lawrence, 209, 220

La Boutique Fantastique (ballet), 57
Lady Bruton (*Mrs. Dalloway*), 166, 168, 174
Lambert, Leonard Constant, 61, 63
landscape, imaginary, 47, 76
Langer, Suzanne, 11–12, 20n17, 20n20
language: failure of, 75–76, 79, 86, 105n7, 124; listening turned into, 150–51; Greek, 122,196,; music as vehicle for exploration of, 134; music related to, 123, 208
language-music relationship, 5–7, 46–47, 118–19; changes between early and later works, 77–78, 155–56; expressive genres, 208; gulf between music and language, 76, 79; language as restrictive, 75–76; literature and music, x–xi, 5–9, 11–15, 17–18; music scholarship, 207–12; music transcends failure of language, 75–76, 86, 105n7; musical patterns in language, 78, 83–84; musical structure in short fiction, 9–17; music/literature triangle, 78; in *Parsifal*, 5, 51, 95, 123; score-text comparisons, 5–6, 11, 20n18; text and music, 9, 11–12, 14–15, 17, 56, 77–78, 85, 198, 207–10, 222–23; word and music in *The Voyage Out*, 78–86
"L'Après-midi d'un faune" (ballet), 35
Laurence, Patricia, 13
Le Sacre du Printemps (Stravinsky). See *Rite of Spring* (*Le Sacre du Printemps*)
Leaska, Mitchell, 98, 121, 241
LeBlanc, Michael, 309n4, 309n7
Lee, Hermione, 2, 58, 114–15, 129
leitmotifs, 235–36, 243, 308
Lepore, Jill, 218
Lerdahl, Fred, 208
Les Tentations de la Bergère ou l'Amour Vainqueur (ballet), 57–58
Leschetizky, Teodor (Theodor Leszetycki), 33, 48–49
Lester, Sally (*The Hours*), 296, 298
Levin, Gerald, 66
Lewis, Wyndham, 269, 270, 274, 281, 283
listening, x; as creation, 155; defensive, 140; individual and, 155–56; meaning-making, 141; moment of being and, 155; as simile for walking, 143; turned into language, 150–51
Lodato, Suzanne, 209
Loeb, Sydney J., 53, 170
London: chimes, 290, 291, 302; noise of, 261–62, 277–78
Lopokova, Lydia, 265
Louis (*The Waves*), 92, 102, 103, 104, 264

MacCarthy, Desmond, 40
machinery: aeroplanes and cars, 267, 270–72, 279; movement and, 267–68; noise intoners (intonarumori), 276–77; sounds of, 261–62
Macnaghten Quartet, 64
Maggie (*The Years*), 190, 195
Mallarmé, Stéphane, 35, 36

Mann, Thomas, 80, 288
Marcus, Jane, 2, 13, 122, 156n9; on *Three Guineas*, 279–80
Marinetti, Filippo Tommaso, 262, 268, 272, 277, 279; "The Battle of Adrianople," 282
Massine, Léonid, 266
Mathiesen, Thomas, 116
McClary, Susan, 294, 309n3
McWhirter, David, 206, 218
meaning, 135, 139, 208; function of, 11–12; indeterminacy of, 15, 147; movement and, 141–42; musical, 6–7, 10–12, 19n9
Mei, Girolamo, 221
Meisel, Perry, 104n1
melodrama, 153, 165–67, 175, 306
melody, 141, 210, 234
memory, 141, 151–52, 206–207
Men without Art (Lewis), 269
mention, concept of, 47
metaphor, x, 135, 211–12, 219
methodology, 182
metrics, mood and, 117
Michaelides, Solon, 115
middle-class education, 28, 30, 47–48
Milton, John, 111, 116, 129
mind/body dichotomy, 188–89
mise-en-abîme effect, 17, 205, 293
Miss La Trobe (*Between the Acts*), 77, 98, 200n6, 215–16, 237
modernism, x, 3, 7–9, 76–77, 87; abstract experience, 6, 19n9, 35–36, 77; nineteen thirteen (year), 28–29. *See also* Futurism; Vorticism
modernist music, 16, 40–41, 229–33; British reception of, 7–9, 65; historically specific concerns, 233–34; serial technique, 106n11, 233, 236, 238, 247, 256n13; silence empowered in, 248; subversive potential of, 242, 247. *See also* Schoenberg, Arnold; Schoenberg, Arnold, works; Stravinsky, Igor; Stravinsky, Igor, works
moment of being, 75; abstract and isolated, 77, 87, 94–95; community experience of, 77–78, 94–95; imagination and, 143–44; from instance to permanence, 82; listening and, 155; music and language interrelated, 99–102; music as interventionist strategy, 189; music enacts, 198; rhythm of, 83–86; as transcending time, 76–77
Moore, George Edward, 14, 31, 49, 84
Morris, Errol, 303–304
Morris, Jan, 268
Mortimer, Raymond, 40
motifs, 90, 235–36; looking glass, 92–94, 103
movement: body and mind linked, 142–43, 188–89, 193; Greek chorus, 116; of individual mind, 149–50; infinity of, 268, 276; between interior and exterior worlds, 139, 144, 146, 156; interiority and, 6, 134, 139, 141–44; meaning and, 141–42; of mind, 135, 139–46; narrative, 149–50
Mozart, Wolfgang Amadeus, 9–10, 34, 53, 64
Mrs. Dalloway (film), 306
Mrs. Dalloway (Woolf), x, 9, 185; as antiwar novel, 162, 164, 174–75, 187; aurality in, 261; *Der fliegende Holländer* associations in, 164–65, 167–68; displaced characters as Jewish, 170–71; intertextuality with Wagner's opera, 15, 162, 171–72, 175–76; Jews portrayed in, 161–79; melodrama, allusions to, 165–67, 175; reflected in *The Hours*, 17, 289, 291, 292, 293, 295, 296; as response to Wagner, 172–73; sexual politics in, 167–68; shivah mourning custom in, 172–76; suicide in, 165–66; theatrical terms in, 165–67; traveler images, 164–65; voyages, allusions to, 164–65; Wagner mentioned in, 55, 290. *See also Hours, The* (Daldry)
Muck, Karl, 50
multimedia, 208–209
Murray, Robert, 116–17
music: absolute, 5, 19n9, 200n11; as abstraction, 141; access to imagination, 140–42; as action-centered, 184, 190; anti- and philo-Semitic discourses, 162; as autonomous, 6, 11, 19n9; communal aspect of, 127, 200n6, 210–11; as cultural capital, 135–36; as dangerous, 119–20, 212; di-

egetic, 161, 174, 210–11, 295–96; Dionysian in, 118–25; discrepancy between use and mention of, 10; failure of language to express, 34, 150–51; formal quality, 37, 123, 145; of fragmentation and acceleration, 268–70; gesture, 83, 88; of Greek chorus, 111–18; immediacy of, 141, 146, 150–51; as interventionist strategy, 189; lack of articulation, 11, 12, 19n9, 199n5; as less important to Bloomsbury Group, 28–29; as linguistic system, 208; as medium of representation, 113; as metaphor, x, 211–12, 219; musical form, x, 2, 5–6, 12, 15, 84, 144–47, 154, 291; musical meaning, 6–7, 10–12, 19n9; as old-fashioned pursuit, 135–36, 139; order in, 37–38, 124, 140; as public, 78; reality and unreality, movement between, 154–55; spirit of, 124; as unifying force in history, 252; water imagery for, 150, 151. *See also* language-music relationship

Music (Russolo), 276

music criticism, 3, 4, 5, 232–33; lack of precedents, 30; by V. Woolf, 3, 246–47; V. Woolf on, 3, 246

music hall, 48, 135, 137–38, 156n4

music of the spheres, 6, 97–99, 141

music psychology, 208

musical analogies: art criticism, 36–37; harmony as social performance, 139–40

musical culture, 46–71

musical drama, 16, 119, 121, 137, 177, 221

musical emotion, x, 5, 8, 84

musical form, x, 2, 5–6, 12, 15, 84, 154, 291; in "The String Quartet," 144–47. *See also* structure

Musical Idea, 235, 237, 253

music/literature triangle, 78

Naremore, James, 214, 215

narrative style, 143–44, 149–53, 218; kinesthetic, 149–50; new, development of, 145–46, 151, 153; stream-of-consciousness, 15, 87, 134, 154, 290–91, 308; third person narration, 98, 192

narrator, 98, 138–39, 146, 148–49, 192; characters merge with, 215–16

Nation and Athenaeum, 3, 57–58

nationalism, x, 166

natural laws, 6, 19n9

neoclassical music, 8–9, 63

"Networks of Noise," 277

Neville (*The Waves*), 91–92, 93, 94, 102, 103

Nevinson, C. R. W., 272, 279, 281–83

Nevinson, Henry, 282

Nietzsche, Friedrich: Attic tragedy, view of, 123–24; *The Birth of Tragedy from the Spirit of Music*, 15, 111, 120–23, 125; *The Case of Wagner*, 111, 122, 160, 176n9; Wagner, view of, 122, 125

Night and Day (Woolf), x, 15, 273; city and imagination, 136, 142–43, 149; contradictory functions of music, 134–35, 144; flame image, 141, 143; formal qualities, 134, 144, 145; movement in, 135, 139–44; music hall scene, 135, 137–39, 142, 148–49, 156n4, 263; musical scenes critique social norms, 134–36, 144–45, 147–49, 152–53; narrative style, 143–44, 146, 149–53; noise in, 142–43; plot trajectory, 139; privacy, illusion of, 136, 137; social control, 136–37; social harmony, 139–40; static visual tableaux, 135–36; theatrical imagery, 136–37, 145

Nijinska, Bronislava, 57, 264, 266, 278, 283

Nijinsky, Vaslav, 35, 39, 277; as choreographer, 264, 265–68; *Jeux* (Games), 275

noise, 265, 270–72, 276–78; Art of Noises, 276–77; in *Between the Acts*, 201n15, 205, 261–62, 280–81; in *Night and Day*, 142, 143; shell shock, 283; in *The Years*, 17, 189–90, 199n1. *See also* aurality

noise intoners (intonarumori), 276–77

North (*The Years*), 277–78

Nose-Diving on the City (Crali), 279

novel: failure of language in, 76; as musical communication, 86–94; reader's relationship to, 101–102. *See also individual novels*

object of analysis, 182

Oliver, Giles (*Between the Acts*), 95–96, 100, 220, 238, 251, 254

Oliver, Isa (*Between the Acts*), 10, 95–98, 100, 211, 213, 220, 236, 238, 239–40, 252, 280
Omega Workshops, Ltd., 262, 269, 271–72, 274
opera, x, 4–5, 47–48; development of, 16, 210, 220–23; German Romantic, 51; Greek chorus as forerunner, 100–101; influence on Woolf's writing, 15, 50; V. Woolf's attendance at, 4, 19n14, 50–55, 95, 101, 121–22, 123. *See also* Wagner, Richard; Wagner, Richard, works
order, music's representation of, 37–38, 124, 140
Orfeo et Euridice (Gluck), 34, 43n8, 53, 59
Orlando (*Orlando*), 66, 207, 212, 215, 219
Otway, Cassandra (*Night and Day*), 135–36, 144
Outline of Musical History (Hewitt), 100–101
outsider narratives, 164, 247–50

Painted Roofs (Richardson), 60
Palisca, Claude, 221
parataxis, 245–46
Parker, Mara, 90
Parry, Hubert, 5
Parsifal (Wagner), 5, 32, 50, 53; music and language interconnected, 5, 51, 95, 123; referenced in *Mrs. Dalloway*, 55; V. Woolf's criticism of, 122–23
passé-ism, 271, 272
Pater, Walter, 97, 134; flame image, 141; moment, concept of, 76–77; "School of Giorgione" maxim, 13, 21, 46, 76, 146
pathetique figure, 88, 106n12
Pepper, William (*The Voyage Out*), 112, 118, 120
Percival (*The Waves*), 91–92, 93, 280–81
performance: as action-centered, 184, 190; entertainment, 16, 185–86, 197; Greek drama, 182–83, 185–87, 196–98; musical, 183–85; primary components, 184, 190, 193, 197; as relational, 184, 197; ritual, 185, 186–87, 194–95; as traveling concept, 182, 183, 199n2. *See also* Greek chorus

performance practice, 4, 183, 199n3
performativity, 183, 185–87
performer-listener axis, 184, 190, 197
period instruments, 58
permanence of artistic creation, 93–94
Philosophy in a New Key (Langer), 11–12, 20n17, 20n20
Phrygian mode, 115
pianola, 29, 41–42
Pindar, 115, 131
Plato and Platonism (Pater), 97
poetic imagination, 95–96
Poetics (Aristotle), 113
poetry, prose as, 99–100, 106n17, 147
Politics (Aristotle), 115
politics and music, ix, 16, 181, 242, 247
"Politics of Comic Modes in Virginia Woolf's *Between the Acts*, The" (Cuddy-Keane), 96
polyphony: in *Between the Acts*, 215, 248, 249; in *The Waves*, 89–92, 94
polyrhythms, 242, 242–44, 265–66
Pomona (Lambert), 63
Portrait of the Artist as a Young Man (Joyce), 263–64
Postimpressionism, 35, 38
Pound, Ezra, 269, 273–74, 277
Powers, Harold, 208
Pratella, Francesco Balilla, 276
Prelude, The (Wordsworth), 98
Prieto, Eric, 209
prime series, 236, 238, 247
primordial world/prehistory, 105n7, 210, 238, 242, 243, 251–52, 253, 254, 262
Principia Ethica (Moore), 31, 84
Problems of Dostoevsky's Poetics (Bakhtin), 89
Proclus, 115
prose: musicality of, x–xi; as poetry, 99–100, 106n17, 147
Proust, Marcel, 59–60
Purcell, Henry, 53, 126

Quilter, Roger, 40–41

radio, 3, 231–32
Ralph (*Night and Day*), 136, 137, 140–41

Ratner, Leonard G., 88, 106n12
Read, Herbert, 267, 268, 269, 276
reader: reader-oriented approach, 101–102; reader-response aesthetics, 101–102; relationship with author and text, 15, 78, 85, 96, 101–102. *See also* audience
Reading of Silence, The (Laurence), 13
reality, modeled on musical experience, 77–79, 84
reception, 7–9, 65, 101–102, 155–56, 292–93, 314
recordings, 3–4, 29, 58–59, 64–66, 210–12
Reed, Christopher, 37
Renaissance, Italian, 220–22
repetition, xi, 86, 99, 223n3, 236–37, 245; motivic, 210, 213–14, 237
representational form, 63
Rezia (*Mrs. Dalloway*), 164
Rhoda (*The Waves*), 77, 84, 86–87, 91–92, 102, 250
rhythm, xi, 1–2, 12, 15, 75; accents, displaced, 242–44, 246; agonistic, 116–17, 125, 237–38; dithyrambic, 115–16; enables risks, 119–20; as order, 124; polyrhythms, 242, 242–44, 265–66; power of, 119–20; of prose, 83–84; role in writing, 120; shared structural, 209, 220, 222; as "soul," 124, 125; spatial, 67–68; synthesis of Apolline and Dionysian, 126–27; temporal and spatial dilation, 82, 83; trochaic, 196, 201n16; unease caused by, 116, 117–18; *The Waves* as, 67; Woolf's exploration of, 242–43; "writing to," 67, 264
Richard (*The Hours*), 289, 292
Richardson, Dorothy Miller, 60
Richter, János (Hans), 49, 50, 53
Rite of Spring (*Le Sacre du Printemps*) (Stravinsky), ix, 41, 57, 62, 66, 120; "Augurs of Spring," 242, 252; first performance, 29, 127, 277, 284n1; rhythm, 241–43, 242, 265–66
ritual, 185, 186–87, 194–95, 198
Rodney, William (*Night and Day*), x, 135–36, 137, 144
Roger Fry: A Biography (Woolf), 1, 2
Romanticism, 8, 98, 141, 167

Room with a View, A (Forster), 80, 104n3
Russolo, Luigi, 276

Sackville-West, Vita, 41
Safranski, Rudiger, 130
Sara (*The Years*), 190–96, 200n15
Schechner, Richard, 185, 186–87, 194–95
Schnabel, Artur, 64, 65
Schoenberg, Arnold, x, 16; Musical Idea, 235, 237; musical objective, 229; prime series, 236, 238, 247; single complete thought project, 235; *Sprechstimme*, 240, 256n13; twelve-tone chromatic scale, 29, 236, 247, 256n13
Schoenberg, Arnold, works: *Five Orchestral Pieces*, 7, 65, 231; *Piano Suite*, Op. 25, 236; *Pierrot lunaire*, 29, 240; *Six Little Piano Pieces*, Op. 19, II, 248, 249; *A Survivor from Warsaw*, Op. 46, 238, 241, 256n13
Schopenhauer, Arthur, 123
Schröder, Leena Kore, 162, 164
Schubert, Franz, 10, 19n15
Schulze, Robin Gail, 199n5
score-text comparisons, 5–6, 11, 20n18
Scott, William, 115
Scriabin, Alexander, 35
Second Viennese School, 7, 8, 231, 255n3
semiotic triangle, 78
Senta (*Der fliegende Holländer*), 162–69, 175
sentimentality, 166–67, 176n8
serial technique, 106n11, 233, 236, 238, 247, 256n13
Seton, Sally (*Mrs. Dalloway*), 166
Shakespeare, William, 12
Shaw, George Bernard, 37
shivah mourning custom, 15, 162, 166, 172–76
"shivering fragments" image, 237, 260, 264, 265, 268, 271–73, 275, 278, 283
Shone, Richard, 262, 271–72, 274
short-story genre, musical structure in, 9–17
Sickert, Walter, 263, 271, 281
sign, 208
significant form, 12, 20n19, 20n20
Silber, Evelyn, 274

silence, 10–11, 12, 83–84; as death, 251; in *The Hours*, 306–307; silencing, 248–50
Silver, Brenda, 104n1
Singing of the Real World, The: The Philosophy of Virginia Woolf's Fiction (Hussey), 13
sister arts, 47
Sitwell, Sacheverell, 231
Skidelsky, Robert, 39
skywriting, 279
Smith, Septimus (*Mrs. Dalloway*), 113, 165–66, 172, 174–75, 279, 282, 306; as model for Richard in *The Hours*, 289, 293–94
Smyth, Ethel, ix, 5, 41, 48, 60–62, 63, 231; argument about *Parsifal*, 53; Woolf's letters to, 5, 18n4, 41, 62, 67, 68, 87–88; *The Wreckers*, 54, 61
Sokolova, Lydia, 265–66
"Song for St. Cecilia's Day, A" (Dryden), 152, 153
Sophocles, 111–17. See also *Antigone*
soul, as spirit of music, 124, 125–26
soundtrack for *The Hours* (Glass), 288–310; "Bell" theme, 295, 302–303, *303*, *304*; cadence, subverted, 295; choreographic function, 306–307; continuity of narrative, 294–95; harmonic patterns, 294; musical examples, *297*, *303*, *304*; piano theme, 294, 298, *298*, 309n5; rhythms, 294; as sound bridge for sections, 307–308; structural role, 291; tables of musical structure, *298*, *299*, *301–302*; texture, 294–95; thematic recurrence, 300, 302; triadic thematic material, 294; variation techniques, 298–99. See also *Hours, The* (Daldry)
Spalding, Frances, 35
Spanish Civil War, 187, 279–80
Sprechstimme, 240, 256n13
stasis, 81–82, 149, 189, 251–52, 264
Stephen, Adrian, 27, 32, 42, 48
Stephen, Helen, 48
Stephen, Leslie, 68, 83, 93, 104n1
Stephen, Thoby, 27
Stephen, Virginia. *See* Woolf, Virginia
stile rappresentativo, 222
Strachey, James, 33

Strachey, Jane Maria, 33
Strachey, Lytton, ix, 9, 27, 31, 43n4; on Quilter, 40–41; on Sydney-Turner, 32–33; view of "The String Quartet," 146
Strachey, Oliver, 33, 48, 154
Strauss, Richard, 8, 19n14, 29, 305, 306; *Elektra*, 51; *Salome*, 51, 53
Stravinsky, Igor, x, 16, 63, 277; opera, 57; polyrhythms, 242, *242*, 243, 265–66; on Proust, 59–60
Stravinsky, Igor, works: *Les Noces* (*The Village Wedding*), 264, 266, 278; *L'Histoire du Soldat*, 230–31; *Octet*, 8–9. See also *Rite of Spring* (*Le Sacre du Printemps*)
stream-of-consciousness narrative, 15, 87, 134, 154; in *The Hours*, 290–91, 308
Street Light (Balla), 269
string quartets, 90, 200n6. See also Beethoven, Ludwig van
"String Quartet, The" (Woolf), x, 9–10, 60, 106n9, 106n10, 278; first-person narration, 146; form and content in, 144–47; fragmentation in, 141, 147, 151–52, 154–55; impetus for, 147; levels of experience, 153–54; narration, 145–46, 148; as romance narrative, 152–53
structure, xi, 1–2, 7–8; architecture of sound, 11, 77, 85–86; geometric figures as, 273; micro-structural level, 235; music as inspiration for Woolf's works, 66–67; musical conversation, 90; nonlinear, 289, 291–92; operatic, in *Between the Acts*, 16, 210; rhythm and, 209, 220, 222; of *To the Lighthouse*, 66; in Woolf's short fiction, 9–17
suffrage movement, 272–73
Suggia, Guilhermina, 63
surfaces, 93; in *The Voyage Out*, 76, 78, 86; in *The Waves*, 93
Susan (*The Waves*), 92
Swithin, Lucy (*Between the Acts*), 10, 84–85, 96–98, 209–210, 213–14
Swithin, Mrs. (*Between the Acts*), 6
Sydney-Turner, Saxon, 32–33, 49, 54, 121
synesthetic perception, 1, 10–11, 35, 75, 263; in *Between the Acts*, 77–78, 95, 101; in *The Voyage Out*, 95

Taruskin, Richard, 8–9
Tchaikovsky, Pyotr Ilyich, 57
temporal and spatial dilation: in *Between the Acts*, 97–98; class-inflected, 243–44; in *Night and Day*, 140–41; "shivering fragments" as, 268–69, 272; in *The Voyage Out*, 76–77, 79, 81–83, 84
texture, xi, 8, 52, 147; in *Between the Acts*, 205–207, 209–10, 213, 215, 219; in *The Hours*, 294–95, 297, 300, 302, 309n5; polyphonic, 15, 248–49, 89–92, 94, 294–95, 297
theatrical performance, 185–87
theme, 213; "Bell," 295, 302–303, 303, 304; piano, 294, 298, 298, 309n5; and variation, 90, 91–92, 102–104
thelxis (enchantment), 113, 123
Thompson, Trina, 6
Three Guineas (Woolf), 30, 187, 279–80, 283
Thynner, Beatrice, 49
Times essay (Woolf), 34
Timothy, Miriam Jane, 50
To the Lighthouse (Woolf), 9, 36, 87, 204, 206, 207, 215; communication through silence as musical, 84; cover design, 268; Forster on, 66; subtitles, 273
Tolbert, Elizabeth, 6, 19n9
tonality, 190, 208, 234
Tovey, Donald Francis, 5
tragedy, 16, 81, 113; Attic, 123–24; dithyrambic rhythms in, 115–16; melodramatic model, 165–66; Rachel Vinrace as tragic figure, 111, 124–26, 128–31
transcendence, 10, 76–77
translation between media/transmedialization, 6, 209
Trevelyan, Elizabeth, 1, 12
Trilby (du Maurier), 169
Tristan und Isolde (Wagner), 39, 51, 123; mentioned in *Jacob's Room*, 68; mentioned in *Mrs. Dalloway*, 55
"Trout" Piano Quintet in A major, D. 667 (Schubert), 10, 19n15
Turner, Victor, 198

unity in discord, 229–30, 238–39, 264–65
unity of the arts, 20n21, 37

unrest problem, 237–39, 244, 248–49
up/down gesture, 88–89, 98
Urrows, David, 209
use, concept of, 47
ut musica poesis, ideal of, 12–13, 46

Valkyrie (Wagner), 36
Vanucci, Pietro, 264
Vaughan, Clarissa (*The Hours*), 289–94
Vaughan, Emma, 1, 48, 112
Vaughan Williams, Ralph, x, 61
Victorian social norms: clothing and propriety, 147–48; critiqued through musical scenes, 134–36, 144–45, 147–49, 152–53; decline of aristocracy, 152–53; harmony, 139–40; music as cultural capital, 135–36; social control, 136–37, 147
Vinrace, Rachel (*The Voyage Out*), 55–56, 75–77; birth of from spirit of music, 125–31; childlike wonder, 82; fusion of Apolline and Dionysian, 126–28; language-music relationship and, 78–86; as tragic figure, 111, 124–26, 128–31; up/down gesture and, 88–89, 98. See also *Voyage Out, The*
Virginia Woolf and the Languages of Patriarchy (Marcus), 13
visual arts, 1–2, 47
visual modernism, 7
visual music, 36–37
Vorticism, 17, 269–70, 272–74, 283
Voyage Out, The (Woolf), 161; aesthetically innovative sections, 79; agonistic rhythm of, 116, 125; ascent and transformed descent trajectory, 79–80, 83–84, 88–89; audience in, 77, 84–85, 87; Beethoven's Op. 111 referenced in, 10, 54, 79–82, 85–86; birth of Rachel Vinrace from spirit of music, 125–31; heroine as pianist, 75–76; language-music relationship in, 75–76; as *Melymbrosia*, 55–56, 113; quote from *Antigone,* 111–12, 115, 116, 130; rhythm of, 83–84, 117; songs from Milton in, 111; synesthetic moments, 95; tempo of, 116, 128; temporal and spatial dilation in, 76–77, 79, 81–83,

84; third person narration, 98; word and music in, 78–86. *See also* Vinrace, Rachel (*The Voyage Out*)

Wagner, Richard, 4–5, 8, 14; on Beethoven, 64; British cult of, 49; as continuing tradition of Beethoven, 56; essay on Beethoven, 66–67; flight from Riga, 165; *Gesamtkunstwerk,* 32, 101, 230, 255n3; influence on Woolf, 49–55, 121–22, 161; neoclassical music drama, 111, 121, 123, 126; Nietzsche's view of, 111, 122, 160; references to in V. Woolf's works, 53; sentimentality in works of, 52, 166–67; V. Woolf's loss of enthusiasm for, 51–52

Wagner, Richard, works: *Das Judentum in der Musik,* 169, 172; *Der Ring des Nibelungen,* 49, 51–52, 169; *Die Meistersinger,* 50, 53, 169; *Die Walküre,* 52–53; *Eine Mittheilung an meine Freunde,* 169; *Lohengrin,* 51; *Siegfried,* 68; *Tristan und Isolde,* 39, 51, 123; *Valkyrie,* 36. See also *Der fliegende Holländer; Parsifal*

Wagner, Siegfried, 50

Wagner's Dramas and Greek Tragedy (Wilson), 167

Walsh, Peter (*Mrs. Dalloway*), x, 163–64, 172

Wandering Jew figure, 160, 162, 164–65, 169–72

Warr, George, 112

Waste Land, The (Eliot), 262

Waves, The (Woolf), 6, 16, 17, 76, 79, 161; aurality in, 261; contrapunctal style, 65, 91; flow of time, 91, 103–104; language-music relationship in, 77; letters and diaries on, 87–88; longing in, 86–87, 91–92; looking glass motif, 92–94, 103; moment of being in, 82; multiple voices in, 89–91, 94; as musical conversation, 89–91; perception as musical, 84; as play-poem, 87–88, 89; polyphonic texture in, 89–92, 94; quartet-like structure, 90; as rhythm, 67; self-definition, 91, 102–103; shock of meeting in, 91–92, 102; theme

and variation in, 90, 91–92, 102–104; Woolf's working method, 66

Webern, Anton von, 65

Weiss, Piero, 221

West, M. L., 115, 118

Whittier-Ferguson, John, 207

Wilde, Oscar, 46

Wilhelmine of Prussia, 49–50

William (*Between the Acts*), 97–98

Wilmot, Fanny ("Moments of Being"), 275–76

Wilson, Pearl Cleveland, 166

Wise Virgins, The (Woolf), 170, 176n8

Wittgenstein, Ludwig, 74

Wolf, Werner, 209

Wood, Henry, 60, 64

Woolf, Cecil, 173

Woolf, Leonard, 292; on concert attendance, 33–34; Jewish background, 170, 172–73, 217; as musical conservative, ix–x; on origins of Bloomsbury Group, 27; passion for music, 27, 30–31; recordings, collection, 65–66; reviews of recordings, 3–4, 58–59; Wagner, view of, 49, 51–52, 58

Woolf, Leonard, works: *Beginning Again,* 28, 56, 59, 162, 170, 173; *In Search of Lost Time,* 28

Woolf, Marie, 173

Woolf, Virginia: active reflection, 188–89; aesthetic concerns, xi, 1–3, 13–14, 76, 78–79, 89, 93–95, 167, 176n9, 182, 189; art-form mixtures, preference for, 230, 232; as audience, 134, 138, 147–48; autobiographical writings, 46; Bayreuth visit, 4, 19n14, 50–51, 54–55, 95, 101, 121–23; book reviews, 48; books as music, 1, 46, 75; as character in *The Hours,* 289, 292, 293, 295; concert attendance, 3, 14, 49–64, 119, 121, 230, 255n2; essays, diaries, and letters, 4, 5, 10, 18n4, 41, 56–58, 62, 67–68, 87–88; on essence of music, 264–65; Greek studies, 111, 113–14, 118, 128–29, 186–87, 200n7, 222; insights into music, 49–51; interest in language-music relationships, 5–7, 118–19; Italy, travel in, 263, 264; Jews, view of, 162,

169–73; meets Nevinson, 281–82; on modernist music, 230–31; music criticism, 3, 29–30, 246–47; music hall, view of, 48, 138; musical background, 2–3, 14, 28, 47–48; as musical conservative, ix–x, 54, 61–62; "new method," 207, 218; note on *Oxford History of Music*, 232; opera attendance, 4, 19n14, 50–51, 54–55, 95, 101, 121–22, 123; "ordinary mind," desire to portray, 223, 229, 268, 277; pacifist stance, 182, 187–88, 217, 279; position in society, 147–48; as proto-interdisciplinary thinker, 185, 186; rhythm, exploration of, 242–43; short stories, 145–47; suicide, 43n8, 59, 294, 295, 305; synesthetic perception and writing, 1, 10–11, 35, 75, 101, 263; Wagner's influence on, 49–55, 121–22, 161; working method, 66

Woolf, Virginia, works, 15; "Anon," 96, 106n15, 106n16, 252, 253–54; "Character in Fiction," 218; *The Common Reader*, 112; "Cracked Fiddles," 271; "A Death in the Newspaper," 271; *Flush*, 63; *Freshwater*, 9; "Impassioned Prose," 83; *Jacob's Room*, 9, 68, 187; on Jane Austen, 102; "The Journal of Mistress Joan Martyn," 56; lectures, 94; "The Mark on the Wall," xi; "Modern Fiction," 143, 229; "Moments of Being: 'Slater's Pins Have No Points,'" x, 275–76; *Monday or Tuesday*, 9, 145–46; "On Not Knowing Greek," 110, 112, 114, 118, 197; "The Opera," 4–5, 138; *The Pargiters*, 63, 187–88; "Poetry, Fiction and the Future" ("The Narrow Bridge of Art"), 9; "Professions for Women," 150; "The Reader," 96; *Roger Fry: A Biography*, 1, 2; *A Room of One's Own*, 101, 150, 262; "A Simple Melody," 47; "A Sketch of the Past," 1, 49, 75, 93, 198; "Street Music," 68, 97, 119–20, 124, 127, 128, 266; "Sympathy," 60; "The Telephone," 268; "Thoughts on Peace in an Air Raid," 180, 188, 191; *Three Guineas*, 30, 187, 279–80, 283; *Times* essay, 34; "Walter Sickert: A Conversation," 263. See also *Between the Acts*; "Impressions at Bayreuth"; *Mrs. Dalloway* (Woolf); "String Quartet, The"; *To the Lighthouse*; *Voyage Out, The*; *Waves, The*; *Years, The*

Woolf scholarship, 2–3, 7, 13
Wordsworth, William, 98
World War I, 36, 151–52, 278, 279, 294
World War II, 65, 262; grand narrative of, 217, 218–19; noise and danger, 280–81
Wyckoff, Elizabeth, 117

Years, The (Woolf), x, 17, 63, 161; "1907" chapter, 189–91; *Antigone* in, 187, 192–94, 196; aurality in, 16, 182, 261, 263; children's' chorus in, 187, 196–98; efficacy in, 16, 181, 186–87, 194–96; "eternal waltz" image, 189–91, 192, 193; Greek drama, connections to, 187, 196–98; musical events in, 181–203; Nijinsky named in, 265; noise in, 17, 189–90, 199n1, 277–78; Ouroboros metaphor, 189, 190–91; as *The Pargiters*, 63, 187–88; process of writing, 206–207; *Siegfried* mentioned in, 68; thought as activity, 188–89, 191–93, 198

Zimring, Rishona, 201n15

www.ingramcontent.com/pod-product-compliance
Lightning Source LLC
Chambersburg PA
CBHW030605230426
43661CB00053B/1851